Francisco de Paula Brito

Francisco de Paula Brito

A Black Publisher in Imperial Brazil

RODRIGO CAMARGO DE GODOI

Translated by H. Sabrina Gledhill

VANDERBILT UNIVERSITY PRESS
Nashville, Tennessee

Originally published in Brazil as *Um editor no impérioi: Francisco de Paula Brito (1809–1861)*, copyright © 2016 by Rodrigo Camargo de Godoi

Cover images: details from Praça da Constituição; the signature of Captain Martinho Pereira de Brito, Paula Brito's grandfather; portrait of Francisco de Paula Brito by Louis Alexis Boulanger (1842, courtesy of the IHGB); a portrait of Simao the mariner (1853, courtesy of the IHGB); Dous de Dezembro press plan; and Constitution Square shortly after the unveiling of an equestrian statue of Pedro I

Library of Congress Cataloging-in-Publication Data

Names: Godoi, Rodrigo Camargo de, author. | Gledhill, Sabrina, translator.
Title: Francisco de Paula Brito : a black publisher in imperial Brazil / Rodrigo Camargo de Godoi, ; translated by H. Sabrina Gledhill.
Other titles: Editor no Império. English
Description: Nashville : Vanderbilt University Press, [2020] | Includes bibliographical references and index.
Identifiers: LCCN 2020019523 (print) | LCCN 2020019524 (ebook) | ISBN 9780826500168 (paperback) | ISBN 9780826500175 (hardcover) | ISBN 9780826500182 (epub) | ISBN 9780826500199 (pdf) Subjects: LCSH: Brito, Francisco de Paula, 1809–1861. | Publishers and publishing—Brazil—Rio de Janeiro—Biography. | Publishers and publishing—Brazil—Rio de Janeiro—History—19th century. | Poets, Brazilian—19th century—Biography.
Classification: LCC Z521.3.B75 G6313 2020 (print) | LCC Z521.3.B75 (ebook) | DDC 070.5092 [B]—dc23

LC record available at https://lccn.loc.gov/2020019523
LC ebook record available at https://lccn.loc.gov/2020019524

In memory of João Batista de Godoy,
my beloved grandfather.

I've seen Daddy sad because nobody buys what he writes. He studied hard and still studies hard, and the other day he had a fight with Lalau, who makes his book—his books, because Daddy has written lots and lots of books—on the machine—those men who make our books on machines are called publishers—but when Lalau isn't here, Daddy calls Lalau all sorts of names that I can't repeat.

HILDA HILST, *O caderno rosa de Lori Lamby* (São Paulo: Globo, 2005), 19.

Contents

Foreword to the Brazilian Edition   *xi*

Acknowledgments   *xv*

Introduction   *1*

PART ONE: THE VENTURES AND MISADVENTURES
OF A FREE PRINTER

1. A "Dove without Gall" and the Court of Public Opinion   13

2. Plantation Lad   19

3. Apprentice Printer and Poet   29

4. 1831, Year of Possibilities   35

5. Bookseller-Printer   49

6. Press Laws and Offences in the "Days of Father Feijó"   61

PART TWO: CONSERVATIVE IMPARTIALITY

7. "A Very Well Set-Up Establishment"   75

8. Newspapers, Theses, and Brazilian Literature   86

9. Workers, Slaves, and Free Africans   100

10. "The *Progress* of the Nation Consists Solely in *Regression*"   113

PART THREE: THE LIFE AND DEATH OF THE
DOUS DE DEZEMBRO COMPANY

11. Man of Color and Printer of the Imperial House   129

12. From Printer to Literary Publisher   147

13. Debts and the Dangerous Game of the Stock Market   157

14. From Bankruptcy Protection to Liquidation   165

PART FOUR: REDISCOVERED ILLUSIONS

15. A New Beginning   179
16. The Petalogical Society   187
17. Literary Mutualism   199
18. The Publisher and His Authors   204
19. Rio de Janeiro's Publishing Market (1840–1850)   220
20. The Widow Paula Brito   228
Epilogue   239

Appendixes   243
Notes   267
References   317
Bibliography   329
Image Credits   339
Index   341

Foreword to the Brazilian Edition

JEFFERSON CANO, Department of Literature,
University of Campinas (Unicamp)

WHEN FRANCISCO DE Paula Brito died, the young journalist Machado de Assis devoted his Comments of the Week column in the *Diário do Rio de Janeiro* to his friend:

Yet another! This year must be counted as an illustrious obituary, where everyone, friend and citizen, can see inscribed more than one name dear to the heart or soul.

Long is the list of those who, in the space of these twelve months, which are about to expire, have fallen into the tremendous embrace of that wanton who, as the poet said, does not discriminate her lovers.

Now it is a man who, due to his social and political virtues, his intelligence and his love of work, had achieved widespread esteem.

He began as a printer and died a printer. In that modest role, he enjoyed the friendship of everyone around him.

Paula Brito set a rare and good example. He had faith in his political convictions, sincerely believing in the results of their application; tolerant, he was not unjust with his adversaries; sincere, he never compromised with them.

He was also a friend, above all a friend. He loved young people because he knew that they are the hope of his homeland, and because he loved them, he extended them his protection as much as he could.

Instead of dying [and] leaving a fortune, which he could have done, he died as poor as he was in life, thanks to the extensive employment he gave to his income and the generosity that led him to share what he earned from his labor.

In these times of selfishness and calculation, we should mourn the loss of men who, like Paula Brito, stand out from the common mass of men.[1]

Half a century later, another statement, this time from the memoirs of Salvador de Mendonça, would become an almost obligatory reference about the role of Paula Brito in mid-nineteenth century Rio de Janeiro:

In Largo do Rocio [also known as Praça da Constituição], outside Paula Brito's establishment, across the street, there were two benches where, on Saturday afternoons, the following individuals would get together regularly to converse about literature: Machado de Assis, then a clerk at Paula Brito's bookstore and press; Manuel Antônio de Almeida, a writer for the *Correio mercantil* and author of *Memoirs of a Militia Sergeant*; Henrique César Muzzio, a physician without a clinic and highly esteemed theater critic; Casimiro de Abreu, poet and clerk in a retail establishment; José Antonio, treasury employee and author of the humorous *Lembranças* [Memories] and, finally, this writer, then a preparatory school student. Many times, as he walked from Paula Brito's shop to his own home across the square, Joaquim Manuel de Macedo, the creator of the Brazilian novel, would come and sit with us, honest and sincere, and more than once he was accompanied by Gonçalves Dias, with his lean body, melancholy aspect, and genial gaze, and Araújo Porto-Alegre, with his bear-like physique and the perennial youthfulness of a healthy soul and body.[2]

Those who compare these two quotations today can easily see how time has imposed on Paula Brito's memory a different meaning from that which was still present in Machado de Assis's affectionate recollection of him. The publisher's political virtues seemed to have been permanently erased, along with his image as the protector of youth. Indeed, Paula Brito's importance during that period seemed no longer to be found in himself but in those with whom he interacted—the most outstanding figures on the literary scene of his time and the future. His was almost a name that hitched a ride in the footnotes of literary history, solely because he kept good company.

Nothing could be more unfair. The book the reader is now perusing reveals a man with a career so rich that historians rarely have the good fortune to find his like; a man who, if he were a fictional character, would be what Lukács called a *type*, in which "all contradictions—the most important social, ethical, and psychological contradictions of a time—are linked in a single living unit."[3] But Paula Brito was not a fictional character, and Rodrigo Camargo de Godoi is no Balzac—despite a reference here and there. He is a historian who is well up to the task imposed by his subject.

"All contradictions" seems like an overstatement, but it is not. The decades between 1830 and 1860 were rife with contradictions, and it is hard to think of any that did not have a deep impact on Paula Brito's life. The intersection of racial and political identities when both were formed through the press would find in a printer descended from slaves a focal point around which the most significant tensions of his time emerged. The intersection of the individual with his enterprising ambitions and dreams and the flow of capital that was seeking new outlets after the definitive end of the transatlantic slave trade would give the publisher opportunities to rise and fall, test the limits of protection, and experience the vicissitudes of speculation.

All of this is skillfully handled by Rodrigo Camargo de Godoi, who shows the reader how these tensions ran through Paula Brito's life and (reprising the "hook" of Lukács's definition) are joined together in a living unit. I hope the reader will forgive this repetition, but there is good reason for it. After all, the idea that the life of the subject, represented in writing, could constitute a unit in which the very (contradictory) unity of the historic process is reflected is common both to the interpretation undertaken by a literary critic and the process of writing undertaken by a historian who devotes himself to a biography. Going beyond writing, does such unity exist? Once again, this is a highly sensitive question for practitioners of both disciplines, and neither will find an easy answer—much less a safe one. For many, of course, it is pointless to pose it, but if we accept the question, this book becomes even more interesting—not by answering it, of course, but by permitting us to think about it every step of the way.

Acknowledgments

ONE COLD MORNING in June 2017, I received a message from Professor Celso Thomas Castilho, of Vanderbilt University, inquiring if I would be interested in scheduling a Skype conversation about a possible translation of my book, which had just been released in Brazil by the University of São Paulo Press. Celso had no idea how happy that message made me, so I would like to begin by thanking him for his hard work, without which the reader might not be holding this book in their hands. In this regard, I would also like to thank my editors for their support throughout the entire process, which involved submitting the original proposal and its approval and publication: Carla Fontana, from the University of São Paulo Press, and Zachary Gresham, from the Vanderbilt University Press. Through them, I extend my thanks to all the workers involved in the production of this book, from the copyeditors to the printers.

The maps that illustrate the book were produced and kindly ceded by my friend, the geographer and professor Tiago Pires. I owe Professor Bruno Guimarães Martins, who also studies the life and work of Paula Brito, a debt of thanks for his generosity in sharing the prints of the publisher's family that he found in the Brazilian Historical and Geographic Institute.

I would like to thank the British Brazilianist and historian Sabrina Gledhill for her superb translation. I cannot say how much I have learned from seeing the solutions she proposed for the English edition. I am therefore grateful to the São Paulo Research Foundation for its grant for the translation (FAPESP Process no. 2018/11281-4), recognizing the central role which that agency has played in promoting scientific research in the state of São Paulo and Brazil. In addition to the translation, FAPESP financed both my original research and the publication of this book in Portuguese. This edition was financed in part by the Coordenação de Aperfeiçoamento de Pessoal de Nível Superior—Brasil (CAPES)—Finance Code 001.

Many thanks to my colleagues at the Department of History and the Research Center on the Social History of Culture (CECULT) at the University of Campinas for their warm welcome. Despite the protests of Silvia Hunold Lara, I can once again affirm that she and Jefferson Cano, Robert Slenes, and Sidney Chalhoub are the mentors who have enabled me to improve as a historian, and who continue to do so. I am also immensely grateful to Flavia Peral, who is responsible for technical and administrative support at CECULT. Without her, our work would be impossible.

At the time I was researching this book, Brazil was a different place. I belong to the generation of historians born between the end of the dictatorship and the beginning of the process of redemocratization—a generation that grew up during what was perhaps the most extensive expansion program for higher education ever seen in Brazilian history. I remember our enthusiasm well, as many, like me, were the first in our families from all parts of Brazil's interior and low-income urban peripheries to have access to university and teaching careers. I would like to see that enthusiasm once again in my students, whom I thank for the daily lessons of perseverance in these difficult times.

Campinas, October 17, 2019

Introduction

ALTHOUGH THE RECORDS are extremely scarce on this point, all indications are that the portrait of Francisco de Paula Brito that illustrates his book of poetry, a posthumous work edited by Moreira de Azevedo, was a lithograph based on a painting unveiled in the headquarters of the Petalogical Society on the evening of December 15, 1862—a year after the publisher's death.[1] In any event, the portrait matches the physical description that Moreira de Azevedo has left us of his friend: a man who was "brown in color, slim, of average height, beardless, and when he died," at the age of fifty-three, "his hair was just starting to go gray."[2] The artist's skill not only managed to capture the features of the late Paula Brito, but the portrait has played an important role as a "place of memory," according to Pierre Nora, whose function "is to stop time, to block the work of oblivion, affixing a state of things, immortalizing death."[3]

Paula Brito cut a good figure by being immortalized with a calm visage, smartly dressed in a sober black coat, white shirt, and tie. In this regard, although it may have been posthumous, this portrait tells us a great deal. If his skin color, which the artist did not attempt to hide, is a manifest sign of his ancestors' experience of slavery, his clothes leave no doubt that this was a citizen of African ancestry who had gained a good position in his society.[4] The son and grandson of freedpersons, he was a merchant, bookseller, printer, and publisher who worked in Rio de Janeiro for three decades, between 1831 and 1861. Indeed, it was through his work and the bonds of

FIGURE I. Posthumous portrait of Francisco de Paula Brito (1863)

solidarity that he formed during his life that made Brito a kind of catalyst in the cultural and literary scene of the capital of Imperial Brazil, gaining renown in his lifetime. In such cases, once a life has ended, no sooner is the body lying in its grave than a profusion of panegyric writings is produced, crystallizing a given image of the deceased for the use and memory of posterity, going beyond portraits and the unveiling of portraits.

The "memorialist construction" built up around the publisher, understood as the transformation of the historical character through history itself, goes through three clearly distinct phases.[5] This is true both in literary history, in the history of books and reading in Brazil, and in studies of Machado de Assis, in which Paula Brito is usually an obligatory presence. Beginning with the first biography published in the *Correio mercantil* newspaper weeks after his death, many of those who wrote about the publisher were unanimous about his altruism, which led to the perception of his first being an "impoverished patron of the arts," then a "pioneering publisher," and, more recently, a "Liberal Freemason."[6] This demonstrates that Francisco de Paula Brito is far from being an unexplored subject and that, in a way, the problem proposed in this book, based on a study of his life, is not unprecedented. Machado de Assis put it very precisely in one of his essays, in which he lavished praise on the French publisher Baptiste Louis Garnier in January 1865: "Speaking of Mr. Garnier, and then of Paula Brito, is to bring them together with a common idea: Paula Brito was the first publisher worthy of the name that we had among us. Garnier now occupies that role, with the differences wrought by time and the vast relations he has established outside the country."[7]

With a view to contributing to the history of print culture in Brazil, this book seeks to turn Machado de Assis's statement, which is well known in the literature, into a question, and on that basis, to attempt to understand the historical conditions that made the emergence of the publisher possible in nineteenth-century Rio de Janeiro.

Although printers like Charles-Joseph Panckoucke were also working as publishers in the eighteenth century, employing a number of practices that were previously unheard of in France's book trade, several authors agree that it was in the first half of the nineteenth century, around 1830, that publishers began to appear as entrepreneurs in the market of printed cultural goods. Therefore, we can initially consider that companies like Blackwood in Edinburgh and Ticknor and Fields in Boston, as well as the Michel and Calmann Lévy brothers in Paris, George Palmer Putnam in New York, and Francisco de Paula Brito in Rio de Janeiro, almost simultaneously became entrepreneurs in the expanding universe of newspapers, magazines, books, and other publications.[8] The defining factor in this process is the gradual specialization of publishers, who began setting themselves apart from traditional printers and booksellers, acting like the other entrepreneurs of the arts that emerged at that time, such as theater impresarios. Thus, according to Christine Haynes, while in seventeenth-century France *éditeurs* were the scholars responsible for compiling and editing works in different genres, the meaning of the term *éditeur* changes dramatically as it designates the "capitalists who assumed the risk of producing the work of a (dead or living) author." Accordingly, "the éditeur was defined by his role in investing capital, both financial and human, to create literary commodities—and monetary profits."[9]

Although in certain cases, as Paula Brito's career demonstrates, the publisher was responsible for the production and sale of printed works, as of the 1830s it was this new actor that, according to Roger Chartier and Henri-Jean Martin, began reorganizing the book world by "controlling authors, putting the printers to work and supplying retail bookstores." In an article co-authored with Odile Martin, Henri-Jean Martin identifies the publication of illustrated books as the beginning of the awareness of the originality of the work of publishers in France, suggesting the importance of the modernization of the printing industry in that process.[10] Addressing this problem, Christine Haynes shifts the focus of her analysis of technological change to politics. According to Haynes, the specialization of éditeurs in France might have come a long way since the seventeenth century, when that branch first appeared during the formation of booksellers' guilds. In the following century, however, a single printer or book merchant could be responsible for the production and distribution chains for printed matter, so much so that by 1820 they were called printer-booksellers. Thus, Haynes believes that the capitalist publisher emerged between 1770 and 1830, in the wake of a series of liberal reforms of the laws governing the French book trade. Such reforms changed intellectual property rights, revised market restrictions, and reduced the powers of censorship bodies. Consequently, individuals who did not belong to the traditional corporations that controlled the book market in the ancien régime were free to go into that business. At the same time, the press laws enacted by the new constitutional regimes to replace the censorship bodies characteristic of the ancien régime had to deal with responsibility for what was being printed, and publishers were part of this new "blame economy," alongside printers, booksellers, and authors.[11]

The bill for a law "against crimes of abuse of freedom of the press" tabled at the June 10, 1826, session of the General Legislative Assembly of the Empire of Brazil demonstrates that, when it came to establishing the legal responsibilities of publishers, the Brazilian situation was similar to that in France. The first articles of Title II of the bill established that those held responsible for press crimes would first be the authors, but since their anonymity was guaranteed by law, printers, publishers, and booksellers would be legally responsible for the content of the printed matter, in precisely that order.[12] Similarly, the dictionaries published in the Empire at that time clearly defined the functions of *editores* (publishers), not confusing them, for example, with printers.[13] However, going beyond legal and semantic abstractions, this book will focus on Paula Brito's life to investigate the historical circumstances that converged to bring about the emergence of the publisher in Brazil—circumstances forged in competition with French publications and through political alliances.

Thus, despite covering the story of five generations of Francisco Paula Brito's family, enslaved men and women who gained their manumission in the eighteenth century, this book focuses mainly on the protagonist's activities between the 1830s and 1850s. His career encompassed watershed moments in Brazilian history in the first half of the nineteenth century. Paula Brito was born just one year after Portugal's Royal Court was transferred to Rio de Janeiro in 1808, fleeing the invasion by Napoleon's troops. The impact of Prince Regent João's flight to the richest part of the vast Portuguese Overseas Empire would be irreversible, culminating in the process that led to the independence and formation of the Brazilian nation state. Moreover, it is important to note that, unlike the Spanish colonies in the Americas, some of which had enjoyed the benefits of printing presses since the sixteenth century, the situation was very different in Portugal's dominions in the Americas. Except for the press of Antônio Isidoro da Fonseca, which operated briefly in Rio de Janeiro in 1747, it was only after the arrival of the prince regent and his family that the Royal Press was established in that city, marking the beginning of the systematic use of printing presses in Portuguese America.[14]

In addition to the Royal Press, the city of Rio de Janeiro also benefited from several improvements made after the arrival of the court, from the Botanical Gardens to the magnificent Royal Library. In the years that followed, the rise of coffee planting in the provinces of Rio de Janeiro, São Paulo, and Minas Gerais produced a political elite that was actively involved

Province of Rio de Janeiro

FIGURE 2. The Brazilian Empire (1846)

in the formation of the Brazilian nation state, while drastically changing the demographics of the nascent Brazilian Empire due to the unprecedented expansion of the transatlantic slave trade. However, it was not just the south-eastern plantations that made use of the abundance of enslaved Africans. Different branches of industry, such as the printing trade, profited not only from slavery but also from the alliances established with the slave-owning elite, as we will see in the case of the publisher Francisco de Paula Brito.

Far from being limited to a recounting the events of an individual's life, there is a vast historical biography on the world of printing. In this regard, Alistair McCleery, in an article on the publisher Allen Lane, defends the importance of the study of the publisher's individual agency to the his-

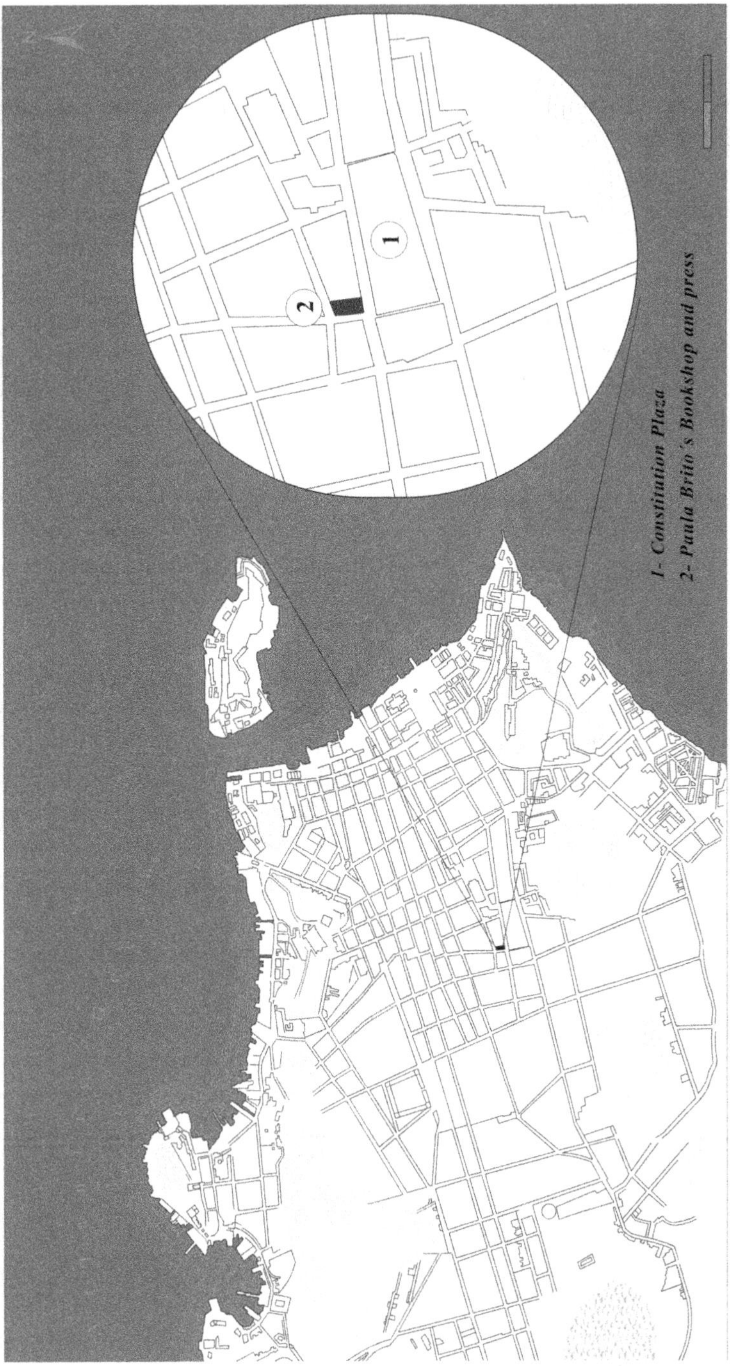

1- *Constitution Plaza*
2- *Paula Brito's Bookshop and press*

FIGURE 3. Rio de Janeiro, the Imperial Capital (1858)

tory of books, considering the application of theoretical concepts such as "the field" and "functional principles" formulated respectively by Pierre Bourdieu and Michel Foucault, to be of little relevance for understanding the publishing market.[15] For the nineteenth century, prime examples of the fruitfulness of such studies include Jean-Yves Mollier's biographies of the Lévy brothers and Louis Hachette, as well as Ezra Greenspan's work on the life of New York publisher George Palmer Putnam.[16] It should be noted, however, that the biographies of publishers fall within a broader context, in which the biographical genre itself, long regarded as "impure," as observed by François Dosse, has been welcomed in the bastions of academia, especially in the last three decades, given the collapse of so-called totalizing paradigms. Since then, craft historians—such as the new British Marxists, the third generation of the *Annales*, and the Italian scholars of "microhistory"—have begun focusing on the experiences and aspirations of flesh-and-blood men and women. Going from individual-agency-centered studies to biography was a major step, and indeed it has been systematically problematized and practiced in the different domains of history, including the history of printing.[17]

Many of the historians who have written about the experiences of nineteenth-century publishers have been able to rely on complete sets of documents, such as the records of Blackwood studied by David Finkelstein at the National Library of Scotland. Considered one of the most complete archives left to us by a nineteenth-century British publishing house, these records enabled Finkelstein to engage in a detailed study of the activities of the company and its directors between 1860 and 1910.[18] In the case of Paula Brito, if similar records once existed, they must have been destroyed in the fire that razed the buildings surrounding the press run by the publisher's widow in the early hours of September 25, 1866. Although the printing workshop was only superficially damaged by the flames, the water the firefighters used to control the blaze damaged most of the late publisher's estate. Thus, writing a biography of Francisco de Paula Brito first required an effort to locate and gather sources. In addition to researching newspapers, initially at the Edgard Leuenroth Archive, and over the past two years using the National Digital Library, I have also studied manuscripts found in different archives and libraries mainly located in Rio de Janeiro.

The story of Francisco de Paula Brito, "the first publisher worthy of the name that we had among us," according to Machado de Assis, will be revisited in this book in four parts. The first, divided into six chapters, deals with the publisher's formative years and activities during the Regency period (1831 to 1841). However, going back to the eighteenth century, we will also see how Paula Brito's family members gradually rid themselves of the bonds of slavery and established themselves as free—and what is more, literate—artisans in Rio de Janeiro. The fact of belonging to a family of freedpersons with a penchant for reading gave the young man access to literacy at a very young age, which made a significant contribution to his apprenticeship as a printer and the development of his taste for poetry. Given the possibilities that emerged after the abdication of Pedro I in 1831, the young Paula Brito decided to buy his cousin Silvino José de Almeida's bookshop, where he later installed a wooden printing press. By becoming a printer-bookseller, Paula Brito was exposing himself to the negative consequences of entering that business, from the threat of having his presses smashed by angry mobs to legal persecution during the Feijó Regency.

Divided into four chapters, the second part deals with the publisher's social ascension in the 1840s. Paula Brito's success as a seller of books, newspapers, and miscellaneous items was essential to the improvements he made in his printing shop. Consequently, that was when Paula Brito became a publisher. Driven by competition with French fictional narratives, the printer-bookseller made the original decision to finance the publication of a work by a Brazilian novelist, the young Teixeira e Sousa. This part of the book also deals with the alliances the publisher formed with Conservative politicians after the coup that declared the majority of Pedro II, well as the organization of labor in his world, both at the press and at home—a microcosm that included foreign workers, hired-out slave women, and free Africans.

After planning the establishment of a large-scale press to meet the needs of Rio de Janeiro's provincial government, Paula Brito founded the Dous de Dezembro company. The third part of this book is entirely devoted to the history of that firm, founded amid the reconversion of capital formerly employed in the transatlantic slave trade to businesses in Rio de Janeiro in the 1850s. The chapters in the fourth and final section deal with the reconstruction of the publisher's businesses after the company failed in 1857. Although he had to scale down his operations and deal with hordes of creditors, some factors enabled Paula Brito to continue printing newspapers and publishing Brazilian authors after his firm went bankrupt. These include the networks of social interactions and personal relationships the publisher-bookseller had formed, such as those established through the Petalogical Society. Furthermore, to expand on this question, part four also discusses the vicissitudes of the book market in Rio de Janeiro, as well as Paula Brito's relations with his authors. At the time, all the raw materials used by printers in Rio de Janeiro were imported, from paper to printing ink, which inevitably affected the cost of books, magazines, and newspapers. There were also serious obstacles to their distribution in the other provinces of Imperial Brazil. Finally, we will see how Paula Brito's widow, Rufina, tried and failed to keep the family business going after his death.

PART ONE

The Ventures and Misadventures of a Free Printer

A "Dove without Gall" and the Court of Public Opinion

O VER THE COURSE of 1833, rumors of the possible return of Emperor Pedro I, who had left for Europe after his abdication on April 7, 1831, began reverberating through the streets of Rio de Janeiro. In 1832, a political faction had been formed in that city with the chief aim of calling for the return of the former ruler whose current title was the Duke of Bragança. They were called the Restorationists or Caramurus.[1] The other two factions active in the city at the time were the Exaltados (Impassioned ones), also known as the Farroupilhas (Ragamuffins), and the Moderates, or Chimangos.[2] As we will see, Moderates and Exaltados had joined forces in Campo da Honra (Field of Honor) plaza, staging the Seventh of April rebellion which forced Pedro to abdicate the throne in favor of his son, who was then a minor. However, as the Moderates gained power, the alliance between those two political identities fell apart.[3] As a result, broadly speaking, while the Caramurus wanted Pedro I to return, the Exaltados were radical liberals who opposed the centralizing project of the Moderates who, in turn, were aligned with the aspirations of the large landowners and merchants of the provinces of Rio de Janeiro, Minas Gerais, and São Paulo.[4]

Just when rumors of the former emperor's return reached a deafening pitch, the Moderates began instrumentalizing the byname Caramuru. At least, so said some newspapers and satirical publications like *O meia-cara*, which observed on November 11, 1833, that "the idea of imminent restoration has given free rein to the Chimangal gang to engage in all sorts of despotism."[5] *Evaristo* backed up that charge by reporting that "the name of Restorationist is given to all those who disagree with the dominant faction [the Moderates] and, through this means, indiscriminately insults honorable Citizens who, dragged off to horrible dungeons, have their hands tied."[6] Indeed, the situation truly began to worsen, both for the Restorationists and the supposed Restorationists, in early December 1833, especially in the evening of the second of that month, Pedro II's eighth birthday.

That night, the Military Society, which, according to the newspaper *A verdade*, "gathered in its bosom all individuals, whether or not they were in the military, who were disgruntled with the Government, and preferably the most brazen Restorationists,"[7] decided to display an illuminated mural that, instead of an effigy of the child-emperor, showed a general who bore a strong resemblance to Pedro I. Some reports state that a justice of the peace was called in, and that, after inspecting the inopportune tribute to the former emperor, he had had the image removed. However, some reports stated that the "indignant populace threw stones at the illumination and the mural, removed it, and stamped on that picture."[8] There were also disturbances at the Theater, where government supporters clashed with backers of José Bonifácio, Pedro II's guardian, whom the Moderates accused of being the Restorationist-in-Chief, allegedly orchestrating a thousand conspiracies from the imperial residence to bring about Pedro I's return.[9]

Three days later, in the afternoon of December 5, over a thousand people gathered outside the Military Society's headquarters in Largo de São Francisco de Paula. It was said that that organization, viewed as a bastion of Caramurus, would be holding an assembly that day. The furious crowd stoned the building and smashed the plaque bearing the society's name. A smaller group is said to have entered the building and ransacked it, tossing furniture and papers into the street. The crowd only left the scene when a justice of the peace appeared.[10] However, not satisfied with the destruction of the Military Society's headquarters, some of them headed for the

FIGURE 4. Praça da Constituição (Constitution Square)

printers' workshops that produced periodicals and pamphlets linked to the Restorationists.

Reports of the incident do not make it clear whether the group first attacked David da Fonseca Pinto's Paraguassú Press before going on to Nicolau Lobo Vianna's Diário Press (Tipografia do Diário), or if they split up and destroyed both workshops at once.[11] In any case, an account by Nicolau Lobo Vianna published a few days later in *Diário do Rio de Janeiro* gives a very clear idea of the afternoon's events:

> doors and windows [were] smashed in, and all the presses, furnishings, and other printing equipment were destroyed; all the printed matter, notices published and awaiting publication, was destroyed, everything scattered in the street, our establishment (through which with immense effort we eke out a living for our large family) was reduced to nothing, or a heap of rubble, and the losses we have suffered are considerable.[12]

The situation was probably very similar at David da Fonseca Pinto's establishment—presses and printed matter destroyed, type scattered in the street, everything reduced to "a heap of rubble." It so happens that the crowd's bloodlust, or rather lust for Caramuru presses and pamphlets, was not sated by ransacking the Paraguassú and Diário. There was a third work-shop to be demolished in Rio de Janeiro, and the horde—which it certainly was from the printers' perspective—headed for Praça da Constitu-ição (Constitution Square).

At about seven p.m., a group "armed with sticks" arrived at Brito and Company's Fluminense Press (Tipografia Fluminense de Brito e Companhia). Shouting "Paula Brito restaurador" ("Paula Brito, restorationist"), they threatened to break in and give it the same treatment meted out to the other two presses. Francisco de Paula Brito must have been overcome with panic. After all, the results of two years of hard work were about to be destroyed. And they would have been, but for the intervention of the justice of the peace of Santíssimo Sacramento parish, José Inácio Coimbra, who ordered the crowd to disperse and assigned a National Guard patrol to guard the printer's door.[13]

The following day, still profoundly shaken, Paula Brito wrote and printed his *Proclamação aos compatriotas* (Proclamation to the compatriots), a one-page document in which he aimed to give a "sincere account" of his "political faith." In it, he refuted accusations that he belonged to the Restorationist faction, declaring himself to be a "true Exaltado." He was a "Brazilian who took up arms among you on the glorious 7 of April [of happy memory], and, enlisted in the national ranks, I protested, defending the Nation, Constitution and Nationality with my life." According to his Proclamation, the confusion had arisen from a "small pamphlet"—perhaps a Caramuru newspaper called *A mineira no Rio de Janeiro*, as we will see in Chapter 5—in which Paula Brito, proclaiming himself a "FREE PRINTER" in capital letters, stated that he belonged to "no party whatsoever."[14]

Meanwhile, the Moderate press celebrated the "lively conduct of the people of Rio de Janeiro on the second, fifth and sixth of December, in which they made the Restorationists disappear."[15] In its Notices section, *Sete d'Abril* mocked the ravaged printers' workshops, observing, for example, that "we really miss the *Escaped Slaves Daily:* now two have just escaped who are even captains. If anyone finds the two maroons, please have them delivered to their master, who is in Lisbon."[16] Ransacked on December 5, the *Diário do Rio de Janeiro*, a newspaper that mainly contained advertisements, including escaped slave announcements, was not published between December 6 and 11, and came out in a smaller format between the twelfth and seventeenth. Therefore, the joke can be interpreted as follows: the "escaped slaves" mentioned in *Sete d'Abril* must have been Nicolau Lobo Vianna and David da Fonseca Pinto, and their Lisbonite "master," Pedro I.

Francisco de Paula Brito did not escape the editor of *Sete d'Abril*'s caustic comments. On December 21, a note in that newspaper's Notices read as follows: "It is false that Mr. *Paula Brito* owes money and obligations to Ripanso and his Brother; it is also false that he is currently occupied with slandering and disparaging them."[17] The style of that section of the Moderate newspaper aimed to amuse its readers through sarcasm. Therefore, the editor meant to say the exact opposite: that Paula Brito did, in fact, owe money and favors to Ripanso and his brother, and had ungratefully slandered and disparaged them. Before learning who Ripanso was, let us take a look at another notice mocking Paula Brito, published in *Sete d'Abril* on January 1, 1834: "It is entirely false that the papers found on Rua da Ajuda, following the destruction of the Diário Press, included the originals of the most infamous notices published in the *Manteiga* signed by the *Patriot* Mr. Paula Brito. This gentleman is a dove without gall, and not a Restorationist at all."[18]

Once again, and through the same sarcasm, the reader was meant to understand the exact opposite. Far from being a "dove without gall," it meant that Paula Brito was as much a Restorationist as the "small amount of printed matter" that his workshop produced, and more than that, he was the author of the notices published in the *Manteiga* (Butter), as the *Diário do Rio de Janeiro* was called, which had been found amid the wreckage of Nicolau Lobo Vianna's press. The insult from *Sete d'Abril* left a deep impression; so much so that, two years later, Paula Brito referred to it in verses he published in *Mulher do Simplício* (Simplício's [the simpleton's] wife):

> And so that you know
> That I am speaking true,
> Just as a certain writer said,
> "I am a *dove without gall*."[19]

However, as early as January 1834, Paula Brito, who wrote that he was "already tired of hearing [what] is being said about me *after the events of December 5, 1833*," once again took up his pen and strips of paper and launched a broadside against the editor of *Sete d'Abril*. It was a lengthy reply that, when printed, took up seven of the eight pages of the January 21 edition of the *Carioca: Jornal político, amigo da liberdade e da lei* (Political newspaper, friend of liberty, and the law). Paulo Brito had printed that newspaper at the Fluminense Press since August of the previous year, which may explain why it was not hard to negotiate that many pages with the publication's editor.

The article had two objectives. First, Paula Brito wanted to make it clear to his readers that he did not owe any money at all to Ripanso and his brother and that he was not the author of the notices published in the *Diário*. Ripanso, as Paula Brito explained, was what "the newspapers of the former opposition" called the poet, journalist, politician, and bookseller Evaristo da Veiga. Thus, after refuting *Sete d'Abril*'s first accusation, he structured the remainder of the first part of the article around an account of his life story, from his childhood to the time of writing. However, although there are some elements of an autobiographical account, [20] the second objective of the article is more of a defense in which the printer, acting as his own advocate, sought to redeem himself before the court that had condemned him. In his words, Paula Brito wanted "to present my defense to the Court of Public Opinion, which it will judge as the supreme Jury." Acquittal by the Court of Public Opinion was essential, because despite his passion, reaffirmed in nearly every sentence of the article, Paula Brito did not hide his desire to restore his "credit." Although he wanted "the good of the Nation," he was not interested in "being anything more than a *printer*."

The events of December 5, 1833, indicate that public opinion, which was in full bloom in the city, [21] also ruled Rio de Janeiro's printing activities with an iron fist. The tension is interesting to see, because before or despite describing himself as a member of a political faction, Francisco de Paula Brito refused to give up the prerogatives of a "free printer." However, there is no doubt that the Restorationist pamphlet that caused him so much grief was unsigned, and Paula Brito tried in vain to exempt himself from responsibility for the content of the publications that came off his presses.

This situation led to two basic problems for nineteenth-century journalism in Brazil: the institutionalization of anonymity and, therefore, the question of attributing legal responsibility for anonymous publications. As we will see, the crowd that almost ransacked Paula Brito's press was acting very much like the judiciary and enforcers of the laws enacted and revised since the reign of King João VI to keep strict control of what was published, and consequently read, in this country. While authors were shielded by anonymity, the printers could be readily identified and, in effect, had to redeem themselves before official and unofficial tribunals, such as the court of public opinion. But looking into this matter more deeply, we should first learn how Francisco de Paula Brito, a young *pardo* (brown, mixed-race) man, the son and grandson of freed slaves, joined the ranks of those printers.

CHAPTER 2

Plantation Lad

IN HIS ARTICLE in *O carioca*, Paula Brito gave a very succinct account of his childhood: "A son of the City of Rio de Janeiro, but raised far away from the perils of [that city], I always lived in the bosom of my family, with parents of small means, until the age of thirteen." However, a little later, the printer associated the color of his skin with the causes of the dire events of December 5, 1833: "I am Brazilian, albeit a man of color, the main cause of the war against me; but it honors me just as much as those of a lighter color than mine glory in being white." Paula Brito concluded by stating: "I am speaking of my nation's business because the Constitution of my Country gives me that right."[1]

It is interesting to note how color and the Constitution intersected in the printer's narrative. Indeed, the Imperial Constitution, enacted in 1824, when Paula Brito was fifteen years old, did not discriminate between Brazilian citizens on the basis of skin color.[2] The way Paula Brito developed his argument a decade later demonstrates the political implications of the absence of a racial clause in the definition of Brazilian citizenship. Despite his *cor trigueira* (brown color), which so incensed his enemies, Paula Brito viewed himself as a full citizen with the backing of the Constitution. And he was not the only one to see himself that way.

Paula Brito belonged to a generation of educated men of color who were born free between the end of the eighteenth century and the first decade of the nineteenth century, reaching political adulthood between the twilight of the First Reign and the dawn of the Regencies, standing out in politics and journalism, among other fields.[3] As we will see, the historical experience of these young citizens *de cor trigueira* was closely linked to the emergence of newspapers and satirical publications such as O *mulato, ou, O homem de cor* (The mulatto, or, The man of color), printed in Paula Brito's press in 1833. Among other demands, they advocated giving that significant segment of society access to public office. First, however, we must consider that the experience of full citizenship by men of color in the first decades of the Empire of Brazil was forged by the experience of freedom in Portuguese America. Because that movement was exemplified by Paula Brito and his family, we will take a look at it in this chapter.

The surname that Paula Brito adopted from his maternal grandfather came from the latter's father and former owner, Portuguese sergeant major Francisco Pereira de Brito,[4] who, together with his brothers Captain José Pereira de Brito and Second Lieutenant Julião Pereira de Brito, left Portugal in the 1720s, crossed the Atlantic and climbed the sierra to reach the mines of Serro do Frio, where it was said that gold and diamonds sprang from the ground.

Sergeant Major Francisco Pereira de Brito owned many slaves who were baptized in the village of Tapanhuacanga, which suggests that Paula Brito's great-grandfather settled there. Seven leagues from the Vila do Príncipe, it was the county seat of Serro do Frio, created as a result of the discovery of gold in those parts in 1714. That precious metal was the cause of the first exodus toward that area in the early eighteenth century. However, the mass immigration intensified in the 1720s, when diamonds were found in Arraial do Tejuco. By the time the governor officially notified King João V of the discovery of diamonds in 1729, the news had already spread like wildfire in Lisbon. Some even suspected that the governor had taken his time to write to the king, because it was said that he had benefited from clandestine mining. Thus, the Crown only extended its administrative, military, and tax apparatus to the extraction of the diamonds in that year.[5]

Between 1725 and 1737, certified church records—basically the baptism and death records found in the Ecclesiastical Archives of the Diocese of Diamantina, Minas Gerais—show that the Pereira de Brito brothers became the masters of most of the enslaved in the Vila do Príncipe area. Considering

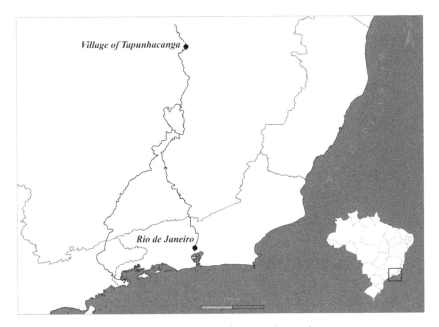

FIGURE 5. The Caminho Novo (ca. 1750)

the cases in which some records may have referred to the same individual, we can estimate that Captain José Pereira de Brito owned roughly twenty-five slaves, while Sergeant Major Francisco Pereira de Brito was the owner of about twenty.[6]

One of the enslaved women the sergeant major owned was Rosa who, after obtaining her manumission, adopted her former masters' surname, becoming Rosa Pereira de Brito. Rosa was born in 1722, and at the age of fifteen, in 1737, while still enslaved, gave birth to a son, Martinho, sired by her master.[7] The boy was not the only child that the sergeant major had with his slave women. Martinho had at least two half-sisters: Marcelina,[8] the sergeant major's daughter with Florência, a black woman, and Natalina, who appeared in the baptismal records of Anna do Ó, a slave of Captain José Pereira de Brito, as the "daughter of Sergeant Major Francisco Pereira de Brito, a free *parda* [brown or mixed-race woman]."[9]

Possibly because he was the master's son, Martinho was freed at the font when he was baptized by Second Lieutenant Julião Pereira de Brito in São José chapel in Tapanhuacanga. As we have seen, Rosa also obtained her freedom and, years later, in 1762, on the occasion of her son's marriage, declared to the vicar of the parish that her name was "Rosa Pereira de Brito, free

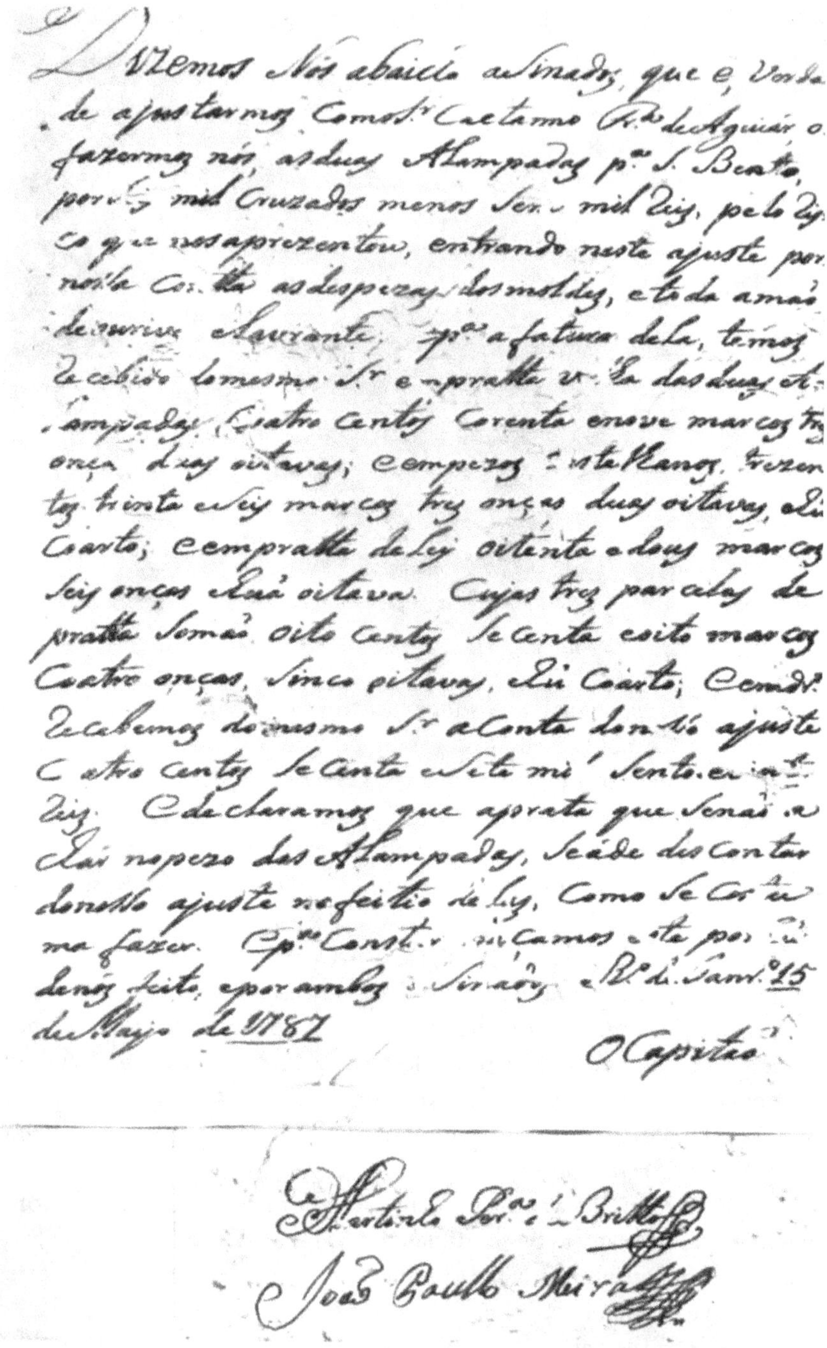

Dizemos Nós abaixo assinados, que é verdade de ajustarmos com o Sr. Caetano R.s de Aguiar o fazermos nós as duas Alampadas p.a S. Bento, por [illegible] mil Cruzados menos seis mil reis, pelo risco que nos aprezentou, entrando neste ajuste por nossa conta as despezas dos moldes, e toda a mão de servir Lavrante, p.a a fatura dela, temos recebido do mesmo Sr. em pratta v.a das duas Alampadas Coatro centos corenta e nove marcos tres onças duas oitavas; e em pezos estelhanos trezentos trinta e seis marcos tres onças duas oitavas, e hu' Coarto; e em pratta de ley oitenta e dous marcos seis onças e huã oitava. Cujas tres parcelas de pratta somão oito centos secenta e oito marcos Coatro onças, sinco oitavas, e hu' Coarto; e em dr.o recebemos do mesmo Sr. a conta deste ajuste Coatro centos secenta e sete mil cento e [illegible] reis. E declaramos que a pratta que se não achar no pezo das Alampadas, se ha de descontar deste ajuste no feitio de ley, como se costuma fazer. E p.a const.a assinamos esta por [illegible] de nós feita, e por ambos assinados. R.o de Jan.ro 15 de Mayo de 1787

O Capitão

Martinho Per.a de Britto

João Paulo Meira

FIGURE 6. Signature of Captain Martinho Pereira de Brito, Paula Brito's grandfather (1787)

black woman, single, born in this parish and presently a resident of Vila do Príncipe who works for a living and says she is forty years old, a little more or less."[10] "Works for a living" says very little about how Rosa supported herself and her children. In any case, she owned at least one slave woman, Maria, of Angolan ethnicity, who died in September 1758.[11] By that time, however, Martinho Pereira de Brito no longer lived near his mother. In 1751, at the age of fourteen, the boy decided to head down Caminho Novo, the road to Rio de Janeiro.

In the first half of the eighteenth century, Rio de Janeiro's strategic geo-political importance in the Portuguese Empire was becoming increasingly clear. Coincidentally, the freedman Martinho Pereira de Brito arrived in that city in the same year as the creation of the Tribunal da Relação (Court of Appeal), whose jurisdiction included the captaincies in the central-south of Portuguese America, from Minas Gerais to Santa Catarina. Due to its proximity with Minas and the disputes between Spain and Portugal over the territories in the Sacramento colony, to the south, Rio de Janeiro became the seat of government of the state of Brazil, and the residence of its vice-roys in 1763.[12] Martinho worked there as a silversmith, a trade he may have learned in Vila do Príncipe. The young man also enlisted in the city's pardo battalion. As a result, in January 1765, Lieutenant Martinho Pereira de Brito, then twenty-eight, lived in the parish of Sé, making a living "from his trade as a silversmith."[13]

Martinho became a renowned artisan, and in May 1787 he was hired to put the final touches on the silver lamps that would adorn the Benedictine monastery's chancel. The contract with then Captain Martinho Pereira de Brito was signed at a time when the manufacture of the lamps had already caused serious problems for the abbot, Friar José de Jesus Campos. Six or seven years earlier, his predecessors had commissioned Caetano Ferreira de Aguiar "graciously to prepare and have made two lamps for the chancel of his monastery." At that time, Caetano was given the silver from the old lamps, as well as a large amount of money. However, time passed and the work was not finished. In view of this situation, the abbot was forced to sign a new contract with Captain Martinho and João Paulo Meira so that they could make the lamps.[14]

According to the contract, the artisans would receive "six thousand cru-zados, less one hundred thousand réis, due to the risk they presented to us." For that sum, they were entrusted with making the molds for the lamps, as well as paying for the services of the goldsmith and silversmith. In the "Current Account of Expenses" attached to the engagement letter signed by the individuals responsible for the project, we find the names of the other artisans involved, including the "woodworker Valentim," who received 32,000 réis for the "molds for the lamps."[15] The woodworker must have been Valentim da Fonseca e Silva, also known as Mestre Valentim, a sculptor and metal, wood, and ivory carver who was known for important urban planning projects in Rio de Janeiro, such as the Public Promenade built when D. Luís de Vasconcelos was viceroy of Brazil. The records for the lamps made for the Benedictine monastery suggest that Captain Martinho had very close ties with Mestre Valentim. As both were the sons of Portuguese men and their enslaved women, they shared similar backgrounds. Furthermore, Valentim was born in Arraial de Gouveia, near Vila do Príncipe, in around 1740.[16]

In 1765, after going through lengthy proceedings to obtain a marriage license, Captain Martinho wedded Anna Maria da Conceição, a slightly younger woman who had been baptized in the See Cathedral of Rio de Janeiro in December 1741.[17] Anna Maria was "the natural [illegitimate] child of Francisca Ribeira, a single, free black woman" and an unknown father. Like the groom, Anna Maria may have been born a slave, as she is described as a *parda forra* (mixed-race freedwoman) in some documents.[18] Although she had submitted all the necessary certificates, the young woman was obliged to give a statement to the Matrimonial Judge at the Ecclesiastical Chamber of Rio de Janeiro. On that occasion, she repeated her declaration that she was "single, free, and unencumbered, and had not promised marriage to anyone except Martinho Pereira de Brito, declaring that she wanted to marry him of her own free will."[19]

The children of Captain Martinho and Anna Maria began coming into this world the year after the wedding. Maria Joaquina da Conceição, in 1766;[20] José, in 1768;[21] and Francisco, in 1771.[22] José and Francisco were baptized in Candelária Church, which suggests that the family lived in that parish. Pinpointing their address even more precisely, the "Almanaque da cidade Rio de Janeiro para o ano de 1792" (1792 almanac for Rio de Janeiro), in which Captain Martinho was listed among the artisans of the "fourth auxiliary battalion of pardo freedmen," states that the family lived on Rua do Cano.[23] Two years later, the 1794 almanac reported that Martinho, described as captain of the Fourth Grenadiers of the third auxiliary battalion of pardo freedmen, lived on Rua do Piolho.[24] In the nineteenth century, that street was renamed Rua da Carioca, and all indications are that Captain Martinho's family lived in that area for generations.

In 1795, the captain's eldest daughter, Maria Joaquina da Conceição, married the carpenter Jacinto Antunes Duarte. Then described as a *pardo forro* (mixed-race freedman), the "son of Anna, the parda slave of José Duarte," her husband was born enslaved in Nossa Senhora do Desterro de Campo Grande parish, Rio de Janeiro. He was baptized in September 1764, and his freedom, together with that of other slaves owned by José Duarte, came six years later, in June 1770.[25] His master had died around that time, and Silvestre Rodrigues, José Duarte's executor, was responsible for the "manumission through coarctation" that the deceased had ordered in his will. Coarctation involved paying for manumission in installments, which was apparently advantageous for masters and slaves in the eighteenth century.[26] In addition to Jacinto, who was valued at 20,000 réis, the pardo Pantaleão, 64,000 réis, the crioulos (Brazilian-born children of Africans) Francisco and Domingos, 30,000 and 38,000 réis respectively, and Maria Benguela, valued at 15,000 réis were freed by the same means.[27] We do not know how each slave went about paying the amount assigned to them. Jacinto was worth 5,000 réis more than Maria Benguela, which leads us to presume that she had recently arrived from Africa. Furthermore, it must be considered that Jacinto was too young to raise a large amount of money. Therefore, his mother, who may have obtained her freedom some time before, could have played a decisive role in his manumission.[28] Years later, when he had to prove that he was free to marry, Jacinto told the Matrimonial Judge that he had left Campo Grande when he was "little," and gone to Rio de Janeiro, where he made a living as a carpenter.

The couple were wed in late April 1795. Two years later, their first child, José, was baptized in See Cathedral in May 1797. Francisco de Paula, possibly one of the younger children, if not the youngest, was born twelve years later, on December 2, 1809. Moreira de Azevedo also mentions that the couple had a daughter named Ana Angélica.[29] The carpenter, Jacinto, his wife, and their children lived in Rio de Janeiro until 1815. That year, when Francisco de Paula was about six years old, the family moved to São Nicolau de Suruí, a district of the town of Magé, a few leagues from Rio.

They moved because Jacinto had leased a plantation owned by the widow Bernarda Pinto Pereira. In November 1810, the widow purchased fifty-two *braças* (about 104 yards) of land in Suruí from Captain Luiz Manuel da Silva Paes Bolina. In the deed of sale drafted in Rio de Janeiro, there is no mention of improvements to the farm, such as houses, mills, or fields. This indicates that Bernarda may have invested more money in the property before

FIGURE 7. Signature of the freedman Jacinto Antunes Duarte, Paula Brito's father (1819)

leasing it to Jacinto.[30] The region had been an important producer of cassava flour since the eighteenth century. Thus, like the farm on which Paula Brito spend a considerable part of his childhood, most of the properties in the Recôncavo Fluminense (Rio de Janeiro bay area) produced cassava flour.[31] The lease that his father signed on August 28, 1815, stated that the farm consisted of "houses with tiled roofs, a flour mill. . . . Two cassava grinding wheels, two copper ovens [and further] items for making flour and a canoe." The lease also included "a beast of burden" and ten slaves who lived on the property, of whom we have the names of eight: José, João, Sebastião, Francisca, Diogo, Violante, Quitéria, and Domingos. Regarding the enslaved individuals, the lease stated that if any of them should die during the period of the contract, Jacinto would have to repay the cost of that loss, which was to be included in the annual payments made to the widow or her heirs. The lease was for twelve years. During the first two, Jacinto was to pay 100,000 réis per annum, and 150,000 réis annually for the remaining ten.[32] Based on the dates in the lease, the Paula Brito family was supposed to return the farm to its owners in 1827.

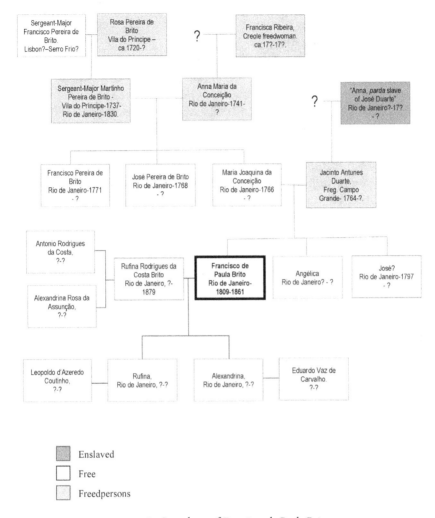

FIGURE 8. Genealogy of Francisco de Paula Brito

Paula Brito returned to Rio before that date. However, he lived on the cassava farm in Suruí between the ages of six and thirteen. His family must have lived in one of the tiled-roof houses, and Maria Joaquina da Conceição may have used one of the enslaved women listed in the lease as a house slave. The young man probably knew all the enslaved people working for his father. It would not be going too far to imagine that Paula Brito's childhood was not very different from that of many other children raised on farms in nineteenth-century Brazil, living amid festivities, early schooling, and slavery. Just another plantation lad.

"Without lessons or teachers," according to his first biographer, he supposedly learned to read and write from his sister Ana Angélica in Suruí.[33] That is unlikely, however, particularly when we see the number of documents his forebears signed that are still extant—as we can see in Figures 6 and 7, which show the signatures of the publisher's maternal grandfather and father. Although historians of reading have observed that it is risky to consider a signature, or better yet, the ability to write one's own name, as an indication of full literacy,[34] such documents show that these men and women who had emerged from slavery in Portuguese America had somehow learned to read and write and taught those skills to their children, perceiving their importance in the conscientiously undertaken process of social advancement.

We do not have enough data to determine to what extent the literacy of Francisco de Paula Brito's family was an exception or the rule among freedpersons in Rio de Janeiro in the latter decades of the eighteenth century. Although we have valuable information on pardo and *mameluco* priests who, despite being excluded from high ecclesiastical posts, received an education and played important roles in the Portuguese Atlantic world, as well as literate pardos and blacks in eighteenth-century Paraíba,[35] historical research has a long way to go to produce a social history of literacy among freed people of color and their free-born descendants. In the long term, however, the effects of this process can be understood when men of color who were one or two generations removed from slavery saw themselves as citizens of a newly created Empire and, with that prerogative, went into the streets and the newspapers to demand their rights.[36]

CHAPTER 3

Apprentice Printer and Poet

FRANCISCO DE PAULA BRITO returned to Rio de Janeiro in about 1823. The thirteen-year-old boy was taken in by his maternal grandfather, the octogenarian sergeant major of the Pardos battalion, Martinho Pereira de Brito, possibly in the house on Rua do Piolho. There are no indications that Paula Brito's parents returned to Rio after their leasehold of the cassava flour plantation expired. Between the time of his grandfather's death and his marriage in May 1833, Paula Brito lived in the home of his cousin, the bookseller Silvino José de Almeida.[1]

At the time, working in the printing business must have been far beyond the expectations of that recent arrival to the city, as Paula Brito's first job was in an apothecary shop. The *Almanach do Rio de Janeiro para o ano de 1824* mentions one João d'Almeida Brito, who lived on Rua detrás do Carmo and is listed as the director of the Santa Casa da Misericórdia Apothecary. This may be a coincidence, but the surname Almeida, shared by his cousin Silvino, and Brito, the same as that of Sergeant Major Martinho, suggest that the young man may have had relatives who were involved in the pharmaceutical trade. However, we know that Paula Brito only spent a few months in that business, because in 1824 he began working at the Imperial and National Press (Tipografia Imperial e Nacional) as an apprentice printer.[2]

As Paula Brito recalled years later, at the time, the Imperial and National Press was run by Brás Antônio Castrioto, who had joined it as a typesetter in 1810, when it was still the Royal Press (Impressão Régia). Before rising to the administrative ranks, Castrioto was also a second clerk and payroll officer.[3] Little is known about the working conditions for apprentices at the Imperial and National Press in Rio de Janeiro. Judging from the wages that apprentices received in another government department, the Imperial Kitchen—just 7,000 réis per month—those young men must have suffered financial hardship.[4] However, the official government press was not the only place where one could learn to be a typesetter. When applying for a job at the workshop where the National and Public Library of Rio de Janeiro would be established in 1822, the typesetter Gaspar José Monteiro stated in his application that he had taught his craft to many people "who are plying their trade at different presses." Gaspar also observed that shortly before, he had "trained several typesetters at the [press] of Silva Porto e Companhia, preparing the workshop for operation."[5]

Certainly, Paula Brito did not decide to become a printer by chance. The considerable increase in the circulation of newspapers and pamphlets during the process of obtaining Brazil's political independence must have stimulated his interest in typesetting and printing presses.[6] From then on, typesetters and printers could find good work opportunities in Rio de Janeiro and beyond. In 1823, for example, the master printer José Francisco Lopes was hired "to direct the national press of the Province of Bahia" in the Town of Cachoeira, with a salary of 400,000 réis per year.[7]

When he started working at the National Press, Paula Brito must have had good knowledge of Portuguese grammar, as this was an essential requirement for aspiring printers. At least, this is stated in the *Manual de typographia braziliense* (Manual of Brazilian printing), published in Rio in 1832 by René Ogier. According to the manual, an apprentice printer's duties ranged from cleaning the workshop to separating and sorting type, as well as copying original manuscripts that would be distributed to the typesetters. To teach the printer's craft, Ogier advised that the process should be carried out slowly and carefully using large type to instill "good habits" and achieve "excellent composition."[8]

However, while Ogier's manual recommended that apprentice printers should have good reading and writing skills, Francisco de Paula Brito must have been outstanding in that regard, since he was given to writing verses. As we will see, at different times poetry played a very important part in Paula Brito's career. As early as 1823, it helped bring him to the attention of the brothers Evaristo and João Pedro da Veiga. In the essay he published in *O carioca*, in which he tried to justify himself before the court of public opinion regarding his close relations with the Veigas—"Ripanso and his brother"—Paula Brito noted that at the age of "fourteen, when, already influenced by love of country, I had written a few verses, I submitted them to for editing to Mr. Evaristo [da Veiga], who will not refuse to confirm the truth of what I am saying."[9]

Evaristo da Veiga was not much older than Paula Brito. Born in 1799, he was twenty-four years old when he met the young man who had just returned from the countryside. Despite his youth and although he had not attended a European university, Evaristo displayed outstanding erudition — he spoke Greek, Latin, French, and English—acquired by reading the books sold by his father, the Portuguese Luís Saturnino da Veiga, who became a bookseller in Rio de Janeiro after retiring as a royal teacher. In 1823, the year he began reading and editing Paula Brito's poetry, Evaristo and his older brother, João Pedro da Veiga, left their father's business to open their own bookshop on Rua da Quitanda, on the corner of Rua de São Pedro. The brothers worked together until November 1827, when Evaristo purchased the bookshop of the Frenchman Bompard, on Rua dos Pescadores, no. 49.[10] The following month, Evaristo began writing for *Aurora Fluminense*, the newspaper that would make him one of the most influential journalists in Brazil, elected twice to the legislature of Minas Gerais province. However, back in 1823, when the future politician was still a fledgling bookseller, it was poetry that brought him and the grandson of the sergeant major of the Pardos together. Like Paula Brito, Evaristo had begun writing poetry at an early age. His first Arcadian poems date from 1811, when he was twelve years old. Therefore, young Paula Brito, "influenced by love of country," found in Evaristo da Veiga the ideal reader, editor, and possibly mentor.

Probably with Evaristo's encouragement, Paula Brito must have written and rewritten verses during the nearly four-year period he spent at the Imperial and National Press. After his apprenticeship, as his first biographer noted, the young man is believed to have found a job, first at the press of René Ogier, and then at that of Pierre Plancher, both French printers.[11] After three decades of experience in the printing business in Europe, Ogier had arrived in Rio de Janeiro in 1826 and thrived there. Twelve years later, when he was applying to be naturalized, he informed the authorities that he owned "a large printing house" as well as "two warehouses of books for sale, paper, and a printing factory," and all of those establishments employed "Brazilian workers."[12] However, Paula Brito did not mention Ogier when he recounted the beginning of his career in O carioca. He only named Pierre Plancher, whose esteem he must have gained, as he was "employed for years as the director of the printing press department."

Paula Brito may have worked for Plancher between 1827 and 1830, when he briefly joined the Second Company of the Third Hunters' Battalion of Rio de Janeiro as an aide. In 1827, Plancher founded the newspaper *Jornal do commercio* in Rio de Janeiro, along with his son Émile Seignot-Plancher and the physician, Joseph Sigaud. That date could coincide with the hiring and inclusion of Paula Brito as a typesetter on the new payroll.[13] In any case, the years he worked with Plancher were important, because as he noted in O carioca, Paula Brito owed the Frenchman "in addition to an enormous debt, the first elements of my little or no wealth."[14]

Pierre-René-François Plancher de la Noé was born in Mans in 1779. After starting out in the typographic arts in 1798, the bookseller-publisher eventually established himself in Paris, more precisely in the Latin Quarter, in 1815. Over the course of seven years of activity in the French capital, Plancher published 150 titles, including works by important names in liberal thinking, such as Benjamin Constant, François Guizot, Madame de Staël, and the Marquis de Lafayette, among others. However, competition in the Parisian publishing market was fierce. In 1820, the year Paula Brito's benefactor gained his *brevet*, there were 254 printer-booksellers in that city, most of them concentrated in the Latin Quarter. Furthermore, Plancher began having serious problems with the law due to the political writings that left his presses. In light of these circumstances, it is easy to infer why Plancher, his wife, Jeanne Seignot, and his son Emile packed up their books, dismantled the presses, and crossed the ocean in search of new markets, arriving in Rio de Janeiro in February 1824.[15]

In Brazil, Plancher established good relations with Pedro I, which was very good for business, as he soon boasted the title of Imperial Printer. According to Marco Morel, if "Plancher was a plebeian and *sans-culotte* in Europe, he became a nobleman in Brazil"—or a "hunchback," the opposition's unflattering term for those who bowed to the emperor. In 1830, the liberal extremist Ezequiel Correia dos Santos openly derided him as an "ugly, hunchbacked, and shameless Frenchman."[16] That may have been when

Pierre Plancher suffered the attack that Moreira de Azevedo mentions in his biography of Paula Brito. On that occasion, the young typesetter apparently dispersed—"with complete poise and calm"—a furious crowd that had broken into Plancher's workshop, incensed by an article published in the *Jornal do commercio*. Moreira de Azevedo may have overstated Paula Brito's heroism, but the difficult political situation in which Pedro I found himself in the late 1830s makes this story credible, at the very least. In any event, it must have been after that incident, in recognition of his bravery, that Paula Brito was promoted to "director of presses" at Plancher's workshop.[17]

It was, therefore, while working for Pierre and Émile Seignot-Plancher that Paula Brito began amassing his "little or no wealth." But a no less important part of the "enormous debt" that Paula Brito owed to the Planchers was the vast technical and above all cultural framework that the Frenchmen had introduced to Rio de Janeiro. It may have been at the Planchers' workshop that Paula Brito learned or improved his knowledge of French—the language from which he would translate some short stories and plays. It may also have been during that period that he was introduced to or established closer ties with freemasonry.[18]

Around 1834, by which time Francisco de Paula was a partner in the Tipografia Fluminense, Plancher returned to France after selling the *Jornal do commercio* and his press to his fellow countrymen Junius Villeneuve and Maugenol for over 50,000,000 réis.[19] When Plancher died in Paris nine years later, Paulo Brito—then the sole owner of the Tipografia Imparcial—was becoming a major businessman and printer in Rio de Janeiro. But let us not get ahead of ourselves, as Francisco de Paula Brito may have not only left Plancher's workshop but the printing business entirely in the late 1830s, if only for a while.

We have more than enough information about the period in which the young printer served as an aide with the Second Company of the Third Hunters Battalion of Rio de Janeiro. In the article he published in *O carioca*, referring to his participation in the overthrow of Pedro I on April 7, 1831, Paula Brito observed: "and as an aide in the 2nd Comp. of the 3rd Battalion of Hunters, I no longer had a life of my own—it was entirely given up to my beloved country." This statement implies that, during the period in which he served as an aide, Paula Brito may have actually set his compositor's tray and type aside altogether. After all, until the creation of the National Guard in 1832, military service was still an important means of social advancement for freedmen and pardos, as it had been for Sergeant Major Martinho Pereira de Brito decades before.[20]

However, with a certain margin of safety, we can surmise that Paula Brito's armed service only lasted from the end of 1830 to April 1831. This supposition is mainly due to the lack of any mention of Second Company in the official records. For example, in 1825, the *Almanach do Rio de Janeiro* only listed the Third Hunters Battalion of Rio de Janeiro, commanded by Colonel Manuel Antonio Leitão Bandeira, whose aide was Gregório Álvaro Sanches. The company which Paula Brito joined may have been formed later. In any event, the young man must have been proud to wear the uniform of the Third Hunters Battalion, which may have been similar to the one advertised in the *Diário do Rio de Janeiro* in March 1837: "For Sale: an embroidered uniform, bandolier, leather cap, and beret, all in good condition, which can serve for any cadet in the 3rd Hunters Battalion; interested parties should go to Rua do Sabão between Ourives and Vala streets, no. 174."[21] The last reference I have found to this subject is in "Hino ao memorável dia 7 de abril de 1831" (Hymn to the memorable day 7 April 1831), written by Paula Brito and printed by Émile Seignot-Plancher. The poem is signed: "Francisco de Paula Brito/Aide to the 2nd Company of the 3rd Hunters Battalion."[22] Therefore, on April 6 and 7, 1831, when the people and the troops came together in Campo de Santana to depose the emperor, we know that Paula Brito was among the troops. He was a soldier-poet.

CHAPTER 4

1831, Year of Possibilities

S ERGEANT MAJOR MARTINHO PEREIRA DE BRITO was a widower when
he died at the venerable age of ninety-three, on July 4, 1830. Paula
Brito, who had lived with his grandfather since he returned to Rio de
Janeiro seven years earlier, may have spent his last moments at his side and
attended his funeral—the sergeant major was buried in one of the tombs
of the Hospício Church, enshrouded in the habit of the Conception confraternity.[1] We do know that it was after his grandfather's death that Paula
Brito moved to the house of a cousin, the pardo bookseller Silvino José de
Almeida, on Praça da Constituição, no. 51.

Silvino had been dealing in books in Rio de Janeiro since at least 1823.
In 1824, his bookshop on Rua dos Inválidos was listed in the city's *Almanach* as the only establishment that worked exclusively with the sale of
books—unlike Plancher, for example, who was not only a bookseller but
was also listed as a printer. In the 1825 edition of the *Almanach*, Silvino's
bookshop is shown at the same address, but that year his cousin Paula Brito's
name appeared as a "bookseller bookbinder."[2] A bookbinder's work was
extremely important at a time when books, whether they were printed in
Rio de Janeiro or imported, were stitched by hand and bound with a cover
tailored to the customer's taste and means. Silvino's clientele included the

Imperial and Public Library of Rio de Janeiro, whose collection contained 975 volumes bound by Paula Brito's cousin between September 1823 and March 1832. In addition to the gazettes and almanacs of Rio de Janeiro, the inventory of works entrusted to the bookbinder include rare books printed between the sixteenth and seventeenth centuries, such as *Sabellii opera omnia* (1560), the *Cancionero general* (1573) and *Fundaciones de los mosteiros de S. Benito* (1601), among other titles.[3]

In 1830, the advertisements for books and periodicals published in the *Diário do Rio de Janeiro* newspaper show that Silvino's shop had moved from Rua dos Inválidos to Praça da Constituição. Thus, in March of that year, anyone interested in acquiring the reprinted edition of *Regimento das câmaras municipais das cidades e vilas do império do Brasil* (City councils of the cities and towns of the empire of Brazil) could find it "in the establishments of Mr. Veigas, Rua da Quitanda, corner of S. Pedro, and Rua dos Pescadores, no. 49; and Silvino José de Almeida, Praça da Constituição, no. 51; price 120 réis."[4] In April 1830, it was also at the bookstore of "Selvino Jozé d'Almeida" that one could subscribe to or purchase copies of *Nova luz brazileira*, a periodical written by the apothecary Ezequiel Correia dos Santos, the leader of the Exaltado faction in Rio de Janeiro.[5]

The radical liberals, or Exaltados, the group for which *Nova luz brasileira* was one of the main outlets, emerged in Rio de Janeiro in late 1829 amid the increased political strife that culminated in the fall of Pedro I in 1831.[6] Silvino certainly maintained close ties with the Exaltados, especially if we observe that, by the end of August 1830, the *Diário do Rio de Janeiro* accused the bookseller of reluctance to sell a certain *Resposta à Nova luz brasileira, ou, Desagravo de brasileiros e portugueses* (Answer to the *Nova luz brasileira*, or, Redress of Brazilians and Portuguese). Although we do not know what that publication contained, its title was symptomatic of a time when the clashes between Brazilians and Portuguese in Rio de Janeiro had intensified. The *Diário's* anonymous writer asked Silvino to shed light on the subject so as "to relieve the troubled public from its suspicions"—he suspects that the bookseller was politically biased when deciding what was sold at his establishment.[7]

Two days later, Silvino published a note in the *Diário* explaining that if he did not sell *Resposta à Nova luz*, it was simply because he had not received any copies of it. However, in case they still judged that he had arbitrarily refused to sell that publication, Silvino told the disgruntled reader to consult the first paragraph of Art. 179 of the "*Constitution* of the forever Independent Empire of Brazil and there they will find the answer."[8] With the Constitution in hand, the reader would see that the answer was short and sweet, since the paragraph cited states that "No Citizen may be compelled to do, or fail to do anything, except by Law." Thus, Silvino made it clear to the "troubled public" that his shop sold whatever he pleased.

However, besides his supposed affiliation to with the Exaltados, the book-seller Silvino José de Almeida was pardo, synonymous with Brazilian in those formative years of that which we now call national identity. To a large extent, that identity was forged in the conflict between Brazilians and Portuguese.[9] The riots that took place on the streets of Rio de Janeiro between March 13 and 15, 1831, became the best-known incidents in that conflict. Involuntarily, according to his testimony in the *Translado do processo a que deu motivo os tumultos das Garrafadas* (Transcript of the inquest on the Bottle Riots), the bookseller Silvino José de Almeida took part in those events.[10]

At around 7 p.m. on the thirteenth, a Sunday, noticing the crowd that was forming in Praça da Constituição, Silvino went to the door of his book-shop and asked why all those people were gathering there. He was told that they were "on their way down," meaning that they were heading for the central streets of the city. Silvino thought nothing of it, closed the shop, and went to bed. About two hours later, the bookseller noticed another gather-ing and opened his window. This time, he saw people filling the streets near the square between Beco da Rua do Piolho and the beginning of Rua do Cano. Once again, Silvino saw the crowd, closed his window, and went to sleep.[11] There is no indication of Paula Brito's whereabouts that night. The gatherings in Praça da Constituição were composed mostly of blacks, par-dos, and a few whites. They included the captain of the Third Hunters' Bat-talion, Mariano Joaquim de Siqueira, the detachment of which Paula Brito was apparently an aide in the Second Company. But that says little, and it is difficult to ascertain if the young man was out in the streets mingling with the crowd, or safe at home with his cousin.

Unlike Silvino, his neighbor Juvêncio Pereira Ferreira, also a "resident of Praça da Constituição with a pharmacy apothecary shop" decided to join the crowd. According to the curious apothecary, there were over four hundred people in the streets, whom he followed on Rua do Piolho and further on. Near Rua das Violas, Juvêncio heard the people who had left Praça da Constituição shout "long live the Constitutional Emperor and the Constitution, the Freedom of the human race"; others "[hailed] the federation, the independence of Brazil, and those shouts were answered by the people who were in the townhouses." It seemed that all was going well until shouts hailing "King Pedro IV and the Portuguese Constitution and the Portuguese" came from the townhouse of João Domingues de Araújo Viana on a corner of Rua das Violas, and a shower of bottles rained from the windows onto the crowd below.[12]

Possibly frightened, the apothecary turned around and was forced to take a different route, because he was told that Brazilians and Portuguese were clashing on Rua da Alfândega. When he got to Rua do Ouvidor, Juvêncio found "a Brazilian youth . . . hatless and very badly beaten so he could hardly walk." The young man told him that he had been attacked by "a number of Portuguese armed with *chuços* and swords" who were shouting "kill the *cabras* [literally, goats] that want to screw us." During the struggle, some of the Brazilians fled while the others confronted the Portuguese, seizing their *chuços*, which were handed over to the justice of the peace of Candelária parish.[13] Meanwhile, Juvêncio was creeping cautiously along, and when he finally got to Praça da Constituição he saw "a lot of folks" calling for vengeance on the Portuguese. Juvêncio found some people in his apothecary shop who had been injured, "two with lead bullets and the others with blows and bruises," who were being treated by a Navy surgeon. After everyone had gone, he followed the example of his neighbor the bookseller and, certainly unnerved by everything he had witnessed, closed the pharmacy.[14]

At around midnight on the fourteenth, Juvêncio awoke with a start, hearing "a crowd that seemed like the marching of regular troops." It seemed like it, but it was not—instead, over two hundred Portuguese armed with *chuços* and swords were shouting "long live the Emperor and the Portuguese nation." The furious crowd stopped outside the pharmacy, threatening to break down the doors and demanding that Juvêncio hand over the *pimpões*, that is, the Brazilians with whom they had clashed the day before, and whom they believed to be hiding there. The apothecary must have been terrified, followed by a sense of relief when he realized that the crowd had decided not to attack him and moved on to Silvino José de Almeida's bookshop.[15]

That day, the bookseller had learned "through hearsay"—most likely from people exasperated by the events who came and went in the bookshop—about everything that had happened on Rua das Violas, as well as hearing about the wounded people treated in Juvêncio's pharmacy. At around midnight, Silvino was also awakened by cries of "Long live His Majesty Emperor Pedro and the Portuguese" and "Brazilians, long live the Constitution," followed by "kill the *cabras.*" Then, "during that affray, tremendous blows were struck against the window panes" of his shop. They were so strong that they shattered the glass. Silvino ran to one of the windows, and as soon as the crowd armed with sticks and swords had spotted him, their cries of "kill, kill" grew louder. The nightmare only ended when José Bernardes Monteiro shouted at them from his townhouse to put a stop to that mischief. The following day, anyone passing through Praça da Constituição could see the bookshop's "broken window cases and panes."[16]

In the article published in *O carioca*, Paula Brito associated his involvement in the events of the "glorious day April 7, 1831" with his desire to "get revenge on the Garrafistas of March, who intended to murder my cousin—*Silvino José de Almeida*—(with whom I was living at the time), breaking the windowpanes and wanting to invade his house."[17] Once again, it is difficult to ascertain whether Paula Brito was in the house at that perilous moment. In any case, he was so enraged by the attack by the emperor's partisans on Silvino's bookstore that the young man decided to take up arms and revolt against despotism. The weapon in question, however, would not be a sword or a *chuço*, in the fashion of the Portuguese Garrafistas, but a quill, the instrument with which Paula Brito wrote his "Hymn Offered to Brazilian Youth on March 25, 1831."

As we have seen, since his return to Rio de Janeiro, Paula Brito had written verses that were read and edited by Evaristo da Veiga. In the "Hymn Offered to Brazilian Youth on March 25, 1831," the young poet began by hailing the Brazilian Constitution granted seven years before, on March 25, 1824, a day remembered in the first stanza as "majestic" and "of eternal memory." However, in later verses the tone of the "Hymn" changes, railing against "enemies" who plotted the "slavery" of the motherland:

> In us, vengeance is reborn.
> Sacred Heroism triumphs,
> Free men do not bow
> To the tyrant despotism.[18]

When reading "Hymn Offered to Brazilian Youth" from the perspective of the confrontations that rocked the streets of Rio de Janeiro in those days, it is easy to perceive the political meaning behind those verses. Young Paula Brito was openly inciting his compatriots to rise up against those who, in addition to attacking his cousin Silvino's bookshops, loudly hailed the Portuguese Constitution and the Portuguese, attacked Brazilians, and threw bottles from the townhouses on Rua das Violas. It was therefore anti-Portuguese propaganda. In this regard, Paula Brito explained that the "Hymn" was written about "The matter of the day, defying the wrath of the enemy of Brazil and his Apostles," meaning Pedro I and his supporters. The poem was well-received for that very reason, so much so that, after reading the manuscript, João Pedro da Veiga, Ripanso's brother, had his clerk tell the young man that he would pay to have the verses printed, immediately offering him 40,000 réis. Paula Brito accepted the money and that very afternoon, put on his straw hat and went to meet his new patron in his bookshop.[19]

The problem was that straw hats were a symbol of the Exaltados. Wearing one was a political act and explains why Paula Brito, who was also pardo, was mocked by some residents and merchants as he walked to João Pedro da Veiga's bookshop, which stood on the corner of Rua da Quitanda and Rua de S. Pedro. Four streets—Quitanda, Ourives, Direita, and Violas—marked the boundary of the Portuguese quarter of Rio de Janeiro, and once the details of publication had been agreed, the bookseller advised the young man to take a different route home to avoid being insulted by the "capitalists" on Rua da Quitanda. Even so, it is very likely that Paula Brito was left the shop a happy man, feeling that he was truly a poet in the service of the "nation and Brazilians."[20]

However, while the Garrafadas inspired Paula Brito's verses, they also encouraged the emperor to take steps in response to the disturbances of the thirteenth to fifteenth of March, appointing a new cabinet on the nineteenth, which was then considered more Brazilian or less Portuguese than its predecessors. It was a palliative measure, because the political crisis in which Pedro I was embroiled had been going on since at least the middle of the previous decade, considerably exacerbated after the death of his father, João VI of Portugal, and his involvement in the succession to the Portuguese throne, to which he had a claim and which he had renounced in favor of his eldest child, Princess Maria da Glória. Notwithstanding, the gulf between the emperor and the General Legislative Assembly of the Empire widened during the second session of the legislature in 1830, increasing the monarch's political isolation—difficulties that Pedro attempted to ease with an ill-fated visit to the province of Minas Gerais in early 1831.

The gathering that Silvino José de Almeida saw outside his bookshop in the evening of March 13 had formed precisely to put an end to the celebrations that supporters of Pedro I, gathered in the vicinity of Rua da Quitanda, were organizing to welcome him on his return. As we have seen, that confrontation resulted in smashed bottles and heads, without forgetting the windows of Silvino's bookshop, which were shattered the following night when the emperor's followers struck back. However, the situation came to a head on April 5, when Pedro I appointed a new cabinet made up of five marquesses and a viscount. The fall of the "Brazilian" cabinet of March 19 hastened the downfall of the emperor himself.[21]

On the sixth of April, "the people and troops," as the saying went, came together in Campo de Santana, which became the Campo da Honra (Field of Honor), to demand that the monarch reinstate the cabinet that had been dismissed the day before. As José Murilo de Carvalho underscored, speaking to that assembly of nearly four thousand people, "it could be said that, in a moment rarely repeated in this country's history, it was a gathering of the elite, politicians, military, and people."[22] However, refusing to accede to the wishes of the people and troops, the emperor eventually abdicated the throne in favor of his five-year-old son, Prince Pedro, in the early hours of April 7, 1831.

Then an aide in the Second Company of the Third Hunters' Battalion, Paula Brito arrived in Campo de Santana at around 1:00 p.m. on the sixth, by which time fewer than one hundred people had gathered there. The young man spent the afternoon and night in the square, where he wrote "some simple poems" on the spot, celebrating Pedro I's abdication. A few days later, Paula Brito went back to João Pedro da Veiga, who once again agreed to pay for the publication of his verses, this time "The Hymn to the Memorable Day April 7, 1831."[23] Printed by Émile Seignot Plancher, the poem began by congratulating the "*brasília* people" who had finally rid themselves of the "ferocious enemy" Pedro I and his "servile party":

> Congratulations, *brasília* people,
> FREEDOM flourishes!
> The perverse one has fallen from the Throne
> Iniquity has succumbed.
>
> Far from us the traitors,
> Far away the servile party,
> INDEPENDENCE triumphed
> *On the seventh of April.*[24]

In the "Hymn to the Memorable Day April 7, 1831," Paula Brito was caught up in the "fraternal union" of the people and the troops, which in "singular equality" raised the "voice in the New World" against tyranny. There are three references to the new emperor in verses that somehow foreshadow a series of laudatory poems to Pedro II that Paula Brito wrote in the course of his life. In one of those references, the truly Brazilian boy emperor was hailed by the "liberated nation":

> Behold the Liberated Nation
> Hails PEDRO THE SECOND
> Born on the fertile Shores
> Of gold-rich Brazil.[25]

The new emperor was, in fact, hailed on the Field of Honor on April 7, amid cries of "Long Live Pedro II," started up by General Manuel da Fonseca Lima e Silva. The congressional deputies and senators in Rio de Janeiro immediately officialized the succession, as well as electing the Trine Provisional Regency, made up of the Marquess de Caravelas, Senator Vergueiro, and General Francisco de Lima e Silva.[26] They were hailed as the "wise regency" in Paula Brito's "Hymn to the Memorable Day April 7, 1831."

The days that followed the "Glorious Seventh of April" were ripe with possibilities for those who lived them. As a result, the young Exaltado Francisco de Paula Brito and most of those who had joined the throng on the Field of Honor believed that a promising new era lay ahead.[27] In addition to better days for the nation, it was also thought that real opportunities in daily life, within the reach of the citizens who took part in the movement, were also in the offing. For Paula Brito, and perhaps many others, those opportunities took the form of a job in the civil service. After all, once Pedro I and his "servile party"—most of whom were Portuguese—had been vanquished, perhaps Brazilians of all colors would have unrestricted access to the bureaucracy. There was no harm in trying, and the young man did just that.

This story would have been different—and might not even have been written—if Regent Lima e Silva had given Paula Brito a position that had opened up in the Senate a few days after the emperor's abdication. In a badly degraded section of the article published in *O carioca*, Paula Brito complained that, after the Seventh of April, "The times and things changed, and because the presses went into decline (as a consequence of the [illegible] revolutions [illegible] my situation was critical)."[28] There is no doubt that the times changed after the Seventh of April, but it does not seem that the presses went into decline at that time. In "Origem e desenvolvimento da imprensa no Rio de Janeiro" (Origins and development of the press in Rio de Janeiro), an article published in 1865, Moreira de Azevedo stated that "the exaltation of the press did not cool but increased in 1831." The historian from the Brazilian Historical and Geographic Institute (IHGB) identified forty-five periodicals circulating in Rio de Janeiro that year, compared with just nine in 1830 and sixteen in 1832.[29]

However, Paula Brito's critical situation was another story. After all, although we know little about what transpired, it could be that Paula Brito's career as an aide in the Second Company of the Third Hunters' Battalion had ended badly. If that was the case, the young man would soon discover that there was little advantage in offering his life to the "beloved country." Thus, going back to his article in O *carioca*, we find that Paula Brito complained about his situation to some friends, saying that he was "unsettled." The young man was advised to go to Regent Lima e Silva regarding "a vacancy in the Senate Chamber." They also told him that Evaristo da Veiga could be very helpful in that regard. Paula Brito sought out the editor of *Aurora Fluminense*, with whom he was close, as we know. Evaristo told him that, although "he did not [have] any friends in the Government"—an observation that was strange, at the very least, since he was a deputy elected by the province of Minas Gerais, and as such, had helped vote in the Trine Provisional Regency[30]—he would give him a "testimonial" that, according to Paula Brito, "not only praised my conduct, but even thought me worthy of employment due to my talents."

Most certainly flattered and armed with that testimonial, the young man knocked on the door of General Francisco de Lima e Silva, a member of the Trine Provisional Regency. Paula Brito handed the document to the regent, who asked him to return the following day with a memorial, "because if there was a vacancy," it would be his. Writing a memorial in less than twenty-four hours, no matter what the subject, may have been the least of his problems. The issue was whether there was a "vacancy" in the Senate Chamber, as Paula Brito's friends had claimed. Therefore, either the regent was unaware of that vacancy or had disingenuously refused to employ Paula Brito, who wrote nearly two years later: "I never again sought out his Excellency and sought to make an honorable living with my labor while continuing the small studies I had begun earlier."[31]

In 1857, the American missionaries Daniel Kidder and James Fletcher were surprised by the number of "mulattos"—"these men with negro blood"—whom they saw studying in the National and Public Library of Rio de Janeiro.[32] The scene the reverends observed in the late 1850s may have been the same twenty years earlier. If it was, young Paula Brito would probably have been one of the "mulattos" in the National Library, absorbed in his studies—"small studies" that could produce big ideas.[33] However, just days after his unsuccessful attempt to enter the civil service, a fresh prospect opened up for the young man: São Paulo.

Although it was an important trading center and a provincial capital, São Paulo was a fairly small city in the early 1830s, nothing compared to Rio de Janeiro and what São Paulo itself would become by the late nineteenth century. In comparison, in 1827, the year when José da Costa Carvalho founded the first press and published the first printed newspaper in São Paulo, the *Farol Paulistano*, there were five printing presses in Rio and twelve newspapers in circulation. However, in 1828, São Paulo became the home of the Law School, consequently becoming an important market for books and other publications.[34] As the *Jornal do commercio* reported on April 19, 1831, it was this prospect that led Paula Brito to plan his move to that city:

> Bookstores and presses are being established in many provinces. In S. Paulo M. Joly, in concert with a business in Rio de Janeiro, brought together a beautiful collection of books and formed a reading cabinet, of which the foremost commercial houses are already subscribers, as well as many university students, which finally had to occur in a city where liberal ideas have developed so readily. But as just one press does not suffice in S. Paulo, Mr. Francisco de Paula Brito, a young Brazilian who is well known for his patriotic poetry, will establish himself in that city and add to the vogue of the reading cabinet of M. Jules Joly. A press and bookstore combined in one establishment must necessarily be very successful in a country where education is so ardently desired.[35]

Just twelve days had elapsed between the publication of "Glorious Seventh of April" and this announcement. Paula Brito's return to the printing business was therefore directly related to Regent Lima e Silva's refusal to give him a job in the Senate Chamber. Far removed from the competitive printing market in the imperial capital, scholarly São Paulo seemed promising. Thus, according to the announcement, Paula Brito planned to start a bookshop and printing press "in one establishment" that specialized in selling and printing books and periodicals.

Nevertheless, Paula Brito's move to the Piratininga highlands never took place. In 1834, when defending himself from accusations of being a Restorationist in the pages of *O carioca*, the "young Brazilian" gave his reasons for refusing to go to São Paulo:

> If I had wanted to be a burden on my friends, I would have used the gift they wanted to give me in May 1831, offering to help with the expenses I would incur at the "C. J. de S. Paulo," where they wanted to send me, which I entirely rejected because I did not want to be a burden on anyone, although with that rejection I helped bring about my own misfortune.[36]

Could "C. J. de S. Paulo" be the Curso Jurídico de São Paulo, the city's law school? In addition to establishing a bookshop and printing press, had Paula Brito planned to study law? If the young man was engaging in scholarly pursuits, why not become a lawyer? There were pardo students at the law school. According to José Murilo de Carvalho, one of the lecturers at that institution refused to speak to those students, alleging that blacks could not be university graduates.[37] No matter what his intentions, Paula Brito clearly had friends who were willing to cover his travel expenses. Nevertheless, as he explained, although it added to his "misfortune," he rejected their aid and decided to stay in Rio de Janeiro.

I have been unable to determine the identity of those friends. However, Paula Brito related in *O carioca* that he once again received the providential aid of João Pedro da Veiga, the patron who had paid for the publication of his "patriotic poetry" in April 1831. If my calculations are correct, this occurred after he had called off his plans to move to São Paulo, sometime between May and October of that year. Thus, without being able to say exactly when, once again we find young Paula Brito on Rua da Quitanda, walking resolutely toward João Pedro da Veiga's bookshop. We do not know if the young man wore his Exaltado straw hat this time, but one thing we can be sure of is that, instead of poetry, he carried a piece of jewelry in his pocket. It might have been a family heirloom, possibly inherited from his maternal grandmother, the wife of Sergeant Major Martinho Pereira de Brito who, as we know, was a renowned silversmith in Rio de Janeiro. Suppositions aside, at that moment, the young man needed money and sought to use it as collateral for a loan from João Pedro da Veiga.[38]

Paula Brito wanted to borrow "a small sum" from the bookseller. In addition to those funds, the young man may have built up his own savings, possibly from the time when he worked for Plancher. However, the answer to the purpose of the money can be read in the "Notícias particulares" (Private news) column in the November 10, 1831, issue of *Jornal do commercio*:

> Francisco de Paula Brito hereby notifies the public, and in particular his friends, that he has purchased from Mr. Silvino José d'Almeida the store located in Praça da Constituição, no. 51, and therefore has the honor to inform publishers and the other customers of said store, that it is still accepting all newspapers and other publications for sale, and, in addition, will produce a new assortment in said establishment. The advertiser hopes to deserve all the esteem he has so far achieved from his friends and countrymen, to whom he will be eternally grateful.[39]

After trying to get a job as a civil servant and planning to move to São Paulo, Paula Brito ended up buying his cousin Silvino's shop. Relying on the esteem of the public in Rio de Janeiro, he also promised to make improvements to that establishment, as we will see in the next chapter. First, however, it would be interesting to answer a question: why did Silvino José de Almeida decide to sell the business after so many years?

Five days after the publication of Paula Brito's announcement in the *Jornal do commercio*, Silvino declared in the *Diário do Rio de Janeiro* that he no longer had any association with the bookshop: "seeing that some gentlemen as still advertising Published works on sale at Praça da Constituição no. 51, and still supposing that the shop belongs to this advertiser . . . hereby declares that the shop is no longer under his management, because he has sold it to Mr. Francisco de Paula Brito." Silvino took the opportunity to ask the editor of *Clarim da liberdade* to pay more attention when producing advertisements because "the manner in which those published in the *Diário* are conceived . . . under the heading Published Works implies that the advertisement was published by the writer [Silvino], who has had no dealings nor could have any dealings with the Editor."[40] As Marcello Basile suggests, the editor of the *Clarim da liberdade*, an Exaltado newspaper published with some interruptions between November 1831 and June 1833, could have been José Luiz Ferreira, a mulatto. The *Clarim* was openly opposed to the moderate government and, in effect, the way Silvino attempted to disassociate

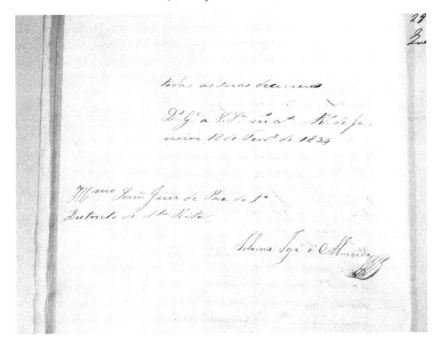

FIGURE 9. Signature of Silvino José de Almeida, Paula Brito's cousin (1834)

himself, not just from the bookshop, but chiefly from the newspaper and its editor, sounded like a political act.[41]

Nonetheless, we would be attributing too much altruism to Silvino if we imagined that he had only sold the bookshop to help a young cousin find a career. The shop was not one of the most important establishments of its kind in Rio de Janeiro and, as we shall see, it was facing strong competition at the time. It might not have been a profitable venture, so much so that Silvino, it seems, believed it would be a promising opportunity to go from being a bookseller to a jailer.

We have seen that immediately after the Seventh of April, Paula Brito had unsuccessfully sought a post in the civil service from Regent Lima e Silva. There are no signs that Silvino followed the same course but, unlike his cousin, he found a job as a "[civil] servant for life in the position of jailer at the Prisons of this Court, by his Imperial Majesty, may God save him."[42] In February 1832, three months after the sale of the bookshop, the lists of slaves sent to the prison by justices of the peace of Rio parishes were signed "Silvino José de Almeida, Jailer of the Prisons."[43] All indications are that

Paula Brito's cousin never returned to the trade of selling or binding books.[44] At the end of 1831, having been appointed by the Moderates, it was not at all strange that the former bookseller should seek to distance himself from the Exaltados, as he did in the *Diário do Rio de Janeiro*. Meanwhile, as he had not been honored with a government post by the *chimangada*, Francisco de Paula Brito, the city's newest merchant, remained loyal to the Farroupilhas.[45]

CHAPTER 5

Bookseller-Printer

A CLOSE READING OF the Books for Sale, Published Works, and Works
to be Published sections of the *Diário do Rio de Janeiro* newspaper gives
a complete picture of the book trade in Rio when Paula Brito entered
that business. In addition to the newcomer, I have found twelve more establishments advertising printed publications in the *Diário* in December 1831.

When it comes to books, the most prominent establishment was Albino
Jordão's shop on Rua do Ouvidor, no. 157, which specialized in "Novels
in Portuguese." It was at Albino's shop that the city's readers could find
titles like *A portuguesa infiel* (The unfaithful Portuguese woman), *Paulo e Virginia* (*Paul and Virginia*), *Aventuras de Telêmaco* (*The Adventures of Telemachus*),
and *Viagens de Guliver* (*Gulliver's Travels*), among others.[1] The two bookshops owned by the Veiga brothers on Rua dos Pescadores, no. 49, and Rua
da Quitanda, on the corner of Rua de S. Pedro, sold "works for the Law
Schools of São Paulo and Olinda." Works by authors like Adam Smith,
Bentham, Malthus, and Ricardo were targeted at scholarly readers. The
Veigas also sold the periodicals *Grito da pátria* and *Simplício velho*, as well as
the political pamphlet *Aparição extraordinária e inesperada do velho venerando ao
roceiro* (Extraordinary and unexpected appearance of the venerable old man
to the peasant).[2] "A few used books and some abridged works" could be

purchased at Mr. Mandillo's Book Shop on Rua da Quitanda, no. 246.[3] The *Diário* also advertised books for sale by private individuals who most likely sold their collections from their homes. In this case, the fourteen volumes of the Portuguese edition of Voltaire's *Philosophical Dictionary* were being sold at Rua dos Ourives, no. 228, while several books in French, such as works by Boulanger and Mirabeau, were available for purchase at "Rua de S. Lourenço, no. 12, across from the Field Barracks."[4]

As for pamphlets, five titles were advertised in the *Diário*. Devoted readers could find the *Folhinhas do Bispado de Mariana e do Rio de Janeiro* (Pamphlets of the Bishopric of Mariana and Rio de Janeiro) at the Home of Mr. Agra, on Rua do Ouvidor, no. 113. On that same street, Émile Seignot-Plancher was selling the *Guia das Guardas Nacionais do Império do Brasil* (Guide to the National Guards of the Brazilian Empire) and *Considerações sobre nosso estado futuro* (Thoughts about our future state). In addition to the Veigas' bookshops, anyone wanting to purchase *Aparição extraordinária e inesperada do velho venerando roceiro* would find it at the establishments of Baptista dos Santos and Francisco de Paula Brito. The pamphlet *Proezas da Cagarilha* could be obtained in any bookshop in the city.[5]

At a time when, according to Moreira de Azevedo, "Journalism had broken with its institution, forgotten its duties, and become a pillory,"[6] it was not surprising to see the large number of periodicals and pamphlets advertised in the *Diário*—nineteen titles, in total. But if the bookshops of Albino Jordão and the Veiga brothers held a virtual monopoly on the book trade, nine of the twelve merchants identified sold periodicals, particularly João Baptista dos Santos, Émile Seignot-Plancher, and Paula Brito. Of these three, Seignot-Plancher was the only one whose establishment ran a printing press in December 1831. This did not mean that his bookstore only sold the output of the presses in the workshop alongside it, like *Jornal do commercio* or *Simplício da roça*. Seignot-Plancher also sold *O ipiranga*, which was printed by the Torres Press.[7] Those who preferred João Baptista dos Santos's shop could find not only *O ipiranga* and *Simplício da roça*, but *Matraca dos farroupilhas*, *Sentinella da liberdade*, and *Grito da pátria*.[8] Paula Brito sold four titles: *O ipiranga*, *Simplício da roça*, *Sentinella da liberdade*, and *O regente*, a newspaper also found in the Tribuno do Povo shop on Rua da Quitanda.[9]

Considering that the newcomer to the business was not the only seller of the periodicals advertised, it is very likely that Paula Brito could not make a living solely from selling publications then, which was also true three decades later. Bookbinding must still have been an important part of his business's activities. It is important to note that the concept of book-shops in Rio de Janeiro in the first half of the nineteenth century was very different from what it is today. They did not just sell books and newspapers. They also offered a vast range of other products, such as cologne, toys, wallets, cigar cases, Havana and Bahia cigars, pocket knives, pens, tea, nail and toothbrushes, razors, combs, and soap, among other items.[10] However, at the end of 1831, although he promised a "new assortment" of merchandise, Paula Brito certainly did not have such a vast stock of products at his disposal. Given the absence of a more varied showcase, all we can do is leaf through the periodicals sold in his shop.

All four—*O ipiranga*, *Simplício da roça*, *Sentinella da liberdade*, and *O regente*—were Exaltado publications. On one hand, this reflects Paula Brito's political stance—as we have seen, even before he dreamed of being a bookseller, he was parading through the streets of Rio de Janeiro in his Exaltado straw hat. On the other hand, it could also have to do with that political group's considerable output of newspapers and journals between 1829 and 1834. Quantitatively speaking, the Exaltados surpassed the Caramurus and Moderates in the publication of periodicals, which largely consisted of small and ephemeral satirical pamphlets.[11]

In this case, *O regente: Jornal político e literário* (The regent: Political and literary journal) is a good example. Published by the Lessa e Pereira Press, there were just two issues, the first of which came out on November 11 and the last on December 15, 1831. An Exaltado pamphlet, it attacked the Moderates, whom it described as the "Antinational, freedom-killing, and recolonizing party," and referred to Father Feijó as a "justice minister who is entirely unschooled in jurisprudence."[12] Similar views about Feijó could be read in *O Ipiranga*.

In its fourth issue, which came out on December 17, 1831, the priest-minister was described as being "as much a layman in the Civil Laws as in the Political Laws of his country."[13] It is important to note that Diogo Antonio Feijó also read these publications and, as we will see, was reflecting seriously on freedom of the press in the Empire at about that time.

The issues of *Sentinella da Liberdade* that Paula Brito sold in December 1831 were edited by Cipriano Barata, one of the top leaders of the Exaltados. The editor and the bookseller may have met in 1831, when Cipriano returned to Rio de Janeiro after spending time in prison in Bahia, accused of Haitianism and Republicanism. Cipriano was arrested once again in Rio and began writing his pamphlets in the jails where he was incarcerated. Among the seven issues of the *Sentinella* published in Rio de Janeiro, Paula Brito's customers could find *Sentinella da liberdade na guarita do quartel general de Pirajá: Hoje preza na guarita de Ville-Gaignon em o Rio de Janeiro. Alerta!!* (Watchtower of freedom in the sentry post of Pirajá headquarters: Today imprisoned in the sentry post of Ville-Gaignon in Rio de Janeiro. Warning!!). [14]

Simplício da roça: Jornal dos domingos (Simplício the peasant: Sunday newspaper), was published by E. Seignot-Plancher's Imperial e Constitucional Press. In the seventh issue, its author stated that "The Moderates' writings is [*sic*] worse than the treasury, than bank notes, than letters of credit from bankrupts." Therefore, he blessed the "Rusguentos [Quarrelsome Ones], and the Rusgas [Quarrels], because at least they give printers a source of income." On the following page, the writer observes that he has heard a Moderate defending the pamphlets written "to uphold law and order," to which he replies, "I don't care about law and order: I want to read the works of the Rusguentos."[15] This was certainly an allusion to the Exaltado newspapers which were avidly read, precisely because of the political diatribes they published. Printing such newspapers might be even more profitable than just selling them. Paula Brito soon realized the potential of the Rusgas and the following year, in addition to selling periodicals, he started printing them at the Fluminense Press of Brito & Co.

In 1832, René Ogier noted in his *Manual de typographia braziliense* that there were nine presses in Rio de Janeiro, listing them by the date they were established in the city. The list included the "Nacional Press, [those] of Nicolau Lobo Vianna, of Émile Signot-Plancher, of Torres, of R. Ogier, of Souto, of Lessa e Pereira, of Guelfier e Companhia, [and] of Thomas B. Hunt e Companhia." The most important was the Nacional Press, given the "quality and variety of type" it possessed. In an observation on the same page, Ogier observed that "In addition to the abovementioned presses, there are one or two that were not listed because they are very small, and more private than public."[16]

Most of these printers, if not all, used "wooden presses." Ogier believed that "iron presses are not suitable for Brazil, particularly in the interior, due to the difficulty in finding craftsmen to repair them if they deteriorate."[17] In 1823, when Minister Martim Francisco Ribeiro de Andrada planned to set up a press in São Paulo, it was proposed that the Nacional Press's iron printing presses be sent to the Ipanema foundry in Sorocaba to serve as a model for the manufacture of Brazilian iron presses, "which would make up for the lack of wooden presses, some of which are already in a highly deteriorated state." However, Gaspar José Monteiro, the typesetter hired to work in São Paulo, wrote to the ministry, informing them that good wooden presses were manufactured in Rio de Janeiro, "where there are machinists who make them . . . with perfection and for a reasonable price."[18] All indications are that Paula Brito had a wooden press when he started his printing workshop, and if it was not on Ogier's list, it may have been because it still numbered among the smaller establishments.

In early February 1832, an advertisement listing the works that Paula Brito was about to publish appeared in *Jornal do commercio*. However, it did not say whether the "tender and loving *Coleção de poesias* [Collection of poetry], and part of the *Obras políticas* [Political works] by Francisco de Paula Brito" that were being sold by subscription for 1,000 réis had been printed at Praça da Constituição, no. 51.[19] Unfortunately, I have also been unable to find *Coleção de poesias* or *Obras políticas*, a title that allows us to infer that Paula Brito was already developing an ambitious intellectual project when he became a bookseller.

We can date the inception of the Fluminense Press of Brito & Co. more confidently by leafing through *Mulher do Simplício ou A Fluminense Exaltada*, a newspaper in verse written by Paula Brito, of which there are only three remaining issues from 1832. They indicate that the bookseller did not own a printing press of any kind before September of that year because the last issue of the series, dated September 4, was printed at the Lessa & Pereira Press.[20] The first three issues of *O conciliador fluminense: Jornal político, histórico e miscelânico* (The Rio de Janeiro conciliator: A political, historical, and miscellaneous newspaper), printed between September 11 and 22, 1832, made it the first newspaper published by the Fluminense Press of Brito & Co. Therefore, the first printing press at the bookstore in Praça da Constituição, no. 51, must have been installed between September 4 and 11.

But Paula Brito was not alone. The very name Fluminense Press of Brito & Co. (Tipografia Fluminense de Brito e Companhia in Portuguese) indicates that it was a partnership. Therefore, if Paula Brito had purchased the bookshop from his cousin Silvino on his own ten months earlier, he needed a business partner to start up the printing operation. However, I have been unable to find that partner's name.[21] There are strong indications that the partnership lasted from mid-1832 to mid-1835, when Paula Brito changed the name of his establishment to the Imparcial Press (Tipografia Imparcial), as we shall see.

Aside from acquisition of a "wooden press," the need for a business partner was justified by the cost of printing in those days. To give an idea of the

TABLE I Newspapers printed by Fluminense Press of Brito & Co. (1832–1833)

Title	Start Date	No. of Issues	Unit Price	Quarterly Subscription	Political Affiliation
O conciliador fluminense	11 Sept. 1832	5	80 réis	2,000	Conciliation
O saturnino	02 July 1833	1	80 réis	–	Moderate
A mineira no Rio de Janeiro	26 July 1833	4	40 réis	–	Restorationist
O carioca	17 Aug. 1833	12	80 réis	–	Exaltado
A baboza	04 Sept. 1833	7	80 réis	–	Exaltado
O mestre José	05 Sept. 1833	3	80 réis	–	Exaltado
O homem de cor	14 Sept. 1833	5	40 réis	–	Exaltado
O evaristo	26 Sept. 1833	5	40 réis	–	Exaltado
O triumvir restaurador	21 Oct. 1833	1	80 réis	–	Restorationist
O meia-cara	11 Nov. 1833	2	80 réis	–	Exaltado
O rusguentinho	29 Nov. 1833	10	–	–	Exaltado

Source: Catálogo de periódicos do Arquivo Edgard Leuenroth (AEL-Unicamp).

prices involved, in November 1834, Ogier presented Evaristo da Veiga with a plan to transform *Aurora Fluminense* into a daily broadsheet like *Jornal do commercio*, which focused on business and politics, with a print run of one thousand copies. The printer attached a simulation of monthly publication costs to the plan, expenses which added up to more than 1,500,000 réis. However, he expected the revenue, chiefly from subscriptions, to surpass 1,800,000 réis, giving a profit of approximately 300,000 réis. Regarding newsroom costs, the editor-in-chief responsible for the political section would be paid 200,000 réis, while the business editor would receive 100,000 réis. Office expenses, such as paper, pens, and ink, were valued at a considerable 91,000 réis. Paper consumption, estimated at forty-nine to fifty rolls of newsprint per month, would cost 225,000 réis, and printing, 648,000 réis, or 27,000 réis for each of the twenty-four issues, with print runs of one thousand copies per issue. In this regard, Ogier observed that it was the best price in Rio de Janeiro, given that the *Diário Comercial* cost 24,000 réis per issue with five hundred copies each.[22]

Therefore, production costs for newspapers and pamphlets could have had something to do with the slow start of the Fluminense Press of Brito & Co., which only gained steam a year after it was established, as of the second half of 1833, as we can see in Table 1. Newspapers were sold for between 40 and 80 réis, depending on the number of pages in each issue. With just three exceptions, most were short-lived, never lasting for more than five issues, which was extremely common during the Brazilian Regency. Paula Brito's press reached its highest initial output in September 1833, when it printed four new periodicals. Regarding the political content of these papers, Paula Brito's Exaltado sympathies notwithstanding, the Fluminense Press of Brito & Co. printed the newspapers of two other political factions active in Rio de Janeiro.

However, the political boundaries were not always clear—at least, this was the case in the pages of *Conciliador fluminense*, whose watchwords were "Conciliation! Order! Unity!"[23] Except for the Restorationist party, which was considered something of a political aberration, the newspaper supported the "unity of April 7" between Exaltados and Moderates.[24] However, if the *Conciliador* was conciliatory, or tried to be, the other newspapers printed at Fluminense Press of Brito & Co. sought to take some sort of stand in the political scene that was unfolding.

None of them proved to be openly Moderate. One exception was *O saturnino*, which, although it avoided taking sides, published a suggestive epigraph in its first and only issue. Attributed to King João VI, in the style of the Moderates who defended the status quo, it read, "it is the duty of the just man, the Patriot, to censure abuses and defend reason."[25] By contrast, seven of the eleven newspapers were Exaltado—*O carioca*, *A baboza*, *Mestre José* (also called *Pai José* and *Carpinteiro José*), *O homem de cor* (which changed its name in its third issue to *O mulato, ou, O homem de cor*), *O meia-cara*, *Evaristo*, and *O rusguentinho*. *O meia-cara* and *O mulato, ou, O homem de cor*, as well as other titles of the Regency pardo press, have been the subject of important studies, one of which even posited that Paula Brito was the editor of *O mulato*, which has been very hard to prove.[26]

The only solid empirical evidence of a link between *O mulato, ou, O homem de cor* and Francisco de Paula Brito is that the newspaper in question was printed at Fluminense Press of Brito & Co. However, a closer look shows that its anonymous editor sought to demonstrate that the persecution of pardos was carried out, among other ways, by excluding those citizens from jobs in the civil service: "there is not a single representative of our colors in Public Employment, and they have excluded us everywhere."[27] This statement harks back to Paula Brito's failed attempt to obtain the post that had opened up in the Chamber Senate two years earlier. However, we should also recall that his cousin Silvino, a pardo, was appointed as a jailer soon afterwards. In this case, the same article explains that not all pardos were Exaltados: "do not be deluded, for the Moderates ignore you because you are mulattoes; leave that infamous and anti-Brazilian party once and for all, [as] it judges you to be inferior to their slaves, and join our exalted ranks."[28] This appeal is repeated in the following issue of *O Mulato*: "Men of color who are shamefully servile to the Moderates, cease to be the instrument of a forsworn and anti-national faction."[29] This is why it is necessary to read these newspapers in the political context that began after the seventh of April, seeking to unveil its grammar amid the clashes between Moderates, Exaltados, and Caramurus. Far from a rejection of the race, what emerges from this press, therefore, is the political articulation of that race.[30]

When assessing these conflicts, we can see that the Fluminense Press of Brito & Co. did not make a living solely from true-blue Exaltado newspapers and satirical publications. It also printed the only issue of *Triumvir restaurador, ou, A lima surda*, a satirical publication that proved to be both Exaltado and Restorationist.[31] *Triumvir* advocated the restoration of Pedro I in its title and epigraph, a poorly rhymed quatrain attributed to the former Emperor: "Give our lives for Brazil; / Maintain the Constitution / Support Independence/ That is our obligation." Taking into account the possibility of his restoration, backed by Britain and France, the editor concluded that the best thing to do would be to "save our party and gain advantages at the Emperor's side, so we can eat the fruits of our crimes and prepare a new 'seventh of April' if Pedro does not want to bow to our invisible ones."[32]

However, *A mineira no Rio de Janeiro: Jornal político e literário* barely disguised its Caramuru ethos. In its "Prospectus," it claimed to support "the SWORN CONSTITUTION, *the Imperial Throne and the Bragança Dynasty*."[33] In the following issue, it described the seventh of April as "doleful," hoping "that it will RESTORE Peace, harmony and foster Brazilian prosperity, lost in a labyrinth of inflamed passions." Two lines later, it wistfully alludes to the "Paternal Government of H. M. Pedro I."[34] In its fourth and final issue, *A Mineira* also charged the Moderate government with "persecuting the friends of the sworn Constitution and the august father of our monarch Pedro II."[35]

The first question that arises after reading the newspapers printed at Fluminense Press of Brito & Co. has to do with the printer's freedom to choose what would be produced by his workshop. The question remains as to whether Paula Brito and his partner were responsible for the content of those publications. There are many indications that Paula Brito was still an Exaltado between 1832 and 1833, the best example being the verses published in *A mulher do Simplício, ou, A fluminense exaltada* during that period.[36] Like the *Marmota*, in its three phases, published between the late 1840s and throughout the 1850s, although it did not always come out regularly, *A mulher do Simplício* was a long-lasting publication by the standards of the nineteenth-century Brazilian press. It was published for fourteen years, from 1832 to 1846. However, the passage of time has not been kind to it, as there are considerable gaps, particularly between 1832 and 1835, the issues that are of the greatest interest at this point.

Joaquim Manuel de Macedo, a leading Brazilian politician and novelist, once wrote that Paula Brito was never "a real poet," and was nothing but a "versifier" lacking in "imagination and even sufficient education."[37] However, the publisher certainly pleased his contemporaries. What is more, he was certainly a talented "versifier" who could compose melodious decasyllables, sonnets, and quatrains. That talent is attested by the longevity of *Mulher do Simplício* and, in the issues we have been able to find for 1832, it was, in fact, an Exaltado publication, as demonstrated by "Answer given to my unknown husband, Mr. Simplício, country poet":

> But let us go on
> To deal with Politics
> Where some of his little verses
> I feel it my duty to refute
>
> [. . .]
>
> He now wishes to hail
> Friends of the Emperor,
> Who should be called
> HM Pedro Abdicator
>
> [. . .]
>
> He calls vile assassins
> Those who are now Exaltados [when]
> Those who have shed blood
> Are the cruel Moderates;
>
> It is they who are preparing
> With premeditated tensions
> For Young Brazilians
> To cut up with swords;

[. . .]

I do not exactly call myself
An Exalted Brazilian woman; -
It is already in my nature
To detest the Moderate filth.[38]

There are references to the Restorationists in "Carta que à Assembleia Geral Legislativa dirige a redatora" ("Letter to the editor from the General Legislative Assembly"), published in the September 4 issue. These verses reveal the Editor's admiration for Madame de Staël:

I heard the sad lamentations
Of a loyal countrywoman,
Wanting but failing to imitate
The publicist *Stael*.

[. . .]

Remember our blood,
Which in April was shed,
By the manipulations of intrigues
Of the Moderate party.

It was they who made war,
Who caused division,
And according to the supreme voice,
It was they who betrayed the Nation.

Due to their atrocities,
Another party came to light;
Thus were born the *rusguentos*
As well as the Caramurus.

[. . .]

Note well that my pen
Is only guided by the common good,

You know, when I detest
Ungrateful Caramurus.[39]

"Hatred of the Moderates," "Ungrateful Caramurus"—these negative feelings must have been superseded by the need to keep the Fluminense Press of Brito & Co. going. Although most of the newspapers printed there in the second half of 1833 were Exaltado outlets, the doors of the bookshop and printing press on Praça da Constituição, no. 51, were not closed to their opponents. However, was printing non-Exaltado newspapers a sign that Paula Brito's political convictions were wavering? Certainly not. It was a matter of money. After all, the printer had just married, and starting a family may have influenced his choices.

Paula Brito had gone back to fetch Rufina, whom he married on May 1, 1833, in the Parish of São João de Itaboraí. On that occasion, standing before Vicar Francisco Xavier de Pinna, "Francisco de Paula Brito, the legitimate son of Jacinto Antunes Duarte and Maria Joaquina da Conceição, received in matrimony Rufina Rodrigues da Costa, the recognized illegitimate daughter of Antônio Rodrigues da Costa and Mariana Antônia Pereira."[40] The records do not state whether Rufina was also pardo, being the daughter or granddaughter of freedpersons. However, her status as a "recognized illegitimate daughter" was underlined and suggests the consensual union of her parents. Nevertheless, the document explains that "both parties [were] born and baptized in the Parish of Sacramento," which is an important detail because it suggests that Rufina and Francisco had known each other for a long time, perhaps since the young man had returned from Suruí, or even before he had gone to live on the cassava flour plantation. It could have been a long-term relationship, and Rufina may well have been the inspiration for the "tender and loving" poems that Paula Brito attempted to publish in February 1832. In any event, marriage brought responsibilities. After living in the home of the late Sergeant Major Martinho and cousin Silvino, Paula Brito was now a husband with a family to support. Therefore, his presses could run for Exaltados, Moderates, and Caramurus alike.

In his article in *O carioca*, Paula Brito openly contradicted himself in this regard. First, he stated that "Periodicals of all Convictions were printed in my workshop" and later that "at my Press, newspapers of the Exaltado opposition party were printed!!! (since not a single one that is Restorationist is printed)!!!"[41] However, his inconsistency was justified in the context of the times. The events of December 5, 1833, when Paula Brito, condemned by the court of public opinion, nearly saw his press destroyed, were directly linked to the publication of newspapers advocating the restoration of Pedro I, such as *A mineira no Rio de Janeiro*.

Until the former emperor's death in Lisbon in September 1834, the news of which reached Brazil in December, rendering Caramurus' platform moot, there was tremendous violence throughout the Empire against the supporters of his restoration. For example, in May 1834, days after the justice of the peace of Arraial do Pilar in Mato Grosso province managed to contain "a riot against an *adotivo* (Portuguese immigrant)," thirty Portuguese were murdered and dismembered in Cuiabá. In addition to killings, the Justice Minister reported looting and rapes, and the victims' families were forced to light lamps and prevented from burying their dead.[42] Paula Brito was therefore right to fear the court of public opinion, for at times it proved to be implacable.

CHAPTER 6

Press Laws and Offences in the "Days of Father Feijó"

IT WAS NOT just the court of public opinion that tried and convicted people, carrying out the sentences by destroying printing presses or murdering Portuguese nationals in Mato Grosso province. There were also press laws in effect in Brazil. This legislation lies at the heart of the problem we will discuss in this chapter: the sharp fall in production of new periodicals at the Fluminense Press of Brito & Co. between 1834 and 1835—as we can see in Figure 10—and its ramifications.

As Table 2 also shows, Brito's establishment only published one new title in 1834 and five the following year, numbers that reflect a broader trend in the Rio de Janeiro press. In 1834, just seven new periodicals were available in the capital, and the following year, there were just eighteen.[1] Since, as we know, just two presses were destroyed and Paula Brito's remained intact, albeit under threat, it is unlikely that the events of December 5, 1833 were

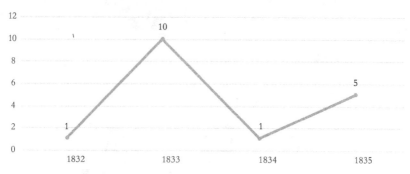

FIGURE 10. Production of periodicals at the Fluminense Press of Brito & Co. (1832–1835).
Source: Catalogue of Periodicals in the Arquivo Edgard Leuenroth (AEL-Unicamp)

the only reason for the drop in the number of publications produced in
1834. A good start for understanding the reasons for that downturn is to
take a look at the newspapers printed at the Fluminense Press—not all of
them this time, as we will follow the clues found in *Sete d'Abril*, a Moderate
paper that showed no sympathy for our printer. In April 1835, while sarcas-
tically comparing the printer to the famous French actor, François-Joseph
Talma, the editor of *Sete d'Abril* claimed that some newspapers were written by Paula Brito himself:

> List of the periodicals said to be scribbled by Mr. Paula Brito—*O simplício
> às direitas, A mulher do simplício, A novidade, A formiga, Café da tarde, Estafeta
> anárquico*, etc., etc., etc., and more recently *Judas e seu testamento*. In this last
> publication he capably played the role of executor [of Judas's Last Will and
> Testament]. And they say that *Talmas* only appear in France![2]

Unfortunately, I have not been able to find issues of *Simplício às direitas,
A formiga, O estafeta anárquico,* or *Judas e seu testamento*. However, like *Mulher
do simplício*, of which we only have the December 1835 issue, issues of *Novidade* and *Café da tarde* still survive. Furthermore, the fact that these newspapers were printed at the Fluminense Press of Brito & Co. increases the
probability that the editor of *Sete d'Abril* was right to say that both were
"scribbled by Mr. Paula Brito."

The Additional Act to the Constitution, enacted in August 1834, stated
that the choice of the new regent who would govern for four years would
be made by census suffrage. These elections, which involved approximately
six thousand voters scattered throughout Brazil, were held on April 7, 1835.
Each voter cast two ballots, choosing two of several candidates for the post.

TABLE 2 Newspapers printed by the Fluminense Press of Brito & Co. (1834–1835)

Title	Start date	No. of issues	Unit price	Quarterly subscription	Political affiliation
A novidade	03 May 1834	3	–	–	Exaltado
Café da tarde	–	5	–	–	–
O justiceiro constitucional	20 June 1835	1	–	–	–
O ladrão	04 July 1835	2	–	–	–
O capadócio	18 Aug. 1835	2	–	–	–
O novo Caramuru	19 Aug. 1835	7	–	–	–

Source: Catálogo de periódicos do Arquivo Edgard Leuenroth (AEL-Unicamp).

Although there were many options—Costa Carvalho, Lima e Silva, Araújo Lima, Pais de Andrade, and Bernardo Pereira de Vasconcelos, to name a few— two candidates polarized the electorate: Holanda Cavalcanti from Pernambuco and Father Feijó from São Paulo Province.[3] Octávio Tarquínio de Sousa describes the brothers Luís Cavalcanti and Holanda Cavalcanti as "a combination of aristocrats and libertarians, arrogant landowners and at the same time liberal agitators." According to Feijó's biographer, Holanda Cavalcanti's partisans in the 1835 elections included Honório Hermeto Carneiro Leão, the future Marquess of Paraná, and one of the leaders of the Conservative party,[4] with whom Paula Brito would establish closer ties in the 1840s. Therefore, it is suggestive that the newspapers the editor of the *Sete d'Abril* claimed to be written by Paula Brito, and which were in fact printed by him, unreservedly supported the candidacy of Holanda Cavalcanti to the detriment of Feijó.

Thus, *A novidade* stated: "the election of Mr. Feijo, [would be] a calamity, worse than any plague and scourge that Divine Providence in its wrath might send against this nascent Empire."[5] *Café da tarde*, in turn, used irony when advocating the same editorial policy. That newspaper certainly got its readers laughing when it stated, for example, that "there is no man like Feijó" and that if he made mistakes, writing "absurdities in the *Justiceiro*," he only did so because he suffered from *almorreimas* (hemorrhoids):

> Do not trust, Voters, what is being put about, that Feijó is very ill, and that
> due to his continuous maladies he cannot take care of the regency: these are
> inventions of Feijó`s enemies: Feijó's disease is not a cause for concern so
> that you should not elect him; his malady, (I have it from a worthy source)
> is *almorreimas*, which sometimes go to his head, and make the priest beat it
> like a madman; but this is of no avail, and only now they prevent him from

riding a horse because they are inflamed; but then we do not want the regent to ride on horseback, but to govern.[6]

However, *Novidade* also provides a highly plausible reason for the fall in the number of new newspapers printed in Rio de Janeiro in 1834. In the opening article in its first issue, which served as a prospectus for the publication, the editor (Paula Brito?) had these flattering words for the prosecutor Antônio de Falcão Miranda:

> A young Brazilian, son of the S. Paulo Law School, whom we respect, we ask his permission to publish from time to time the *Novidades* (news) of this city, promising never to perturb him with any responsibility, so we will not offend public morals, religion, the fair sex, the law; nor will we discuss *restoration*, as long as, for the soul of its captives, he lets us entertain the public already tired of waiting for improvements in the Nation.[7]

Following the wave of restorationism that swept through Rio and other parts of the Empire in late 1833 and early 1834, was the government—and consequently the justice system—keeping a closer eye on the press? As the editor of *A novidade* asked the prosecutor for "permission to publish from time to time," that is very likely. Indeed, this vigilance must have inhibited the publication of new titles. But the situation worsened the following year, particularly for the opposition newspapers, when Feijó defeated Holanda Cavalcanti and became Sole Regent.[8]

In late May 1836, then Regent Feijó wrote to Paulino José Soares, demonstrating how much the "abuses" committed by some periodicals and presses in Rio were worrying him. On that occasion, Feijó insisted that the law should be enforced, no matter whether it was by the chief of police or the municipal judge.[9] His letter singles out one newspaper in particular—*Raio de Júpiter* (Jupiter's lightning bolt), which was then the target of implacable persecution, along with *Sete d'Abril* and *Pão de açúcar*. According to *Sete d'Abril*, the government had declared "*war* and *war* to the death, persecution and extermination" against *Raio de Júpiter* because that newspaper had seriously questioned the legitimacy of the 1835 election.[10] In a matter of days, *Sete d'Abril* was also charged with the "crime of abuse of the press."[11] In the case of *Pão de açúcar*, which was charged with the same offence in April 1836, the editor of that newspaper, José da Cruz Pirajá, had to come forward and take responsibility for the publication, as the printer responsible for publishing the newspaper was under siege. And who was he? None other than Nicolau Lobo Vianna, the owner of the Diário Press, which was destroyed in December 1833. Pirajá pleaded, "If it is a crime to speak frankly, do not take revenge on one who has no part in it. Spare the not-guilty printer: let the lightning bolts of revenge fall on us."[12]

The regent's "war on the press," waged in April and May 1836, was also the subject of heated debates in the Chamber of Deputies. During the May 13 session, Figueira de Mello, who, along with Bernardo Pereira de Vasconcelos and other deputies, was in the opposition to Feijó's government, discussed the matter in his response to the emperor's Speech from the Throne. The deputy charged that "many periodicals have disappeared due to the ministry's persecutions, and even typesetters, who are not at all responsible for the newspapers, have been arrested."[13] In April 1842, Paula Brito published a letter in *Jornal do commercio* stating that, as in "the days of Mr. Feijó," newspapers were being accused of press crimes and, as a result, he had nearly ended up behind bars:

> As long as I have had a printing press, I have only stopped printing one newspaper, after having produced several issues; that was the *Cidadão*, and this was because of some less-than-honest articles that came out in them; but *Esbarras, Fado dos Chimangos* and others have never dishonored my workshop.
>
> In the days of Mr. Feijó, I saw newspapers accused the day they were published; I was heavily beset and finally I was under indictment for more than two years! Because of *Bússola da Liberdade*, I was ordered to present those responsible within two hours on pain of arrest![14]

In the context of the debate in which he was taking part, involving a lawsuit against the Widow Ogier, this letter says a great deal about the political stance that Paula Brito adopted after the Age of Majority coup. However, it does not specify to which "days of Mr. Feijó" the printer was referring—whether it is between 1831 and 1832, when the priest was justice minister, or between 1835 and 1837, when he was regent. During both periods of Feijó's political career, there is solid evidence that publishers and printers were persecuted for press crimes. In 1832, the lengthy criminal case brought against Joaquim d'Abreu Gama and Nicolau Lobo Vianna, both of whom were arrested and convicted of publishing the Restorationist newspaper *O Caramuru*, produced some of the most complete case records on such crimes that I have found in the course of my research. The records state that the printer was captured in an ambush set up by Chief Constable Luiz Manuel Álvares de Azevedo, who had "invited him in an official letter" to appear at his home "for the good of public and national service." Vianna was arrested there without being informed of the charges against him.[15] Two years later, when the Moderates began clamping down on the opposition press, Paula Brito fell afoul of the law due to the publication of *Seis de Abril Extraordinário*, a newspaper which certainly was another that did not survive the ravages of time.

The case became public when *Diário do Rio de Janeiro* published a list of proceedings in 1840.[16] At the time, Paula Brito made a point of issuing a note clarifying "that my case has already been *tried and [I was] acquitted*; and thus I am free of the only charge I suffered as the printer of the newspaper *Seis d'Abril*, which was born in 1834."[17] Again, it is necessary to read the note in the political context of the late 1830s. But before we move in that direction, we must understand how the law affected publishers and printers at a time when writing might not be as risky as printing.[18]

The report that Feijó presented to the Legislative Assembly in May 1832, when the priest was justice minister, already pointed out that "the license of writing" was a "cause of no less fecund immorality." Feijó began his reflections in a somewhat indulgent tone, discussing how the "prestige of the press offers itself to the . . . uncertain judgment" of "a still ignorant people" and "a fiery youth, whose years are appearing on the horizon of a still poorly established and little clarified freedom." Following the Minister's assessment, this "uncertain judgment" could explain why "any man of letters, and without morals, spreads false principles with impunity: he attacks the private and public life of the honest citizen: inflames passions and disrupts society."[19] Feijó resented the law's inability to "punish these abuses," particularly because there were ways in which a writer could evade responsibility for his writings:

> Measures must be taken so that the writer cannot deceive the good faith of the readers, hiding his name, perhaps [a] very despicable [one], nor escape the prompt punishment of his temerity. Insults, slander, and threats, which the law of October 26 of last year so wisely classified as police crimes, when published, should be prosecuted in the same way: simplified proceedings, prompt sentencing, will allay the resentment of offended honor: the dread-

ful consequences of wounded self-esteem will be avoided, and the audacity of a man without honor and without manners will be contained.[20]

The legislation in question was the Law of October 26, 1831, which, as a supplement to the measures taken to suppress the tumult in the streets of Rio de Janeiro after the Seventh of April, prescribed "how to prosecute public and private crimes" while addressing "police crimes." In article 5 it stated that "minor physical offenses, insults, and *unpublished* slanders, and threats, will be considered police crimes, and as such will be prosecuted."[21] In fact, Feijó wanted insults and slander to be prosecuted as "police crimes," which were unbailable offences when caught in the act.[22]

However, as the "writer discovers many means of escape," the minister's reflection on abuses of "license to write," going beyond punishment, rested on the problem of responsibility. According to the lawyer Paulo Domingues Viana, punishment of press crimes could be meted out in three ways. In the first, based on so-called common law, or the "English system," all those involved in producing the writing—the author, printer, and publisher—are held responsible, and as such, are considered respondents and/or co-respondents. The German system was quite similar, in which, apart from mutual responsibility, showed no sign of being voluntary, which was characteristic of the third, the Belgian system, also known as the "chain of responsibility." It is precisely with this system that we must concern ourselves, for, as Viana observes, it was not exclusively Belgian.[23]

The cornerstone of Imperial Brazil's criminal law regarding press offenses, the "chain of responsibility system" was clearly explained in the first decree on that matter, issued by King João VI on March 2, 1821. The law in question sought to establish a complex middle ground between "the obstacles which the prior censorship of writing posed to the propagation of truth, as well as the abuses that unlimited freedom of the press could bring to religion, morality, or public peace." It was a difficult balance to strike because, while prior censorship was abolished, another kind of censorship was introduced through prosecutions, because printers were obliged to submit two sets of proofs for examination. If the printed matter was found to contain "anything that is contrary to religion, morals, and good habits, against the Constitution and the Person of the Sovereign or against the public peace," publication would be halted "until the necessary corrections are made." Booksellers, who were obliged to report which books they sold, and printers were thus liable to confiscations, fines, and imprisonment. In the case of "seditious or subversive writings," His Majesty explained who would be "responsible before the courts of these my realms due to the nature and consequences of the doctrines and assertions contained in them": "firstly, their authors, and when these are not known, the publishers, and finally the sellers or distributors, in the event that they have knowledge of or are complicit in the dissemination of such doctrines and assertions."[24] The principle of the chain of responsibility had been established.

Prince Pedro's regency began a few weeks after João VI returned to Portugal. In the ensuing months, the prince regent, who was then a liberal ruler in the vacuum left by the Liberal Revolution of 1820 in Oporto (Porto), signed two major decrees regarding the press and reading practices. The first allowed all books except those considered obscene through the Rio de Janeiro customs house, and the second allowed freedom of the press in accordance with the regulations of the Lisbon Cortes.[25] However, the issue of anonymity came into the debate when, in a communiqué issued on September 24, 1821, the board of directors of the National Press (Tipografia Nacional) expressed its opposition to that practice.[26]

Certainly, the communiqué suited the board's immediate aims, as it was more interested in avoiding "responsibility for the printing of writings" by ensuring the compulsory identification of authors and publishers. However, insofar as it indirectly suspended the chain of responsibility system enshrined in the Decree of March 2, 1821, the communiqué ended up going beyond such interests. Other printers could and would certainly benefit from this regulation. After all, if printers only "printed books," as defined by Silva Pinto's Portuguese dictionary,[27] why should they be incriminated by the content they printed? Pedro may have agreed that the chain of responsibility contained serious contradictions. So much so that, in the ordinance signed on January 15, 1822, the prince simultaneously halted publication and confiscated all copies of Heroicidade brasileira (Brazilian heroism) and determined that the board of directors of the National Press "should never consent to printing anything without publishing in the publication the name of the person who must answer for its contents."[28]

However, that ordinance was short-lived. Four days later, the all-powerful minister José Bonifácio revoked it as follows: "The Prince Regent hereby sends through the same Secretary of State, to declare to the said board that it must not obstruct the printing of anonymous writings; because the author must be held responsible for any abuses they contain, even though his name has not been published; and if this [name] is withheld, the publisher, or printer [will be held responsible] according to the law regulating freedom of the press."[29] In addition to reestablishing the chain of responsibility principle, the Ordinance of January 19, 1822, officially established the right to anonymity, a practice which, in Marcello de Ipanema's view, was the "old and terrible poisoned tree of the Imperial press." The ordinance would only be overturned in the Republican Constitution of 1891.[30] Anonymity was an important political weapon, so it had to be preserved. This is because, according to José Murilo de Carvalho, "many politicians wrote in newspapers in which anonymity enabled them to say what they would not dare [utter in] the Senate Chamber."[31] Therefore, despite a few amendments, subsequent legislation did not make any substantial changes in this system. This would be seen in the well-structured press bill presented to the National Constituent Assembly in October 1823.[32]

In its first article, the bill abolished censorship, and in the second, it stated that in the Empire of Brazil "anyone was free to print, publish, sell, and buy books, and writings of all kinds without any responsibility, other than in the cases stipulated in this law."[33] However, such cases were numerous, and the punishments meted out included prison sentences, fines, and exile.[34] The bill also set out the details of the qualification of the offenses and the formalization of the charges, as well as the election of the judges in charge of such cases and the procedures that would guide their work. The bill was considered so comprehensive that, after the first reading in the House, a deputy called for a "second reading to be dispensed with because [it] takes too much time and it is no use hearing so many articles [read] again."[35]

As we have seen, article 16 reaffirmed the established principle of the chain of responsibilities:

> 16. For abuse, in any of these cases, the author or translator will be held responsible; when they are not named or, when they are, they are found to reside outside the Empire, responsibility will fall on the printer; and for abuses committed in writings printed in foreign countries, responsibility will fall on those who publish them or sell them in this Empire.[36]

Articles 3 and 4 were key and supplemented the investigation of these responsibilities, at least those of the printer:

3. All writings printed in the Empire of Brazil must show the place and year of the printing, and the name of the printer: anyone who prints, publishes, or sell any writings without [fulfilling] these requirements will be fined 50,000 réis, and whoever buys them will lose the copies that have bought, and twice their [face] value.

4. Anyone who falsifies any of the requirements mentioned in the preceding article shall be fined 50,000 réis, and when such falsification attributes the publication to any person in the empire, the fine will be doubled.[37]

The bill made it obligatory to publish an imprint statement, requiring, on pain of fines, that information be provided about the place and year of publication and the name of the printer. Therefore, while the authors' anonymity had been preserved, that of the printers had not, as they were obliged to "undersign" all the works that left their presses, no matter what they contained. In effect, in the case of anonymous subversive writers, the printers would be the first to be identified. The press bill was debated in the Constituent Assembly about a month later, during the sessions held on November 8 and 10. The debates did not go beyond article 6 because, after an intense power struggle between the deputies and Pedro I, the Constituent Assembly was arbitrarily dissolved.[38] However, eleven days later, the press bill became law through the Decree of November 22, 1823, without any changes, and the compulsory identification of printers and publishers was maintained, along with remaining silent regarding authors' anonymity.[39]

The Constitution granted in 1824 did nothing to change this situation.[40] However, in June of that year, Joaquim Gonçalves Ledo presented the Chamber of Deputies with a new "bill against crimes of abuse of freedom of the press." Although it failed to advance, it is interesting to note the solutions Ledo proposed to the matter of responsibilities. Title II of his bill is entirely devoted to the subject, deciding immediately in the first article that "the person responsible for any writing, and of any nature whatsoever: 1 the author of the writing, 2 the presenter of it," and in article 3 that "in the absence of the author and the presenter, those held responsible are: 1 the printer, 2 the publisher, 3 the seller." Printers, publishers, and merchants would only be exempt from the considerable fine of one million réis if they presented a "signed statement of responsibility" in which "the signature is recognized by a notary." In article 6, the obligation to publish an imprint statement was reaffirmed.[41]

In September 1830, a new law came into effect, instigated by the Speech from the Throne at the opening of the Legislative General Assembly. On that occasion, Pedro I demanded that deputies take action regarding "the need to repress by legal means the continuing abuse of freedom of the press throughout the Empire."[42] As in Gonçalves Ledo's bill, Title II of the new law established "Responsibilities" according to the principle of successive guilt that had been in force since 1821—that the printer, publisher, author, and finally the seller would be held responsible for any "printed or engraved" matter. Therefore, authors would only be held responsible for their manuscripts, which would be the responsibility of the printers if they went to press.

A short time later, in December 1830, the enactment of the Empire's Criminal Code brought new laws on freedom of the press into effect. While article 7 of the Criminal Code, regarding cases of "abuse of the freedom to communicate thoughts," added little to the previous laws, from then on such offences were considered common crimes.[43] However, the Criminal Code did usher in one innovation—the compulsory registration of publishers, printers, and lithographers, as well as the obligation to send a copy of every printed item to the public prosecutor's office.[44]

The law was unfavorable for printers in many ways. Therefore, the only way for men like Francisco de Paula Brito, Nicolau Lobo Vianna, and other owners of presses throughout the country to avoid falling afoul of it was by presenting letters of responsibility signed by the authors. Paula Brito had to do so when he was called before the courts for printing *Bússola da liberdade* (Compass of freedom). As we have seen, if he had not had the letter of responsibility at hand, according to his own account, he would have gone to jail.[45]

Feijó's relations with the press were far from cordial, especially in 1836. He even attempted to reorganize press legislation through the Decree of March 18, 1837, which provided guidance for prosecutions and sentencing in crimes of that nature. However, the system of responsibilities remained unchanged, with just one important addition in article 8, which stated that printers and publishers could only present letters of responsibility that had been recognized by a notary on the same day or prior to the date of publication.[46] However, this decree was revoked shortly after Feijó fell from office. Finally, in the days of the Conservative Return, the reform of the Criminal Code carried out by Bernardo Pereira de Vasconcelos put press crimes within the jurisdiction of chiefs of police.[47]

However, Paula Britos's problems with the law did not go that far. After an uncertain start, like all beginnings, the son of the freedman Jacinto and grandson of the captain of the Pardos Battalion purchased his cousin's bookshop, added a printing press, and, along with a business partner, printed newspapers with different political leanings. As a result, he was prosecuted and nearly saw his establishment ransacked and destroyed. Most likely for that very reason, as of October 1835 Paula Brito opted for impartiality—at least in the name of his new press, the Tipografia Imparcial de Brito, or Brito's Impartial Press. The times and desires were changing.

PART TWO

Conservative Impartiality

CHAPTER 7

"A Very Well Set-Up Establishment"

THE JUNE 22, 1844, issue of *O Brasil*, a Conservative newspaper edited by Justiniano José da Rocha, contained an advertisement on page four titled "Aproveitável Aula de Meninas" (Useful class for girls). It was for a girls' school that had been located on Rua do Piolho, no. 118, for a time and had just moved to Beco da Barreira, no. 23. At that institution, "run by a respectable lady and her daughters," the students learned "reading and writing, four types of mathematics, needle and scissor work in the known styles and tastes," "music, dancing, etc. etc. ensuring strict education in the civil, moral and religious parts." The ad honestly admitted that the establishment did not have "the renown of the great schools" of Rio de Janeiro. Nevertheless, it promised "reasonable prices" and the advantage of having the "students entrusted to the care and vigilance of yet another person." However, the part that really interests us is this: to bolster the school's credibility, the ad listed some of the "gentlemen" whose daughters studied there: "and this can be certified, among many others, by the [following] gentlemen—Major Schoukow (of Largo de S. Francisco de Paula), Lieutenant Colonel F. Ferreira Gomes, José Pedro Fernandes, Cantalice, Manuel Alexandre da Silva,

FIGURE 11. Portrait of Francisco de Paula Brito by Louis Alexis Boulanger (1842), courtesy of the Instituto Histórico e Geográfico Brasileiro (IHGB; Brazilian Historic and Geographic Institute)

José Maria de Sousa and Francisco de Paula Brito, all of whom have their daughters or persons belonging to them [enrolled there]."[1]

Paula Brito's daughters, Rufina and Alexandrina, whose birth we will discuss further on, were respectively nine and six years old. It may be that only the older girl attended lessons in Beco da Barreira when the ad was published. At any rate, by the mid-1840s, their father already served as an

FIGURE 12. Portrait of Rufina Rodrigues da Costa Brito, Paula Brito's wife by
Louis Alexis Boulanger (1842), courtesy of the Instituto Histórico e Geográfico Brasileiro
(IHGB; Brazilian Historic and Geographic Institute)

role model—he was a "gentleman" whose example should be followed by
his peers. Broadly speaking, the following chapters deal precisely with this
question—that is, they attempt to understand how, from the mid-1830s to
the 1840s, Francisco de Paula Brito managed to establish himself as a merchant, printer, and publisher with a reputation in Rio de Janeiro that qualified him as a "poster child" for his daughters' school.

FIGURE 13. Portrait of Rufina, Paula Brito's "fille aimée" (beloved daughter) by
Louis Alexis Boulanger (1842), courtesy of the Instituto Histórico e Geográfico Brasileiro
(IHGB; Brazilian Historic and Geographic Institute)

That story may well have begun in October 1835, when, after closing
the Fluminense Press, Paula Brito became the sole owner of his business,
changing its name and address. As announced in the *Diário*, the press was
still in the same old Rocio, as some still called the Praça da Constituição.
However, the new establishment was bigger, with two entrances, one on
the tree-shaded plaza and the other on Rua de São Francisco de Paula. Maps

FIGURE 14. Portrait of Alexandrina, Paula Brito's youngest daughter by
Louis Alexis Boulanger (1842), courtesy of the Instituto Histórico e Geográfico Brasileiro
(IHGB; Brazilian Historic and Geographic Institute)

of the city show that this was Rua da Lampadosa, which, running parallel
to Praça da Constituição, ended in Largo de São Francisco de Paula. In any
event, Paula Brito's "private office," to which anyone interested in "secret
publications" should go, was strategically set up on that street, far from the
curious eyes on Praça da Constituição. In times of press persecution, discre-
tion was essential. The announcement also showed that Paula Brito's part-

ner's departure from the business was not recent. His name is still unknown to us, preserved in a sheaf of yellowed pages or a roll of microfilm that is yet to be found. However, of all these changes, the most significant was the name of the press, which went from Fluminense to Tipografia Imparcial de Brito, or Brito's Impartial Press.[2]

Above all, this new name suggests political neutrality. It was certainly a proactive way of preventing assaults like those of December 1833, which may have still been fresh in the publisher's mind, and possibly of avoiding lawsuits. We should recall that, at the time, there was another press with the same name in São Paulo, owned by Silva Sobral.[3] Furthermore, being "Impartial" might be very good for business. Our publisher had been aware of that since he started printing periodicals—although he proclaimed himself an Exaltado, he always stressed that he was "a free printer." Thus, we will see, just like the former Fluminense Press, true to its name the Impartial Press would produce Regressionist (later known as Conservative) newspapers, as well as Liberal ones. However, there was nothing impartial about the press's owner. After his Exaltado years during the Regency, the publisher initially flirted with the Liberals, particularly during the campaign to declare Emperor Pedro II an adult. However, he moved on to the Conservatives and stuck with them for the rest of his life. These alliances were key to the printer's social ascent, which can be gauged by Paula Brito's performance as a merchant selling a range of wares, as well as the technical improvements made at his printing press.

The *Almanak administrativo, mercantil e industrial do Rio de Janeiro* (Business, commercial and industrial almanac of Rio de Janeiro) was first published by the Laemmert brothers, Henrique and Eduardo, in 1843 and circulated for forty-five years, virtually throughout Pedro II's lengthy reign. Better known as the *Almanak Laemmert*, it provides a fairly complete picture of the establishments that published and sold printed materials in the imperial capital in most of the 1840s. Table 3 shows that, less than ten years after he founded the Impartial Press, Paula Brito was facing growing competition in Rio's printing sector. We can see that the number of presses listed in the *Almanaque* for 1844 grew steadily until 1850.

Competition certainly gave newspaper editors and owners an edge in negotiations with the printers. As a result, they could hire the ones that tendered the best offer. This may have been the case with *O cidadão*, a weekly newspaper published between December 1838 and May 1839—a respectable output of fifty-seven issues. Proclaiming itself to be "yet another soldier

TABLE 3 Establishments printing and distributing printed matter in
Rio de Janeiro (1844–1850)

Year	Presses	Lithographers	Bookshops
1844	12	3	10
1845	16	3	9
1846	15	3	11
1847	18	3	12
1848	21	3	14
1849	22	4	14
1850	25	4	15

Source: *Almanak Laemmert*, Seções Tipografias, litografias e livrarias das edições de 1844 a 1850.

that joins the ranks of the friends of truth and the prosperity of our nation,"[4] the newspaper was printed by three different presses. The first three issues were printed by the Crémière Press, the fourth to eighth by Paula Brito's Impartial Press, and the ninth and tenth by the Brasiliense Press. The paper went back to the Crémière Press to print its eleventh to thirty-first issues before once again turning to the Impartial Press for the remainder of its run.

This was not the case with lithographers, because the number of establishments changed very little during that period. Until Brito & Braga lithographers opened on Rua do Ouvidor, no. 51, the foreign-owned establishments of Heaton & Rensburg, Ludwig & Briggs, and Victor Larée held the monopoly on producing prints, portraits, maps, and bills of exchange in Rio de Janeiro.

Following the trend observed for printing presses, between 1844 and 1850 the number of bookshops rose somewhat steadily. Some booksellers had been active since the first Regencies, such as Albino Jordão and João Pedro da Veiga. However, like lithography, the book market in the imperial capital was dominated by foreign merchants—about 60 percent of the fifteen bookshops listed in the 1850 almanack.[5] The number of foreign booksellers, particularly from France and Belgium, also grew over the course of the 1840s. Without a doubt, this phenomenon played a major role in galvanizing that sector. Booksellers such as the Garnier Brothers, Firmin Didot, and Desiré Dujardin mainly established themselves as affiliates of major European companies interested in expanding their markets. As a result, it could be difficult to compete with these *marchands de livres*, who were directly connected to their Parisian suppliers.[6]

Clashes involving municipal authorities and French printers residing in Rio may have occurred on occasion, as the case of the typographer Bintot in May 1848 attests. On that occasion, the representative of the French Legation in the capital sent a confidential note to the Ministry of Foreign Affairs requesting explanations about the violence perpetrated against Bintot by city council bailiffs, as well as his imprisonment in the Aljube prison. The previous year, the French citizen had been charged with not officializing the operating permit for his business and repeatedly ignoring notifications to negotiate the fees and outstanding fines. Finally, when a bailiff sought him out at his press, there was an argument and the Frenchman tried to pull the papers from the official's hand, for which he was arrested. Only later was it discovered that the permits for Bintot's press were entirely in order, and the bailiff was at fault for not having duly checked the accounting department's records. Therefore, the city council attorney who drafted the report on the case did not rule out the possibility that the bailiff "was engaging in corruption," trying to take advantage of the foreigner.[7]

Going back to the data for the 1850s, it is important to note that five of the fifteen booksellers were also printers like Bintot. Agostinho de Freitas Guimarães owned a bookshop on Rua do Sabão, no. 26, as well as a printing press further down the same street, at no. 135. The Laemmert brothers owned the Universal Bookshop on Rua da Quitanda, no. 77, and the Universal Press on Rua dos Inválidos, no. 61B. Junius Villeneuve, the owner of the newspaper *Jornal do commercio*, had a bookshop and press at the same address, Rua do Ouvidor, no. 65, as did Crémière, at Rua da Alfândega, no. 135, and Soares e Cia, on Rua da Alfândega, no. 6.[8]

This was the case with Francisco de Paula Brito as well, although the owner of the Impartial Press does not appear even once among the "book merchants" listed in the *Almanak Laemmert*. We know this because an extensive catalog of books for sale at the shop on Praça da Constituição, no. 64, appeared in the *Gazeta dos tribunais* in early May 1845 (see Appendix 3).[9] This catalog presented the readers with a list of over two hundred books, originally divided into the main languages read in nineteenth-century Brazil. The predominance of French—65 percent of the catalog, or 131 titles— suggests that, like his competitors, Paula Brito may have maintained contact with European suppliers. However, some Portuguese titles, such as *Cânticos Líricos*, *O Filho do Pescador*, and *Três dias de um noivado* by Teixeira e Sousa, Marins Pena's farces, and *Olgiato* by Gonçalves de Magalhães, were printed by Brito's press.

TABLE 4 Catalog of Paula Brito's bookshop, *Gazeta dos tribunais*, 1845

Langage	Number of Titles	Percentage
Latin	10	5%
Italian	2	1%
Portuguese	53	26%
French	131	65%
English	7	3%
TOTAL	*203*	*100%*

Source: *Gazeta dos tribunais*, no. 227, vol. III, 6 May 1845, pp. 3–4 (appendix 3).

Even so, according to the *Almanak Laemmert*, Paula Brito was only a bookseller *ipsis litteris* as of 1852, because his name finally appears in the "Book Merchants" section after he founded the Dous de Dezembro company.[10] However, the Laemmert brothers' omission in the 1840s is significant, as it suggests that Paula Brito's activities as a bookseller were far from his main priority. Therefore, books were just another type of merchandise among the many others for sale in his shop. These included tea—"the best," as Paula Brito advertised in verse and prose in the newspaper *O farol* in August 1844:

The best Brazilian tea, as well as tasty tea from India, are on sale at Paula Brito's shop selling paper, books, snuff, office items, etc., Praça da Constituição, no. 64.
Those who have the *good taste* to enjoy
The *good taste* of tea
May leave a *good taste* by showing,
They have *good taste* as well.
It is the house style to have blue paper bags with a printed label.[11]

In 1834, the Fluminense Press's situation had been far from ideal. As we have seen, there was a sharp drop in the number of new titles being printed, certainly due to the prosecution of printers and newspaper owners. Furthermore, Paula Brito was having a hard time receiving payment from some debtors,[12] who must have included newspaper editors. The situation would have been dire if the printer had depended solely and exclusively on the press for his living. But he did not, because most of his income came from the "bookshop," or better yet, the "shop selling paper, books, snuff, office items, etc." There is no record of Paula Brito having sent books to the National and Public Library of Rio de Janeiro, but in 1853, the merchant did send a bill for "several objects for a total of 14,000 réis" to the librarian Friar Camilo de Monserrate.[13] Therefore, it was thanks to the diversification of his business that Paula Brito managed to get through that difficult period for newspaper publishers and grow. In other words, during and after the storm of the latter years of the Feijó Regency and through most of the 1850s, the merchant's success subsidized the success of the printer.

That he was indeed successful is attested by the fact that, in late October 1844, Paula Brito purchased a "large mechanical press." Described as "the biggest and most complete [equipment] from Europe, transported to the Americas," it originally belonged to the owners of O Despertador. When that newspaper ceased publication, the press—"without ever having operated in the hands of its first owner"—came into the possession of Paula Brito. Barely disguising his enthusiasm, the printer announced in the first column of O Brasil on October 31, that finally his establishment was "now able to produce all kinds of printed materials, no matter how many copies, with the ease and advantages that can be obtained from such machines." And he added: "From now on, not only will this paper [O Brasil] be distributed as early as possible, but the public will soon have other larger publications for which the entire establishment is already very well set up."[14]

According to the Manuel nouveau de typographie, until the mid-1830s there were basically three types of printing presses. The wooden kind were widely used; all-iron presses, or Stanhopes, were made in the UK; and finally, there were mechanical steam-driven cylinder presses.[15] There are no indications that Paula Brito's acquisition was a two-cylinder press like the one invented by the German watchmaker Friedrich Köenig. That steam-powered press revolutionized the publishing sector, printing up to 1,300 sheets per hour. Dupont observed that Köenig's press was first used to publish the London Times in 1814.[16] However, it was certainly expensive. In 1853, the editor of Correio do Brasil estimated that importing and setting up a new mechanical press would cost a considerable five million réis.[17] In 1848, Justiniano José da Rocha, then the owner of the Brazil Press, calculated that investing in that sort of equipment would only be feasible if his newspaper managed the feat of garnering two thousand subscriptions. Only then, said Rocha, would "a mechanical press [provide] advantages that compensate for its higher price and other inconveniences." In the same article, in response to the editor of the Correio da tarde, who had accused him of being envious by making his newspaper a daily, Justiniano said that even if he managed to get two thousand subscribers, he would not need the equipment because "one of the best mechanical presses in Rio de Janeiro is the property of our personal friend."[18] Francisco de Paula Brito? Very likely, the answer is yes.

Paula Brito may have been one of the first printers in Rio de Janeiro to own a mechanical press. When he purchased his, not even the National Press had anything like it. It was only the following year that the Finance Minister and Secretary of State, Manuel Alves Branco, authorized the purchase of a mechanical press for the National Press.[19] The *Correio mercantil*, one of the daily newspapers circulating in Rio, would only buy one a decade later.[20] It was therefore by selling tea, books, office supplies, and other products that, by the mid-1840s, Paula Brito had surely become the owner of one of the finest presses in Rio de Janeiro, for a time superior to the National Press. In the next chapter, we will see what was printed at that "very well set-up establishment."

CHAPTER 8

Newspapers, Theses, and Brazilian Literature

ETWEEN 1835 AND 1851 Francisco de Paula Brito's Impartial Press printed approximately twenty-eight newspapers.[1] Some of them, as we have seen in the case of *O cidadão*, were also printed by other presses during the course of their publication. Another important point is the political diversity of those papers. As we will see, Paula Brito became a staunch ally of the Conservative party. Nevertheless, for the good of the business, he continued to be a "free printer," as the Impartial Press printed opposition and government newspapers. Many of them attacked each other, like *O Brasil*, which was conservative to its core, and *A regeneração*, which was linked to the Liberals who supported the early declaration of the young emperor's majority. Unlike the Regencies, during that period a clearer distinction seems to have been established between the roles of printers and publishers on one hand and editors and authors on the other. At least, this is suggested by the editor of *A ortiga*, one of the newspapers printed at the Impartial Press:

First of all, we will say that as the editor of this paper, Mr. Printer, under whose power we find ourselves, and there being agreement between us and

him in all things, that is, principles, good faith, and money, the various articles which, from now on, will be the responsibility of their authors, under
the *heroic names* they adopt, for example—*canoe* (we will define this at the
opportune time) *clarion, tightrope, trumpet*, etc., etc., thus giving our printer
and publisher the glory of good typographical execution, if he does it, and
our eternal recognition, which will go hand in hand with our existence, for the secrets
he keeps about us, although that is the greatest distinction a public printer
can have.[2]

In many cases, perhaps most, printers and publishers had no connection
whatsoever with the political or apolitical opinions of the newspapers they
printed. Therefore, as their authors were entirely responsible for their written content, it was up to the printer—in this case, Paula Brito—to ensure
the graphic quality of the publication and the anonymity of its authors, as
the law required. When each played their part, a pact was established among
the parties that was based on "principles, good faith" and, it is important
to note, money. Table 5 and Figure 15 show the variety of titles printed
by Paula Brito's Impartial Press, as well as the production indicators. The
press campaign to declare Pedro II's majority must have been reflected in the
increased number of new papers published in 1840, the most significant year
of that period. However, in addition to political broadsheets, the Impartial
Press also printed Catholic, literary, and scientific journals. The scientific
publications included the following medical journals: *Revista médica fluminense, Revista médica brasileira, Arquivo médico brasileiro*, and *Anais de medicina
brasiliense*. A closer look at these publications would confirm a continu-
ity among them, as, except for the *Arquivo médico brasileiro*, edited by Dr.
Ludgero da Rocha Ferreira Lapa, the others were linked to the Imperial
Academy of Medicine of Rio de Janeiro.[3]

In 1844, Paula Brito printed some issues of *Arquivo médico brasileiro: Gazeta
mensal de medicina, cirurgia e ciências acessórias* (Brazilian medical archive:
Monthly gazette of medicine, surgery, and accessory sciences). However,
its editor seems to have been unhappy with the printer, whom he blamed
for delays in the publication and consequently the distribution of the journal. Clearly annoyed, he published a notice in the journal asking the printer
to make a public apology to its subscribers. Paula Brito did not overlook
the taunt and published his response right below the editor of the *Arquivo
médico brasileiro*'s notice, blaming the delay on the overwhelming amount of
work at the press. As a result of that episode, Dr. da Rocha Ferreira Lapa

TABLE 5. Periodicals printed by Francisco de Paula Brito's Impartial Press (1835–1851)[1]

Periodical	First Issue	Last Issue
Revista médica fluminense[2]	07 Mar. 1833	Mar. 1841
A mulher do Simplício	12 Dec. 1835	30 Apr. 1846
Seleta católica	Jan. 1836	Sep. 1837
O guarda nacional	06 Feb. 1836	26 Feb. 1836
o atlante	05 May 1836	30 Aug. 1836
O católico[2]	17 Feb. 1838	02 July 1838
O cidadão[2]	15 Mar. 1838	25 Oct. 1838
O popular	07 Apr. 1838	07 Apr. 1838
D. Pedro II	23 June 1838	14 Sept. 1838
O pregoeiro[2]	05 Jan. 1839	16 Jan. 1839
Simplício endiabrado	07 May 1839	07 May 1839
A ortiga	10 Aug. 1839	07 May 1840
O monarquista do século XIX	17 Aug. 1839	07 Sept. 1840
A liga americana	31 Oct. 1839	20 Feb. 1840
O homem do povo[2]	26 Feb. 1840	12 Nov. 1840
O propugnador da maioridade	19 May 1840	21 July 1840
O filho do Brasil[2]	04 July 1840	13 Oct. 1840
O grito da razão	17 July 1840	17 July 1840
A regeneração	18 Aug. 1840	30 Mar. 1841
O Brasil[2]	16 June 1840	2 June 1840
Revista médica brasileira	May 1841	Mar. 1843
A gazeta dos tribunais	10 Jan. 1843	29 Dec. 1846
O gosto[2]	05 Aug. 1843	7 Sept. 1843
Arquivo médico brasileiro[2]	Aug. 1844	Sept. 1848
O brado do Amazonas	5 Apr. 1845	31 May 1845
Anais de medicina brasiliense	June 1845	Sept. 1851
A marmota na corte	7 Sept. 1849	30 Apr. 1852
O Tamoio	15 Jan. 1851	29 Mar. 1851

Source: Catalog of periodicals in the Arquivo Edgard Leuenroth (AEL-Unicamp).
1. Initially printed by Brito & Co.'s Fluminense Press.
2. In addition to the Impartial Press, some issues were printed by other presses based in Rio de Janeiro.

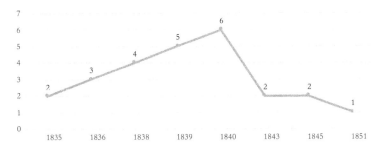

FIGURE 15. New periodicals printed by Francisco de Paula Brito's Impartial Press (1835–1851). Source: Catalogue of Periodicals in the Arquivo Edgard Leuenroth (AEL-Unicamp)

must have decided to dispense with the Impartial Press's services and have the journal printed at Berthe & Haring's Press on Rua do Ouvidor, no. 123.[4]

However, Paula Brito maintained good relations with the publishers of the *Anais de medicina brasiliense* (Annals of Brazilian medicine), the journal of the Imperial Academy of Medicine. In early June 1846, the beginning of a new volume of the publication, the editor, Dr. Francisco de Paula Cândido, mentioned the "efforts and intelligence of the printer," to whom he owed "not only the improvement of the new and larger format, which the journal will have from now on, as well as the considerable reduction in the work load of the editors of scientific articles, as Mr. Paula Brito was responsible for proofreading, etc., and other detailed tasks."[5] Days later, on June 30, the "diligence and care of Mr. Paula Brito" in printing the journal were once again underscored at the Annual Session of the Imperial Academy of Medicine. According to the minutes for that session, Paula Brito was entrusted with the "publishing and distribution" of the journal, being remunerated with copies of the publication, an agreement that relieved the Academy of the "risk of financial losses due to a lack of subscribers."[6] However, his remuneration depended on that institution's budget. In 1847 and 1848, His Majesty's government appropriated just 1,600,000 réis for the Imperial Academy of Medicine, which was a paltry sum compared to the 20,120,000 réis earmarked for the Academy of Fine Art.[7]

These amounts suggest that Paula Brito was not well paid for his work. In any event, the connection between the printer and the physicians at the Imperial Academy of Medicine may have had one advantage: the publication of theses defended at the Rio de Janeiro School of Medicine. The Law of October 3, 1832, which reorganized the medical and surgical schools of Rio de Janeiro and Bahia, covered the subject of theses in article 26, clearly

TABLE 6. Medical theses published in Rio de Janeiro and listed in the
Arquivo médico brasileiro (1844–1845)

Press	Number Printed
Americana	2
Comercial—E. C. dos Santos (Niterói)	1
Impartial—Francisco de Paula Brito	12
Imperial and Constitutional—Villeneuve & Co.	1
Imprimerie Française	1
N. L. Vianna	4
Teixeira e Cia.	1
Brazil—J. J. da Rocha	2
Diário	4
Francesa	1
Universal—Laemmert	11

Source: *Arquivo médico brasileiro: Gazeta mensal de medicina,
cirurgia e ciências acessórias*, Rio de Janeiro, 1844–1845.

stating that no student could be awarded the title of Doctor of Medicine
without defending a thesis written in Portuguese or Latin, according to the
regulations of each institution. What interests us here is that the law stipulated that these theses had to be "printed at the candidates' expense."[8] As a
result, newly graduated doctors became an important clientele for printers
in the two cities that housed the Empire's medical schools. An overview of
this market in Rio between 1844 and 1845 can be obtained from the titles
published in the "Medical Works" and "Medical Works Published in Rio de
Janeiro" sections of the *Arquivo médico brasileiro*. As shown in Table 6, forty-
two theses were printed at eleven different presses during that period, as
reported in Dr. da Rocha Ferreira Lapa's journal.

In the mid-1840s, the Impartial Press and the Laemmert brothers' Universal Press were the go-to establishments for young doctors in Rio wanting
to print their theses. The good service provided to the Imperial Academy
of Medicine when publishing and distributing its journal may have been a
determining factor behind the twelve theses printed by Paula Brito, which
put him at the top of the ranking. In some cases, physicians associated with
the Imperial Academy were professors at the Medical School, which was
based in the former Jesuit college. For example, as the editor of the *Anais de
medicina brasiliense*, Dr. Francisco de Paula Candido maintained close contact

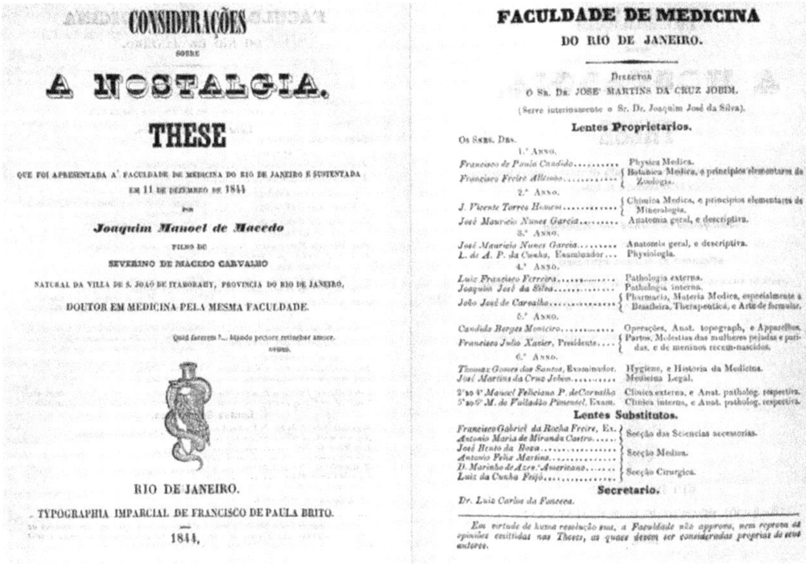

FIGURE 16. Title page of *Considerações sobre a nostalgia* (On nostalgia), thesis by Joaquim Manuel de Macedo (1844)

with Paula Brito. He was also a lecturer who taught first-year students at the Medical School.[9] Therefore, networks formed since the 1830s, when Paula Brito began printing the *Revista médica fluminense*, certainly contributed to newly graduated doctors' preference for going to Praça da Constituição, no. 64, to print their theses. This was the case with Dr. João Arnaud de Araújo Lima, a native of Campina, near the town of Santa Luzia do Norte, Alagoas, who had his *Dissertation on Amenorrhea or Suppression of Menstrual Flow* printed there in 1844, as did his classmate, Dr. Joaquim Manuel Macedo, the author of *Considerações sobre a nostalgia* (Considerations on nostalgia), a thesis printed by the Impartial Press that same year.[10]

Shortly before obtaining his medical degree,[11] Dr. Macedo wrote a novel entitled *A moreninha* (The brunette), published in a limited edition at the Tipografia Francesa, or French Press. Saint-Amant, the owner of the establishment located on Rua de São José, no. 64,[12] had clearly offered the best terms to the budding novelist, who must have paid for it out of his own pocket. However, the book sold out in a few months. It was such a success that in April 1845, the publishers Dutra & Mello embarked on a campaign in the *Diário do Rio de Janeiro* to enlist subscribers—from among "lovers of literature, and especially the fair sex, to whose grace and kindness the gal-

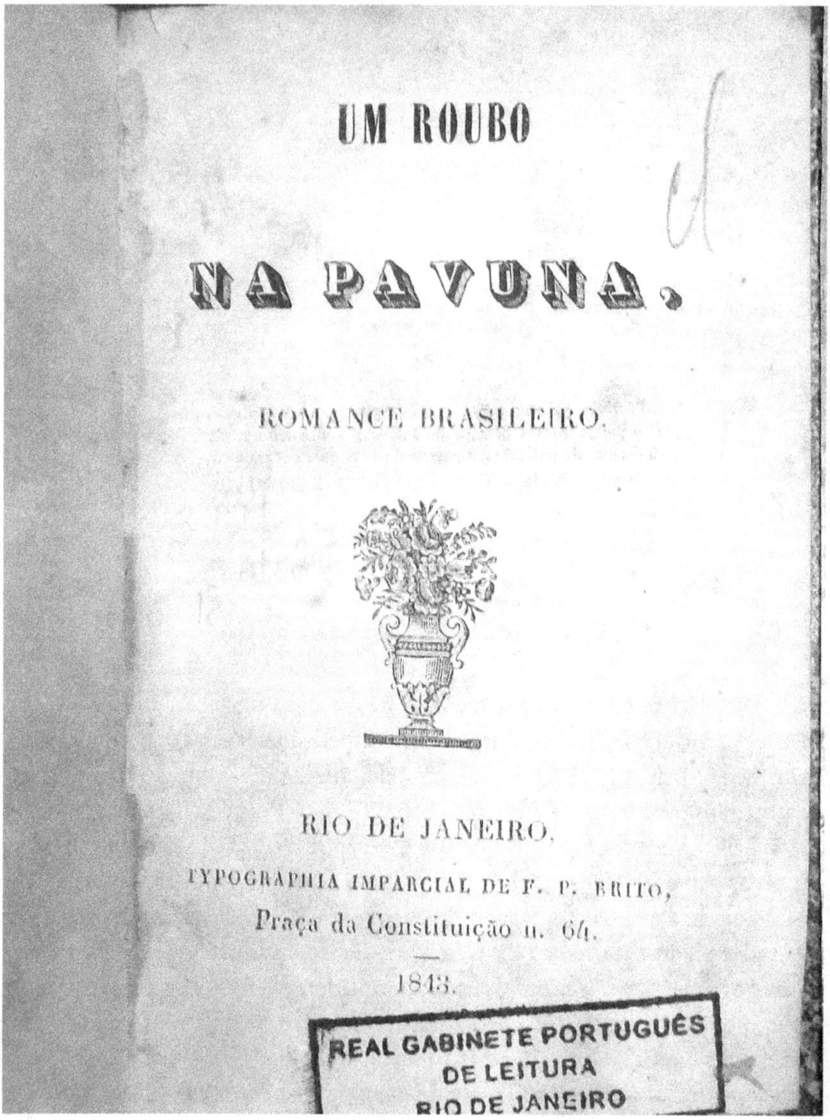

UM ROUBO

NA PAVUNA,

ROMANCE BRASILEIRO.

RIO DE JANEIRO.

TYPOGRAPHIA IMPARCIAL DE F. P. BRITO,

Praça da Constituição n. 64.

—

1843.

FIGURE 17. Title page of *Um roubo na Pavuna* (A robbery in Pavuna),
novel published in 1843

lant *Moreninha* owes a debt"—for a new edition of the novel. Subscriptions could be purchased at the bookshops of the Laemmert brothers, Paula Brito, and Bender, and the new edition would be illustrated with "five fine prints portraying the most important scenes in the story."[13]

Although he helped sell subscriptions for the second edition of *A morenina*, along with the Laemmert and Bender bookshops, Paula Brito played a very important role at a time when novels seduced both the intellectuals and ordinary readers of Rio de Janeiro. In 1836, following the French model, *O chronista* (The chronicler) was apparently the first work in that genre to be serialized in that city's newspapers. The footer of the first page was reserved for the readers' entertainment, and soon, following the European example, French novels colonized that space. In 1839, however, the *Jornal do commercio* began publishing prose fiction written by Brazilian authors, which was a novelty at the time. Paula Brito, Justiniano José da Rocha, and João Manuel Pereira da Silva were the first Brazilian authors to publish serialized novels in the *Jornal do commercio*. One striking feature of these early narratives, going beyond adapting the genre of the novel to Brazilian characteristics, was the legitimization of a conception of national literature, built up in opposition not only to Europe but also to the provinces, with Rio de Janeiro as its hub.[14]

In the course of this process, literary publishers emerged in Rio de Janeiro. When it comes to novels with Brazilian DNA, a goodly number of pages were written before Macedo published *A moreninha* in September 1844. When serialized novels—Brazilian or foreign—invaded Rio's newspapers, the owners of those publications realized that they were a magnet for readers. However, despite the narratives published in *Jornal do commercio* in 1839, the performance of the "Brazilian novel" had not yet been tested in book form. This occurred in May 1843, when Paula Brito printed and sold by subscription the "Brazilian novel" *Um roubo na Pavuna* (A robbery in Pavuna).[15] It was a small-format, eight-page book by an anonymous author who dedicated it to his "dear mother." We do not know whether the novel received good reviews, or whether Paula Brito was just the printer or if he took the risk of publishing it himself after purchasing the manuscript from its author—later identified as Luís da Silva Alves de Azambuja Susano.[16]

About a month after the publication of *Um roubo na Pavuna*, in June or August 1843, Antonio Gonçalves Teixeira e Sousa serialized his work *O filho do pescador, romance brasileiro original* (The fisherman's son, an original Brazilian novel) in *O Brasil*, a newspaper then printed at the Impartial Press.[17] As soon as the final installment had come out, Paula Brito published it as a book in a single 152-page volume sold at his bookshop for 1,000 réis.[18] Thus, Texeira e Sousa's work paved the way for many other novels and short stories in nineteenth-century Brazil—they were only published in book form after reaching their readers in installments found in the footers of newspapers. Success during that initial stage certainly ensured the second, which made the newspapers' serialized novel sections a well-calibrated gauge of the market for publishers. However, the publication of *Um roubo na Pavuna* and particularly *O filho do pescador* in serial and book form begs at least two questions: was Paula Brito aware of Rio de Janeiro readers' interest in Brazilian novels or—as the printer and publisher of books and newspapers—was he deliberately intervening in the development of that interest?

In the prospectus for *Arquivo romântico brasileiro*, a periodical that publicized the novels Paula Brito published as of February 1847, we can find some significant answers to these questions:

Having recently developed in our readers an excessive taste for reading novels, or novellas, which is the same; and our newspapers serializing French novels almost daily, we observed that not a few readers, after the serialized novels are finished, will buy them in booklets, thus paying twice, once with the newspaper subscription, and again when buying the booklets, which will not happen with a regular publication that publishes novels; for once the issues in which the novel is published are purchased, or subscribed, there is nothing left to do but the binding, and there you have a beautiful and clear volume of novels. This has been attempted more than once, because such publications have been unsuccessful, and never for lack of subscribers; for the reason is that when starting to publish a novel in a publication produced for that purpose only, the major newspapers also begin to publish it, and subscribers having the same novels as [those serialized in] the daily newspapers do not renew their subscriptions, and so the publication of novels dies a slow death: this was the case with the *Arquivo Romântico*.

Notwithstanding these sad examples, we will undertake a publication with the above title, which will only publish Brazilian novels; that way no one will publish them but us, and only us.[19]

In 1847, the taste for novels was recent and growing. Paula Brito perceptively observed that readers who were eager to follow their plots were willing to pay twice for the same work, by subscribing to the newspaper and buying the book. His publication aimed to eliminate that extra expense by serializing novels in fascicles that could be collected and bound when the last installment was published. However, to ensure the project's success, publishing Brazilian authors was the only way to deal with the unfair competition of translations. After all, at a time when bootlegging French books was a common practice, it was impossible to purchase exclusive publication rights for a specific novel. Thus, the key to survival was the exclusivity ensured by the publication of Brazilian authors—"no one will publish them but us." Therefore, the publisher's first justification of the preference for Brazilian novels was based on the realities of the marketplace. Nevertheless, there were other reasons:

> Two advantages will result from this, or rather three: first, by writing about our own things, we will get to know our country, our antiquities, and all our things better; second, it adds to our literature, which is already vast; third, it stimulates the genius of our young people, who spurred by example have hurled themselves into the writers' arena. In view of these advantages, we hope that all lovers of novels will subscribe to this publication, which is 500 réis per month, giving a page and a half, on good paper, good type, forming a clear edition. The *Arquivo romântico brasileiro* comes out every Saturday, when it is not a holiday. The publishers started their career by publishing the Brazilian novel by Mr. Antonio Gonçalves Teixeira e Sousa, which bears the title: *Tardes de um pintor, ou, Intrigas de um Jesuíta* (Afternoons of a painter, or, Intrigues of a Jesuit). The public's favorable reception of *Filho do pescador* and *Fatalidades de dous jovens* (Fates of two young men) by the same author, made us turn to this novel, which, on a larger scale, is far superior to those two.[20]

Following Paula Brito's reasoning, the nationalist argument preceded the justification of market forces. The first was based on the need to promote a Brazilian literature crafted by Brazilian authors. From a publisher's perspective, publishing national authors meant first offering a product that stood apart from the French translations that swamped the newspaper footers and bookstores of Rio de Janeiro. Indeed, the novels of Teixeira e Sousa, an author already known to and well regarded by the public, would be perfectly suited to the pages of the *Arquivo romântico brasileiro*, whose serialized works were printed at the Teixeira & Co. Press, an establishment in which Paula Brito had been a partner since 1845.

The eldest son of a Portuguese merchant and a free parda woman, Teixeira e Sousa was born in Cabo Frio, Rio de Janeiro Province, in 1812. Due

Antonio Gonsalves Teixeira e Sousa

Nasceu na cidade de Saco Fruto em 28 de Março 1812

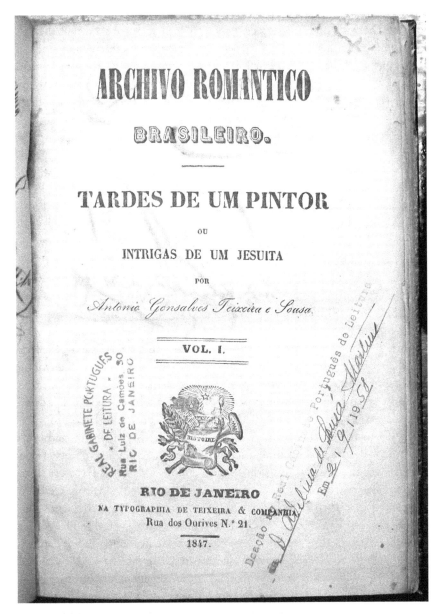

FIGURE 18. Title page of Antonio Gonçalves Teixeira e Sousa's novel *Tardes de um pintor* (Afternoons of a painter), and the author's portrait on the frontispiece, published in the Brazilian Romantic Series by Paula Brito

to his father's financial struggles, he was forced to leave school at the age of ten and make his living as a carpenter. When he was thirteen, he moved to the provincial capital to hone his craft. In around 1830, the young man returned to Cabo Frio, seriously ill with a lung disease. In the following years, Teixeira e Sousa suffered a number of misfortunes, losing his siblings and his parents, and decided to return to Rio. However, during his convalescence in Cabo Frio, he had devoted himself to his studies. During that time, according to Joaquim Norberto, who published a biography of Teixeira e Sousa in the journal of the Brazilian Historical Geographic and Ethnographic Institute, the young man "not only read but avidly devoured all the books that came his way." According to his biographer, love of learning and the adversities of life were the ingredients that brought about Teixeira e Sousa's transformation: "The hymn of consolation had poured into his soul, tortured by loss, and the rude worker became a poet!"[21]

Young, pardo, a lover of learning and poetry. His affinities with Paula Brito were considerable, and in 1840, it was precisely that publisher who took him in "with the smile of satisfaction on his lips, and used his work, providing him with a livelihood."[22] The biographer chose the right verb, because he was certainly correct in saying that Paula Brito "used" Teixeira e Sousa's work, "providing him with a livelihood" in exchange. The young man quickly learned the art of printing and the tricks of the book trade, becoming Paula Brito's business partner in the Teixeira & Co. Press, located on Rua dos Ourives, no. 21. That combination press and bookshop was active from 1845 to 1849, when Teixeira e Sousa—by then married with children—decided to become a schoolmaster in Engenho Velho.[23] However, it was the literary skills of Teixeira e Sousa, described as a "fruitful writer, imaginative novelist, inspired poet," that were first recognized and "used" by Paula Brito in his publishing endeavors. In addition to the novel O filho do pescador, Paula Brito printed the Cânticos líricos (Lyrical songs), verses whose second volume, published in 1842, was dedicated to Judge Paulino José Soares de Sousa, the future Viscount of Uruguai. In 1844, it was the turn of Três dias de um noivado (Three days of an engagement), another book of poetry. Then, in 1847, came the epic A independência do Brasil (The independence of Brazil), in twelve cantos, considered by a contemporary reader to be replete with "infinite beauty."[24]

The Impartial Press would also publish works by other Brazilian authors. In addition to Teixeira e Sousa, Impartial's catalog also included Gonçalves de Magalhães and Martins Pena, primarily the author of skits and farces.

However, despite Paula Brito's efforts to publish novels, plays, and books of poetry by Brazilian authors, possibly with a view to creating a market for Brazilian literature, the number of such works was smaller than the other categories in the publisher's catalog, such as Medical School theses and political speeches. According to the catalog of works produced by Paula Brito's presses, collected and published by Eunice Ribeiro Gondim in 1965 and recently expanded by José de Paula Ramos Júnior, Marisa Midori Deaecto, and Plínio Martins Filho, it included three novels, four books of poetry and thirteen plays, compared with, for example, thirty-five medical theses and fourteen speeches by illustrious politicians such as Martins Francisco Ribeiro de Andrada, Francisco Gê Acayaba de Montezuma, and Paulino José Soares de Sousa.[25] Nevertheless, the publication of Brazilian novelists, playwrights, and poets by Paula Brito would gain fresh impetus with the founding of the publishing firm Empresa Dous Dezembro.

Therefore, to recap a few points, we have so far seen that, after founding the Impartial Press, Paula Brito managed to expand the business, buy a mechanical press, print several newspapers and journals and numerous Medical School theses, and take a chance on publishing Brazilian authors who could successfully rival French translations. But after all, who built Thebes, the city of the Seven Gates? In other words, who composed, printed, and distributed these publications? How was the world of work organized around Francisco de Paula Brito?

CHAPTER 9

Workers, Slaves, and Free Africans

THE FACT THAT many authors consider Paula Brito to be Machado de Assis's first "boss" has made a major contribution to the publisher's inclusion in literary studies in general and specific research into the works of the author generally regarded as Brazil's greatest writer.[1] Nevertheless, the young Machado was not his only employee. Many other workers found jobs at Paula Brito's bookshop and presses. Thus, going beyond the time period covered by this part of the book, particularly due to a lack of data, in this chapter we will look at the three decades in which the publisher was active in Rio de Janeiro, from November 1831, when he began selling books and sundry items, until his death in December 1861. In fact, Paula Brito's posthumous inventory would be a good place to start, as it contains references to some of his staff.[2]

In addition to the cost of renting the building that housed the printing press, gas, medicine, the deceased publisher's funeral, and mourning for the family, the inventory also included debts incurred from "the wages of clerks, from the wages of newspaper deliverers and collectors, from workers' salaries." Noting individually listed cases, we find that Francisco Germano da

Silva had been Paula Brito's clerk, and the publisher's widow and executrix owed him 550,000 réis for his wages for March 1860. The deliverers, who may have walked the streets of Rio de Janeiro distributing the newspapers and magazines printed by Paula Brito to their subscribers, were Antonio Francisco de Araújo, who was owed 104,580 réis, Manuel José Rodrigues, 34,000 réis, and Moisés Antonio Sabino, 20,000 réis. Compared with the clerk's salary, the wages of the deliverers were not high, possibly reflecting the unskilled labor involved, and perhaps because they were teenagers and children. Unfortunately, the inventory does not provide more detailed information about these workers. The "List of creditors of the late Francisco de Paula Brito" merely states "Miscellaneous Workers at the Press for the period of two weeks. 257,800 réis." The inventory also fails to mention any enslaved individuals among the late publisher's chattels, which does not mean that Paula Brito did not own slaves during his lifetime—on the contrary.

Regarding free workers, *Marmota fluminense* provides more precise data about the 1850s. During the expansion of the Empresa Dous de Dezembro, which will be discussed in the next part of this book, Paula Brito published an announcement in that newspaper stating that he had hired *"monsieur* Therier, a skilled portrait artist and lithographer, engaged in Paris."[3] Clemant Bernard Louis Therier had arrived in the imperial capital on February 25, 1853, with a view to working for the Brazilian publisher.[4] Therier was not the only Frenchman Paula Brito hired, as there are references to the fact that Dous de Dezembro employed between thirty and forty workers, including Brazilians and Frenchmen.[5] However, as early as 1856, the numerous financial problems that pushed that company into bankruptcy were already severe. In fact, Louis Therier left Dous de Dezembro in May 1856, partnering up with another Frenchman, Martinet, to start a new lithographic business in Rio de Janeiro.[6] This case is very similar to that of the typographer Luiz de Sousa Teixeira who started his own company after leaving Paula Brito's press in February 1853.[7] There is no evidence that Luiz de Sousa was apprenticed at Paula Brito's press. However, back in the 1840s, this case may bear some resemblance to that of Teixeira e Sousa, who, as we know, learned the printing trade from Paula Brito and started his own business with the help of his former employer.

Given the lack of records, I had to look for data on the organization of work in the publisher Paula Brito's world from a variety of sources dating from a range of time periods. However, this search was more promising thanks to the implementation of Decree no. 384 of October 16, 1844, issued by Manuel Alves Branco, then finance minister and secretary of state. Except for the National Press, the purpose of this law was to regulate the collection of an annual tax, called a patent, on printers throughout the Empire. This tax, which was different in each region, varied in towns, coastal cities, cities in the interior, and the capital, as it was calculated on the basis of the number of free and enslaved workers those establishments employed:

> Art. 1. All presses in the Empire, with the sole exception of the National Press, shall be subject to an annual Patent Tax, pursuant to Article 10 of the Law of October 21, 1843, according to their size, which shall be regulated as follows:
> § 1 The Presses that employ up to fifteen free workers shall pay:
>   In towns   20,000 réis
>   In cities in the interior   40,000 réis
>   In coastal cities   60,000 réis
>   In the Imperial Capital   80,000 réis
> § 2 Those which employ from sixteen to thirty free workers will pay double the taxes above, according to their category, and four times as much if they exceed that number [of workers].
> § 3 The employment of enslaved workers, alone or together with free workers, no matter how many [are enslaved], will subject the press to payment of an additional one-tenth of the tax, according to their category.[8]

Article 2 of the law stated that these workers included typesetters, printers, beaters, and apprentices. The third and fourth articles stated that, at the end of each fiscal year, the owners of the presses had to provide the tax office with a full list of all workers, free and enslaved, employed in their establishments.[9]

Justiniano José da Rocha launched a direct attack on the "Machiavellian minister" Alves Branco's Decree no. 384 in the columns of his newspaper. Lest we forget, *O Brasil* was a Conservative paper in a Liberal administration, which explains da Rocha's effort to discredit all of the ministry's tax and tariff policies.[10] Attempting demonstrate the unfeasibility of the law, the journalist focused on three very important points for our discussion. Here is the first:

> Of all the means of calculating the worth of a press, the minister has chosen the worst: the number of workers is not always a gauge of the work of

a press; furthermore, each press is a school where a multitude of boys will learn that trade, perform some light and unskilled tasks there, but be of no use to the business. Counting these boys in order to use them to increase the imposition of the tax means punishing the owner of the press for the very charity with which he helps these youths, giving them a useful future occupation. What printer will take in an apprentice, knowing that he will be taxed for it? Thus, we will soon see the art of printing, which has developed so greatly among us, which provides sustenance for hundreds of families, wither away due to the lack or scarcity of new workers. Thus we will find that this extraordinary number of Brazilian boys, found in abundance in our printing presses, preparing for a means of making a living that does not make them a burden on their parents, instead making them useful, will dwindle bit by bit until they disappear entirely![11]

Although the services the youths provided are described as "light and unskilled" and Justiniano da Rocha's argument was based on the importance of apprenticeships for young boys, his words suggest these workers were an important part of daily life at printing presses. Many of them must have become printers, which may have been the case with Luiz de Sousa Teixeira at Paula Brito's press. Thanks to the enactment of Decree no. 384, we should know how many apprentices were actually employed in Brazilian presses, if it were not for a second problem that da Rocha mentioned. Printers could easily evade the tax. All they had to do was reduce their workforce during the taxable month by dismissing workers and apprentices. Nevertheless, since "not all [presses] do regular bookkeeping," there was a third obstacle to the application of the law. Based on his vast experience in the business, da Rocha pointed out that usually printers' tax bookkeeping was fairly unorthodox, which would greatly hinder the application of a law based on "books that do not exist."[12] From that perspective, Decree no. 384 would first require presses to take a different approach, obliging them to keep more accurate tax records. In any event, the law was implemented, and in February of the following year, printing presses appeared among the other categories of tax collected in Rio de Janeiro.

In 1845, there were sixteen presses in Rio de Janeiro. Dividing this number by the amount collected, a mere 292,000 réis, we find that each establishment paid the City Revenue just 18,250 réis, well below the 80,000 réis required for printers in Rio that employed up to fifteen free workers. According to the figures published in the *Diário*, Justiniano José da Rocha

TABLE 7 Patent tax collected by the tax office of the city of
Rio de Janeiro in February 1845

Patent Tax	Amount
Patent tax on spirits for consumption	16,005,912 réis
Patent tax on cattle for consumption	9,112,200 réis
Patent tax on horses and animals entering the city	60,000 réis
Patent tax on auction and fashion houses	1,600,000 réis
Patent tax on printing presses	292,000 réis

Source: "Recebedoria do Município da Corte, fev. de 1845," Diário do
Rio de Janeiro, 4 Mar. 1845, p. 2.

was quite right in warning that the law would certainly be flouted. It may be that few establishments in Rio voluntarily submitted accurate lists of their workers to the city's tax collectors.

Other sources indicate that slave labor was widely employed in Rio's printing presses. In this regard, there are records showing that Paula Brito hired at least one slave to work in his press, a Creole named Francisco who had escaped from his master, João José de Mattos, in August 1858.[13] The slave was shrewd, known throughout the city to the point that he had received a benefit performance at the São Januário Theater, and told everyone that he was a freedman by the name of Francisco José de Mattos. The fugitive slave advertisement describes him as "very well dressed and barefoot, and he has a scar under his chin and lacks the tip of a finger right on his right hand." When he fled, Francisco was selling fish in Praça do Mercado (Market Square), but he had previously worked at the Customs Office and "at Mr. Paula Brito's business as a beater"—that is, he was responsible for inking the press.[14]

Antônio, a black slave "aged twenty to twenty-one, of very good appearance" was another fugitive who fled his master wearing "striped trousers and a blue shirt" in November 1831. The ad announcing his escape merely states that Antônio was a "printer" without specifying the type of work he did or where he had been employed.[15] If he was a compositor, Antonio must have been able to read and write, like the Creole slave of Colonel Antônio da Costa Barros, a resident of Valongo, who also decided to flee in August 1830. A repeat fugitive, the captive who claimed to be a freedman called himself Mascarenhas, and was described in the advertisement that Colonel Barros published in the Correio mercantil as "short, thin, with small features, well spoken, able to read, write, and count well."[16] However, literate slaves like Mascarenhas could be considered an "island in a sea of illiterates," to borrow an expression coined by José Murilo de Carvalho.[17] Thus, it is not surprising that most slaves employed in presses were printers and beaters. Unlike the roles of compositors and proofreaders, the work of printers was considered hard unskilled manual labor.[18] This was the case with Teodoro, who was born a slave of the *Jornal do commercio* in March 1844. He learned the printing trade but was never taught to read and write. In 1862, Teodoro, who was not only a printer but a practitioner of the Afro-Brazilian martial art/dance, *capoeira*, was involved in the death of another slave, for which he was tried and convicted. During one of the interrogations to which he was subjected, "he responded that his name was Teodoro, the slave of Júnio Villeneuve & Co., a Creole, born in Rio de Janeiro, who does not know his age, *printer, cannot read or write*, residing on Rua do Ouvidor, no. 55."[19] Max Fleiuss reported that the first Alauzet press used at the *Jornal do commercio* was operated by six slaves, two of whom were compositors, a specialized skill for which literacy was a basic requirement.[20] In fact, the founders of the Fluminense Printers' Association, a mutualist, activist society of Rio de Janeiro Printers, included an enslaved compositor.[21]

In 1846, African slaves were also employed as printers at Heaton & Rensburg, "the largest lithographic establishment in Brazil" according to the American traveler Thomas Ewbank, who also described Mr. Heaton's astonishment at hearing that in the United States a lithographic printer earned ten to fifteen dollars per week. Ewbank soon learned from the owner of the press that "here, one thousand réis [50 US cents] is a good wage and slaves do not cost us even a quarter of that."[22]

It was not unusual for free and enslaved individuals to work side by side in a range of businesses in Imperial Brazil, from printing presses to major establishments like the Baron of Mauá's shipyard in Ponta da Areia.[23] As Mr. Heaton told Mr. Ewbank, the use of slave labor was good business for the printing sector. However, except for the hired-out Creole slave Francisco, studies show that Paula Brito employed very few of his male and female slaves at the press. Thus, although contemporary authors warned that "it was hard to conceive of a system whose impacts are more dire and extensive than those resulting from the existence of domestic slavery,"[24] this was precisely the case with our publisher.

Although references to Paula Brito's "poverty" should be seen in context and were written after the death of a bankrupt man who left numerous debts, it was all too familiar to those who knew and wrote about him.[25] However, the fact that the publisher's human chattel in the mid-1830s consisted of just one enslaved woman does not contradict that image. It is difficult to determine exactly when the publisher purchased the African slave named Maria, from the Congo nation. If she arrived in Rio de Janeiro after the enactment of the law of November 7, 1831, that abolished the African slave trade by making it illegal to enslave captives who disembarked in Brazil, Maria would have been one of the 750,000 Africans unlawfully enslaved in that country between 1831 and 1850 and Paula Brito would have been yet another of many slave owners who benefited from the contraband of Africans to his country.[26]

What we do know, however, is that in September 1837, Maria Conga was described as "thin and very sallow, [with] full breasts, round, [a] well-shaped face, small eyes, thick eyelids, short hair."[27] Depending on the length of time she was enslaved in Brazil, she may have spoken Portuguese with some difficulty, retaining the vocabulary and accent of her original African language, possibly spoken in the area of the River Zaire in central western Africa.[28] We can also deduce the type of work Maria did—domestic service being the most plausible. However, like other urban owners of the limited slave workforce, individuals and families who were generally poor and owned one or two slaves, Paula Brito may have hired out Maria's services as an additional source of income.[29] According to an advertisement for hired-out slaves published in the *Diário do Rio de Janeiro* in May 1837, Paula Brito did make use of this arrangement. It stated that "the Brito Press" was hiring out "a serious and skilled girl" for 12,000 réis. That was a high price compared with the 320 réis estimated for the same year by Frederico Burlamaqui as the "average (daily) wage of a common slave."[30] But this was not the case with the "serious and skilled girl" who was far from being a "common slave"—she was described as being perfect for "private domestic service," ideal "for working in a decent house, because her good qualities demand it. She can do anything, and takes care of everything in a loyal, cleanly, and ready manner."[31] The timing suggests that the slave woman may have been Maria Conga. However, we cannot rule out that it may have been another slave woman owned by Paula Brito.

We have seen that Paula Brito married his wife, Rufina, in Itaboraí in May 1833, and the family grew after the birth of their daughters. Their eldest child, Rufina, who was named after her mother, was born on December 28, 1834, and Alexandrina arrived on April 17, 1837.[32] Therefore, even if she was hired out to other households, Maria Conga's labor must also have been essential at Paula Brito's home between the births of the two girls. After all, Rufina was pregnant with Alexandrina when the couple's elder daughter was less than three years old. Among other tasks, Maria Conga must have supplied the house with water from the popular Carioca fountain, located near Paula Brito's house, carrying a jar on her head. Maria may have also have washed the family's clothes at the same public fountain while chatting with other laundresses and water carriers.[33] However, there are no indications that Maria was not hired out during this period, serving other masters and handing over an agreed share of her wages to Paula Brito at the end of each week or work period. We may never know if this happened, nor will we find out why Maria decided to flee at the end of August 1837, four months after her mistress gave birth to her second daughter.

On August 24, Maria "disappeared" from Paula Brito's home, wearing "a red striped dress, a crimson shawl and a cloth wrapper, fine and new." The fact that she was well dressed suggests that Maria had enjoyed some privileges in the Paula Brito household. However, this does not exclude the possibility that Rufina and her husband were very harsh, to the point of making the African woman's enslavement unbearable. In this regard, the Liberal newspaper *O grito nacional* did not hesitate to accuse the Conservative Paula Brito of "treating his slaves very harshly, having lost the friendship of his groomsman for that reason."[34] Although it was written in the context of the political clashes between Liberals and Conservatives, the newspaper editor's concerns help provide a plausible explanation for Maria's escape. It also suggests that Paula Brito owned other slaves, whose names and details are unfortunately unknown to us. Two weeks after the enslaved woman escaped, the publisher printed an advertisement in the *Diário* asking "anyone who catches her or hears news of her, to deliver her or report her to the house on no. 66, Praça da Constituição, and receive a reward from Mr. Francisco de Paula Brito."[35] However, we do not know what happened to Maria, who decided to decamp from this story in her "cloth wrapper, fine and new."

Maria Conga's services must have been sorely missed, particularly by Rufina, who had to do all the housework and take care of the children—Alexandrina was still a baby. Even so, Paula Brito would only try to ease the situation the following year by hiring "a good black woman who can wash and starch clothes [and] cook," most likely to serve his family.[36] Nevertheless, if the problem was finding domestic help, it would soon be resolved. Paula Brito had just been granted the services of two free African women from the Cassange nation called Graça and Querubina who had been rescued from the patache *César*, a ship impounded for the illegal human trafficking of Africans in May 1838.[37]

When it was captured, the *Cesar* was smuggling 202 Africans into Rio de Janeiro. After they were rescued, 191 of them, including Graça and Querubina, were sent to the House of Correction, where they remained until July 11. Then, following their official registration, they were distributed to private dealers by the Third Civil Court Judge and interim Orphans' Court Judge of Rio de Janeiro.[38] In early August, in keeping with the judge's decision, Registrar José Leite Pereira published a statement in the *Diário do Rio de Janeiro* urging all those who had been granted free Africans from the *César* to pick up their letters and receipts of payment for the Africans at his office in Rua do Sabão.[39] Paula Brito was one of the dealers who responded to the notice. After enduring the Middle Passage across the Atlantic, Graça and Querubina were embarking on their new lives in the publisher's household.

About eleven thousand Africans were rescued, freed, and placed under the custody of the Brazilian government between 1821 and 1856. These measures resulted from bilateral agreements between Brazil and Great Britain that formed mixed commissions to judge ships allegedly involved in human trafficking. As of 1817, these agreements established that the men, women, and children found aboard those ships would be freed. However, before being granted full manumission, they were obliged to perform fourteen years' compulsory service. Thus, Africans rescued from the Atlantic slave trade were either distributed to public institutions in Brazil or offered to private dealers, also known as *arrematantes* (bidders).[40] Graça and Querubina Cassange would only be fully manumitted in August 1854, after sixteen years' service to the publisher and his family. Cassange was the name of a large slave market located West of the River Kwango in Angola, so their "nation" may not have identified the African women's birthplace and merely be the place where both women were sold before being put aboard the *César*.[41] Once they were handed over to Paula Brito, we can surmise that Graça and Querubina worked as domestic servants, doing work similar to that possibly performed by the enslaved Maria Conga. Paula Brito may even have made some money by hiring out the African women's services—a common practice among *arrematantes* that the jurist Perdigão Malheiro harshly censured.[42] We can also surmise that one of them worked as a nanny to help raise Rufina and Alexandrina, the publisher's daughters. Even so, Graça and Querubina were not the only African women Paula Brito was "given."

In April 1839, the British warship *HMS Grecian* captured the brig *Leal* about fifteen miles off the Brazilian coast, Northwest of Cabo Frio. The *Leal* was carrying 361 Africans, and the mixed commission based in Rio de Janeiro considered it a "good prize." Therefore, the Portuguese owner of the *Leal*, Antonio José de Abreu, its captain, Luiz da Costa Ferreira, and its pilot, Manuel dos Santos Lara, were put on trial. Guimarães denied that he was the owner of the vessel, while the captain and pilot declared that "the Africans seized aboard the *Leal* were traveling as settlers to an African port." Despite their feeble excuses, all three were acquitted.[43]

Paula Brito was granted the services of at least one African man rescued from the *Leal*, a youth named Fausto of the Sunde nation. Sunde or Mossunde was on the South bank of the River Zaire, also in central western Africa,[44] which suggests that Fausto, Graça, and Querubina may have spoken similar languages, which would have been important—particularly from the standpoint of the recent arrival. Records of the other Africans rescued from the *Leal*, such as the *malungos* Isaac and Jovita, both from the Muteca nation, enable us to calculate that Fausto was between eleven and thirteen years old when he disembarked in Brazil. However, he died of unknown causes about a year after entering Paula Brito's house.[45]

In March 1845, records produced by the clerk for free Africans show that the publisher was using the services of six individuals.[46] Fausto had passed away by then; therefore, in addition to Graça and Querubina, there were four more Africans in his employ. Another list, produced in 1861, states that Paula Brito was granted the services of Claro and Agostinho, two African men from the Quelimane nation.[47] We have very little information about Claro. Nevertheless, thanks to the records resulting from a misunderstanding involving the manumission of another individual named Agostinho, we do know that the African granted to Paula Brito was sent to the House of Correction in May 1855 and remained there until October of that year. After that, Agostinho was transferred to the Santa Casa de Misericórdia charity hospital, "where he should still be found," according to a letter to the chief of police of Rio de Janeiro dated August 1862.[48]

Another free African woman whose services were granted to Paula Brito was called Maria Benguela. There are no records of when, much less from which ship, Maria was rescued. However, in June 1857, Paula Brito decided to transfer her services to Fernando Rodrigues Silva, a notary and clerk in the town of Valença. However, the Orphans' Court Judge ruled against the move when he found that the publisher owed Maria Benguela two

years' wages.[49] The annual salary of a free African placed in the care of the
Curator of Free Africans was 12,000 réis. No matter how deep Paula Brito's
financial troubles may have been during the bankruptcy proceedings of the
Dous de Dezembro company, precisely between 1856 and 1857, failing to
deposit Maria Benguela's wages sounds like negligence. In fact, willingly or
not, the African woman would only be able to go on to Valença after the
24,000 réis had been paid.

Beatriz Mamigonian demonstrates that the working arrangements established between dealers and their Africans were no different from those
between masters and slaves. The historian shows that most of the free Africans studied in her vast research were employed in domestic service. In her
assessment, this type of unskilled labor drastically reduced those individuals' prospects of autonomy after manumission. The few free Africans with
specialized skills were carpenters and bricklayers, and no Africans rescued
from slave ships were found to be working in commerce or mechanical pro-
fessions.[50] In addition to these services, the bookbinding workshop set up at
the House of Correction, Rio de Janeiro's first working prison, may have
become a place where some free Africans could receive vocational education as of 1850, when Queirós Law definitively banned the transatlantic
slave trade. According to Carlos Eduardo Moreira de Araújo, although they
were far from being criminals, many of these workers spent long periods in
the House of Correction, mainly employed in building the prison that held
them.[51] However, some of them must have learned the bookbinding trade
and, once freed, they might have found employment in the city's workshops. Therefore, Agostinho, Claro, and even Fausto may have worked for
a time at Paula Brito's press.

In any event, having been granted the services of seven individuals, one
of whom is not identified, Paula Brito found himself in a respectable position in the ranking of private *arrematantes* in Rio de Janeiro. Although the
Decree of November 19, 1835, clearly stipulated that "the same person will
not be granted more than eight Africans, unless a larger number of them is
needed for the service of a National Establishment," some private dealers
in Rio enjoyed the services of eight to twenty-two individuals.[52] Such con-
cessions primarily reflected the social prestige of the men and women who
received them, as they were supposedly chosen by virtue of their "recognized probity and character," according to a Notice from the Department
of Justice to the Orphans' Court Judge dated December 1834.[53] However,
the selection the individuals who received the services of free Africans

was determined by bureaucrats and members of the imperial government, becoming synonymous with political favor, granted in exchange for political support.[54]

This is made patently clear by an episode that took place in the Chamber of Deputies on May 11, 1839. On that day, the provincial representatives were engaged in a heated debate about the appointment of budget committees. In his speech, Deputy Navarro rejected charges of corruption in the previous cabinet, where the Conservative Bernardo Pereira de Vasconcelos had been Home Secretary and Justice Minister.[55] At one point in his impassioned speech, which received a rebuke from the president of the House, Navarro declared:

> I cannot speak without agitation; I am not a statue.
>
> And let us not say, gentlemen, that the minister [Bernardo Pereira de Vasconcelos] corrupted this deputy. When an African was wanted, the minister granted him: is there any corruption in that? It is most vile for anyone to be corrupted with two or four Africans; it is most vile for anyone to assume that such corruption is possible. Now what was the ministry doing in this case? It was calculated that for the sake of those Africans, he should not sour a deputy, lose that vote, and send him swiftly over to the opposition, which occurred when [the minister] was not willing to do as they wished.[56]

Navarro was cobbling a shoe intended to fit Deputy Antônio Carlos Ribeiro de Andrada Machado e Silva, José Bonifácio de Andrada's brother, who immediately retorted by giving this explanation about the Africans he had received:

> MR. ANTÒNIO MACHADO—It is to explain wrong facts, which this young man set forth, that I have asked for the floor. . . .
>
> The young deputy has erred once again, perhaps because he misunderstood the lessons that Mephistopheles of Brazil taught him. A wretched person here [Antônia de Moraes] and my correspondent asked me, as I had some relations with the ministry, to speak in her favor about acquiring the services of some Africans; I requested [them] on behalf of Antônia de Moraes and they gave her two boys; I requested [them] on behalf of Jerônimo Francisco de Freitas Caldas, and they gave him two. I believe that they are not means of corruption . . .
>
> MR. NAVARRO—I have not requested any.

MR. ANDRADA MACHADO—I do not know; nor did I ask for myself, because
I do not need any government [for that]; I have provided services to Brazil
that the honorable deputy will never render.[57]

This discussion confirms the importance of free Africans in the political
bargaining during the Imperial period. Clientelist networks were formed
around the concession of these workers, binding "wretched" people like
Antônia de Moraes to deputies and ministers with the shackles of grace and
favor.[58] In this sense, the cabinet formed on September 19, 1837, headed by
Bernardo Pereira de Vasconcelos, seems to have distributed the free Africans'
services lavishly. Published in O Brasil in October 1840, an article by Justiniano José da Rocha, who was also an *arrematante*, stated that "there was
an immense clamor and fuss made by the messrs. who are in power today
regarding the September 19 cabinet's distribution of Africans."[59] Defending
the cabinet's policies in the press, just as Navarro had done in the Chamber
of Deputies, da Rocha tried to explain to his readers that "[if] the number
of these Africans were known, it would be seen that the enemies of the ministry were just as well apportioned, or more, as its friends."[60]

In 1837, all indications are that Paula Brito, then a staunch Liberal-
Andradist, was leaning more toward Antônio Carlos Ribeiro de Andrada
Machado e Silva. Consequently, according to Justiniano José da Rocha, the
publisher would be among the enemies of the September 19 cabinet who
were "well apportioned" with the services of free Africans. Nevertheless,
Paula Brito would not remain a Liberal and Andradist for long. After the
definitive reorganization of the parties and the "Age of Majority Coup,"
the publisher joined the ranks of the Conservatives.

CHAPTER 10

"The *Progress* of the Nation Consists Solely in *Regression*"

I N 1850, AN anonymous writer in the Liberal newspaper *O grito nacio-nal* observed that the Conservative Paula Brito had "learned, and *poorly*, the French language in the home of a Frenchman, Mr. Plancher." In his turn, Joaquim Manuel de Macedo wrote that Paula Brito had "learned it sufficiently." Despite the fact that the publisher was not an authority on the language of Montaigne, he managed to translate a few plays, satires, and poems by Évariste de Parny.[1] And if we trying to identify the time when the publisher expressed a Conservative conscience, supplanting the Exal-tado politics of his youth before the Liberal and Conservative parties were even formed, one translation may provide a significant clue. It was not a play that Paula Brito translated, but one he did not:

Mr. Editor—Having learned that I am said to have been the translator of the play entitled: *O rei se diverte* [The king has fun]—[and] not wanting to steal the glory of the actual translator, nor be the target of the censure that has been expressed; I hereby declare that I not translated any plays for the Fluminense Constitutional Theater, except for the—*Abrasadores* (Incendiaries)—staged a long time ago, which did not please, despite being very decent, and having scenes with good morals. I beg you, Mr. Editor, to kindly publish these lines from your colleague and friend—Francisco de Paula Brito.[2]

O rei se diverte was a Portuguese translation of *Le roi s'amuse*, a play by Victor Hugo whose political content had already caused a stir in Paris, where its performances were suspended by the censors the day after it opened in November 1832. Looking to amuse himself, Francis I, the king in question, perpetrated all kinds of atrocities. Among them, he seduced the daughter of his fool, who sought to get his revenge on the perverse and perverted monarch by plotting his assassination. However, at the end of the play, it was the innocent girl who died. When it opened in Rio de Janeiro four years later, Justiniano José da Rocha harshly criticized *O rei se diverte* in his review published in *O cronista*. Da Rocha found fault with many aspects of the play, which extended to all the "depredations of the Romantic school," focusing first on its immorality and second on the desecration of a king. When reading da Rocha's review in the context of the series of theatre reviews that preceded it, the historian Jefferson Cano demonstrated that those essays were just another trait of the Conservatism inspired by Benjamin Constant which had emerged in the mid-1830s.[3] At the time, concepts like liberty and equality were undergoing a profound reappraisal, gradually adapting to Regressist interests. Thus, da Rocha's reviews were, according to Cano, "a scathing critique of Liberal mistakes." This stance extended and, more than that, informed how a play like *O rei se diverte* should be received by the critics, as it was also considered immoral from the political point of view.[4]

Possibly feeling a stronger interest in protecting his image and business, Paula Brito may have simply wanted to avoid controversy. However, in this context, his objection to seeing his name associated with the translation of *Le roi s'amuse* is open to interpretation. In his appeasing note, the publisher openly stated that he had translated *Os abrasadores*, a play that had not been a popular success but at least was "very decent" and contained "scenes of good morals."[5] Furthermore, Paula Brito wrote that he did not want to "steal the glory" of the actual translator and, at the same time, wanted to avoid being the target of criticism aimed at the Victor Hugo play. Although he does not refer to Justiniano José da Rocha's review in *O Cronista* directly, the publisher and journalist may have been going through a similar process after the fall of Feijó and the rise of the Regressists in 1837: both events had quenched the Liberal and, in Paula Brito's case, Exaltado fires that blazed in their hearts during the early days of the Regency. Emphasis should be given to the word "process" because it seems we are not seeing an abrupt change—a Regressist and Conservative epiphany. It is likely that, for Paula Brito, it began with the prosecutions he endured during Feijó's regency due to the publication of periodicals such as *O Seis de Abril Extraordinário* in June 1834, or, going a little further back in time, to the attempt to ransack his press in December 1833.

These speculations are plausible. However, a close reading of Paula Brito's early newspaper in verse could provide the ideal angle for viewing this process. As of 1835, *A mulher do Simplício* might have continued to be *Fluminense* (from Rio de Janeiro province), but gradually ceased to be *Exaltada*. Despite its name, following Paula Brito's leanings, the newspaper went from being Andradist to Maiorista (supporting the early declaration of Pedro II's majority), and ended its days as a Conservative or Saquarema publication.

Paula Brito's enthusiasm with the Andradas was clear in *A mulher do Simplício* in March 1837, when at the end of a long blank verse poem on page eight, the newspaper's ostensibly female editor concluded:

> *Vivas* are sung to the Loyal ANDRADAS
> Who played a part in this Great Enterprise,
> And to whom Brazil already owes so much!
> Let the World know what we joyfully celebrate:
> COUNTRY, CONSTITUTION, PEDRO THE SECOND.[6]

The different fonts originally used in the magazine seem to underline the key words of Paula Brito's political convictions at the time: loyalty to the Andradas, to Country, Constitution, and Emperor Pedro II. For the editor—"Simplício's wife"—the publisher's poetic persona, the São Paulo Liberals were the main agents of Brazil's Independence, a fact that should be taken into account during the Senate elections of 1838: "I am convinced that the Voters / Have a vivid memory / Of how much our ANDRADAS / Did for Independence."[7] After José Bonifácio de Andrada's death, his brother Martim Francisco Ribeiro de Andrada entrusted Paula Brito with the publication of the manuscript of *Elogio acadêmico da Senhora D. Maria Primeira* (Academic elegy for Queen Maria I), recited at the Royal Academy of Sciences in Lisbon in March 1817. The publisher's note that Paula Brito printed in that edition is very interesting, as it demonstrates how, in some cases, his publishing activities were closely related to his political principles:

> His excellency Mr. Martim Francisco Riberito de Andrada having offered us, as a sign of the friendship with which he honors us, and which we are far from deserving, the manuscript of the present *Elegy*, we are delighted to publish it as another sign of the veneration and respect we have consecrated to the ever-lamented ashes of the patriarch of our Independence.
>
> May this small service of ours, along with others we have done, become in the eyes of his distinguished brothers (to whom Brazil owes so much, and to whom it has been so ungrateful), always worthy of the esteem we so far from deserve, insofar as we are worthy of it.
>
> Francisco de Paula Brito
> *Publisher Owner*[8]

As we will see, this tendency would increase in the 1850s, when the Conservative publisher showed some reservations about publishing Liberal authors, particularly the young José de Alencar, who is now considered one of Brazil's leading Romantic novelists. However, in 1839 Paula Brito was a staunch supporter of the Andrada brothers. During the months that followed, Antônio Carlos de Andrada would become one of the leading architects of the early declaration of Pedro II's majority, a political maneuver by the Liberals to curb the supremacy of the Regressist Party, which had been in power since the fall of Feijó in September 1837. Without a doubt, all his life Francisco de Paula Brito was a loyal subject of his Imperial Majesty, "the Savior of Brazil," as he described Pedro II in a sonnet dedicated to the emperor in December 1839. In this sense, the Liberals' Age of Majority Coup in 1840 fueled Paula Brito's sympathies for that party's leaders. After all, at that time, both professed the same creed, summed up in verse by Paula Brito, hiding behind the persona of the female editor of *A mulher do Simplício*: "Only PEDRO and the Constitution / Brazil can save: / *He who governs at eighteen, / Can at fifteen govern.*"[9]

On the night of July 24, 1840, the day after Pedro II was declared an adult, when the Liberal cabinet headed by Antônio Carlos Ribeiro de Andrada was formed, Paula Brito recited a lengthy poem in the presence of the young monarch, the princesses, and the audience at the São Pedro Theater. It must have been unbearably tedious for a fifteen-year-old to listen patiently to those 111 verses, which began:

All hail, for thee, Lord, this golden Day
of your Acclamation! O tender Pedro
Brazilian Monarch—all hail the glory
of thy grateful people in acclaiming thee!
Motherland! The happy homeland strips off this mourning,
That for so long thy grief shows us;
Brazilian People, generous and docile,
You no longer have to fear the hideous arm
Of fallacious anarchy.[10]

This passage is interesting because it shows that Paula Brito viewed the emperor's adulthood as something of a new age of prosperity and order, in which the homeland had finally exorcised the ghost of Regency anarchy. However, in a short time, the enthusiasm of *A mulher do Simplício, ou, A fluminense exaltada* regarding the directions taken after Pedro II's celebrated coming of age dwindled considerably. In a poem entitled "Ora o homem tem razão" ("Why, the man is right"), "Simplício's wife" wondered:

Does adulthood
produce the desired effects?
The promised equality,
In the order of its precepts
Do the peoples find it was in vain?
Why, the man is right![11]

Implicitly, for every question the editor poses, the answer is a resounding no, an expression of her political disillusionment with those formerly considered "firm, illustrious, liberal, and honorable" leaders of the nation, namely the Liberal cabinet of July 24. Moreover, several questions arose, some of which were of vital importance to Paula Brito, as well as to the Empire's other citizens of African origin—"mixed" and "brown" people:

Could someone have disposed [the Emperor]
Among a people that is so *mixed*,
To despise due to his appearance
The citizen devoted
To the Throne, the Law, and the Nation?
Why, the man is right.

[. . .]

> Will those who are deserving
> *Even if their color is brown,*
> Find recognition
> Or continue with the usual
> Tomorrow yes, today no?
> Why, the man is right.[12]

According to José Murilo de Carvalho, intense public participation made July 23, 1840, seem like April 7, 1831, redux. Nine years later, the elite, people, and troops returned to the streets of Rio de Janeiro, this time with a view to enthroning a monarch instead of overthrowing him.[13] From this perspective, that is, the viewpoint of those who were hailing the new emperor in the streets, the effective beginning of the Second Reign signaled social changes that, in the ensuing days and weeks, did not occur. Thus, in the above verses, Paula Brito showed that he was not only aware of his own situation but that of all the citizens of color who were devoted "to the Throne, the Law, and the Nation," who were once again left high and dry. Meanwhile, many of the ships that were still afloat were slavers who continued to land on the nation's beaches even though the slave trade had been banned since 1831:

> Will we have to see the peoples,
> And some authorities,
> Trafficking in new blacks,
> Which in the towns and cities
> The classes go on mixing?
> Why, the man is right.
>
> Or will the law be banned
> That prohibits the traffic,
> So that then it will permit
> This, daughter of ignorance,
> Inhuman slavery!
> Why, the man is right.[14]

The illegal trafficking of Africans and the exclusion of citizens of color were inseparable themes in Paula Brito's mind. The problem is that this factor alone does not explain the publisher's Conservative turn, as Liberals and Conservatives had turned a blind eye to the smuggling of enslaved Africans since the 1831 law was enacted. Lest we forget, in 1837 alone, after the rise of a Regressist cabinet headed by Bernardo Pereira de Vasconcelos, fifty-seven thousand Africans entered Brazil illegally.[15] However, according to verses published in *A mulher do Simplício*, the Liberals who backed the declaration of Pedro II's majority had not lived up to Paula Brito's expectations.

This may explain why the publisher became openly Conservative at some point between 1840 and 1841, as another poem attests. In verses dedicated to Paulino José Soares de Souza, the future Viscount of Uruguai, Paula Brito wrote, paraphrasing Camões: "Scenes change, politics change, / Your party descends, the opposition rises / (Party that was mine)."[16] In this poem, published in *A mulher do Simplício* in December 1841, Souza is often called a "patron." Furthermore, the title, "Grateful Tribute," implies that Paula Brito had in some way and for some reason received a favor from the Conservative leader, which was soon explained in one of the verses:

> More than once, Sir, I have sought you out,
> Always for the unfortunate,
> (I have not yet asked for favors for myself)
> I find you frank, fair, and open.
> The more I look for you, the more I find you.[17]

If favors were "our nearly universal mediation," according to Roberto Schwarz,[18] as the above verse demonstrates, it was certainly Paula Brito who established closer ties with Souza. However, in addition to the future Viscount of Uruguai, Eusébio de Queirós, the chief of police of Rio de Janeiro and another major Conservative leader, also received a fulsome sonnet by Paula Brito, published in the same issue of *A mulher do Simplício*.[19]

The Liberal press, in its turn, did not leave Paula Brito's habit of flattering Conservative leaders with his poetry unscathed. In 1856, on the occasion of the death of the Marquess of Paraná, the editor of *O grito nacional* would describe as a "fresh-water poem" the sonnet in honor of the late Conservative leader that Paula Brito distributed at the Lírico Theater. The editor accused the publisher of having "mixed up our first day, the day of Brazil's emancipation, with the fate of a man who did not play the smallest part in that majestic event!" And after quoting the first two stanzas of the sonnet, he concluded: "Oh pooh, nothing but adulation! What foul-smelling toadying!"[20] Also in 1856, *O grito nacional* would make fun of another sonnet that Paula Brito recited when Paulino José Soares de Souza, then called the "hero of the *chouriços*," returned from a trip to Europe. According to the editor, "From the foot of Sugarloaf Mountain, Mr. Paula Brito addressed to His Excellency a speech in verse, with the title of sonnet, which was much applauded by the bystanders, and by some forty thousand more from the neighborhood who joined him for this *noble* end."[21] Thus, returning to *A mulher do Simplício*, we can see that the verses published in 1842 showed that its editor's Conservative turn was in fact consistent: "Here, readers, so far / Are our causes as they are: / The *progress* of the nation / Consists solely in *regression!*"[22] Therefore, like the Regency, his Exaltado days were a thing of the past: "If I once cried out ardently / Iron, fire, Exaltation; / Today, experienced, I merely ask for / Order, peace, sweet unity."[23]

However, Paula Brito's backing for the Conservatives was not limited to the sonnets and verses published by the female editor of *Simplício*. It also extended to the ballot box. The publisher belonged to the group of Brazilians that the Imperial Constitution defined as "active citizens." That is, he was one of the select few who were eligible to vote because they were born free, were not "criminals pronounced in quarrels or investigations," and had an "annual net income of 200,000 réis through property, industry, commerce, or employment." In fact, once the candidates had been chosen in the primaries, it was citizens like Paula Brito who voted for deputies, senators, and provincial council members.[24] In the August 1849 elections, Santíssimo Sacramento Parish had thirty-eight Conservative voters.[25] Paula Brito's fellow electors were physicians, landlords, civil servants, judges, and even the Justice Minister, Eusébio de Queirós. However, in addition to voting Conservative, Paula Brito sometimes served as a member of the electoral council, which he did in the December 1848 elections. Serving alongside Antônio Joaquim de Azevedo, the publisher was secretary of the council chaired by Antônio Saldanha da Gama, the justice of the peace of the second district of Santíssimo Sacramento Parish.[26]

The previous year, when he was an alternate, Paula Brito had been involved in a dispute with the chairman, the Liberal justice of the peace and police chief, Joaquim Pinheiro de Campos. The disagreement arose when Pinheiro de Campos decided that he should put the ballots in the ballot box himself. None of the electoral officials opposed the chairman, but Paula Brito noticed that the police chief was carefully scrutinizing each vote before casting it. The publisher protested that each elector should be able to cast his own vote. The police chief retorted that he was doing so to prevent voter fraud, which, according to him, had occurred in previous elections in that parish. Paula Brito was outraged at the chairman's accusation because he had presided over the previous elections, so the charge of fraud fell on him. Thus, the publisher's response was a counteraccusation. Paula Brito asked whether Pinheiro de Campos was making a point of examining each vote to determine whether it "sided with the government or not." The other officials present backed Paula Brito, and Councilman Barreto Pedroso reportedly declared "that the ballots should enter the box without going through customs." Grudgingly, Pinheiro de Campos was obliged to accept the publisher's protest.[27] In 1847, the country was going through the so-called Liberal quinquennium (1844–1848). Thus, by questioning Pinheiro de Campos's actions in that year's elections, Paula Brito was merely defending the interests of the Conservative party, a revelation that may have given rise to the rumor that spread in Rio de Janeiro regarding his supposed appointment as chief of police in March 1848.[28]

Meanwhile, *O grito nacional*, one of Rio de Janeiro's Liberal newspapers, attacked the publisher at every opportunity. That publication circulated in Rio for the respectable period of a decade, between 1848 and 1858, and in August 1849, precisely during the elections, Paula Brito's name began to appear in its pages in articles like the following:

> Setting aside the *impartial* Francisco de Paula Brito, deserter from the party, and who due to *his birth*, and COLOR, never should have done it; even though it was an advantage for the Liberals; because they do not want men *who serve in election times to engage in* CERTAIN *transactions*; letting our fellow countryman who (to be fair) does not pretend to be white, but yet is mixed up with the whites, the *only* ones who have positions in this country of *bodes* and *caibras* [*sic*] (goats), as they call them.[29]

As we can see, the political use of race transcended the chronological boundaries of the Regency period, certainly enjoying a long career in the political language of the Empire. As in the first years following the Seventh of April 1831, once again, skin color was linked to and emerged from political discourse. According to *O grito nacional*, pardo and mulatto were synonymous with the Liberal party. Therefore, although he did not want to be white, but was always "mixed up with the whites," Paula Brito was perpetrating a double betrayal. By abandoning the Liberal cause in the early 1840s, the publisher was also seen to be betraying his color. However, the fact that Africans and people of African descent were joining the Conservative party during the Second Reign belied *O grito nacional*'s free association. For example, to the extent that significant spatio-temporal proportions should be respected, in the 1880s the freedman Cândido da Fonseca Galvão, the self-proclaimed Obá II, African prince of Rio de Janeiro, fiercely defended the Conservatives in articles published in minor newspapers in that city. It is also worth noting that in the 1870s the activities of the *capoeira* gangs, or Maltas, such as the famous "Flor da Gente" (Flower of the People) from Glória Parish, were always willing to fight—in the broadest sense of the term—for that party's interests. In Recife, pardo men organized through the Society of Mechanical and Liberal Arts sought political support from the leaders of the Conservative party in Pernambuco province.[30]

Going back to the pages of *O grito nacional*, we will see that, after accusing Paula Brito of betraying his color by becoming a Saquarema, the newspaper also sketched out a highly unflattering biography of the publisher. The aim of this long article, published in January 1850, was to contest a piece by Próspero Diniz published in *A marmota da corte* in December 1849 which was, according to the editor of *O grito nacional*, "*most impertinent and insulting toward the noble and enlightened French Nation.*"[31] Paula Brito would go down in history as the "insinuator or advisor" of Prospero Diniz. That is why *O grito nacional* felt it necessary to disclose its version of the publisher's past to all its readers:

> Francisco de Paula Brito, it is rumored, went from being a *bad* tailor, working in the house of an old black female greengrocer, lived in Rua dos Barbonos to become a printer, where he learned *and poorly* the French language in the house of a Frenchman *mister* Planchér [sic], the first owner of the establishment and the newspaper *Jornal do Comercio* [sic]. Opening a small shop in Largo do Rocio, it is said that he set up a small print shop at the *expense* of several citizens, to print the proclamations that spread on April 3, 1832, and from then on he marched, always belonging to the liberal party, offering verses to all the members of that party, especially to the Great Andradas, who were removed from power soon after the Age of Majority: seeing that the wind *blew bountifully* toward the side of the party with which he then

waged war, to general astonishment, (except ours) this *political mountebank* burnt the *rotten incense, and the lowest and vilest flattery* for the members of the ministry of forty-one, particularly Mr. Paulino José Soares de Souza! So, it went on; and aided by luck, with the HAPPY purchase of a mechanical press for 101,000,000 réis, soon afterwards spending a few thousand réis raised through the lotteries, and the income from the *best* tea and yerba mate, the *best* snuff and the *best* couplets to the catacombs of the dead, finally, with the hope of fifty million from the Provincial Assembly to set up a printing press, which publishes official acts; and so many other millions and privileges to extract castor oil etc.[32]

According to the editor, Paula Brito, who had become a printer because he was a bad tailor, was nothing but a "political mountebank" who had abandoned the Liberals when he saw that "the wind *blew bountifully* toward the side of the party with which he then waged war." Effectively, attempting to decipher the editor of *O grito nacional*'s argument, we can see that his article bore witness to a time when Paula Brito was already a prominent printer and merchant in Rio de Janeiro. Therefore, he made a point of explaining to his readers that the publisher's success could only be due to the patronage of the Conservative party and its leaders, such as the Viscount of Uruguai.

In a way, *O grito nacional* was right, particularly when it came to a grant that Paula Brito had expected to receive from the Provincial Assembly of Rio de Janeiro since 1848. In early June 1848, the publisher had applied to the Assembly for a loan in Provincial bonds totaling 50,000,000 réis. The newspaper *O Brasil* gave a detailed explanation of what Paula Brito intended to do with that enormous sum:

1. Set up a large-scale press, of an official nature, with modern improvements, thereby lowering the price of publications currently produced among us.
2. Create a daily newspaper with a fine format and clear printing in which he will publish FREE OF CHARGE acts of the government, as well as those of the Assembly; these, however, through agreements to be stipulated later.
3. Add to the establishment a lithographic press, book binding workshop, stationery, and bookshop, etc., all in the best possible taste, which is lacking in the province, etc.
4. Teach the art of printing to twenty young men from Rio de Janeiro Province, four of whom it will send, at its own expense, to learn stenography, to make them—stenographers of the Provincial Assembly.

5. That will have the right to print any and all works in order to standardize books, and other printed matter from tax offices, etc.

6. Allowing him to repay the amount requested to the province's coffers within eleven to twelve years.[33]

The idea was to set up a modern press that could meet the needs of Rio de Janeiro's provincial government. The key point is that Rio de Janeiro province had been a bastion of Conservatism since the administration of President Rodrigues Torres had ended in 1836. According to Ilmar Rohloff de Mattos, the extent of its sway went beyond the boundaries of the provincial government, as Rio de Janeiro became a laboratory "in which the Saquaremas tested measures and assessed actions they sought to extend to the general administration when implementing the decisions of the General-Government, always with the final aim of establishing order in the Empire."[34] One of the fronts favored by successive Conservative administrations in Rio de Janeiro province, according to Ilmar Mattos's key study, was public schools, as their leaders soon discovered the political effectiveness of education.

By taking education beyond the school system—which was also important to the Saquarema leadership—to include instructing the public through the consumption of publications and, consequently, ideas, Paula Brito was linked to the historical process Ilmar Mattos described. This went beyond being a voter and electoral officer ready to defend his party's interests, or a poet whose Conservative muse was always willing to sing its leaders' praises. Paula Brito was one of the citizens recruited by the Saquaremas to implement an ambitious plan to build the Imperial State while establishing themselves as the masters of that state. Ordinary citizens, such as men of letters, doctors, teachers, and, in our case, publishers, joined the Conservative cause.[35] However, that process was highly transactional. At least, this is what Paula Brito's relations with the Viscount of Uruguai suggest, as well as the indignation of O grito nacional's editor at the wind that "blew bountifully" in the publisher's direction after his Conservative turn. The benefits could take the form of government grants like the one Paula Brito was attempting to obtain from the Provincial Assembly of Rio de Janeiro.

Despite O grito nacional's criticism, the press hailed Paula Brito's initiative. Two days after reporting on that matter first-hand, Justiniano José da Rocha returned to it in O Brasil. In another article, Paula Brito was described as "one of our most intelligent printers, most zealous about the progress of his art. . . . A well-known, highly admired citizen," the owner of "one of the best presses in Rio," equal to the foreign presses in that city. Da Rocha saw nothing but advantages in granting the loan to Paula Brito. According to the editor, the National Press was not just a burden on the public coffers but technically outdated, "one of the slowest of our major presses," because, in his assessment, "the government is a terrible administrator of industrial firms." In his view, the solution was what we now call private enterprise.[36] Da Rocha also explained that the new business would be established on the other side of Guanabara Bay, in Niterói, the provincial capital. Furthermore, he gave a more detailed explanation of how the loan would be made through the concession and sale of bonds. According to the editor of *O Brasil*, the amount of the loan could be considered small compared with the cost of publishing the official gazette, which was roughly 40,000,000 réis.[37]

The following month, the newspaper *O americano* enthusiastically announced that the commission appointed by the Provincial Assembly of Rio de Janeiro to deliberate on issuing bonds had approved the proposal submitted by Paula Brito, "our foremost printer," with just one vote to the contrary. Respectfully, the newspaper criticized the recalcitrant deputy, reaffirming that the grant "could be in no way prejudicial to the financial interests of the Province."[38] However, the publisher was not the only printer who had his eye on provincial bonds, as "the two tenders in which Mr. Paula Brito has bid should not embarrass us or make us hesitate about the subsequent confirmation of the Assembly." In this regard, Paula Brito must have written a memorial reporting "his constant efforts . . . commitment and constant dedication to his work." For these and other reasons, also according to *O americano*, public opinion clearly favored Paula Brito. However, it was up to the deputies to make the final decision.[39] In 1848, in addition to Paula Brito's Impartial Press and the National Press, there were nineteen other printing establishments in Rio de Janeiro.[40] There is no concrete evidence of this, but the provincial government may have opened a prior tender for the granting of bonds, which made all other printers possible competitors.

Despite his credentials, the backing of public opinion, and close ties with Conservative politicians, all indications are that Paula Brito did not receive that loan in bonds from the Province of Rio de Janeiro. However, two years later, the publisher tackled a fresh project that resumed and expanded the plan devised in 1848. The idea was to establish one of the most ambitious publishing houses in the Empire—the Empresa Tipográfica Dous de Dezembro.

PART THREE

The Life and Death of the Dous de Dezembro Company

CHAPTER 11

Man of Color and Printer
of the Imperial House

A MID THE CLASHES between Liberals and Conservatives in the Rio
de Janeiro press, we can see that the instrumentalization of race in
political discourse continued after the early years of the Regency era,
when newspapers such as *O mulato, ou, O homem de cor* (The mulatto, or, The
man of color) were published. Thus, in the early 1850s, the liberal newspaper *O grito nacional* accused the Conservative Paula Brito of being hostile
to "people of color," both regarding his slaves and in relation to the black
women with whom he shared the ferry when traveling to Niterói:

> Today, this *notable* [Paula Brito] rejects *people of color*, starting by massacring
> his slaves, having therefore lost the friendship of his groomsman; and he
> is generally *attributed with the paternity* of an article inserted in the *Niterói*, a
> newspaper published in his press, in partnership with Mr. Candido Martim
> Lopes, in Niterói, asking the steamboat administrator not to let *black women*
> [stand beneath] the awning because since he had to make those journeys to
> take the air in the house with the *large tamarind tree*, which he had rented on
> the seashore, HE FOUND THE SINGING OF THOSE BLACK WOMEN MOST
> IRKSOME!!!!!!![1]

Despite the weight of these accusations, the reference to African descent as expressed by the editor of *O grito* does not sound like a disparagement of Paula Brito. According to his opponents' argument, it was way the publisher treated other men and women of color that put him in a very bad light. Therefore, it can be considered that, as references to the color of individuals began to disappear from the description of witnesses in civil and criminal cases in the "former slave-owning Southeast," and before the acceptance of racial theories changed practices and discourse,[2] free citizens of African descent like the publisher Francisco de Paula Brito fought and were challenged in the political arena as individuals with full political rights under the 1824 Constitution.[3] As a result, in the political debate in the press, skin color could emerge as a factor that reinforced ties and alliances.

Paula Brito took a stand on the virtues of free men of color in an episode involving Simão, a free black sailor from Cape Verde who worked as a coal stoker aboard the *Pernambucana*, a steamship that sank on October 8, 1853, during a voyage from Rio Grande do Sul to Rio de Janeiro. All told, forty-two people died in the disaster, but thirteen passengers were saved by Simão's stamina and selflessness. In the weeks that followed, the Portuguese African sailor became a celebrity in Rio de Janeiro, where the Trade Association raised funds on his behalf. In early November, Simão had an audience with Pedro II, who offered him a reward of 400,000 réis, as well as a medal. Portuguese officials also came forth to celebrate the sailor's heroism.[4] In his turn, Paula Brito analyzed the matter in an article published in *Marmota fluminense* on November 8 that was suggestively titled "Black Simão: It is Not Color that Makes a Hero but His Deeds!"

> The unfortunate incident of the sinking of the steamship *Pernambucana* led to the emergence, in 1853, of a hero, a black man who, full of courage and love for humanity, hurled himself into the sea, not once but many times, and risking his life every time, thus saved many passengers on [the ship], and they only looked to him! This is all the more commendable because, being *black*, all those whom he saved were *whites*, including married ladies, maidens, and children, whom he respected and inspired, filled with self-confidence! Tired from the struggle, feeling weakness in his legs, the cold of the sea, he stretched himself on the beach once, and rubbing [his legs] with sand, was thus able to restore the circulation of the blood and achieve his aim, as far as his strength could go, and circumstances allowed!

SIMÃO

Heróe do Vapor Brasileiro Pernambucana

FIGURE 19. Portrait of Simão the mariner, given to the Marmota Fluminense's subscribers (1853). Image courtesy of the Instituto Histórico e Geográfico Brasileiro

Is this *black* man not worthy of a state pension? We are told that in the city a fundraiser is being organized for him; that act is praiseworthy, beautiful, and even a duty; but this alone is not enough; in such cases the government should take the initiative and encourage others to do the same if they should find themselves (God forbid) in the circumstances of Black Simon! So many people saved from the wreck by one man. . . . it is such an extraordinary story that it must be cherished by those with a loving heart, and love of humanity.

Honored be the newspapers that have been actively engaged in this [effort].

In the next issue, we will provide a portrait of this hero.[5]

The promise would be kept, and *Marmota fluminense*'s subscribers did receive a portrait of Simão in the following issue (see Figure 19). However, it is important to note that, in a time when, far from being omitted, references to the color of free Brazilian citizens of African descent were often made in the political press, Paula Brito turned the episode involving Simão into an opportunity to take a stand in this truly national debate.[6] Although the sailor was a Portuguese subject born in Cape Verde, for Paula Brito this may have been an opportunity to stress the value of free men like himself, who were the children and grandchildren of manumitted slaves. Therefore, when extolling Simão's feat—"a hero, a black man"—the publisher could have had occasional interlocutors in mind, possibly some linked to the Liberal Party, such as those who three years earlier had accused him of rejecting people of color.

In addition to the article and portrait published by the Empresa Tipográfica Dous de Dezembro, Paula Brito also wrote a poem, "Simão, Hero of the *Pernambucana*," in which he hailed the sailor as a "man of strength and valor." In one of the final verses, Paula Brito recalled that "Our monarch is the first / To give the sublime example, / Of not knowing how / To make men's color a crime." It should be recalled—as we will see further on—that at this point Pedro II was the main shareholder in the major publishing enterprise founded by Paula Brito who, in his turn, concluded the poem with this declaration: "Virtue has no color."[7]

In itself, the need to add this maxim attests to how much color prejudice was part of the daily experience of citizens like him. However, when purely racial barriers were imposed on the free movement of such men, it could give rise to controversy—especially when the men of color being barred were respectable merchants and slave owners. At least, this was the case when Paula Brito was blackballed by the Fluminense Club just a few weeks after the wreck of the *Pernambucana*.

In the second half of 1853, the businessman Augusto Carlos Gonçalves e Souza lavishly refurbished the former police station in Praça da Constituição, next door to Paula Brito's shop and press, transforming it into "the most flamboyant building to strut in the imperial capital."[8] Soon, the Fluminense Club would open there, a novelty that caused quite a stir in Rio de Janeiro. Then, in mid-October, the *Correio mercantil* published the "Regulations for the Fluminense Club." Thirty-three articles drafted by its creator and owner provided a detailed explanation of the institution's aims and operations. As for its aims, the first article stated:

> The establishment called the Fluminense Club is owned by the businessman Augusto Carlos Gonçalves e Souza, and aims to provide the polite and polished people of this city's society with a gathering place, where they can find a pleasant pastime in the licit entertainments allowed in such establishments in the main cities of Europe.[9]

A "gathering place" for the "polite and polished people of . . . society," the club would accept three types of members—founding, ordinary, and occasional.[10] It would offer a variety of "pastimes" during its opening hours, which were from 9 a.m. until midnight. On the club's premises, members and their families could read Brazilian and foreign newspapers and play billiards, chess, backgammon, and bagatelle—card games were only permitted on ball nights. The club would also provide several rooms for music, dining, dancing, and smoking, and a special salon for tea and refreshments. Then, of course, there were lavatories and a cloakroom.[11]

Breathless with excitement, an anonymous writer in *Diário do Rio de Janeiro* described its elegant premises as follows: "The large and numerous rooms of our club are adorned with all the luxury and good taste of the loveliest establishments of this kind that are offered to us in the major cities of Europe, where amenities are intertwined with the caprices of fashion and the voluptuousness of the arts." According to the same author, the club would mainly be appreciated by foreigners who spent long seasons in Rio—illustrious visitors who could best "judge our customs and our civilization."[12] Subscriptions for membership in the Fluminense Club were advertised in the newspapers, and believing themselves to belong to polite society, large numbers of people barraged the businessman with applications. However, he soon found himself in a serious predicament. After all, on what basis should he select "polite and polished people"? Who would be the best representatives of "our customs and civilization"? Before the opening ball, which would be attended by the Emperor and Empress, he did not think twice and crossed off the names he deemed unfit to join his select club from the list of subscribers.

Voices thundered from newspaper columns demanding explanations from businessman. The *Jornal do commercio* referred mockingly to the "blue-blood club."[13] In *Correio mercantil*, a reader signing himself Zebedeu observed that some people he knew had been "crossed off [the list] because they were deemed unworthy," despite being "highly qualified to belong to such an establishment." Therefore, the warning to the club owner was clear: "Mr. Augusto [Carlos Gonçalves e Souza], if you want to get any results from your efforts and expenditures, do not permit or commit injustices that will only be a detriment to you."[14] In the same newspaper, the "Country Pros-ecutor" stated in a letter addressed to his "Country Lawyer" that he had left the club, which "seemed to be considerably reduced in numbers" after a friend of his was "crossed off"—"does [the distinguished gentleman] know that not all country folk are known in the city, and for that, fie! *I cross it off doubly*." At one point, the missive from the Country Prosecutor inquired, "Why would Mr. P. B. be excluded?"[15]

The initials P. B. must have referred to Paula Brito. Writing in *Diário do Rio de Janeiro* without pseudonyms, José Silveira do Pilar, who had recommended some people for membership in the Fluminense Club, addressed that institu-tion's management, "demanding that they give the true reason for crossing off the name of Mr. Francisco de Paula Brito from the list of members he [Pilar] had proposed." If they did not explain themselves, José Silveira threatened to go to the chief of police so that "in his presence," he repeated, "they can formally declare the powerful reason they had to eliminate the name of Mr. Francisco de Paula Brito from the list of members," since he was "as worthy of belonging to that association as any of the other gentlemen."[16]

We know almost nothing about José Silveira do Pilar.[17] In any event, just three days after writing in the *Diário*, he once again demanded explanations from Fluminense Club in the *Jornal do commercio* regarding the rejection of Paula Brito's name. In this new article, after reaffirming that the publisher was a man of good social standing, because "his relations are not such that do him discredit," José Silveira pointed out the reasons for his exclusion: "I am told that the noble administration gave as the *cause* for the line that crossed Mr. P. Brito's name off the list of proposed members of said club, that this gentleman is a man of color!!"[18]

José Silveira argued that it was wrong to believe that the segregation of men of color was a sign of civilization. European courts such as that of the French emperor, which was surrounded by "*Moors* and even *Africans*," proved the contrary. Even Brazil was rich in examples of this kind. "Do you not see some seats of our *parliament* occupied by men of the *color* of he whom you now expel from your midst?" wrote José Silveira. Even Pedro II "is not *ashamed* to have *Moorish* men in his Court and by *his side*, and some of them are great enlighteners and adornments of the nation?"[19] Although he was far from being a Moor, but instead the son and grandson of Creole freedmen, Paula Brito himself could also be seen in the emperor's presence on certain occasions, such as the time when he wrote and printed his "Sonnet to the Press, Dedicated to His Imperial Majesty Pedro II" in Quinta da Boa Vista Palace.[20] As we know, Paula Brito also maintained good relations with major politicians, particularly the leaders of the Conservative party. Furthermore, outside the political sphere, prestigious institutions such as the Conservatório Dramático Brasileiro (Brazilian Theater Conservatory), the theater's official censorship body in Rio de Janeiro, also recognized the publisher's merits.[21]

Therefore, it is difficult to gauge the impact of the Fluminense Club's rejection of Paula Brito. Although the publisher was always "mixed up with the whites" as a known and recognized figure in the political and literary worlds of Rio de Janeiro, sometimes men like Mr. Augusto Carlos Gonçalves e Souza would remind Paula Brito, his wife, Rufina, and their daughters, now young women aged eighteen and fifteen, of the burden of the family's slave ancestry. However, going beyond friendship with the publisher, the indignation expressed by José Silveira do Pilar and the "Country Prosecutor," which was certainly read and possibly shared by readers of Rio de Janeiro's daily newspapers, was due to the fact that, at the time, Paula Brito was the distinguished owner of Brazil's largest publishing venture. By late 1853, he was not just an ordinary man of color. In fact, this may have been the reason for a good part of the uproar.

It also reflects the importance of the Empresa Dous de Dezembro, a corporation founded by Paula Brito in the late 1850s. Originally a printing firm and later a literary publishing house, it must have received an influx of the capital previously employed in the transatlantic slave trade. In the first half of the nineteenth century, Brazil had received about 80 percent of the captives that embarked from Africa. Percentages aside, the commerce in human beings was a highly lucrative business, generating profits of roughly

500 percent. The definitive ban on the slave trade imposed by Law no. 581 of September 4, 1850, also known as the Eusébio de Queirós Law, brought an influx of capital valued at 16,000,000,000 réis into the country.[22]

Both the end of the slave trade and all the money it generated had been expected for some time. In 1846, for example, the Interior Ministry's response to a request for a grant by the Frenchman André Gaillard for his paper mill in Andaraí stated that "Brazil needs to import factories not only to use the capital that will be unemployed and lost with the cessation of the [slave] trade, but also to bring from Europe fruitful and intelligent colonization."[23] Therefore, some of the money from transatlantic slave traders was expected to finance the country's incipient industrial development, as indeed occurred with the proliferation of new businesses established in Rio de Janeiro as of 1851.[24] From that year until 1865, a total of 76 corporations and 515 limited partnerships were registered in that city's Business Tribunal.[25]

Therefore, no one was surprised when the winds that filled the sails of the slave ships before the advent of steamships began blowing favorably for the merchants and entrepreneurs of Rio de Janeiro in the run-up to the 1850s. Paula Brito saw the opportunity to carry out his long-held dream of establishing "a large-scale press" according to the proposal submitted to the Provincial Assembly of Rio de Janeiro in 1848. Clearly, that project did not go ahead as planned. There are many possible reasons for that, from the failure of the Provincial Assembly to grant him the fifty million in bonds, or even that another printer tendered the winning bid. Speculation aside, we do know that two years later Paula Brito returned to and expanded the project, transforming it into the prospectus for his printing business Empresa Tipográfica Dous de Dezembro.

During the over six-year period between its inception and its liquidation, Dous de Dezembro had two very different formats. The first was explained in the prospectus, a document drafted by Paula Brito in 1850 and published the following year.[26] In addition to the company's by-laws, the plan also functioned as a subscription agreement. In the copy I have located, the agreement was reached between the publisher and Father Joaquim Ferreira da Cruz Belmonte, a Portuguese grammar and Latin teacher at the Seminário Episcopal de São José (St. Joseph's Episcopal Seminary), on April 1, 1852.[27] Certainly because of its contractual nature, the plan took pains to explain the venture's advantages to its readers and potential shareholders. The line stating that the company had as "protectors and first shareholders Their Imperial Majesties," that is, it was constituted under the auspices of

EMPREZA TYPOGRAPHICA

DOUS DE DEZEMBRO

DE QUE SÃO

PROTECTORES E PRIMEIROS ACCIONISTAS

SUAS MAGESTADES IMPERIAES

E ORGANISADA POR

FRANCISCO DE PAULA BRITO

EM 2 DE DEZEMBRO DE 1850.

400$000 Rs. PERTENCE ESTA ACÇÃO Rs. 400$000

Ao Ill.mo Snr. P.e Joaquim Ferreira de Cruz Belmonte

PLANO

§ 1.º Esta Empreza tem por fim e objecto principal desenvolver a arte typographica em todo o Imperio do Brasil, e auxiliar o progresso das Sciencias e das Letras, por meio da divulgação de obras, nitidamente impressas, modeladas ao gosto moderno, e vendidas por preços commodos.

§ 2.º Para preenchimento d'estes fins, capitalisar-se-ha uma SOMMA de SESSENTA CONTOS de RÉIS, dividida em 150 Acções de quatrocentos mil réis cada uma, e este capital vencerá o juro de seis por cento ao anno, sendo metade pago em Junho, e outra metade em Dezembro de cada anno.

§ 3.º Os Accionistas, alem do juro estipulado, receberão gratis um exemplar de quaesquer jornaes que pela Empreza sejão impressos a sua custa.

§ 4.º O Emprezario não fica obrigado á amortisação do capital, senão depois de findos seis annos, que tantos durará a Empreza.

§ 5.º Ficam hypothecados ao pagamento do capital e juros, os Estabelecimentos que o Emprezario actualmente possue na praça da Constituição ns. 64, 66 e 78, cujo inventario, com as competentes avaliações, será patente aos Snrs. Accionistas, que desejarem vêl-o, e será devidamente registado. Todos os mais bens que o Emprezario possa vir a possuir, por qualquer forma que seja, ficam igualmente hypothecados.

§ 6.º São transferiveis as Acções por meio de endosso regular, o qual será averbado no livro dos talões para a percepção do juro pelo portador.

Rio de Janeiro 1.º de Abril de 1852.

O EMPREZARIO,

Fran.co de Paula Brito

TYP. DA EMPREZA — DOUS DE DEZEMBRO

Praça da Constituição n. 64

1851.

FIGURE 20. Dous de Dezembro press plan

Pedro II and Empress Teresa Cristina, was an essential part of those guarantees. Moreover, the date chosen for its founding—December 2, 1850—and the fact that the company was named after that date were highly symbolic. Being Pedro II's birthday, that date was one of the Empire's most important national holidays.[28] I do not know if Paula Brito was the first, but he certainly was not the only printer to honor the emperor with a reference to his natal day. In São Paulo, Antônio Louzada Antunes founded the Dous de Dezembro Press, which was also active in the 1850s and associated with the development of book publishing in that city.[29] However, in Paula Brito's case, there was a slight conflict of interest. As we know, the publisher was born on December 2, 1809,[30] sixteen years before His Imperial Majesty.

When subscribing for shares in the company, the Emperor must have been impressed with its scope—so much so that he awarded Paula Brito the title of Printer of the Imperial House, which the publisher not only began blazoning on the books and newspapers he printed but also displayed on the front of his business premises. By December 1851, Paula Brito had completed the refurbishing project that transformed his former home on Praça da Constituição into the company's headquarters. All that was lacking was the City Council's authorization to make changes to the front of the building, where he had added doors and windows opening onto the street. It also displayed the Emperor's coat of arms "as a printer of the Imperial House."[31] The Emperor and Empress's protection of Dous de Dezembro resulted from long and patient efforts that Paula Brito had been making since the mid-1830s. However, after Pedro II was declared an adult, in addition to Conservative politicians, Paula Brito had established closer ties with the monarch and his consort. In this regard, their dealings must have been done in practice, going beyond the sphere of grace and favor and flattering poems. When he died, Paula Brito owed money to the emperors of Brazil—300,000 réis to Pedro II and 120,000 réis to Teresa Cristina. They were relatively small amounts, compared to the other debts listed in the inventory of his estate after his death, but they were significant from the perspective of the networks of support that the publisher had forged during his lifetime.[32]

The printing company's prospectus was divided into six articles. The first covers the benefits the firm would contribute to the "art of printing throughout the Empire of Brazil." To do so, it would further the "advancement of science and literature" while undertaking a commitment to the quality and affordability of the printed matter. The second and third articles dealt with the price at which shares were offered, as well as the advantages for shareholders:

Art. 2. To fulfil these objectives, the SUM OF SIXTY MILLION RÉIS will be capitalized, divided into 150 shares worth four hundred thousand réis each, and this capital will bear interest at six per cent per year, half of which will be paid in June and the other half in December of each year.

Art. 3. The shareholders, in addition to the stipulated interest, will receive a free copy of any newspapers that the Company prints, at its own expense.[33]

Paula Brito needed 60,000,000 réis in start-up capital for his venture. To have an idea of how much that sum represented within the context of the printing business in Rio de Janeiro, the government budget for 1850 to 1851 allocated 33,000,000 réis to the National Press, which was increased to 40,000,000 for the following two-year period.[34] In 1850, the National Press had "six French iron printing presses, three similar English [presses], and a mechanical press," and employed "eighteen compositors, fifteen apprentices, a master printer, a type keeper, eight printers, twelve apprentices, and a janitor who serves as a doorman."[35] Considering that Paula Brito intended to establish a press that, as he himself would say "has no betters in this city," and imported equipment from France for that purpose,[36] the 60,000,000 réis needed to set up the company, divided in 150 shares worth 400,000 réis, was not at all exceptional compared to the amounts allocated to the operations of the National Press. However, in addition to capital, the plan also set share yields at 6 percent per annum. In cash, that amount was equivalent to 24,000 réis paid in two installments. On its own, it was a modest sum, but when multiplied by one hundred shareholders, no less than 2,400,000 réis of the company's annual revenue would be set aside to amortize the interest.

However, to promote the shares, the publisher had to offer the advantages for shareholders that were covered in article three of the prospectus. Thus, in addition to annual interest, they would each receive a copy of the publications printed by the press, a measure that was somewhat paradoxical because, on one hand, it attracted new shareholders, but on the other, it eliminated 150 potential purchasers of those publications. The final three articles of the prospectus deal with the guarantees offered to shareholders:

Art. 4. The businessman [Paula Brito] is not obliged to amortize the capital for the first six years of the Company's existence.

Art. 5. The establishments that the businessman currently owns in Praça da Constituição, nos. 64, 66, and 78, whose inventory, with the appropriate appraisals, will be apparent to the Shareholders who wish to see it, being duly registered, will be used as collateral for the payment of capital and interest. All the more assets that the Entrepreneur may possess in whatever form are equally mortgaged.

Art. 6. Shares are transferable through regular endorsement, which will be recorded in the book of receipts for the perception of interest by the accountant.[37]

Therefore, Paula Brito was exempt from amortizing the capital raised from the shareholders within the period of six years initially provided for corporation's existence. In article five, most importantly, the publisher pledged all his assets as collateral, including any assets that might be purchased in the future. Finally, the prospectus detailed the manner in which shares and interest would be recorded. Meanwhile, Paula Brito turned to the pages of *A marmota na corte* in his effort to distribute shares in the company, as illustrated by an ad in *Guanabara* magazine published in June 1851:

Tuesday July 1, issue no. 7 of this scientific and literary journal is published with two illustrations and interesting articles by messrs. Macedo, Porto-Alegre, Capanema, Freire Alemão, Burlamaque, Magalhães, and others.

Subscriptions are available for 5 réis for six months or 10 réis per year. Subscribers must renew their subscriptions by the thirtieth of this month.

People who acquire shares in the printing firm—Dous de Dezembro—will immediately receive free of charge (in addition to future publications) *Guanabara, Anais de medicina,* A *marmota na corte,* and interest on the shares, which is the same as that for government bonds. Interested parties should inquire at the shop of Paula Brito, Praça da Constituição, no. 64.[38]

Government bonds might be a good investment,[39] but only Dous de Dezembro's shareholders would also receive copies of *Guanabara* magazine, *A marmota na corte,* and the medical journal *Anais de medicina.* Even so, not everyone was happy with the price at which shares were offered. In July 1851, an article in the Niterói-based newspaper *O commercio* suggested that the capital raised from the initial public offering had already been spent, because Paula Brito had just imported "machines supplementary to his workshop" from France. The writer also explained, indicating the possible expansion of the market, that the publisher intended to "propagate in the provinces literary publications produced in Rio, and vice versa." From this perspective, Paula Brito was compared with the famous actor João Caetano due to their contributions to Brazilian literature in their respective fields. Being compared to the leading actor and theater impresario in Brazil in the mid-nineteenth century was very flattering indeed. Thus, the curious metaphor the author employed—the "chick turning in the egg . . . is about to hatch!"—summed up the importance of Paula Brito's venture for the "prosperity and progress" of literature in the country. Despite his poultry praise, the author concluded his article on a critical note: "We regret that the price of the shares was not more affordable; Mr. Paula Brito should think of men of letters and not of the capitalists, and the former, not the latter, should be his sole shareholders."[40] After all, how could a scholar come up with the 400,000 réis needed to become a shareholder of Dous de Dezembro? The question was rhetorical, as the writer was accusing Paula Brito of neglecting men of learning in favor of capitalists.

Without hesitation, Paula Brito leapt into the fray and issued a precise rebuttal to the writer from Niterói in an article published in *A marmota da corte*. After giving brief thanks, the publisher went straight to the point: "If you permit me . . . I will give the reason for not dividing the shares in my Printing Firm into amounts [valued at] less than 400 [thousand réis], like shares in Niterói, Botafogo, Buses, Freight Trains, Monte de Socorro [*sic*], and others in this city."

As the publisher explained:

First of all, I need ready capital that will serve to finance the fulfilment of commitments I was obliged to undertake to uplift my business (which has no superior in this city) to its present state, as can be attested by messers. E. Laemmert, Nicolau Lobo Vianna, and Fortunato Raymundo de Oliveira, who assessed it (to serve as the basis for calculating the share [values]; and as I saw that, to make use of their funds, our capitalists do not need the cash advantages I am offering them, because we have bonds, treasury bills, banks, etc., to employ them with infallible guarantees (if there are such things in life); so I offer them my newspapers, or those in which I am a partner. Well now, if all the shares were issued, the newspapers I would give to my 150 shareholders at 400 [thousand réis] could not be given for 300 [thousand réis] Now, the newspapers that I would give to my 150 shareholders at 400 [thousand réis], if all shares were issued, I could not offer them for 300 [thousand réis], if they were [issued at] 200 [thousand réis], or 600 [thousand réis], if they were [issued at] 100 [thousand réis]. I could, of course, have conceived my plan in another way; I thought about it; in no case, however, would I have a large number of shareholders, and the reason for that I will give in the future. Moreover, 400 [thousand réis] is a regular sum; interest of 6 per cent, and newspaper subscriptions, rise almost 1 percent per month, a profit that can attract strangers, who have no relations with me, who do love or hate me, to be my shareholders; but my friends, those who have affection for me, and on whom I can rely, merchants and capitalists with whom I have had relations and transactions, will accept the shares at 400 [réis], when I resort to them; and just as they take them at that value, they would take a larger quantity, because they know me, esteem me, praise my efforts, encourage me, and protect me; they are confident in me, not on my goods and chattels; they are confident in what I can do because they can see what I have already done.[41]

When justifying the price of the shares and consequently the need to offer copies of the printed matter to shareholders, Paula Brito was following an essentially simple line of reasoning. Basically, it might have been something that truly concerned him a great deal when he conceived the Dous de Dezembro printing company. The publisher needed capital to invest in his workshop, but how could he attract the attention of investors, of capitalists, especially those who were not among his circle of friends, given the ample availability of profitable investments in Rio de Janeiro at that time—"bonds, treasury bills, banks, etc.?" The data on corporations registered with the Business Tribunal of Rio de Janeiro in 1851 and 1852 give a clear idea of the competition that shares in Paula Brito's company faced in the capital's stock market. According to Table 8, the publisher had good reasons for offering additional incentives for Rio de Janeiro's investors to purchase those shares, which is what he did by offering his publications to potential shareholders.

In his response to the article in the *Commercio*, Paula Brito mentioned some of the companies listed in this table. They included Monte do Socorro, which was registered with the Business Tribunal in January 1851 and described as being in the savings and loan business. It had capital of 400,000,000 réis divided into four thousand shares valued at 100,000 réis apiece, much less than Dous de Dezembro's share price. Similarly, shares in Paula Brito's company cost more than those in the Companhia Brasileira de Paquetes a Vapor, traded at 350,000 réis apiece, and Companhia de Navegação do Rio Inhomirim, traded at 300,000 réis. It should be stressed that this company, which provided steamship services between the ports of Estrela and Rio de Janeiro, had the same amount of capital as Dous de Dezembro. Indeed, the strategy of using free publications to lure poten-

TABLE 8 Corporations registered with the Rio de Janeiro Business Tribunal in 1851 and 1852

Name	Date Registered	Purpose	Capital (réis)	Shares into which capital is divided	Duration
Banco Comercial do Rio de Janeiro	08 Jan. 1851	Savings and capital allowances	5,000,000,000	10,000 at 500,000	20 years
Monte do Socorro	10 Jan. 1851	Savings and loans	400,000,000	4,000 at 100,000	Indefinite
Companhia Brasileira de Paquetes a Vapor	22 Jan. 1851	Coastal shipping from Rio de Janeiro to Pará	720,000,000	2,000 at 350,000	Indefinite
Companhia Seguros Marítimos—Regeneração	08 Feb. 1851	Insurance for ships of all flags	360,000,000	300 at 1,000,000	20 years
Companhia de Navegação do Rio Inhomerim	20 Mar. 1851	Steamship transportation between the port of Estrela and Rio	60,000,000	200 at 300,000	Indefinite
Companhia de Seguros Contra o Fogo—Argos Fluminense	20 Mar. 1851	Insurance for [houses] residences, goods, etc.	1,000,000,000	1,000 at 1,000,000	Indefinite
Companhia Fluminense de Ônibus	20 Mar. 1851	Bus transportation for passengers from the city to the outskirts	Indefinite	–	10 years
Companhia de Seguros Marítimos—Nova Permanente	15 May 1851	Ship and freight insurance	400,000,000	400 at 1,000,000	10 years
Companhia de Seguros Marítimos—[illegible]	19 Aug. 1851	Ship and freight insurance	400,000,000	400 at 1,000,000	30 years
Companhia de Seguros Contra o Fogo—Phoenix Fluminense	22 Oct. 1851	Insurance for homes and goods	1,000,000,000	1.000 at 1,000,000	Indefinite
Companhia Caixa Econômica do Rio de Janeiro	25 Oct. 1851	Savings bank	Indefinite	–	Indefinite
Companhia de Navegação por Vapor—Macaé e Campos	07 Jan. 1852*	Shipping between Rio, Macaé, and Campos	Indefinite	–	20 years

Source: "Mapa das companhias e sociedades anônimas registradas no Tribunal do Comércio da Corte do Império, desde a execução do *Código comercial* até dezembro do corrente ano," in José Thomaz Nabuco de Araújo, *Relatório do Ministério da Justiça*, 1866. Companhia de Seguro Mútuo Contra o Fogo, whose purpose was insuring buildings, real estate, and goods, was registered in 1852 and 1853.

*No more companies were registered by the Business Tribunal on Feb. 1, 1854.

tial shareholders may have been the publisher's only option. As Paula Brito observed, this would not have been possible if the press's shares were distributed for, say, 300,000 réis. All he could do was hope that the moneyed class enjoyed reading his publications. However, it did not work out very well, and the publisher eventually gave up on this practice, allowing his shareholders to choose to receive an additional 10 percent in cash on the value of their annual premiums instead of the periodicals.[42]

Nevertheless, during the early days of Dous de Dezembro's existence, Paula Brito's tactic seems to have achieved a modicum of success. One year after the company was founded, a financial statement published in *A marmota na corte* showed that all but nineteen of the seventy-five shares had been issued. It also listed the names of the forty-four shareholders, which included influential figures in the art and political worlds of Imperial Brazil, such as Minister Ângelo Muniz da Silva Ferraz, Viscount of Abrantes, the physician and novelist Joaquim Manuel de Macedo, and the artist, author, and diplomat Manuel de Araújo Porto-Alegre, Baron of Santo Ângelo.[43]

However, a more complete list of the printing company's shareholders appeared in *Guanabara* magazine in 1856. Entitled "Shareholders of the Empresa Dous de Dezembro who, as such, received *Guanabara*," it is made up of 118 names, including 104 men, 11 women, and three companies. A comparison of the list of shareholders who received *Guanabara* magazine with that published in the *Almanak Laemmert* provides a rough idea of the social backgrounds of some of the Paula Brito's company's shareholders.[44]

According to Figure 21, there is a significant number of merchants and capitalists among the shareholders listed in *Guanabara*. The merchants included Antônio Pereira Ribeiro Guimarães, a tobacco and cigar wholesaler; João José Fernandes d'Azevedo, who sold timber for the civil construction and shipbuilding industries; and Commander Patrício Ricardo Freire, who bought and sold gold, silver, and jewels; as well as merchants who may have been of lesser means, such as Manuel José Ferreira, who owned a grocery store. Other merchants could easily be classified as capitalists, like Francisco José de Mello e Souza, a cattle merchant and director of the Banco Comercial e Agrícola (Commercial and Agricultural Bank) of Rio de Janeiro. The capitalists included the Baron of Mauá, as well as men from his circle such as Antônio Ribeiro Queiroga, listed in the *Almanaque* as the "partner responsible and manager of the Banco Mauá, MacGregor e Companhia." The Banco do Brasil was represented by two of its directors, João Henrique Ulrich and Militão Correia de Sá. The abovementioned Minister

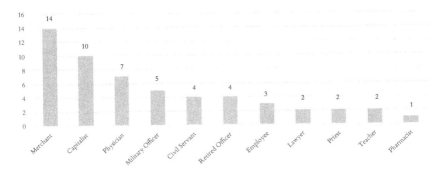

FIGURE 21. Backgrounds of Empresa Dous de Dezembro's fifty-four shareholders. Source: "Acionistas da Empresa Dous de Dezembro que, como tais, receberam o Guanabara," Guanabara, t. III, 1856. "Guia do Rio de Janeiro ou indicador alfabético da morada dos seus principais habitantes; altos funcionários, empregados, negociantes, capitalistas, proprietários, fabricantes, artistas, industriais, etc., mencionados em seus lugares competentes no *Almanak Laemmert* de 1858."

Silva Ferraz could also be classified as a capitalist, chiefly due to his role as a director of the Companhia Seguradora Contra a Mortalidade dos Escravos (Slave Mortality Insurance Company) and secretary of the board of the Companhia de Seguros Marítimos e Terrestres (Maritime and Land Insurance Company). In addition to the bankers and insurance magnates, the shareholders also included the owners of educational establishments such as the business partners Dr. Mateus da Silva Chaves and Dr. Rufino Soares de Almeida, the owners of the Colégio Marinho secondary school.

Another significant group among the shareholders of Paula Brito's company was made up of physicians. Surgeons like Frederico João Ormerod, Francisco José de Sá Júnior, and Marcos José Pereira do Bonfim, as well as Dr. Ludgero da Rocha Ferreira Lapa, the former editor-in-chief of the *Arquivo médico brasileiro*, whom we have met before. The doctors were followed by officers, active and retired. Chief among the active officers was certainly Warship Captain and Naval Battalion Commander Manuel Francisco da Costa Pereira. The retired officers included Lieutenant Libório José de Almeida, who was still active in 1858 as captain of the Niterói police.

Four civil servants were found among the shareholders: police registrar Antônio Xavier de Mello; finance ministry clerk Augusto Henrique Gonzaga; secretary Feliciano Zeofrido Rangel Maia; and José Joaquim dos Santos, who worked as a customs official. Regarding the three shareholders classified as employees, they all worked at banks in Rio de Janeiro. Antônio José Marques de Sá was a "Treasury Official at the Banco do Brasil"; Manuel José da Costa Ludovico worked as first clerk at the Banco Rural e Hipotecário (Rural and Mortgage Bank); and Ricardo Soares da Costa Guimarães was the treasurer at the Caixa Econômica savings bank in Rio de Janeiro. Along with Antônio Alves Ferreira, the only pharmacist among the shareholders, there were also two priests, two lawyers, and two teachers. Thus, in addition to Father Joaquim Ferreira da Cruz Belmonte, whom we have met before, the other shareholding clergyman was Canon Joaquim de Oliveira Durão, curate of the Imperial Chapel, synodal examiner of the Episcopal Curia and professor of Dogmatic Theology at the São José Seminary. The attorneys were João Caldas Vianna and senator and judge João Antônio de Miranda. Finally, the teachers were Gabriel de Medeiros Gomes, who taught Latin and "national grammar" at Colégio Pedro II, and Commander João Maria Pereira de Lacerda, who taught geometry at the Naval School.

The occupations of the shareholders listed bolster the argument of the anonymous writer in the *Commercio* newspaper, according to whom Paula Brito had turned his back on the literati in favor of capitalists and businessmen. The small number of teachers who owned shares in the company confirms the journalist's assertion. Although the prospectus for the Empresa Dous de Dezembro stated that one of its aims was to promote "the advancement of science and literature," Paula Brito was also a capitalist and a merchant, and as such, he sought to prioritize the most efficient sources of capital required to set up and run his business.

That tactic worked, for a time. However, Paula Brito soon began trading shares at 100,000 réis, most likely with a view to making them accessible to a larger swath of the public, and not just merchants and capitalists. Meanwhile, the company kept growing.

CHAPTER 12

From Printer to Literary Publisher

H AVING COMPLETED THE refurbishing that transformed his home into a printing establishment, Paula Brito focused on building a "large store" with two fronts, one facing Praça da Constituição and the other fronting onto Rua da Lampadosa, where Dous de Dezembro's lithography and engraving workshops would be installed.[1] Not that these projects went without a hitch—on the contrary. In mid-1852, Manuel Francisco da Silveira Freitas, "the owner of a home situated on Rua da Lampadosa, no. 35," obtained a court order to stop construction from the Municipal Judge of the First Court of Rio de Janeiro. Paula Brito's neighbor claimed that, "to the detriment of his property and in violation of his right of ownership," the building would "pour water" into his back yard. As a result, a bailiff ordered the bricklayer José Tavares de Souza, the carpenter Manuel Joaquim da Costa Júnior, and all the other craftsmen working on Paula Brito's construction project to put down their tools. However, the publisher was in a hurry to get the building done. He quickly reached an understanding with Silveira Freitas, after which he sent a petition to the judge stating that he wanted to "continue with his project without causing problems" and "undertook to demolish anything that might cause any harm to his neighbor's property, having agreed this with [that neighbor]."[2] The problem was solved and work continued. Soon, the building would house the machinery Paula Brito had imported from Europe.

Two months later, the publisher announced on the first page of *Marmota fluminense* that he was distributing "Júlia," a waltz for the flute, the first lithographic work produced by the workshops of the Empresa Tipográfica Dous de Dezembro. "In addition to the printing press, set up on a large scale, we now have—*Lithography, Engraving, and a Bookbinding Workshop*," the businessman announced with great satisfaction. The advertisement also stated that part of the company's equipment was on its way, while another part was being cleared through customs. Furthermore, the steamship *Tay* was taking new orders from the publisher to Europe.[3] In late 1852, Paula Brito promised his shareholders that in four to six months, Dous de Dezembro's workshops would be completely installed.[4]

It is hard to determine how many printing presses Dous de Dezembro owned in the course of its existence. In 1856, the newspaper *Courrier du Brésil* reported that the company "owned different rooms, where there is a printing workshop with thirteen presses, from manual to more complex [ones]."[5] However, lawsuits brought against the publisher in the Business Tribunal suggest that, between 1854 and 1856, Dous de Dezembro's workshops were equipped with at least three lithographic presses and two Stanhope presses. We do not have detailed information about the lithographic presses, but the printing press invented by Lord Stanhope in the late eighteenth century, which bore his name, may have been manual but was made entirely of iron. This innovation had a considerable impact on productivity.[6] In any event, a leaflet for Dous de Dezembro possibly printed between 1853 and 1855 demonstrates the magnitude of the growth that Paula Brito's business achieved during that period. In it, we can see that in addition to numbers 64 and 68 on Praça da Constituição, the company had also come to occupy 31 and 33 Rua da Lampadosa, while the shop, with a vast range of articles on sale, was located at 78 Praça da Constituição, on the corner with Rua de São Jorge. The leaflet shows the printer of the Imperial House alongside his most illustrious clients, such as the Imperial Academy of Medicine, the Auxiliary Society for Brazilian Industry, the Colégio Marinho secondary school, the Baron of Mauá's companies, and "other Scientific, Literary and Industrial Associations." The company's workshops are described as follows:

Large-Scale Printing Press
>   with the proportions [required] to print quickly, neatly, tastefully and
>   at affordable prices, all works, no matter how difficult they may be.

Lithography
>   for business cards, trade labels, labels for apothecaries, wine and liquor,
>   circulars, maps, and
>   many more
>   engraved, written, or autographed, always clear and to modern tastes.

Engraving Workshop
>   for records of the various official documents and anything else that is
>   engraved.

Large Bookbinding Workshop
>   which prepares, both in paperback and hardcover, all works, even the
>   most delicate, songs, etc., and in which one will always find
>   complete assortment
>   of
>   blank books for
>   retailers
>   government offices
>   and
>   private writing
>   in folio, quarto, octavo, the best one could desire, both fully bound, partly
>   bound, in soft cover, etc.[7]

If it were not for the difficulties the publisher was beginning to face at that time, one could even believe that the company was doing extremely well. Of course, advertising brochures can be biased and should be interpreted carefully. However, the leaflet indicates that the construction of the warehouse, begun in 1852, as well as the importation of new equipment, had definitely been completed.

Soon, Paula Brito began issuing shares at a lower price. As we saw in the previous chapter, the company's shares were originally valued at 400,000 réis, with an annual return of 6 percent paid in two installments. In October 1853, however, an advertisement published in the Supplement to *Marmota fluminense* referred for the first time to shares valued at 100,000 réis. The return on those shares was still 6 percent. The difference was that, instead of receiving all of Paula Brito's publications, shareholders opting for these shares would only receive a free subscription to *Marmota fluminense*.[8] However, in addition to increasing the number of shareholders, the distribution of shares at a lower price was probably due to the transformation of Dous de Dezembro from a printing firm into a literary publishing house. Implemented over the course of 1854 and officially begun the following year, this transformation went beyond changing the company's name. The publisher was fully confident and ready to take the most ambitious step in his career. Accordingly, Paula Brito began the process of seeking approval of the articles of association of a new company through a petition sent to the Interior Ministry of the Empire in April 1855:

> Sir.
>
> For the consideration of Your Imperial Majesty, Francisco de Paula Brito hereby submits the articles of association of the "Empresa Literária Dous de Dezembro," and relying on the favor of the powers of the State, due to the services that he has rendered to the nation through his art, and hopes to render on a larger scale, if [this petition] is well received and in any event sponsored by Your Imperial Majesty:
>
> I humbly request that Your Imperial Majesty approve or deny [this petition] as your imperial will shall see fit.
>
> > Expecting to Receive Mercy
> > Rio de Janeiro, April 17, 1855
> > *Francisco de Paula Brito*[9]

Although it was sent to the Imperial Minister and Secretary of State for Business, who was then Luís Pedreira do Couto Ferraz, it was standard practice to address the petition directly to Pedro II. In another document, the publisher also asked the emperor to become a patron of the venture. It should be noted that, to convince "the powers of the State," Paula Brito based his argument on "the services [he had] rendered to the nation through his art," as well as those which he hoped to "render on a larger scale." Indeed, the articles of association of the Empresa Literária Dous de Dezembro literary publishing house show that it was set up on a much larger scale than that which was proposed for the printing firm. Paula Brito's request got through the Empire's red tape without any serious setbacks in late April 1855. On

TABLE 9 Corporations registered with the Business Tribunal of Rio de Janeiro in 1855

Name	Date Registered	Purpose	Capital (réis)	Shares into which capital is divided	Duration
Companhia de Vapores Santista	11 Jan. 1855	Transporting passengers and cargo between the city of Rio de Janeiro and Santos	130,000,000	200 at 250,000	10 years
Empresa Provincial de Transportes	03 Feb. 1855	Transporting goods from Macacos to Pavuna	500,000,000	2,500 at 200,000	30 years
Associação Colonial do Rio Novo	05 Mar. 1855	Importing families and farming land in Rio Novo	300,000,000	3,000 at 100,000	Indefinite
Imperial Companhia Seropédica Fluminense	23 May 1855	Breeding silkworms and growing mulberry trees	400,000,000	1,600 at 250,000	20 years
Companhia Niterói e Inhomerim	25 May 1855	Steamship transportation in Rio de Janeiro's bay	2,400,000,000	12,000 at 200,000	Indefinite
Companhia Estrada de Mangaratiba	04 July 1855	Transporting passengers and cargo	100,000,000	2,000 at 50,000	10 years
Sociedade Fluminense [Illegible]	19 July 1855	Livestock breeding	250,000,000	500 at 500,000	20 years
Companhia União Campista and [illegible]	06 Aug. 1855	Shipping between Rio de Janeiro and Campos	400,000,000	50,000 at 200,000	Same
Companhia Farol Agrícola e Industrial	16 Nov. 1855	Founding an agricultural school in Rio de Janeiro City	10,000,000,000	50,000 at 200,000	25 years

Source: "Mapa das companhias e sociedades anônimas registradas no Tribunal do Comércio da Corte do Império, desde a execução do *Código comercial* até dezembro do corrente ano," José Thomaz Nabuco de Araújo, *Relatório do Ministério da Justiça*, 1866.

the twenty-fourth of that month, the application reached the Crown, Sovereignty, and National Treasury Councilor, who in early May expressed a slight reservation about the duration of the company. That minor matter was soon dealt with, and, in a matter of weeks, the government issued Decree no. 1.610 of May 23, 1855, authorizing the incorporation and approving the articles of association of the Empresa Literária Dous de Dezembro.[10]

The articles of association were divided into fifteen provisions. After briefly describing the company, the first article set out the amount of the company's equity capital, as well as the number and nominal value of its shares:

> The company—Dous de Dezembro—made up of large-scale press [including] printing, lithography, stamping, and bookbinding, hereby becomes an association with the above name, which will have equity capital of 500,000,000 réis in 2,500 shares of 200,000 réis apiece.

If the share prices seem reasonable, the new company's capital is impressive. Compared with the minor sum of 60,000,000 réis required to set up the press, in 1850, Paula Brito's literary publishing house needed a capital of no less than 500,000,000 réis, divided into 2,500 shares of 20,000 réis each. The fifteenth and final article of the articles of association stipulated that the literary publisher would have a duration "at least twenty years," until 1875. As we will see, Paula Brito did not live to see that year, much less his company. However, as Table 9 demonstrates, twenty years was the average duration for other corporations registered with the Business Tribunal in 1855. Table 9 also shows that the literary publisher's capital of 500,000,000 réis was indeed massive. Even so, it was nothing compared to the 10,000,000,000 réis of the Companhia Farol Agrícola e Industrial, an agricultural and industrial firm.

The new Dous de Dezembro company had more equity capital than six of the new companies registered. As for the literary publisher's shares, in addition to the situation of the former shareholders of the Dous de Dezembro printing firm, whether they owned shares with a nominal value of 400,000 or 100,000 réis, the articles of association stipulated that the shareholders who owned the 400,000-réis shares had the advantage, as they automatically owned two shares of 200,000 réis. The holders of 100,000-réis shares could either pay the difference or redeem their shares and no longer own stock in the company (articles 11 and 12). By giving up his business establishments and property to the company, Paula Brito became the owner of five hundred shares (article 12), which represented, in imperial currency, the considerable sum of 100,000,000 réis. In this regard, the articles of association also stated that Paula Brito would continue to run the company as "the administrator of the association, if it deems that to be appropriate." To this end, he would receive an income or a share in the company's annual income (article 8). There were even guidelines regarding the possibility that Paula Brito might travel to Europe, "for the benefit of the association" (article 10). However, in addition to having a share in the profits and the possibility of foreign travel, Paula Brito could also be rewarded for the expansion and diversification of the business:

> Art. 9. For every new speculation, or new branch of the company, that the administrator has in view, such as type casting, making business cards, playing cards, printing domestic and foreign books, their sale, orders from Europe, as well as the legislation of this country, by order of the Government, and some others, the board may award him a bonus or give him a percentage, which will only occur when the advantages of any of these ventures have been determined.

It was up to the company's directors to decide how much Paula Brito would receive "for each new speculation, or new branch" into which the literary publisher ventured. In its turn, the board was responsible for "managing all businesses, cash, and the respective bookkeeping" (article 7). The appointment of the company's directors and their roles, including in the event of Paula Brito's death, were covered by articles 13 and 14:

> Art. 13. The board will sit for two years and can continue to serve at the end of that period if reelected; the order of its members will be regulated by votes, as usual. The hiring and firing of the treasurer and employees will be done freely by [the board]; that of heads of workshops and workers [will be done] by the administrator, by his orders, or as agreed.
>
> Art. 14. In the event of the death of the administrator, or any inconvenience that hinders the progress of the association, the board shall take the necessary steps to continue or cease [operations], observing what is decided at the general meeting.

The articles of association of the Empresa Literária Dous de Dezembro were more complex and detailed than the business plan for the printing firm. Once created, the literary publisher would be much larger than its predecessor. However, putting the articles of association into practice would not be an easy task. Paula Brito knew this and relied on the government's protection to incorporate the company:

> Art. 5. The board itself, together with the administrator Francisco de Paula Brito, or he alone, will request from the State powers any assistance deemed appropriate, giving all the necessary reasons for such measures.
> Art. 6. For the assistance that has been provided to the association, the Government is entitled to have any work it deems appropriate done at its establishments, without paying any more for it than the prices set by the National Press, or any other government workshops identical to those of the association.

In the event of government aid being provided, the articles of association offered the state the right to print whatever it wanted at the company's workshops. However, regardless of the enactment of Decree no. 1.610, the incorporation of the Dous de Dezembro literary publisher depended on the largesse of the "State powers." Article 5 stated that the government could offer any "assistance deemed appropriate," but Paula Brito had a clear idea about how the state could help him. He explained this in an application to the Interior Ministry, which in turn referred it to the Chamber of Deputies, as we can see in the report of proceedings on August 6, 1855:

> From the Minister of the Empire referring the request in which Francisco de Paula Brito asks the imperial government to take four hundred shares, without dividends for five years, from a company that intends to be founded with the title—Literary Publisher—to the committee on Commerce, Industry, and the Arts.[11]

Doing the math, the publisher expected the government to invest 80,000,000 réis in Dous de Dezembro through the purchase of four hundred shares with a nominal value of 200,000 réis apiece. Paula Brito also wanted the shares acquired by the government to have no entitlement to interest for five years. In the Chamber of Deputies, the publisher's request was referred to the

Committee on Trade, Industry, and the Arts, which, a few days later, at its August 10 session, issued the following opinion:

> In order to be able to give its opinion on the inclusion of Francisco de Paula
> Brito, the industry and arts committee requires that the government, through
> the ministries of the Interior and the Treasury, be asked for information
> about the company's advantages, the possibility of tendering, and the sub-
> sidy to be paid, and their opinion on such points.[12]

The Interior Ministry's assessment of the advantages of the literary publishing firm, following the request of the Chamber of Deputies Committee on Trade, Industry, and the Arts, would be addressed during the September 4 session.[13] However, while the petitions came and went between the ministries and the Chamber, Paula Brito explained why he needed government funding to readers of *Marmota fluminense*. The grant would be used for the "prompt payment of partial creditors" of the printing firm.[14] Thus, the merger of the two companies was linked to the payment of debts. And, as we will see, at this point some of Paula Brito's creditors were already suing him in the Rio de Janeiro Business Tribunal.

Enriched by customs tariffs, the Treasury held most of the nation's money. As a result, any commercial, industrial, or banking venture depended on the generosity of the State.[15] Thus Paula Brito was not alone in applying for such aid. For example, in 1856, the Imperial Companhia Seropédica, a silk manufacturer, obtained a grant of 120,000,000 réis from the provincial government of Rio de Janeiro divided into four yearly installments. Those funds were to be invested in its silk mill, the purchase of land and equipment, hiring free workers and setting up silkworm nurseries.[16] In 1855, Paula Brito himself had obtained an important government concession, confirmed by Decree no. 1717 of January 23, 1856, which gave the publisher the right to produce chromolithographed playing cards for five years at the Dous de Dezembro company's workshops, using a sophisticated ten-color printing method.[17] Paula Brito spared no efforts and used the columns of *Marmota fluminense* to try to convince the public of the benefits his literary publishing firm would bring to the country. The improvements to the art of printing being made in France, under the aegis of Napoleon III, served the Rio de Janeiro publisher very well to remind not only his subscribers and readers, but also honorable deputies and ministers, of his company's importance:

A person of the art, well informed, assures us that last year the French government spent 200,000 francs (70,000 réis) on the printing of the—*Imperial Typog-
raphy Specimen*—for the Paris exhibition. They say it is a done in very good
taste, with only one hundred copies printed.

France, like the United Kingdom, Germany, Belgium, and the United
States, knows the value of the printing press, and the resources that are drawn
from it; as for us! . . . we had better keep quiet so that we are not regarded
with suspicion.

To our correspondents, we will take charge of the purchase of this work,
which should be a printing monument, which will do honor to the reign of
Napoleon III. The pages of books make kings eternal.[18]

Whereas European governments recognized the importance of printing,
and therefore of the press, things were very different in Brazil. However,
the year 1856 was beginning and an advertisement for shares in the literary publishing firm that appeared in *Marmota fluminense* on January 1 suggests that the subsidy required from the government was still not guaranteed.[19] We will see later on that, instead of subscribing for shares in Dous de
Dezembro, the government eventually approved a loan of 80,000,000 réis.
However, it came too late and, lacking timely government aid, the company
was forced to file for bankruptcy protection.

CHAPTER 13

Debts and the Dangerous Game of the Stock Market

IN 1854, JOÃO Ferreira da Cruz Forte published his two-act comedy *O jogo do burro, ou, A febre das ações* (The fool's game, or, Stock market fever). The play follows the misadventures of Frederico, an ambitious young man who is in love with Lala, against the backdrop of Rio de Janeiro's stock exchange in Praça do Comércio. The young woman's father, the merchant João Dias, is opposed to their courtship because he considers Frederico to be a good-for-nothing and wants Lala to marry his close friend and fellow merchant, Lourenço Mendes. This is basically the plot of the comedy, which, in addition to Frederico and Lala's love story, revolves around the stock market fever that was sweeping Rio de Janeiro at the time:

LALA — I don't know for certain yet . . . but, my dear Frederico . . . what can I do? . . . You know very well that Daddy is not the sort of man who gives in easily . . .

FREDERICO — We will see . . . for now you only need to stand firm, anyway
. . . A month is enough . . . In this resistance is our salvation . . . I tell you . . .
You know what's going on in this city with the stock market? . . . It's a yellow fever . . . a terrible game . . . the devil's afoot . . . it's a game that takes
your shirt . . . it's like they're all mad . . . Anyone who has skill and energy
and a scrap of wealth will make rivers of money! . . . you can make a fortune in an instant . . . Your father also trades there . . . He may already have
made more than fifty million . . .
LALA — Really? . . . but what does that have to do with our situation, my dear
Frederico? . . .[1]

In the remainder of the scene, the young man tells his beloved that he,
too, has been profiting from the "game of shares." In addition to Frederico,
other characters want to join in the game and spare no effort to do so. Ger-
trudes, Lala's mother, has sold the slaves Florindo and Luciana without hesitation so her husband could buy shares at the bourse in Praça do Comércio. For the same reason, the sacristan pawned off his only slave, a retired
officer pawned his uniforms and furniture, a teacher sold all his books, a
civil servant, his wife's jewels, and an apothecary, all his wares. At the stock
market in Praça do Comércio, the scene of the second act, the companies
distributing shares have absurd names, such as the Imaginary Bank of the
Five Parts of the World, with funds that could be realized with brown-paper
certificates, the Aerostatic Steam Packets to the Moon in Twenty Seconds
Company, the Gold Company for the Exploration of Metal in Sugarloaf
Mountain, the Fantastic Speed-Teaching Company for army recruits and
wet nurses "through the ultra-new electric umbrella method in twenty-four
hours," and the Odoriferous Company "for waste and filth in the city using
patchouli extracts." In the end, after making a fortune with shares in the
Aerostatic Steam Packets to the Moon company, Frederico saves João Dias
from going bankrupt due to the crash in shares in the Fantastic Speed-
Teaching Company. And, as the reader may already have guessed, our hero
also wins his beloved's hand.

Around the time of the publication of that comedy, Paula Brito's *Marmota fluminense* published a caricature that also portrayed that "fool's game."
Entitled "A febre da praça" (Stock market fever), it does not refer directly to
Cruz Forte's play, but portrays "the people in a state of tumult" due to shares
in the Banco do Brasil, the Banco Hipotecário mortgage bank, and "the rail-

A FEBRE DA PRAÇA EM 1854.

FIGURE 22. Stock exchange fever

way and gas lighting companies."[2] Looking closely at the picture, just below the donkey's head, on the pediment supported by the columns, we see the emblems of the companies in whose shares the merchants—represented by clerics, military men, and capitalists in coats and top hats—were purchasing wildly. Thus, both the cartoon and comedy provide an interesting insight into that singular moment when corporations were causing a furor in the Imperial capital.

However, the long-term effects of that singular moment were extremely harmful. At least, this was the assessment of Sebastião Ferreira Soares, who focused on understanding the financial crisis that led to the collapse of the Banco Souto in September 1864. According to Ferreira Soares, the recycling of capital from the slave trade had undeniable benefits for "the material improvement" of the country. However, "Commerce in Brazil was not yet sufficiently familiar with the development and management of industrial corporations, nor for banking operations, when they appeared in great profusion in the Rio de Janeiro market." Indeed, the "immoral game of usury in all classes of society" stemming from the trading of the shares in those companies was one of the main drivers of the crisis.[3]

The collapse of the Banco Souto per se is not relevant here. However, the causes and immediate effects of that "immoral game of usury" on corporations established in Rio de Janeiro is extremely pertinent. Paula Brito, who had founded Empresa Tipográfica Dous de Dezembro in late 1850, was about to establish his literary publishing house at a time when stock market fever was starting to burn in Rio de Janeiro's bourse. However, like yellow fever, which occasionally caused death and desolation, stock market fever could also be fatal. According to Ferreira Soares, the stock speculation that plagued Rio de Janeiro began with a blunder by the Marquess of Paraná in 1854—"great men, great mistakes," concluded Ferreira Soares. In 1853, the Minister of the Interior, the Viscount of Itaboraí, planned the merger of Rio de Janeiro's two main banks, Banco Comercial and Banco do Brasil to centralize the credit system and regulate the circulation of currency. In the meantime, the cabinet fell in September 1853, and it was up to the powerful Minister Honório Hermeto Carneiro Leão, the Marquess of Paraná, to conclude the merger.

The storm broke out when Paraná authorized the distribution of shares in the new Banco do Brasil at 10 percent interest, triggering the furore in the stock exchange. According to Ferreira Soares, as soon as the measure was implemented "the organization of banking and corporate plans for several companies began, and without being legally incorporated, their shares were distributed and issued in the market, bought and sold at a higher or lower premium."[4] What seems to be the key issue behind the "fool's game" or "stock market fever" was the lack of capital underlying the creation of so many corporations and banks. Paula Brito is a good example of this, since the incorporation of the Dous de Dezembro literary publishing house depended on funds from the Treasury. Now, the very need for a government subsidy suggests the fragility of the Rio de Janeiro stock market. Therefore, between 1854 and 1857, a period that coincides with a thwarted attempt at expansion and consequent bankruptcy of Paula Brito's company, "those were years when a great deal of money was lost in Rio de Janeiro's market; and in this immoral game of the stock market many unwary individuals sacrificed their wealth, and the good clever capital profited."[5] The debts that played a very important role in the Dous de Dezembro debacle indicate that Paula Brito was one of the unwary.

Between 1853 and 1856, many of Paula Brito's assets were seized to be auctioned off due to lawsuits brought in the Business Tribunal of Rio de Janeiro—the most important assets were his lithographic and printing presses. The Business Tribunal was an institution recently created by the Business Code enacted in June 1850, shortly before the enactment of the law definitively banning the transatlantic slave trade to Brazil. In this regard, 1850 was a unique year in the history of the Second Reign because, in addition to the Business Code and the Eusébio de Queirós Law, another equally important law promulgated that year was the Land Act—a trinity essentially linked to a single issue. Thus, while one law banned the "infamous trade," another regulated latifundia as a means of compensating landowners deprived of a constant supply of African captives, and finally a third regulated business activities, anticipating the return of assets previously employed in the lucrative trade in human beings.[6] In other words, Paula Brito and the other merchants in Brazil were subject to a new mercantile law that had just come into effect in the shadow of the abolition of the African slave trade.[7]

Among the Business Tribunal records filed in the National Archives of Rio de Janeiro, I have found nineteen cases against the publisher, through which it is possible to follow the progress of Dous de Dezembro's bankruptcy. According to the provisions of the mercantile legislation adopted in 1850, a business lawsuit was carried out in three stages. First, conciliation was sought between the parties before the parish judge of the nearest parish. In the cases studied, Paula Brito did not attend any of the conciliatory hearings to which he was summoned. Therefore, without conciliation between the parties, the case was referred to the Business Tribunal, where the debt was judged through a ten-day legal action which, as its name implies, obliged the debtor to pay the debt plus interest and court costs within ten days. When this did not happen, judicial enforcement followed, at which time the debtor's assets were assessed and auctioned off to pay the creditors.

Paula Brito was sued by four of his suppliers, including Saportas e Companhia and Eugênio Bouchaud, dealers who supplied Rio de Janeiro's printers with a varied range of items. In October 1853, Paula Brito did not redeem the bill of exchange for a little more than a million that he had signed when he purchased "printing items" from Saportas e Cia. It is interesting in this case that the document was endorsed by Luiz Thorey, an importer of French printing presses and supplier of printing items. During the execution of the debt, as early as November 1854, Paula Brito very nearly lost two of his Stanhope presses.[8] De Bouchaud's "large foundry and type store" was the place where Rio de Janeiro's printers found "a vast variety of fantasy types, state-of-the-art vignettes of all genres, as well as a rich collection of emblems . . . printing ink, French boxes, boughs, twigs, roller trimmings, roller molds, dies, *biseaux* [bevels], setting rules, brushes, and all the accoutrements of the typographic art."[9] Paula Brito had spent 500,000 réis or so on type for his workshop at Bouchaud's establishment in January 1856. However, the bill only was paid in December, after the supplier had gone to court to have "two iron lithographic presses complete with their accoutrements, in very good condition" seized and auctioned off.[10]

Francisco José Gonçalves Agra, a merchant based on Rua do Ouvidor, struggled to receive over 1,000,000 réis that the publisher owed him for the purchase of tea and paper in January 1854. In this case, the payment was divided into five installments of 250,000 réis at interest of 1.5 percent per month. A written promissory note was issued for each installment, the first of which fell due on the fifth of March and the last on the fifth of July. Paula Brito failed to honor any of them, and when he received a court order to pay all five, the publisher nearly lost three lithographic presses. Calculating the total value of the assets to be auctioned off, each press must have been worth about 460,000 réis. However, the equipment was spared because the debt was paid in a notary's office the month after the assets were attached.[11] The debt contracted with Gonçalves Agra reinforces the importance of tea among the articles sold by Paula Brito, in addition to novels and periodicals. Ads regularly published in *Marmota* featured that product among the many items sold in the bookstore, such as stamped paper, cigars, office supplies, dolls, playing cards, and an "endless variety of interesting things."[12]

Like Gonçalves Agra, the wholesaler Adriano Gabriel Corte Real also supplied "interesting things" that were sold by retailers like Paula Brito. In October 1855, the publisher spent over 3,500,000 réis on unspecified "goods" purchased from Corte Real. On that occasion, the publisher managed to negotiate much longer payment terms, as the promissory note only came due in nine months, in June 1856. Even so, just a few weeks after that date, Dous de Dezembro filed for bankruptcy protection, leaving it to the company's shareholders to make decisions about the payment of the publisher's debts. Little pleased, or not at all, Corte Real and his attorney proceeded with the ten-day legal action against Paula Brito, who, in turn, did not even attend the conciliation hearing, much less the hearing at the Business Tribunal, where he was judged in absentia.[13]

While owing his suppliers considerable sums, Paula Brito also found it difficult to pay debts of less than 300,000 réis. In May 1855, João de Souza Monteiro, a resident of Rua Nova de Sao Francisco da Prainha, executed a promissory note from the publisher worth 188,649 réis. The document was not transcribed or attached to the case file, which makes it hard to determine the nature of the debt. In any case, if he had not paid his creditor with interest, including court costs, Paula Brito would have lost a fully equipped Stanhope press,[14] which would have been a terrible deal, since a Stanhope with all its accessories could cost nearly 600,000 réis, three times the amount of the debt.[15] The widow Mariana Augusta d'Oliveira received from Dr. Joaquim Pereira de Araújo, a homeopathic doctor whom we will get to know better later, a promissory note worth 300,000 réis that Paula Brito had signed in March 1855.[16] All indications are that the note was for a loan, as the publisher had turned to the doctor on other occasions to try to restore his company's financial health. Mariana Augusta d'Oliveira did her best to reach an agreement in the tribunal of the justice of the peace of the third district of Santíssimo Sacramento parish, but, as usual, Paula Brito did not attend the hearing. This time, however, the lawsuit filed by the widow and her attorneys did not go on for long. Perhaps embarrassed by seeing a creditor in mourning, Paula Brito offered to redeem the promissory note, paying it in a notary's office, plus interest and fees.[17]

In most cases where assets were attached, by stating that he was ready to pay his debts, Paula Brito managed to be named the depository of his printing and lithographic presses. As a result, the equipment remained in the workshop while the publisher sought a means of saving them from being sold at auction. However, there were cases in which the equipment actually was auctioned off. In late March 1854, Paula Brito borrowed 1,000,000 réis from Bernardino Ribeiro de Souza Guimarães. The promissory note stated that it would be redeemed "in exactly two months." However, Paula Brito failed to keep that promise, and his creditor began taking steps to recover the loan.[18] A warrant of attachment was issued in late September. According to the valuation of the assets involved, they were "two Stanhope presses in perfect condition and all their accessories," each valued at 600,000 réis.[19] In late October, auction notices were posted in the courthouse and published in Rio de Janeiro newspapers. We can imagine Paula Brito's reaction when he leafed through the *Diário do Rio de Janeiro* on October 25, 1854, and read the dreadful edict on the third page.[20] This time, the publisher managed to save at least one of the presses. In December, Souza Guimarães informed the Business Tribunal that he had received 700,000 réis from the publisher, a considerable part of the debt. From that point on, the fate of one of the presses becomes uncertain. Souza Guimarães asked the judge to recalculate the debt and continue the attachment of the other press. The judge upheld the petition and a new warrant of attachment was issued. However, the records for the proceedings do not show whether the publisher managed to save that press. All indications are that he did not.[21]

In any event, the foreclosure auction notices published in the newspapers made the Dous de Dezembro company's difficulties public. Certainly aware of the news, and fearing that promissory notes signed or simply endorsed by Paula Brito would go unpaid, long-standing creditors flocked to the Business Tribunal. In these cases, the publisher may have been surprised when José Antonio de Oliveira Bastos, a merchant established at Rua da Alfandega, simultaneously protested four promissory notes signed by Eugênio Aprigio da Veiga, which totaled a considerable 4,600,000 réis. Eugênio Aprigio had moved to Campos dos Goytacazes, so Paula Brito was responsible for the debt in Court, as an endorser. However, the lawsuit may have gone well in Campos, for the case was abruptly closed.[22] Then there was Duarte José de Puga Garcia, who had lent 500,000 réis to the publisher as far back March 1848. However, Puga Garcia's lawyer reported that Paula Brito had not paid of interest on the loan since October 1853. Thus, although it only began in November 1855, the litigation dragged on until October of the following year. The execution notices were not concluded, but a statement by Puga Garcia's legal representative said that the slow proceedings were "due to the delays that the petitioner [Paula Brito] has requested."[23]

In 1856, the situation worsened, and, faced with the bankruptcy of his company, Paula Brito had plausible reasons to "request delays."

CHAPTER 14

From Bankruptcy
Protection to Liquidation

P AULA BRITO DID everything in his power to prevent Dous de Dezembro from filing for bankruptcy protection and folding. The fact that
he borrowed nearly 3,000,000 réis from the homeopathic physician Dr.
Joaquim Pereira de Araújo in April 1856 clearly demonstrates that he was trying to save his business. The previous year, Paula Brito had already signed
a promissory note for 504,000 réis lent to him by the same doctor. Therefore, considering capital alone, Paula Brito owed the homeopathist more
than 3,500,000 réis. The promissory note signed when the loan was issued
in April stipulated that it had to be repaid in June at interest of 2 percent
per month.[1] The extremely short deadline suggests that the publisher was
hoping that Dous de Dezembro's finances would regain the health they had
enjoyed in the early days or, at best, that the government grant would finally
come through. However, considering, for example, the sum that Paula Brito
owed to his supplier Corte Real, his debts at that time easily amounted to
7,000,000 réis. It was enough to buy about eleven Stanhope presses or fifteen lithographic presses like those used in Dous de Dezembro's workshops.

It was these mounting debts that led the publisher to call a meeting of shareholders and creditors to decide the company's fate. Based on the agreement reached at the meeting held on October 21, 1856, the initial idea was to liquidate the company without declaring bankruptcy, a decision that had important and—for Paula Brito—negative implications. An out-of-court bankruptcy protection document was signed in the presence of all those present, including the vice-butler of the Imperial House. It contained four clauses. The first two covered the company's debts and the situation of its shareholders:

1. That all debts contracted up to this date will be halved.
2. That from this day forward, all premiums will be suspended for the length of time that a Commission, which will be responsible for overseeing the establishments, deems fair, given the current state of affairs.[2]

The summary write-off of no less than half of the company's debts is strong evidence of the magnitude of the crisis. It was followed by the suspension of premiums, that is, the interest due on shares would not be paid from that date onward. Judging from the case of Father Joaquim Ferreira da Cruz Belmonte, which completely belies the financial statements published in *Marmota fluminense*, shareholders had not seen the color of that money for more than two years.[3] Thus, few shareholders would have been surprised by the measure. The third clause of the document dealt with the supervision "of the establishments":

3. That the said Commission be appointed, consisting of three members, including creditors and shareholders, with full powers to verify the assets and liabilities of the company and liquidate it so that all creditors are paid, as mentioned above. This Commission will direct and operate the establishments, being empowered to appoint a manager of their trust, keeping Mr. Francisco de Paula Brito in the administration proper of the establishments under the direction of the said Commission.[4]

Paula Brito was clearly reluctant to give up the helm. Therefore, if the commission, through a manager, was taking over the "direction" of the business, the editor would not give up his place in its "administration." "Direction" and "administration" are synonyms that make it clear that Paula Brito intended to stay on as the CEO of Dous de Dezembro until the bitter end, which was achieved with the assent of those present. The fourth and final clause specifically concerned a mortgagee, to whom Paula Brito offered the bookstore as collateral, including the building on Praça da Constituição, no. 78.[5] The numerous creditors listed in the inventory for the publisher's estate included Viscount Ipanema, with whom, through a "mortgage deed," Paula Brito's widow had inherited a debt of 6,000,000 réis. It is possible that the mortgagee was Ipanema, to whom Paula Brito may have already lost the property, as it was not listed among the assets in the publisher's estate.[6]

The bankruptcy protection document also pointed out that the shareholders and creditors acknowledged, "on the one hand, the zeal and good faith of the same Mr. Francisco de Paula Brito and, on the other, the impossibility of continuing [to run] the company in its present state." This recognition is important, as it ultimately meant that, at least, they were absolving the publisher of moral responsibility for the state in which the company found itself. Then it appointed the commission that would oversee the liquidation of Dous de Dezembro. It included Adriano Gabriel Corte Real, who, as we know, was one of the publisher's suppliers, and creditors Antônio José Gonçalves de Souza and José Antônio de Araújo Filgueiras.[7]

Therefore, after that bankruptcy protection agreement was reached out of court, Paula Brito continued to run Dous de Dezembro for the remainder of 1856. However, the liquidation of the company was not entirely free of conflict, as not all creditors and shareholders attended the October meeting, and some of them were not happy with the decisions made at the time. The homeopathic doctor and usurer, Dr. Joaquim Pereira de Araújo, was among the creditors who were dissatisfied with the decisions reached—so much so that, when the doctor sued Paula Brito the following year, the publisher was obliged to write a letter in his own hand justifying how the arrangement was reached:

> Judging myself insalvable [*sic*] in October last year, I summoned, through circulars and announcements to my creditors (and among them to Dr. Araújo) to explain my situation to them. Gathered together in their vast majority, they understood that by declaring bankruptcy—judicially—all would be lost; because, after the workshops were closed, the typesetters laid off, the machines [illegible], for the six or eight months the process lasted, little or nothing would be profitable, so they settled on the bankruptcy protection agreement. . . . This document was later signed by many creditors, and Dr. Araújo was the only dissenting party who wanted to sue me.[8]

Paula Brito claimed that, although the company was in trouble, it would be unwise to declare bankruptcy, as that process would drag on for months. However, reading Paula Brito's explanation, it is important to stress that "the vast majority" did not mean all creditors and shareholders. Thus, in addition to the lack of consensus, by proposing the liquidation of the company in this informal and amicable manner, Paula Brito was in breach of mercantile law, providing an opening for dissatisfied creditors and shareholders deprived of the guarantees offered them by the Business Code to take legal action against him. Was the publisher really acting in good faith as he tried to show? We do not know, but regardless of good or bad intentions, it is certain that he was acting illegally. As summarily decreed by article 797 of the Business Code, "every merchant who ceases his payments is understood to be insolvent or bankrupt."[9] Thus, the creditors and shareholders who opposed the bankruptcy agreement signed in October 1856 had the law on their side. Among the malcontents, besides Dr. Joaquim Pereira de Araújo, we have found another well-documented case in records of the Business Tribunal—that of the Portuguese grammar and Latin teacher at the São José seminary, Father Joaquim Ferreira da Cruz Belmonte.

In February 1857, through his lawyer, Father Joaquim went to the Business Tribunal of Rio de Janeiro to claim back the 400,000 réis he had paid for share number 109 in Empresa Tipográfica Dous de Dezembro. The priest had subscribed for the share in April 1852, and according to his complaint, he had not been paid interest since July 1854. However, since the lawsuit did not stress the interest, what the cassocked shareholder wanted was the repayment of the capital he had invested. According to that document, in a section that directly refers to the bankruptcy protection agreement, "The defendant [Paula Brito] claimed that the said company had been liquidated, conducting its activities without . . . appearing to be bankrupt under the law or being declared insolvent by the competent authority."[10] Concerned about his investment of 400,000 réis, the priest was afraid that the publisher, who was flouting mercantile law, might simply fail to pay him. If this was what the priest truly feared, we can picture him crossing himself when he leafed through the newspapers and read that Paula Brito would be putting all of the company's assets on the auction block on April 28, 1857, at 4 p.m.

The publisher had hired Joaquim José de Castro Bittancourt to organize the auction of his assets. According to the catalog that was distributed as an insert of the *Diário do Rio de Janeiro*, a copy of which would be attached to Father Joaquim's lawsuit, Paula Brito intended to sell off all of Dous de Dezembro's property: "the entire contents of its major book-shop, and the engraving, bookbinding and lithography workshops, a large amount of bound works, the same in paperback, a large amount of musical scores, as well as building no. 68 in the same place [Praça da Constituição]."[11] Regarding books and periodicals, the nearly nine hundred titles listed in the auction catalog were divided into fifty lots. Each of them was organized according to a certain thematic order, perhaps to attract buyers with specific tastes. Lot 12, for example, consisted exclusively of works by Gonçalves de Magalhães, while lot 13 contained novels and plays by Joaquim Manuel de Macedo. Similarly, some were comprised of opera librettos, such as lot 20, and others contained plays, like lot 28. There were also lots with a scientific bent, such as lot 26, which consisted mainly of medical books, as well as lots made up of works in a variety of genres in the French language, such as lot 36. In addition to these printed items, the catalog stated that the following were also for sale:

More than 6,000 different musical scores, such as polkas, waltzes, schottisches, romances, *modinhas*, etc., as well as about 2,000 fashion plates from those already distributed with *Marmota*.

More than 20,000 prints and [pictures of] saints and virgins, portraits, caricatures, etc.

There are certainly 100 different works, whose number will go from 35,000 to 40,000 volumes.

None of the Stanhope presses was included in the auction, which suggests that Paula Brito intended to stay in the printing business. Thus, in regard to equipment, the catalog listed "a complete lithography press," "an engraving press with about 150 copper plates of all invocations," as well as "a binding workshop." The property located on Praça da Constituição, no. 68, described as having "two fronts," would be auctioned off the same day at 5:30 p.m. The terms and conditions of the auction were as follows:

1. Everything is sold as is.
2. Cash on delivery.
3. All buyers will give a deposit upon bidding.
4. The lots will be delivered on the following day.
5. Buyers are requested to examine the lots before the auction, as after the auction no complaints will be accepted.

6. For those who do not wish to comply with these conditions, it would be wise not to tender a bid.

7. The auctioneer's commission is 5 percent.

Possibly due to bad weather, as a heavy storm broke out in Rio de Janeiro that afternoon,[12] the auction was postponed until May 8. The change of date was providential for creditors who were worried about recouping debts, as it allowed them to get themselves organized. The indefatigable Father Joaquim, for example, brought witnesses against the publisher on May 6, two days before the auction. Domingos Pereira Arouca, Antonio Joaquim Cardoso d'Almeida, and Antonio de Miranda Marques testified before the third district municipal judge in the service of the Business Tribunal. The Portuguese blacksmith Domingos Pereira Arouca, thirty-two, a resident of Rua da Vala, said he knew "because he had heard" that, in order to "form" the printing company, Paula Brito had begun distributing shares valued at 400,000 réis, and that, also "because he had heard," he knew that the company had ceased operations with the consent of shareholders, but not as the Business Code required. Domingos knew that the priest was a shareholder of Dous de Dezembro and "that the company has been liquidated and sold at auction . . . all the assets still belong to the defendant . . . without any as a guarantee for his creditors."[13] Antonio Joaquim Cardoso d'Almeida, also Portuguese, twenty, a resident of Ladeira de João Homem who worked as a "bookkeeper in several commercial establishments," reinforced the same points underscored by Domingos Pereira Arouca. He said that he knew that "the defendant is auctioning off all his assets as [was] made public in the newspapers, and for that reason had no assets at all as collateral for his creditors."[14] Similarly, Antônio de Miranda Marques, a thirty-four-year-old merchant from Rio de Janeiro who lived on Rua Nova do Livramento, said that Paula Brito had indeed traded shares with a nominal value of 400,000 réis to "set up his printing business" and that, "in view of announcements made by the defendant," he knew about the shareholders' meeting. Furthermore, "because it has been made public in the papers," the witness confirmed that Paula Brito was "auctioning off all his printing-related assets."[15]

However, in addition to holding the auction initially scheduled for the afternoon of April 28, Paula Brito had made another major decision. On the twenty-sixth, in compliance with the law, the publisher filed for bankruptcy for the Empresa Dous de Dezembro.[16] Notwithstanding the out-of-court settlement with some of his creditors and shareholders and the attempt to keep the presses in operation for the months to come, Paula Brito found himself at an impasse. However, filing for bankruptcy two days before the auction was nonetheless a strategy, as it meant the possibility that the money raised through the auction could go into the company's bankrupt estate, whose fiscal trustee was the creditor João Manuel da Silva.[17] Possibly instructed by his legal counsel—he had engaged the lawyers Augusto Teixeira de Freitas and Joaquim Theodoro de Souza Soares—Paula Brito was trying to protect the proceeds of the auction from the avarice of certain creditors and shareholders, particularly the priest and the doctor.

Going back to April 27, the day before the auction was due to be held, the wary homeopathist asked the second court of the Business Tribunal to place a lien on Paula Brito's assets for an amount that would ensure that his creditor received what he was owed. News of the auction of Dous de Dezembro's assets was already spreading through the newspapers and the physician feared that he would finish up empty handed.[18] Then, like the shareholder-priest, Dr. Souza Soares also presented witnesses who confirmed before the judge that Paula Brito was indebted to him and that the publisher had announced the auction of his assets. On that day, the witnesses for the doctor were the Portuguese Francisco Marques Guimarães, a twenty-five-year-old clerk, and Francisco José Martins Neto, also Portuguese, a twenty-nine-year-old merchant.[19] Therefore, by April 28, the day the auction was supposed take place, the vigilant Dr. Souza Soares had already obtained a lien on the publisher's assets—"as many as will guarantee the amount" that he was owed.[20] However, as the reader already knows, the auction was postponed until May 8, possibly going on until the tenth or twelfth, as reported by the *A pátria* newspaper, published in Niterói:

> Today, there continues the auction of Paula Brito, who is experiencing the displeasure of losing his life's work. However, he has the consolation that he can still keep working, and he has done well to take that decision because there is still time: as he is freed from the encumbrances that bind him to the *Dous Dezembro* [sic] company, he has the power to make a new life, and if he leaves the credit calculations [behind him], I assure you that he will still be happy. Credit is money that must always be repaid, and when the resources to be used are lacking, creditors do not want to know that, or about anything but their money, in fact, there comes a torrent of epithets of rogue, thief, dodger, etc., etc., however honorable and happy the man is. Our society is not yet constituted so that it knows how to distinguish the unhappy but

honorable man from the happy and dishonorable; when dealing with money, men seem to lose their minds, their judgment is clouded. I wish we could hope to see Brazilian society renewed![21]

The unnamed journalist was seeking to hearten Paula Brito who, writing in *Marmota fluminense*, thanked him for his considerations. The publisher began his article, in which he gave a positive assessment of his career since 1831, by addressing Pedro II. Therefore, if there was any consolation for the bankruptcy of his company, it was that Paula Brito was convinced that he was playing an important role in a larger project. In addition to the advancement of Brazilian printing, it involved the perpetuation of his beloved monarch's achievements:

> If we have done anything for our country, and for history to tell of him and his second Reign what surely would not be said if minds like ours had not done so much and so desperately; that the arts to which we are dedicated owe much to us; that artists owe us a great deal, having come from our workshops in no small number; that we have greatly committed ourselves to political parties from 1831 to this day; this is something no one is unaware of; it is justice that cannot be denied us by the greatest notables of our country.
>
> Our conscience at ease, we do not complain about what we have suffered, nor regret what we have done.
>
> Money has never been, is not, and will not be our idol.
>
> With experience—of men and things—we will continue to walk the road of life, only with more reserve is true, and a little more caution. . . . We have never done anything ostentatious, because, always knowing the fragility of our position, we have always been afraid to climb so that, a new Icarus, we would not have to plummet, melting our wings.
>
> Although we are nothing, if we should generate a review of our actions, what we have done, and what has been done with us; more than one artist, more than one merchant, would serve as an example of our modest history, just as we are sure that it would trouble more than one person.
>
> Rio de Janeiro, May 13, 1857
Francisco de Paula Brito[22]

The creditors, however, cared little or nothing for all that. If this historian has not been traduced by the handwriting and, above all, the abbreviations used by the clerk José Luiz de Araújo Barros, the total value of Empresa Dous de Dezembro's assets sold at auction was 9,800,000 réis.[23] Without hesitation, the day after the auction Dr. Souza Soares requested and obtained a seizure warrant, that is, the sequestration of 3,625,000 réis, enough to cover the amount of the loan, interest, and the costs of the lawsuit brought against Paula Brito. The money from the auction was being held by the auctioneer, at his residence on Rua do Hospício, when the bailiff Tertuliano João Batista and the registrar Jose Luiz de Araújo Barros went there to execute the warrant.[24] As a result, just over one-third of the total amount raised at the auction was placed in the Public Deposit Vault to await the outcome of the lawsuit.[25]

Paula Brito refused to accept that decision. To ensure that the entire amount obtained through the auction went into Dous de Dezembro's bankrupt estate, the publisher instructed his lawyer, Augusto Teixeira de Freitas, to ask the Business Tribunal judge to lift the sequestration order. In his petition, the attorney considered the procedure of these notices to be "odious," as they put his client in the invidious position of a "suspect debtor." The defense claimed that Paula Brito had acted in openly and transparently, which made it unfair to treat him like a bad debtor, and the auction was only held to "prevent further losses and pay his creditors."[26] When contesting the embargo, Dr. Souza Soares's lawyer did not deny Paula Brito's "probity," stressing that "it is true that misfortunes put him in a state of insolvency, as one should not only deduce from the out-of-court bankruptcy protection agreement reached with some of creditors."[27] According to Dr. Souza Soares's counsel, the October 1856 meeting was further evidence that Paula Brito could not pay his creditors. Therefore, to ensure his client's peace of mind, the sequestration should be maintained, and the auction money placed in the Public Deposit Vault and pledged in favor of the doctor.

In July 1857, the fiscal trustee appointed to oversee Dous de Dezembro's bankruptcy proceedings, João Manuel da Silva, also came forward to ask the judge to put those funds into the company's bankrupt estate.[28] Cunningly, the doctor's lawyer pulled an argument from his sleeve that seemed infallible to him when he challenged the trustee's request: "the bankruptcy had not yet been filed" when the dispute began between his client and Paula Brito. The lawyer based himself on article 830 of the Business Code to state that "it clearly implies that only judgments that grant execution after bankruptcy can be halted; it only mentions future and subsequent executions."[29] However, the chief and special judge of the second Business Tribunal, Antônio Thomaz de Godoy, ruled that the bankruptcy of Paula Brito's printing company had been filed in time. Thus, against the doctor's wishes, all of the money raised at auction was included in the company's bankrupt estate.[30]

At the same time, Father Joaquim Ferreira da Cruz Belmonte was still on his own personal crusade. Shortly before the ruling in favor of the Dous de Dezembro's bankruptcy trustee, Paula Brito's lawyer asked to see the Ordinary Lawsuit filed by the priest. The mere request to view the case outraged Father Joaquim's legal representative, Dom Brás Nicolau da Silveira, who argued, referring to Title XV of Book III of the Philippine Ordinances, that Paula Brito had not yet come forward, having failed to attend the conciliatory hearings held by the justice of the peace.[31] However, possibly thanks to the same Title XV,[32] the judge allowed the publisher's lawyer to see the filing. Without stating why he did so, Paula Brito dropped the case at the end of June 1857. In the end, he was ordered to repay the 400,000 réis owed to the Latin teacher at the São José Seminary.[33]

The second meeting of creditors of the now-defunct Dous de Dezembro company took place on September 25, 1857. Held in the courtroom of the Business Tribunal, the gathering was chaired by the judge of the first Business Tribunal, Firmino Rodrigues da Silva, and attended by João Manuel da Silva, the trustee of the bankrupt estate, as well as Paula Brito and twenty of his creditors.[34] The purpose of the meeting was to identify all creditors and deal with the bankruptcy. Judge Rodrigues da Silva presented the attendees with the full report on the proceedings, "from their inception to the present state," and suggested to the creditors that the debts be consolidated. Paula Brito proposed a new settlement with his creditors, this time before the judge, in accordance with the Business Code:

> I propose to keep the little that remains in my business, that is, the Dous December company, for the amount of 10,000,000 réis payable in five years, also contributing 2,000,000 réis, which together with the 4 [million] he will receive from the Government (if the purchase of the lithographic press goes through), [illegible] of 6,000,000 réis, money belonging to the orphans of the late Doctor Júlio, which has been spent on the establishments, appear in the balance sheet as a privileged debt. I undertake, however, to pay 10,000,000 réis in the short term if I can obtain them, either from the Powers of the State, or from any friendly associate, or valuable means provided to me.[35]

The number of bankruptcy creditors listed in the inventory for Paula Brito's estate totaled 130 names.[36] Among them, with the consent of those present at the meeting, the publisher gave preferential treatment to the orphans of a certain "Dr. Júlio" (no surname given), possibly a shareholder or creditor. Paula Brito also reported that he had negotiated the sale of lithographic press to the Government, which may have been interested in acquiring the equipment for the National Press. However, once the press had been sold, the publisher pledged that the money raised would be used to pay the 10,000,000 réis with which he purchased what was left of Dous de Dezembro from his creditors. Therefore, despite the fact that his company had gone bankrupt, Paula Brito intended to carry on.

The Report from the Commission Entrusted by the Imperial Government with the Notices of October 1 and December 28, 1864, to Investigate the Main and Accidental Causes of the September 1864 Crisis, which, as its lengthy title explains, sought to shed light on the collapse of the Banco Souto, reported that in 1857 Paula Brito and forty-eight other businessmen went bankrupt in Rio de Janeiro, victims of the "corporate fever and [the] game of shares." In absolute figures, the document states that Paula Brito had assets of more than 43,000,000 réis, and a liability of an astonishing 187,000,000 réis.[37] Still, whether with the help of the "Powers of the State" or "any friendly associates," which were blurred in the financial policy practiced in the empire, Paula Brito wanted to keep going.

It was small consolation that Dous de Dezembro went bankrupt weeks before the global crisis that began in the United States reached Rio de Janeiro. The crisis triggered by a sharp rise in prices following the discovery of gold in California was devastating for the book publishing business. Like Francisco de Paula Brito, countless publishers and booksellers closed their doors in that troubled year, 1857.[38]

PART FOUR

Rediscovered Illusions

CHAPTER 15

A New Beginning

S HORTLY BEFORE HE fell ill in December 1861, Paula Brito could still be seen "at the door of his workshop, wearing plain work clothes, with a smile on his face [and] a quip on his lips."[1] However the publisher's characteristic smile and quip must have vanished during the long months between 1856 and 1857, when the Dous de Dezembro negotiated bankruptcy protection and eventually went into liquidation. During this difficult phase in his career, the bookshop on no. 78, Praça da Constituição, on the corner with Rua de São Jorge, closed its doors, and *Marmota fluminense*, first issued in 1849, nearly ceased publication. In May 1857, Paula Brito announced that he was going to stop publishing the newspaper, arguing that working as its editor-in-chief had become difficult because his "spirit was overcome by the shock of constant disappointments." The publisher also confessed that he had been seriously thinking of giving up his "typographic mission."[2] However, *Marmota fluminense*, as well as its editor's "typographic mission," were spared by the fall of the Caxias ministry on May 4, 1857.

After the death of the Marquess of Paraná, the president of the Ministerial Council had been the war minister, Luís Alves de Lima e Silva, Marquess and future Duke of Caxias. The cabinet took office on September 3, 1856, the second to be installed since the conciliation of political parties.[3] In

February of the following year, while the liquidation of Dous de Dezembro was still under way, Paula Brito launched *O moderador*, published twice a week and entirely focused on the government. Considering that it ceased to be as soon as that cabinet fell, never going beyond its fifteenth issue, we can confidently deduce that Paula Brito had received government funding to cover the costs of its publication. Thus, it lavished praise on the Caxias ministry, as we can see in *O moderador*'s prospectus:

> It is to the current ministry that we owe the implementation of a broad and generous policy which has given us the state of prosperity in which we find ourselves, which has opened up the field of discussion to [people of] all capacities and made them co-participants in the state government. Undoubtedly, it is to the ministry's policies that we owe the death of the parties, so that in their stead the nation appears, manifesting its desires, imposing its will. To this wise and prudent policy we owe, above all, the extinction of the pains and passions with which the activity of Brazilians was consumed.[4]

It seems nonsensical to refer to a "state of prosperity" when he was struggling with the liquidation of his business. However, the belief in the benefits of party conciliation outweighed such troubles. *O moderador*'s pages lionized the late Marquess of Paraná and his cabinet, while the battle waged with the opposition press was open and constant—namely against the *Correio mercantil*, the *Diário do Rio de Janeiro*, and the *Correio da tarde*.[5] In an article entitled "Brief Considerations on Current Politics," the unnamed writer, certainly Paula Brito, explains that the conciliation of the parties was much more advantageous than the old bipartisan system that had set Liberals against Conservatives, especially when observing that under that system, "the sanctuary of favors was closed to anyone whose emblem was not the symbol of the ruling party, and the intelligentsia were thus cast out from within the government when they lacked the characteristic imprint of its principles or were averse to contradictions and despotism."[6]

The writer believed that, as long as the party coalition was in place, access to state benefits was open to both Liberals and Conservatives. A year later, in May 1858, it was precisely to this "sanctuary of favors" that Paula Brito returned to say his prayers. When the cabinet fell and *O moderador* consequently ceased publication, Paula Brito changed his mind about shutting down *Marmota fluminense*. As he himself explained, in an exasperated tone: "The fall of the ministry brought about the demise of *O moderador*, a ministerial publication, and we are therefore forced to [continue publishing] *Marmota* until the end of this six-month period. Yet another setback!"[7] *Marmota fluminense* came out twice weekly during the first half of 1857, although it no longer published fashion plates or sheet music, as it had done during the golden days of Dous de Dezembro.[8]

At the end of that period, the publisher decided to sell space in *Marmota fluminense* to "a friend," who began publishing a series of political articles. This strategy must have aimed to prolong the newspaper's life for a while. However, when he announced the deal, Paula Brito took care to explain to his readers that *Marmota* now had an anonymous co-editor. He declared that he was not responsible for anything published in regard to politics, "limiting our humble pen and those of our devoted friends . . . to those facetious articles that it [the pen] has always dealt with in the most select and convenient portion, in addition to the usual reviews and transcripts."[9] Later we will see that running a newspaper like *Marmota fluminense* was crucial for any publisher in the nineteenth century. Indeed, it was worth his while to ensure that it stayed in circulation.

Although he had thought seriously about leaving the printing business, Paula Brito reconsidered that as well. In mid-1857, the publisher began selling printing items in Rio de Janeiro on commission, supplying them to his "printer colleagues in all parts of the Empire." It was no secret that Francisco de Paula Brito knew Rio's printing industry better than most. As a result, although the sources are not clear about the success of his commissions, Paula Brito was able could guarantee that his clients received only the best for their workshops.[10] However, as early as February 1858, just before he started dealing in used printing materials,[11] the publisher was on the lookout for a property in the city. In an advertisement, he wrote that he needed "[an] inexpensive house [in which to] set up an entirely commercial establishment to serve his large clientele well and soon, doing everything he is qualified to do." He preferred the area near "Rua do Cano and Rua de S. Pedro, from Rua dos Ourives to [Rua] Direita."[12] In just a few days, he found a building on Rua do Cano. By mid-March, Paula Brito had set up a new printing, lithography, and bookbinding business at that address.

The size of the new establishment was minuscule compared to the workshops of the now-defunct Dous de Dezembro company. From this perspective, we can understand Paula Brito's anger when he read a report in *Correio mercantil* on the travels of the Methodist ministers Kidder and Fletcher in Rio de Janeiro. At one point in their narrative, the Americans declared that "the largest press in Rio de Janeiro belongs to Mr. Paula Brito, who is a man of color." The reference to his skin color was not a problem, but saying that he owned the Brazilian capital's largest press after his company had gone bankrupt was an overstatement that had to be contested. After all, a great many creditors were still hot on his heels. Perhaps for that reason, the day the travelers' report was published, Paula Brito wrote the following letter to the *Correio mercantil*:

> To the Editor—Although the value of the work of Messrs. Fletcher and Kidder is undeniable, I must nevertheless declare that my printing establishment was never, nor is it, the *foremost* in this capital, as it is said, although it is large and important, and has cost me millions of sacrifices. Above all, *I have to struggle with the difficulties with which all those in my condition struggle*, as those gentlemen rightly say. The truth above all.
> I am, etc.
>
> Francisco de Paula Brito
> *Santíssimo Sacramento, November 15, 1858*[13]

Although in 1856 Empresa Tipográfica Dous de Dezembro had as many as thirteen printing presses, from the most basic to highly sophisticated models, the inventory for Paula Brito's estate only lists ten presses in 1862—of which two large ones and a small one included all their accessories, while the others were "unmended."[14] In any case, the reason for moving the press to Rua do Cano was simple—after being closed for months, the bookstore would reopen on Praça da Constituição.[15]

Gradually, Paula Brito's business ventures regained some of their previous vitality. The state of the "good and cheap" bookshop's furnishings suggests that this was a fresh start marked by difficulties. About four years after the bookshop reopened, Paula Brito's inventory showed that it contained "old pine shelving," possibly used to display books and other merchandise, "two very old wooden chairs," "one long table," "six stools," and "one office stool."[16] However, despite being arranged on old shelves, soon the books, tea, and other goods were within the reach of longstanding customers. Paula Brito must have restored his credit with his suppliers, because his advertisements show that he was selling a wide range of wares, from dolls that shed tears to English soap. In the case of stationery, books, periodicals, and other printed matter, a lengthy catalog listing ninety-three items appeared in *Marmota* in late April 1858.[17] The prints on sale included portraits of the Viscount of Uruguai and the Marquess of Olinda, leading lights of the Conservative party. Music lovers could buy sheet music for Mr. Moura's *Miscelâneas* for piano and flute, or the "*Bouquet das Brasileiras*, a musical album with fourteen pieces for piano and voice." Religious patrons could purchase the Novena of St. Rita or the Life of St. Prisciliana, while Freemasons would find the *Guia para a abertura e encerramento das lojas do Rito Escocês* (Guide to the opening and closing of Scottish Rite lodges).[18]

The number of plays for sale reached twenty-four titles, especially the works of Martins Pena, which sold for 300 to 1,000 réis. Novels, a total of five titles, were sold for about 2,000 réis per volume. Books of poetry, thirteen titles in all, were priced from 1,000 to 3,000 réis.[19] According to the Dous de Dezembro company's auction catalog, in addition to the 911 books listed by title, Paula Brito and the auctioneer Castro Bittancourt put over six thousand pieces of sheet music and twenty thousand prints on the block. Going beyond the catalogs, it is almost certain that what was left unsold after the auction returned to the shelves. However, while it was clear to everyone in Rio de Janeiro that Paula Brito was beginning to recover from bankruptcy, the legacy of his debts was considerable. Unless he could rid himself of that burden, he knew he would struggle to thrive. The solution the publisher found was to resort to a very common form of government subsidy at that time: the lotteries.

The Proceedings of the Chamber of Deputies are full of such requests: lotteries whose funds were employed for various purposes. At the May 31, 1858, session, for example, the deputies discussed a request for four lotteries "for the benefit of the works and needs of the parishes of Montes Claros, Contendas, São Romão, Januária, Barra das Rio das Velhas, and Curvelo, in the province of Minas Gerais." Similarly, the nuns of the Convent of Our Lady of the Conception, in Olinda, asked the chamber for "a lottery held in Rio de Janeiro to repair their convent," and the Fluminense Library was granted two lotteries to build "a house to store its books."[20] Thus, in mid-May 1858, Paula Brito sent an application to the Chamber of Deputies for five lotteries that were to run for eighteen months. Like other merchants who resorted to this form of financing, Paula Brito also asked the government to advance him the lottery funds to be raised. Although the application does not reveal how much money was involved, Paula Brito made a point of explaining how he planned to invest it. Part of the funds would be used to pay off Dous de Dezembro's debts. Without the grant, the pub-

lisher argued, it would not be possible to "discharge the debts or be reha-
bilitated in the market within five years." And five years was a long time,
since Paula Brito, in his second point, stated that he intended to transform
his business establishments into a kind of printing school for the "Brazilian youth who want to learn" there. He also claimed that, with the lottery
money, he could resume his plan to "make his large-scale press useful to
literature, authors, and translators." Finally, he explained that he wanted
to travel to Europe, "in order to study in Germany, England, France, and
Belgium what might be useful for printing and its accompanying branches,
which are all still lagging far behind among us."[21]

The fixation with "large-scale" printing persisted, an idea that, as we
know, had been brewing in the publisher's mind at least since the late 1840s.
His desire to go to Europe was first documented in the mid-1850s, when
he made a failed attempt to create the Dous de Dezembro literary publishing company. Although it would never happen, this time his departure was
actually scheduled. Paula Brito informed the deputies that he wanted to
embark on the packet steamer in February 1859. Concluding his request,
the publisher justified it by recalling his professional career, political affiliation, and patriotism:

> Based on the foregoing, and on all that you know of the applicant, allow him
> to enter into minute considerations which would fully justify the reason for
> his request; however, you need only remember, most august and honorable
> gentlemen, how much he has been doing since 1832 as a printer, as a political
> co-religionist for many of you, and as a hard-working man wholly devoted
> to the glory and prosperity of the land of his birth.[22]

As soon as it reached the Chamber of Deputies, the request was dis-
patched to the Finance Committee, which was made up of three deputies,
Sampaio Vianna, Torres Homem, and Paula Santos. About six weeks later,
the committee issued its first opinion, observing the need to consult the
Finance Ministry, as it alone could assess the usefulness of the company,
the means for getting it off the ground, and the assurances that it would
be viable. A few weeks later, as early as mid-July 1858, instead of award-
ing him the five lotteries, the Ministry granted the publisher a loan, as his
establishment was deemed "useful and worthy of protection."[23] This was
not the first time that year that the publisher had been favorably treated by
the Finance Ministry. In late January, Paula Brito obtained an important

concession that authorized his new establishment to sell copies of all the legislation and other government publications, formerly a monopoly of the National Press.[24]

Thus, the loan specifications were made public in the Chamber of Deputies session of August 26. When granting it, the Finance Ministry reported on the grant requested by the publisher in 1855, which asked the government to subscribe for four hundred shares in the Dous de Dezembro printing company in order to turn it into a literary publisher. However, in 1855, the loan was not issued in time. Therefore, two years later, the Finance Ministry suggested that the Chamber of Deputies Finance Committee consider the loan as an alternative to lotteries. The committee approved the suggestion:

> Art. 1. The government is authorized to issue a loan to Francisco de Paula Brito, up to the amount of 80,000,000 réis for as long as it deems appropriate, and with the conditions that are the least burdensome to the treasury, so that the same Paula Brito can make improvements to his printing establishment.
>
> Art. 2. The government will demand the necessary guarantees for the solution of this loan, and may accept as collateral the establishment of the same Paula Brito, if it is sufficient for that purpose.
>
> Art. 3. Provisions to the contrary are hereby repealed.
>
> Palace of the Chamber of Deputies, 18 August 1858—
> F. de Paula Santos—Sampaio Vianna[25]

It is unclear whether that vast sum of money was at least partially disbursed. Paula Brito's inventory suggests that it was not, as it included numerous residual debts from Dous de Dezembro, which shows that not all of the company's former shareholders and creditors had been paid. Moreover, Paula Brito changed his plans and did not travel to Europe in February 1859. Staying on in Rio de Janeiro, he decided to take a chance on a project involving the City Council, an institution that had long been highly profitable for the city's printers.

Any printing company that was awarded a contract with the City Council stood to benefit on two fronts: first, by supplying the municipal offices with the forms used by the bureaucracy—bills, notices, budgets, and warrants; second, by also producing a daily or periodic gazette on the Council's sessions and acts. In this regard, the archives contain a number of petitions from Rio de Janeiro's printers offering and demanding to provide services to the municipal government.[26] With an eye on that potential client, in early May 1859, Paula Brito sent the Council a highly advantageous proposal that, in addition to supplying printed materials, envisaged the creation of an exclusive weekly gazette for the publication of the minutes and everything the Council wanted to make public. Paula Brito promised that the gazette would be distributed free of charge to the councilors and employees of City Hall, as well as being sent to the other councils in the province at his own expense. The first issues of this "municipal gazette" would be distributed along with *A marmota* to attract the attention of potential subscribers. All this would cost the municipal coffers 3,600,000 réis, paid in twelve monthly installments.[27]

The city councilors considered the proposal advantageous. Two weeks after the document reached the Council, Paula Brito was the "owner-editor" of the *Arquivo Municipal*, "a gazette especially devoted to the publication of the acts of the . . . Most Illustrious Council." According to its prospectus, the *Arquivo Municipal* revived an initiative of Ezequiel Correia dos Santos who, in 1834, printed some issues of the *Gazeta Municipal*.[28] However, as we will see, in two years the publication would become obsolete, ceasing publication for lack of readers. In any case, the creation of the *Arquivo Municipal* in 1859, along with the loan process the previous year, demonstrates that the solidity of the prestige and political alliances the publisher had forged. However, other ties were equally important in Francisco de Paula Brito's career. And, of course, the network surrounding the Petalogical Society merits special attention.

CHAPTER 16

The Petalogical Society

T HE SOCIAL COLUMNS published in *Marmota fluminense* indicate that the
Petalogical Society was born in the early 1830s, shortly after Paula Brito
purchased his cousin Silvino's bookshop, which gradually became a
gathering place: "The Petalogical or Petalogy Society, a society that, as its
name implies, deals only with *petas*, is an association of more-or-less educated people who have gathered for about twenty years in one of the loveliest and best-known venues in this city."[1] As the owner of that venue, the
publisher became the founder of the society, an association that for more
than two decades was based on the informal conversations of those who
flocked to it—that is, until its sessions and news of its members' participation in Rio de Janeiro's Carnival and civic festivities began appearing frequently in the press in the early 1850s.[2]

According to the *Dicionário da Língua Brasileira*, the Brazilian Portuguese
dictionary compiled by Luiz Maria da Silva Pinto,[3] a contemporary of the
founding of the Petalogical Society, *peta* was synonymous with *petorra*, a
kind of game that was very popular among young men of that time. It is
also defined as "squid" and "a small hatchet used to prune trees," as well as
"a dark spot that occasionally appears in horses' eyes." Figuratively speaking, *peta* also meant "fabrication," and this was the meaning employed when

187

naming the society—that is, an association devoted to the study of lies. When its sessions and minutes began appearing in the *Marmota fluminense* as of January 1853, readers of Paula Brito's bi-weekly could get a better idea of the topics discussed.

Generally speaking, the minutes of these meetings followed the format of the Annals of the Chamber of Deputies published in the *Jornal do commercio*. They even borrowed the procedural model for the Chamber's sessions.[4] Accordingly, the minutes contained some variation of a digest, a description of the topics for discussion, and the order of the day. At a session held in January 1853, one of the first to be documented, the topics for discussion consisted of "verbal offices" in which the members engaged in telling *petas*. Fabrications like these: "an end has been put to the *capoeiras* that had been disturbing the streets of the city of Rio de Janeiro, and not a single one has appeared since," and "through the energetic measures taken by the authorities, naked men are no longer seen on the beaches, so that families can henceforth, without fear, appreciate the beautiful, fresh, and enjoyable scent afforded by the majestic, well-finished balcony of the Public Promenade."[5] That is, while the *capoeira* gangs continued to roam the city streets, matrons and young ladies were still exposed to the bare backsides of men enjoying a cooling dip at the beaches of Rio de Janeiro. The order of the day, in turn, invariably contained a joke.

Sessions of the Petalogical Society began informally. All it took was for a group, small or large, to enter the bookshop with a view to engaging in pleasant conversation. "At 7 p.m., with eighteen members present, the session opened without any formalities, that is, without reading and approving the minutes of the previous session."[6] "The session began without ceremony. Those present were members who wished to get together, and the lamp of style was lit."[7] In this sense, one of the most complete descriptions of what actually took place during Petalogical Society meetings was provided by Machado de Assis in one of his articles in the series "By Chance" published in the *Diário do Rio de Janeiro* four years after Paula Brito's death. Although lengthy, this extract uniquely evokes the spirit of that society:

> This book [*Lembranças* (Memories), by José Antonio] is a memoir—it is a memoir of the Petalogical Society in its earliest days, Paula Brito's Petalógica—the Procópio Café its day—where all sorts of people gathered, politicians, poets, playwrights, artists, travelers, mere amateurs, friends, and curiosity seekers—where all topics were discussed, from the removal of a

ministry to the pirouette of a fashionable dancer; where everything was debated, from the high C from the chest of [the Italian tenor] Tamberlick to the speeches of the marquess of Paraná, truly neutral ground where a budding writer came across a councilor, where an Italian singer conversed with a former minister.

Reading José Antonio's book makes me nostalgic for the Petalogical Society—not because it contains all the characters in that association; I miss it because it was in the golden age of the original Petalógica that José Antonio's poems were written and the first edition of *Lembranças* was born.

Everyone had their family at home; this was their family away from home—*le ménage en ville*—entering meant taking part in the same supper (the supper here is a metaphor) because the Lycurgus of that republic saw it that way, and that is how everyone who crossed that threshold saw it as well.

Do you want to know the latest news of parliament? You just had to go to the Petalógica. Of the new Italian opera? The new book just published? E★★★'s most recent ball? The most recent play by Macedo or Alencar? The state of the market? Rumors of all sorts? You didn't need to go any further—just go to the Petalógica.

Scattered all over the surface of the city, the petalogicians would come and go there, just passing through, picking up and spreading gossip, analyzing rumors, sniffing out news, all that without taking a minute away from their own business.

Just as conservatives and liberals enjoyed free entry, *lagruistas* and *chartonistas* did so as well; on the same bench, at times, they discussed the superiority of the divas of the day and the advantages of the additional act; the sorbets of José Thomaz and confidential appointments equally warmed people's spirits; it was a veritable *pèle mèle* of all things and all men.[8]

The press revealed few clues as to the identity of those men. *Marmota fluminense* generally used pseudonyms when referring to petalogicians, such as Carijó, Papagaio, and Cubatão.[9] There was also a curious method for admitting new members. For example, a captain in the reserves was such a joker and liar that he merited a recommendation from a petalogician. On one occasion, the military man had told him that after coating the razor-sharp edge of his sword with oil to prevent it from rusting, the following day he found over five hundred severed tongues from mice that had licked the oil during the night.[10] Similarly, for several months, from September 1853 to February 1855, readers of Paula Brito's bi-weekly were able to read, with some inter-

TABLE 10. List of some Petalogicians found in Rio de Janeiro newspapers

Name	Occupation
Antônio Luiz de Sayão[1]	Lawyer (*Almanak Laemmert*, 1855, p. 390)
Virgílio José de Almeida Campos[1]	Clerk of the Orphans' Court (*Almanak Laemmert*, 1855, p. 118)
Joaquim Manuel de Macedo[1]	Writer, physician, first secretary of the IHGB, and teacher of modern, medieval, and Brazilian geography and history at Pedro II Imperial College (*Almanak Laemmert*, 1855, p. 86, 91, 405)
Francisco Pedro de Arbues da Silva Muniz e Abreu[1]	Lawyer and secretary of the Appeals Court of Rio de Janeiro (*Almanak Laemmert*, 1849, p. 75; 1863, p. 162)
Herculano Luiz de Lima[1]	Customs warehouse manager (*Almanak Laemmert*, 1877, p. 248)
João Antonio Gonçalves da Silva[1]	Teacher of ancient and medieval history and geography at Pedro II Imperial College (*Almanak Laemmert*, 1857, p. 104)
João Ribeiro de Carvalho[1]	Possibly a merchant (*Almanak Laemmert*, 1857, p. 501)
Francisco Correia da Conceição[1, 2]	First secretary at the Brazilian Theater Conservatory (*Almanak Laemmert*, 1857, p. 329)
Severiano Rodrigues Martins[1]	Physician, Rua do Cano, no. 68. (*Almanak Laemmert*, 1854, p. 372)
Basílio José de Oliveira Pinto[2]	Definitor in the Confraternity of the Glorious Martyrs St. Garcia and St. George (*Almanak Laemmert*, 1855, p. 341)
João Caetano dos Santos[3]	Director and impresario at the São Pedro de Alcântara Theater (*Almanak Laemmert*, 1855, p. 319)
Antonio Gonçalves Teixeira e Souza[4]	Writer and beginning literacy teacher at the Engenho Velho public school, later appointed clerk of the Business Court (*Almanak Laemmert*, 1855, p. 88; 1856, p. 111)
Constantino Gomes de Souza[4]	Physician (*Almanak Laemmert*, 1862, p. 461)
Laurindo Rebello[4]	Poet (Diário do Rio de Janeiro, 07 Nov. 1860, p. 1)
[Augusto Emílio] Zaluar[4]	Poet and director of the Zaluar College on Rua do Catete, no. 175 (*Almanak Laemmert*, 1854, p. 346)
[Antônio de] Castro Lopes[4]	Physician (*Almanak Laemmert*, 1857, p. 461)
José Antònio [Frederico da Silva][4]	Poet and first officer at the Rio de Janeiro War Arsenal (*Almanak Laemmert*, 1855, p. 233)
[Francisco Duarte] Bracarense[4]	Musician at the Imperial Chapel (*Almanak Laemmert*, 1855, p. 137)
[Joaquim Maria] Machado de Assis[4]	Journalist and librarian of the Brazilian Arcadian Society (*Almanak Laemmert*, 1862, p. 397)
Carlos José do Rosário[5]	Lawyer and second clerk in the accounting division of the Treasury Department (*Almanak Laemmert*, 1859, p. 197)

Name	Occupation
[José Maria da Silva] Paranhos[6]	Future Viscount of Rio Branco; politician; in 1855, Minister of the Navy (*Almanak Laemmert*, 1855, p. 55)
Eusébio de Queirós [Coutinho Matoso da Câmara][6]	Politician, leader of the Conservative Party
Justiniano [José da] Rocha[6]	Politician, journalist, and writer; in 1855, a deputy for Minas Gerais and, in the same year, a professor of "Jus Gentium" at the Military School (*Almanak Laemmert*, 1855, p. 61, 232)

Sources:

1. "Notícias diversas," *Correio mercantil*, 17 Sept. 1859, p. 1 (Thanks to the city's public sanitation company containing a list of some members of the Petalogical Society).
2. "Discurso pronunciado na igreja do Santíssimo Sacramento, no dia 15 de janeiro de 1862, por ocasião da missa e funeral que a sociedade Petalógica mandou celebrar em comemoração a alma do seu finado fundador e sócio o Sr. Francisco de Paula Brito," *Correio mercantil*, 16 Jan. 1862.
3. *Diário do Rio de Janeiro*, 22 Sept. 1863, p. 3 (Announcement of a mass for the soul of João Caetano dos Santos ordered by the Petalogical Society).
4. "O Carnaval," *Gazeta de notícias*, 21 Feb. 1887, pp. 1–2 (Memorial text by Mello Morais Filho about Carnival celebrations in Rio de Janeiro in the mid-1850s).
5. "O Sete de Setembro," *A marmota*, 16 Sept. 1859, p. 1 (Transcript of a chronicle from Revista popular signed Carlos, certainly Carlos José do Rosário, identified as a member of the society).
6. "Herculano Lima," *Gazeta de notícia*, 1 Feb. 1888, p. 1 (Obituary for Herculano Luiz de Lima).

ruptions, *Memória sobre as manias do Mundo da Lua* (Memoir of the manias of the Lunar World), written "in order to obtain the *honorable* title of Member" of the Petalogical Society. It was an anonymous account of a fantastic voyage by the author, his wife, and daughter through the routes of magnetism to the Lunar World. There, with the eye of an ethnographer, the traveler observed the customs of the Lunatics, "weak, bloated, and yellow folk" and watch a play—the comedy *A. B. C. do amor, ou, A escola da roça* (ABC of love, or The country school), which was also published in *Marmota fluminense*.[11]

There are indications that the society had over a hundred members,[12] which corroborates Machado de Assis's report that petalogicians were "scattered all over the surface of the city," However, only the major daily newspapers occasionally make it possible to identify some of those individuals. Consisting of twenty-three names, the list shown in Table 10 is quite short. However, mainly combined with information provided by *Almanak Laemmert*, it gives us an idea of the backgrounds of some of the associates.

Table 10 demonstrates that the society's membership included well-known men from the literary world, such as novelists Joaquim Manuel de

Macedo and Antonio Gonçalves Teixeira e Souza, both of whom were published by Paula Brito, as well as eminent politicians like Eusébio de Queirós and José Maria da Silva Paranhos, Viscount of Rio Branco. However, the Petalogical Society also welcomed doctors, lawyers, civil servants, teachers, actors, and musicians.

In addition to the meetings held at Paula Brito's bookshop, where these men told tall tales and enjoyed a good laugh, there were times when the Petalogical Society engaged in philanthropic activities. This was the case in April 1855, when two enslaved children were manumitted through a subscription among its members.[13] In January 1859, the society organized a benefit at the São Pedro Theater for Filipo Tati, an Italian opera singer who was experiencing serious hardship in Rio de Janeiro.[14] However, in the 1850s the Petalogical Society began playing an increasingly prominent role in the daily life of Rio de Janeiro, particularly in the two most important events in the city's calendar: Carnival and civic festivities commemorating Brazil's Independence.

Regarding Carnival, the Petalogical Society's participation coincided with the ramifications of an official attempt to do away with the traditional Entrudo. According to historian Maria Clementina Pereira Cunha, who studies the samba of Rio de Janeiro, the Entrudo could be summed up as the "custom of getting wet and filthy with wax limes or satsumas filled with scented water, using needles, wooden bowls, tubes, and even bath tubs—every sort of container imaginable that could hold water and be thrown." In addition to the water sports, it involved "the use of talcum powder, 'vermilion,' paint, flour, eggs, and even mud, tar, and fetid liquids, including urine or 'wastewater.'"[15] Like Pedro II, Paula Brito loved the merrymaking that was considered by many to conflict completely with the ideals of civilization that some intended to impose on the Empire of the Tropics. The publisher was so fond of the Entrudo that he must have been seen soaking wet, throwing and being hit by wax limes during the revels. At least, an article published in *Marmota fluminense* after the first police onslaught against those festivities during the 1854 Carnival allows us to form that mental picture.[16]

Paula Brito's carnivalesque side was certainly not unknown to his contemporaries, as he also employed his poetic talents to write lyrics for its songs—*lundus* and *modinhas*. One of them, the *lundu* "A marrequinha" (The little duck), set to music by the maestro Francisco Manuel da Silva, was sold "exclusively" at his bookshop in early August 1853. In a playful tone, the lyrics alluded to the curvaceous lines of young ladies:

The flirtatious eyes
Of the charming young lady
Make me think of
Her lovely little duck

Young lady, have no fear,
Release the duck,
If not I will die,
I will be no more.

If dancing Brazilian style
The young lady moves her body
How she plays by jumping
Her lovely little duck.

Young lady, have no fear, etc.[17]

The 1854 ban on the Entrudo was one of several repressive measures carried out by Alexandre Joaquim de Siqueira, a judge in Vassouras parish who
had become Rio's chief of police in April 1853. The new chief's eagerness
to regulate the city was soon felt by different segments of society. First, by
sellers of lottery tickets, who were forbidden to sell their wares in the streets
of Rio de Janeiro; then, by coachmen, all of whom were supposed to regis-
ter with the police department and undergo tests of aptitude and skill.[18] The
edict that decreed the end of the Entrudo was first published in the press in
January 1854, warning revelers that "anyone who takes part will be fined
four to twelve [thousand réis], and if they cannot pay it, will spend two to
eight days in jail." Slaves caught enjoying themselves could be sentenced to
up to "eight days in jail if their master does not have them punished in the
prison with one hundred lashes." The edict was also clear when ordering
the destruction of all wax limes found by the police.[19]

Some people went to jail during Carnival because they insisted on taking part in the Entrudo.[20] However, opinions differed as to the repressive
measures. Some believed that they were a sign of progress because, as one
journalist remarked, "the masked balls for Carnival were magnificent; from
the barbaric game of limes everyone has gone on to [engage] in the entertainments of civilized countries."[21] Nevertheless, some disagreed: "Our

Entrudo was no good because innocent little oranges gave some profit to [Brazilians]. Then came the foreign masks, the dominoes, and the immoral masked balls."[22] As we have seen, Paula Brito was most certainly a fan of the Entrudo. In *Marmota fluminense*, he lamented the suppression of the revels, observing that he felt a "strong attachment to the Entrudo," and adding, "we feel [this] in our soul, because for us, there is nothing better." The publisher believed that the ban on the Entrudo directly affected the poor residents of the capital: "In Rio de Janeiro, the upper class and middle classes have a surfeit of entertainments; but the poor folk—the people—per se, lead a dog's life; they eat, because they must eat to live; and they sleep because they have nowhere to kill time: aside from that, they are permitted no other enjoyments."[23] However, despite the best efforts of Chief Siqueira and his men, with every passing year it became clear that the Entrudo had not died. To the joy of people like the publisher Paula Brito, the revels had "nine lives."[24]

The city's first major Carnival associations emerged in the void left by the police chief's bans in 1854. This was the case with the Congresso das Sumidades Carnavalescas (Congress of Carnival Luminaries), a society created by a group of young writers and poets linked to the *Correio mercantil*.[25] The Sumidades Carnavalescas' objective was clear: "the enthronement of European carnival . . . whose splendid purple [will drive away] forever the ragged cloak of the cursed Entrudo."[26] During the Carnival of 1855 they paraded opulently through the streets of Rio for the first time, displaying the "sumptuousness and brilliance of the costumes . . . all historical, all with the greatest propriety." Although it failed to exterminate the Entrudo, the Congresso das Sumidades Carnavalescas inspired the creation of the Sociedade União Veneziana (Venetian Union Society), which paraded along similar lines for the first time during the 1857 Carnival.[27]

In 1854, the Petalogical Society planned to present the public with "a triumphal float" the following year, possibly inspired by the innovations promised by the Congresso das Sumidades Carnavalescas. However, despite the enthusiasm of over one hundred of its members,[28] the society did not parade through the streets, instead focusing its activities on the area outside its headquarters on Praça da Constituição. From that time forward, the doors of the Petalogical Society were an obligatory stop for the parades of all the main Carnival associations. These occasions were generally well documented in the newspapers, such as the Carnival of 1857, when the Sociedade União Veneziana and Congresso das Sumidades Carnavalescas stopped there, while "numerous rockets rose in the air amid enthusiastic cries and thunderous applause."[29]

Such congratulations were to a certain extent natural, since many petalogicians belonged to the Congresso das Sumidades Carnavalescas.[30] However, because of the crisis that struck the Dous de Dezembro company that year, the Carnival of 1857 was not the happiest of times for Paula Brito. "Due to lack of money, the heat, the yellow fever [epidemic], and many other circumstances, all of this passed us by," wrote the publisher, who confessed that he had no heart for the festivities: "Because we have not left the house, we find no pleasure in any of these things, for our minds are tirelessly occupied by others."[31] The Petalogical Society halted its activities for a few months after Dous de Dezembro went bankrupt. Its meetings only resumed the following year, after Paula Brito had reopened the bookstore. On September 7, 1858, five months after the resumption of its meetings, the Petalogical Society played a more active role in the civic celebrations of Brazil's Independence.[32]

As Hendrik Kraay indicates in a book on the political ramifications of civic celebrations in Rio de Janeiro, in 1848 the number of national holidays was reduced from seven to three days: March 25, September 7, and December 2. The historian points out that this apparent streamlining was possibly linked to the rise of the Conservative cabinet that marked the beginning of that party's dominance in the ensuing years. Thus, establishing as national celebration days the anniversaries of the Constitution and Brazilian Independence and the Emperor's birthday followed a specific interpretation and political instrumentalization of the festivities.[33] In the case of September 7, between mid-1850 and mid-1860 unofficial celebrations flourished in Rio de Janeiro, organized by civic associations. The first of these, established in 1855, was the Ipiranga Society, which was linked to the Liberal Party and brought together nearly nine hundred members. In 1856 and 1857, the celebrations organized by the Ipiranga Society included nocturnal lighting, bands, fireworks, artillery salutes, parades, and a *Te Deum*. This initiative was such a success that it inspired the creation of similar associations, such as the Sociedade Independência Brasileira (Brazilian Independence Society), Sociedade Festival 7 de Setembro (Seventh of September Festival Society) and Sociedade Independência Juvenil (Young People's Independence Society).[34]

Also inspired by the Ipiranga Society, according to Kraay, the Petalogical Society also played an active role in the Independence Day festivities. Thus, on September 7, 1858, the Rio de Janeiro press reported that the petalogicians

FIGURE 23. Constitution Square shortly after the unveiling of an
equestrian statue of Pedro I in 1862

had gathered in "a permanent session at their headquarters in Largo da Constituição, which was brilliantly lit and adorned with Brazilian flags, flowers,
patriotic couplets, etc."[35] The following year, the society attracted attention
by lighting its headquarters entirely with gas lamps, according to a corre-
spondent from Rio Grande do Sul who was passing through the city.[36] Not
only that, but the petalogicians illuminated the entire Praça da Constituição
in the same fashion. This was a somewhat expensive gesture that was nevertheless feasible thanks to the contributions that poured in from every part
of Rio de Janeiro, including Quinta da Boa Vista, the imperial palace, from
the purses of Pedro II and Empress Teresa Christina. Some criticized the fact
that Paula Brito and company should have importuned their majesties with
a request for money for the lighting project. Thus, in the columns of *Correio mercantil*, a reader signing himself Epaminondas registered this protest:

> We will be permitted to criticize the procedure of the worthy members of
> the Petalogical society when they asked Their Imperial Majesties for a finan-

cial contribution to the festivities. . . . Church feasts, rockets, and cherry bombs are in fashion [illegible], spending money on that and abandoning the unfortunate who are in such need of the aid of others.[37]

On the other hand, a columnist for *Revista popular*, Carlos José do Rosário, who has been identified as a petalogician, defended the society in one of his fortnightly columns: "With limited resources, it first turned to it friends to help it with its efforts to illuminate Praça da Constituição. . . . The Petalogical Society has performed a blameless act, highly praiseworthy and unmerited [*sic*] of any criticism."[38]

After Paula Brito's death, the Petalogical society also took part in festivities such as the unveiling of the controversial equestrian statue of Pedro I in Praça da Constituição. It was controversial because it was not just a decorative monument portraying the first emperor mounted on a handsome steed and holding the constitution in his hand, surrounded by Amerindians symbolizing Brazil's main rivers. Above all, the statue was a specific interpretation of the nation's history, according to which its independence was viewed as the work of Pedro I and the constitution a mere concession from that monarch. Therefore, the active participation of Conservatives in the construction of that monument and the staunch opposition of the Liberals regarding its political significance set the tone for the intense debate in the newspapers that marked the unveiling of the statue.[39]

Hewing closely to the political leanings of its departed founder, the Petalogical Society sided with the Conservatives by celebrating the monument. In fact, its members lavished praise on the French sculptor Louis Rochet. In the evening of March 22, 1862, the petalogicians were invited to gather outside the society's headquarters "to attend the event they intend to hold on that same day for Mr. Rochet, for his magnificent work on the equestrian statue." On that occasion, when the anthem of the arts was sung and Eusébio de Queirós, the president of the committee charged with commissioning the monument, gave a speech, Rochet was presented with a bust of himself sculpted by Chaves Pinheiro. Shortly thereafter, on April 1, the Frenchman received the title of honorary member of the Petalogical Society.[40]

Nevertheless, although the Petalogical Society had inspired the creation of other associations, such as the Palestra Fluminense Society in Rio de Janeiro and the Petalogical Societies of Niterói and Pernambuco,[41] all indications are that the organization founded by Paula Brito did not live on for many years after his death. In *Diário do Rio de Janeiro*, Machado de Assis once again reported on the Petalogical Society's participation in celebrations of Independence in 1864, the year that it ordered masses for its founder's soul.[42] Soon, references to it became increasingly scarce until they disappeared entirely. The society's existence ended up being intertwined with that of Paula Brito, making them inextricably associated elements.[43]

However, the Petalogical Society's activities were not limited to lively sessions, carnivals, civic festivities, and occasional philanthropy. As we have seen, if political alliances were vital to the publisher's business, the society was no less important. "So, you see, my friend, that this useful institution will have produced no small number of benefits," Paula Brito observed in 1853. "It gives rise to patrons, projects, employees, jobs, everything, in short, that it, those who turn to it, or those who take part in it could want."[44] In fact, Paula Brito turned to the Petalogical Society as early as October 1860 to carry out another publishing venture, the last in his lifetime: the Auxiliary Fund for Dramatic and Musical Compositions.

CHAPTER 17

Literary Mutualism

I N THE MID-NINETEENTH century, plays were such popular reading
material that the publication of comedies, dramas, farces, and librettos made many publishers rich, as the successful careers of the brothers
Michel and Calman Lévy in France exemplify. Michel Lévy had a background in theater and was well aware that the audience was eager to read
the latest hits presented on Parisian stages.[1] A similar phenomenon was also
occurring in Brazil, which was attested by the deputy for São Paulo when he
submitted a bill to the Chamber of Deputies aimed at protecting the rights
of the authors of those works: "The theater, Mr. President, [is] generally
viewed as the literary genre that the public most enjoys."[2] Its popularity
could also be gauged by the contents of publisher Paula Brito's catalogs.

According to the list of books for sale that was published in *A marmota*
after the bookshop reopened on Praça da Constituição,[3] the reading public of Rio de Janeiro had a marked preference for plays and opera librettos.
Martins Pena's comedies sold for 600 réis, and he was undoubtedly a best-
selling author. The location of Paula Brito's shop was also a factor—it was
just a few steps away from the São Pedro Theater, whose director was the
actor and Petalogical Society member João Caetano dos Santos. The foot
traffic in the shop could be tremendous on show days. According to Jean-

Yves Mollier, in his analysis of the situation in France, "The opening of a comedy, of a drama, was never planned without the sale of the printed text that same evening, in a room in the theater or somewhere in the vicinity."[4] Paula Brito was also well aware of what was going in Rio's other theaters. A good example in this regard is the story of the publication of Joaquim Manuel de Macedo's play *Luxo e vaidade* (Luxury and vanity), in 1860. Staged for the first time on September 23 at the Ginásio Dramático Theater by the newly founded National Theater Company, the play was considered the "rebirth of the Ginásio," the home of the "school of realism" in Rio de Janeiro, which had been struggling since the middle of 1858. In the weeks following the opening of the play, Paula Brito worked hard to gather subscriptions for the publication of *Luxo e vaidade* while publicizing the growing box-office and critical success it gained with each performance.[5]

A total of eight hundred subscriptions were raised, and the "List of Subscribers" and "Supplementary List of Subscribers" published as an appendix to that volume demonstrate that the play was a huge success. The lists also indicate that this sales method also included wholesalers, as other booksellers and traders subscribed for considerable numbers of copies. Antonio José Gonçalves Guimarães, a bookseller-printer located at Rua do Sabão, subscribed for fifty copies, the same number shown for Henrique Laemmert, the owner of the Livraria Universal (Universal Bookstore). Domingos José Gonçalves Brandão, in turn, subscribed for one hundred copies, while José Martins Alves, an agent of the *Correio mercantil* in Bahia, subscribed for forty, certainly with a view to selling them in that province.[6]

Similarly, Paula Brito also purchased the rights to plays originally published in Lisbon. As soon as his bookstore reopened in 1857, the publisher became a representative of Teatro Moderno (Modern Theater), a "collection of dramatic works performed to public acclaim in national theaters" in Portugal.[7]

Paula Brito was aware of the keen interest in reading plays in Rio de Janeiro and other provinces. Thus, in October 1860, it was none other than Joaquim Manuel de Macedo, the author of *Luxo e vaidade* and other plays and novels published by Paula Brito, who first mentioned the publisher's new venture in a column published in *Jornal do commercio*.[8] According to Macedo, Paula Brito intended to "revive" an idea set out in 1856 in the articles of association of the Dous de Dezembro literary publishing house. The aim of the new plan, which Macedo called an "Auxiliary Fund for Literature" was to publish plays "until its funds reach an amount that permits operations of broader scope." Naturally interested in financing the project, Rio de Janeiro's theater impresarios and companies mobilized to help Paula Brito. Macedo wrote that the National Theater Society and the director of the São Pedro Theater immediately offered to hold benefits to raise funds for the project. All told—according to the columnist's estimate—their efforts produced the tidy sum of 3 million réis. Macedo also observed that the project would create a system of awards to provide incentives for Brazilian playwrights. Finally, he explained that, this time, Paula Brito was not alone, because he had entrusted the drafting of the articles of association to the Petalogical Society. "Who would have thought that the famous Petalogical Society would be involved in work that belies its name! The society of fabrications coming up with truths!"[9]

When quoting Macedo's article in *A marmota*, Paula Brito commented that he had been mulling over the idea for over a decade. Indeed, the first articles of association of the failed Dous de Dezembro company expressed the publisher's desire to aid the advancement of literature throughout the Empire. Despite being deferred several times, the plan finally had a chance of becoming a reality. Perhaps that is why, this time, Paula Brito called on the Petalogical Society to help him, justifying this decision on two grounds:

1. To give the Petalogical Society, which I have created, a means of entertainment and recreation in reading and judging dramatic plays, thus wishing for a group of young men, many of whom are skilled and well-educated, from the best classes in society, to do more than they have done in the past, belying its name with its efforts on behalf of dramatic and musical works.
2. Realizing the benefit that I requested and the other, which was liberally offered to me, through a commission or commissions, of which I will be part, ensuring that everything is so well and clearly carried out that the public is not unaware of the least thing about it.[10]

While the first paragraph makes it clear that the Petalogical Society was directly involved in drafting the Fund's articles of association, the second says little about the "benefit" that would finance the project. Paula Brito must have expected some government funding. However, the unofficial nature of the Petalogical Society presented an obstacle, as Law no. 1083 of August 22, 1860, had recently been enacted to regulate all associations active in the Empire, irrespective of their nature. For a society to operate officially, its articles of association had to be approved by the State Council.

Therefore, the association that met informally at Paula Brito's bookshop and took part in Rio de Janeiro's Carnivals and civic festivities would have to be regulated. When he presented the readers of *A marmota* with the articles of association of the Auxiliary Fund for Dramatic and Musical Works (not the Auxiliary Fund for Literature, as Macedo had called it), Paula Brito explained that there were complications regarding the Petalogical Society that prevented it from running the project. Nevertheless, to streamline the process of establishing the Fund, the publisher stated that he had submitted the articles of association to the Imperial Secretary of State for Business and was awaiting the decision of the State Council.[11]

The document's nineteen articles regulated the operations of the Auxiliary Fund, stating that its main objective was to raise and manage funds that would be used to reward and finance the production of Brazilian works:

> Art. 1. A prize is hereby created, which for now will be from 200 to 600 [thousand réis], to be bestowed on the best dramatic or musical work, according to its merit.
> Art. 2. The awarded works will remain the property of the Society, but their authors will be entitled to 10 percent of any net benefit that may be derived from them, whether [from] renting, selling or printing them.[12]

The Auxiliary Fund sought to focus on the dual use of a dramatic play—that is, staged performances and publication in book form. Other organizations whose articles of association were analyzed by the State Council during the same period also proposed financing publications. The Gabinete Português de Leitura (Portuguese Reading Library) of Maranhão, for example, stated among its objectives: "When the interests of Association so permit, collecting worthy works in the Portuguese language, reprinting rare books and publishing interesting manuscripts in the same language."[13] In its turn, the Grêmio Literário Português (Portuguese Literary Guild) of Rio de Janeiro intended to "advance the development of letters as much as possible through publications produced by the institution," particularly memoirs, biographies, poetry, and "small articles in prose" collected annually in a French *in-quarto* volume of up to three hundred pages. However, the guild's articles of association did not allow the funds to be used to finance the publication of political tracts, "novels in general," "light comedies," and translations.[14]

In the end, by seeking to finance the staging and publication of plays, the Auxiliary Fund was proposing a kind of literary mutualism. As historians have pointed out, the purpose of mutual aid societies was to defend the interests of workers, mainly through material aid, the promotion of better working conditions, and the education of their associates.[15] If they could not make a living from their writings, authors who failed to obtain a position in the civil service would certainly have struggled in the nineteenth century. From the humble role of clerk, as was the case with Teixeira e Souza, to the highest diplomatic posts, as was the case with Gonçalves de Magalhães, joining the ranks of the imperial bureaucracy was a matter of survival for the vast majority of Brazil's poets, playwrights, and novelists.[16] Thus, while far from solving the problem, the Auxiliary Fund for Dramatic and Musical Works was an alternative form of remuneration for writers, in this case playwrights who penned dramas and comedies. Even if they surrendered ownership of their work to the Fund, the selected authors could make a few thousand réis from the products of their quills. In fact, by all accounts, everyone stood to gain, because the publisher certainly had his eye on a highly lucrative market.

Unfortunately, in early February 1861, the State Council rejected the Fund's articles of association. The counselors who examined the documents— the Viscount of Sapucaí, the Marquess of Olinda, and José Antônio Pimenta Bueno—concluded that the entity was not an association: "This Session does not see any association whose articles are to be examined, whether or not to be approved; it sees an individual organizing a regulation for its intended purpose, not to govern an association." If by chance there was a company behind the Fund and it was "legitimately constituted," its articles of association would have to be redrafted. Otherwise Paula Brito should "request its incorporation in accordance with the Laws and Decrees governing the matter."[17] A few days later, the *Diário do Rio de Janeiro* reported that the "company in favor of literature" conceived by Paula Brito had not been approved "because it is incorporated into the Petalogical Society."[18]

Paula Brito died a few months later. Due to lack of time or lack of enthusiasm, he set aside the task of reorganizing the Petalogical Society in accordance with the laws governing associations. In any case, his failed attempt to create the Auxiliary Fund for Dramatic and Musical Works demonstrates the publisher's interest in promoting Brazilian literature and its authors while trying to make a small profit. The way relations between the publisher and the authors took place in practice, going beyond the unrealized projects, is the subject of the following chapter.

CHAPTER 18

The Publisher and His Authors

T HE SON OF a wealthy Portuguese merchant based in Barra de São João, on the north coast of Rio de Janeiro province, Casimiro de Abreu spent over three years in Portugal with a view to improving his business skills. His father, José Joaquim Marques de Abreu, spared no effort to turn his son into a top-notch trader. However, much to José Joaquim's chagrin, young Casimiro's talents lay more in poetry than in commerce. While in Portugal, he published some poems in literary magazines. In January 1856, the company based at the Dom Fernando Theater in Lisbon staged *Camões e o Jaú* (Camoens and the Javanese), a one-act play by Casimiro de Abreu that was published by the Panorama Press a few months later. On that occasion, the contract between Casimiro and the Portuguese publisher stated the following:

I, the undersigned, hereby declare that I have contracted with Mr. Antonio José Fernandes Lopes, publisher and established proprietor with a book store on Rua Aurea, no. 227 and 228, to reprint my verses, which will be entitled *Primaveras* [Spring], of the ones that I already have collected and others that I will collect in Rio de Janeiro, where I intend to print the first edition to present to my friends; and the said Mr. Lopes [will] reprint as many editions as he pleases, but on condition that it will be two years from the date of that first edition I intend to publish in Rio; furthermore, he may also include in the reprints that are to be made the poetry written by me that has been published in his literary journals, *Panorama*, and *Ilustração Luso-Brasileira, which have been bought and paid for and belong to him now and in perpetuity*, and my original one-act play entitled "Camões e o Jaú" for which I sell the rights to him and for which I have received payment on this date. And because we have signed this contract, I am obliged not to contract with anyone else regarding the reprinting of these works, nor to reprint them on my own, subjecting me to the laws of this and my own country; furthermore, Mr. Lopes is obliged to deliver in Lisbon to me or by my order, one hundred bound copies of the abovementioned *Primaveras* for each of the reprints he publishes, which copies represent the value of the sale and assignment [of rights] I made to him. Lisbon, July 12, 1856. Casimiro d'Abreu.[1]

When he arrived in Rio de Janeiro, Casimiro's baggage contained a published book and another that had been previously contracted with a publisher. Nevertheless, the edition of *Primaveras* published in Rio de Janeiro by Paula Brito was far from being just a gift for friends, and can be considered a commercial edition, sold by subscription and over the counter in the city's bookshops. There is strong evidence that Casimiro had cheated the Portuguese publisher, because after the poet's death, his mother, Luíza Joaquina das Neves, went to court over the matter.[2]

Upon his return to Rio, at his father's insistence Casimiro went to work as a clerk at Câmara, Cabral & Costa, which owned tapioca, gum, arrowroot, and grain stores at two addresses in the city.[3] However, the clerk insisted on remaining a poet, and before long Casimiro's verses began appearing in the newspapers and journals of Rio de Janeiro. As early as April 1858, he confirmed to Francisco do Couto Sousa Júnior, an old school friend, that he intended to publish a collection in book form:

– Rio de Janeiro April 1, 1858 –

Dear [friend] –

Could you please, and if it is not too much trouble, send me the issue of the *Popular* that contained "Virgem loura" [Blonde virgin] because I have lost the manuscript and do not know in which issue of the [*Correio*] *Mercantil* it came out.

I want to go on arranging and amending all my foolish blunders, as I am getting ready, in January, on my birthday, to bring to light a volume of poetry and then . . . who knows? You should prepare yourself as well, because I want subscriptions; but we have plenty of time, that business will start in September or October—you know very well that I do not work at full throttle.

Continue holding me in your esteem and believing that I am – Your sincere friend –

Casimiro JM. d'Abreu[4]

The copious correspondence between the poet and Sousa Júnior, who lived in Porto das Caixas, Rio de Janeiro province, shows that Casimiro moved heaven and earth to see his poetry published in book form. In late April, the poet confessed to his friend that he was starting to cut back on the publication of his verses in the press because, after all, "having to publish [them in] a book, one must not show them all in the newspapers."[5] Soon afterwards, in July, when he heard that Gonçalves Dias had just arrived on the latest British packet steamer to dock in Rio, Casimiro wrote that he intended to ask the celebrated poet for "a critical review—of my book of poetry." In the same letter, Casimiro revealed that he wanted it to be a small volume so that "all my verses are not included, which I will reserve for another book, since many poems are unfinished or require revision."[6]

It was most likely during this period that he engaged the services of Paula Brito to print the book. The publication was originally supposed to be financed through subscriptions. To a point, that method was a sound one, because by relying on a large number of loyal subscribers, he could, for example, print enough books to avoid remaindering a large number of copies. The subscription system also indicates that, wary of the risks, publishers refused to cover the full cost of publishing some titles, even if they were the "songs of a young poet whose heart is beginning to awake . . . like nature's smiles in spring," according to the *Correio mercantil*, in an article reporting that Casimiro was preparing "a posy of his loveliest productions, which will be published under the title of *Primaveras*. Subscriptions are accepted at the address of the publisher, Mr. Paula Brito."[7] Thrilled by the news he had read the day before, Casimiro once again wrote to his friend Francisco:

– Rio – July 13 – 1858

Mon cher –

– Yesterday in the miscellaneous news [section] the *Mercantil* made the grand
announcement that subscriptions are available for my poetry—I beg you
also to announce, quite simply, that subscriptions are being accepted at the
office of the *Popular*, and in a few days I will send you some lists. By the way,
I want to know what you think about including my portrait in the volume:
should I do it or not? I think not, and if the poetry of Teixeira de Melo (very
close to being published) does not contain one, I will not be so foolish as to
put one in mine—I recommend reading the book by Teixeira de Melo that
it will be entitled—*Sonhos e sombras* [Dreams and shadows]—and I think it
will be the best thing to come out; I have never seen lovelier poetry.
  – Goodbye, *I* . . . give *you* a hug *and I* am, *as allways* [*sic*]

Your dear friend,
Casimiro Abreu[8]

In late July, subscriptions for *Primaveras* were sold in Rio and the out-
lying area. Casimiro sent lists to Francisco in Porto das Caixas, entrusting
him personally with collecting names at the Military School, the Naval
Academy, and the Medical School of Rio de Janeiro—"because I want to
be read by the lads." A certain "Freitinhas" must have sent subscriptions
from Queimados and Cantagalo, which Casimiro added up hopefully: "I am
firmly convinced that I will cover the printing costs, which is my desire."[9]
However, despite the efforts of the poet and his friends, they failed to raise
enough money to publish the book. Apparently, Paula Brito would not
print a single verse without first seeing the color of the thousands of réis
agreed for publishing the work.

  The money eventually came from the pockets of the poet's father.[10] However, Mr. Marques de Abreu did not finance the book without setting some
pre-conditions, which made Casimiro very unhappy: "He wrote to my masters' business, saying that if they think this will make me do my work better,
they can provide me with the necessary amount."[11] José Joaquim had little
interest in his son's poetic tendencies; what he really wanted was to see Casimiro do well at his job. To be sure, from the perspective of a Portuguese man
who made his fortune by trading in lumber, leaving more than 150,000,000

réis in his will,[12] *Primaveras* was nothing but a youthful whim. A whim that, to Casimiro's despair, was slow to be fulfilled. He wrote to his friend, "No news about my book yet!" And he continued, "Paula Brito says it will be ready in June, but I believe it won't even [come out] by the end of the year; the man cozens me and I endure it all with my usual negligence."[13] Whether Paula Brito was cozening him or not, we do know that *Primaveras* only came out in September in a "clearly printed paper edition on Holland paper."[14]

Although Paula Brito helped Casimiro distribute some copies, possibly to those who had paid for subscriptions at his bookshop, the poet's letters show that he made strenuous efforts to ensure that his book reached the other subscribers. In October, for example, Casimiro sent thirty copies to Sousa Júnior, recommending to his friend that, if any were left over, he should send them to Nova Friburgo, "in the care of Freitinhas," or sell them at the price set by Paula Brito.[15] In the following weeks, *Primaveras* won critical acclaim, although it did not sell well enough to cover the cost of publication.[16] Casimiro died a year after the book was released, at the age of twenty-one, six months after his father's death. When dictating his will, afflicted with an advanced stage of tuberculosis, the poet recalled his debt to Paula Brito: "I do not recall the total amount, [being] the remainder for the printing of my poetry."[17]

Paula Brito had only printed and distributed Casimiro de Abreu's book, leaving the selection of the works published and, more importantly, the cost of publication, to the poet himself. However, in other cases, Paula Brito purchased manuscripts and paid for the publication of original works at his own expense and risk. Therefore, in addition to striving to set up a large-scale press, the publisher was also looking to finance the publication of Brazilian authors. In 1855, the articles of association of the Dous de Dezembro literary publishing house clearly included the "protection . . . of authors by rewarding their works [and] purchasing their manuscripts." For that purpose, it earmarked the fabulous sum of 20,000,000 réis "to be used as the association sees fit, both in its interests and in the interests of literature, authors, and translators."[18]

Although I have not been able to find contracts between Paula Brito and his authors similar to the existing agreements of the publisher Baptiste Louis Garnier,[19] articles in the literary section of *Marmota fluminense* indicate that Paula Brito was purchasing the rights to publish literary works. The novel *Maria, ou, A menina roubada* (Maria, or, The kidnapped girl), by Teixeira e Sousa, which was initially serialized in September 1852, was preceded by a note stating that "To engage all people of different tastes in reading our

TABLE 11. Selection of works by Joaquim Manuel de Macedo published between 1844 and 1861

Title	Genre	Publisher
Considerações sobre a nostalgia[1, 3]	Thesis	Tipografia Imparcial de Francisco de Paula Brito, 1844
A moreninha[1]	Novel	Tipografia Franceza, 1844
		Tipografia Americana de I. P. da Costa, 1845
O moço loiro[1]	Novel	Tipografia de Carlos Haring, 1845
Rosa[3]	Novel	Tipografia do Arquivo Médico Brasileiro, 1849
Vicentina[3]	Novel	Empresa Tipográfica Dous de Dezembro, de Paula Brito, 1854
O forasteiro[2]	Novel	Tipografia de Paula Brito, 1855
Os romances da semana[3]	Novel	J. M. Nunes Garcia, 1861
A carteira do meu tio[3]	Novel	Empresa Tipográfica Dous de Dezembro, Paula Brito, 1855
O fantasma branco[2]	Play	Empresa Tipográfica Dous de Dezembro, 1856
O primo da Califórnia[3]	Play	Tipografia de Francisco de Paula Brito, 1855
Luxo e vaidade[1, 2, 3]	Play	Tipografia de Francisco de Paula Brito, 1860
A nebulosa[1, 3]	Poetry	Tipografia Imp. e Const de J. Villeneuve e C., 1857

Source:
[A] Catálogo da Biblioteca Brasiliana USP, www.brasiliana.usp.br
[B] José de Paula Ramos Jr., Marisa Midori Deaecto, and Plinio Martins Filho, eds., *Paula Brito: Editor, Poeta e Artífice das Letras*, 2010.
[C] Catálogo de Obras Raras da Biblioteca Nacional do Rio de Janeiro, catcrd.bn.br.

newspaper, *we have just hired one of our novelists*, whose writing is already known to the public for many and varied works."[20] When the first install-ment of the novel came out in *Marmota fluminense*, another note informed its readers that "Our endeavor, from today onwards, will be to encourage Brazilian talent, offering advantages to those who devote themselves to the belles-lettres, and prove themselves worthy of public praise and every sac-rifice we can possibly make."[21] In addition to Teixeira e Sousa's novel, the publisher's first literary venture, Paula Brito also published a considerable number of works by Joaquim Manuel de Macedo.

The publisher once wrote in *Marmota* that "Dr. Joaquim Manuel de Macedo . . . has insisted on having a rapport with me since the time when, as a Latin student, he was writing *Odes ao Barata* (Odes to Barata) in 1832, in the village of Itaboraí." From then on, he had taken pride in that associa-tion. "He always takes pleasure in appreciating my ideas, perhaps because he has as yet nothing to regret, and God forbid [he should]."[22] A selection of thirteen of Macedo's works published between 1844 and 1861, the year of Paula Brito's death, indicates that the two men were indeed very close.

Table 11 shows that seven of the thirteen works selected were published by Paula Brito, which suggests that although the publisher and the author may have disagreed on politics, that was not a problem where publishing was concerned. Macedo was elected provincial deputy and general deputy for the Liberal Party in several legislatures, and *A carteira do meu tio* (My uncle's wallet), a work published by the Conservative Paula Brito in serialized and book form, was a frontal attack on the conciliation of political parties backed by the Conservatives. Therefore, it was not unreasonable for the advertisements published in the press to describe it as "opposition satire."[23] However, the two men's conflicting ideologies may have been overcome by Macedo's success with the reading public. His early novels were published by a different press, perhaps at his own expense. However, between 1854 and 1856, five books came out with Dous de Dezembro's imprint. In this regard, the publication of *Vicentina* is a good example. The original novel was originally published in installments in *Marmota fluminense* in March 1854.[24] Meanwhile, the book version was ready for publication, as Paula Brito offered it to the company's shareholders as a premium.[25] The following year, when *A carteira do meu tio* was first serialized in *Marmota fluminense*, Paula Brito published an article stating that the "advancement of literature" in many cases required the "sacrifice of profits" for the newspaper:

> For the advancement of literature, the editorial team is undoubtedly striving to obtain important original works from Brazilian pens, and is happy to be able to start today the lovely joco-serious story of *A carteira de meu tio*, in addition to a new novel from Dr. Macedo, which may begin on Tuesday.
>
> The editors sacrifice all *Marmota*'s profits to the present day in order to reach the number of subscribers it wants to have in the future, which it hopes to achieve, based on its six years of existence, and seeing that every year it receives valuable contingents of new subscriptions from the public.[26]

The records do not show the retail price of these "important original works from Brazilian pens." Even so, the announcement indicates that "Brazilian literature" was a major draw for the newspaper, and Paula Brito spared no effort to publish it. However, sometimes a great deal of effort was not required to provide readers and subscribers with such delights. For example, in 1859, Bruno Seabra, a literato from Paraná who was living in Rio de Janeiro, became seriously ill. Stricken with violent fevers, the young man urgently needed money to pay his debts, including what he owed to the pharmacist who supplied him with medicine. Amid all these difficulties, he wrote a novel and sought out Paula Brito, who purchased the manuscript—on what terms we do not know. In any case, according to the author of the account originally published in the newspaper *A regeneração*, "with the income from *Paulo*, the poet was able to pay his debts, considering himself very fortunate at a time when his recovery was very much in doubt."[27]

Paulo, Bruno Seabra's novel, followed the same course as the works of Joaquim Manuel de Macedo—it was serialized in *Marmota* before being published in book form.[28] Thus, it is clear that owning a literary journal was of vital importance for nineteenth-century publishers, and not just in Rio de Janeiro. By the early 1850s, the US publishing market was absorbing novels with print runs in the hundreds of thousands, such as Harriet Beecher Stowe's *Uncle Tom's Cabin* and *The Wide, Wide World*, by Susan Warner. However, literary magazines run by publishers, such as *Putnam's Monthly*, later *Putnam's Magazine*, and *Harper's Monthly* continued to play a decisive role in that market. Similarly, according to Mollier, Louis Hachette's *Journal pour tous*, which reached an impressive print run of seventy-five thousand, was a "laboratory for author recruitment." The same thing happened in Britain with *Blackwood's Magazine*, published since 1817.[29]

This is highly significant because Paula Brito, who was aware of the value of a publication like *A marmota*, had a serious falling-out with the newspaper's founder, Próspero Diniz, who was born in the province of Bahia. The bi-weekly, which sometimes had print runs of more than one thousand copies,[30] went through three different stages. During the first stage, from September 1849 to March 1852, it was called *Marmota na Corte* and belonged to Próspero Diniz, who was introduced to Paula Brito by Manuel de Araújo Porto-Alegre shortly after Diniz's arrival from Bahia. Paula Brito himself tells us how their meeting came about:

> Having arrived in [Rio], Mr. Próspero Diniz in September 1849 came to my house and, wanting to publish a newspaper, recalled the titles *Luneta*, *Marmota* (Groundhog), *Marmota fluminense*, and I don't know what else; it was my opinion that Mr. [Diniz] should continue writing under the title of his newspaper in Bahia—*Marmota*—so we agreed that a new newspaper should be called *Marmota na Corte* (Marmota in Rio), a recollection that was later corroborated by Mr. Porto-Alegre, the first person who told me about Mr. [Diniz].[31]

The honeymoon with the Bahian writer was short-lived, and money was at the root of their troubles. "After just one issue was published, Mr. [Diniz] demanded that I give him 60,000 réis per month; a few days later he wanted 80,000 réis, and finally 100,000 réis, because the newspaper was so influential and was selling well," explained Paula Brito, who thought it absurd "to pay 100,000 réis per month to an employee for a few *articles* he wrote *without being responsible for anything else* [!]"³² Their problems worsened when Diniz decided to return to his home province in December 1850, promising to continue collaborating with the newspaper, whose title he still owned. After calculating the wages owed, Paula Brito paid him for "that month up to the present day." At first, Diniz kept his promise, but to Paula Brito's indignation, he then launched a newspaper entitled *Verdadeira Marmota de Próspero Diniz* (Próspero Diniz's Real Marmota). Soon afterwards, after moving to Recife, Pernambuco, he started up *A marmota pernambucana*. Meanwhile, just as Diniz was starting up *Marmotas* in the northern part of the Empire, Paula Brito was still editing and printing *A marmota na corte*, whose readership was growing steadily.³³

In September 1851, when Dous de Dezembro was just getting started, the Bahian newspaper editor returned to Rio de Janeiro and sought Paula Brito out to receive the money he was owed. At the time, the publisher only wanted to pay him for the original articles Diniz had submitted while he was away. But the Bahian wanted more. Justifying his demands with the excuse that the money would go to his mother, Diniz managed to get Paula Brito to pay him half the newspaper's profits—"about 360,000 and some réis"—which the publisher rounded up to 400,000 réis. ³⁴ Paula Brito was clearly angry with the journalist, but even so, he entered into a "new agreement" with him:

> I reached a new agreement with Mr. [Diniz], who wanted the same 100 [thousand] réis he had received in 1849, [which] I did not want to give him because the circumstances had changed, and I was sure that *A marmota* would no longer sell as well as it had back then. If this is what transpired, how can Mr. Diniz say that he created and then handed over *Marmota* to me, which I took over to make a fortune? . . . Make a fortune from *Marmota*! . . . What an idea!³⁵

Paula Brito might not have been getting rich from *Marmota*, but he was still unwilling to give it up. The following extract is wonderful because, in addition to showing that the publisher was furious about Diniz's behavior, it gives us a glimpse into the working relations between Paula Brito and the journalists in his employ:

> Mr. [Diniz] started writing in September, and that month I paid him 90,000 réis for the news of his arrival. I opened a 2,000 réis subscription for four months to see if I could get more advantageous entries; But Mr. [Diniz's] influence was waning, like all things in this world, so I set him a monthly fee of 60,000. Mr. [Diniz] became ill, and in that time he wrote nothing until the end of January (as can be seen from his article on his sufferings); I always paid him 60,000 réis, taking it to his home, while he was bedridden; but once Mr. [Diniz] had recovered, and seeing that he could not, or would not write, I told him in March that he would be dismissed from the editorial staff at the end of the month if he carried on with such negligence; Mr. [Diniz] then began writing, and indeed, in April, he wrote a few articles (always one to two pages); but seeing that, despite these much-publicized articles, *A marmota* was not selling, and to support it I was obliged to pay (as I have always paid) several other employees (as well as those who honor me their manuscripts), and publishing songs, fashion plates, etc., which is what the readers like most these days; I told Mr. [Diniz] that he was no longer part of the editorial staff, and accordingly I paid him 60,000 réis for April, for which he issued a receipt, as usual.[36]

Considering the amounts that Próspero Diniz received, the monthly wage of a *Marmota* employee must have been about 60,000 réis in 1852. That year, an *arroba* (about 14.7 kilos) of rice cost 1,000 réis, a bushel of beans cost 2,050 réis, and an *arroba* of beef jerky cost 2,800 réis.[37] From the point of view of a basic diet, such wages might have been satisfactory. However, in Diniz's case, the outcome was not at all amicable. The former editor saw himself as the owner of the newspaper's name, which Paula Brito contested, claiming that there were several papers in the Empire with the same name. Próspero Diniz also accused Paula Brito of "mutilating" his articles, and Paula Brito concurred, as he considered Diniz's writing offensive.[38] After Próspero Diniz's departure from the newspaper in late March 1852, Paula Brito became the sole owner of *A marmota da corte*. He renamed it *Marmota fluminense: Jornal de modas e variedades* (Rio de Janeiro province Marmota: Newspaper of fashion and varieties) and continued publishing it under that title until late June 1857, when, after Dous de Dezembro went bankrupt, it changed its name to *A marmota*.

Active for more than a decade, it is no exaggeration to say that *A marmota*'s longevity was a major feat in the history of the nineteenth-century Brazilian press. The loyal subscribers who ensured its success included Miguel Archanjo Galvão, a civil servant who made his career in the Ministry of Finance. According to receipts found among manuscripts in Brazil's National Library, dated between 1859 and 1861, when he was a clerk, Galvão paid his subscription for the biweekly publication religiously.[39] In 1861, the "periodical published by the learned Mr. Francisco de Paula Brito, the artist *par excellence*," was recommended by A. C. Azevedo Coimbra as being highly beneficial reading for Brazilian families. In the same article, he named the "skilled pens" of its collaborators: "of the distinguished poet Antônio Gonçalves Teixeira e Sousa; of the erudite publicist, Dr. Justiniano José da Rocha; of the learned Moreira de Azevedo; of the talented poet, Bruno Seabra, and Messrs. Machado de Assis, Bráulio Cordeiro, José Morais e Silva, Castanheda Júnior, Leo Junius, Rodrigues Proença, and other young men of recognized talent."[40] However, this Pleiad did not include an author who already enjoyed considerable prestige. Although he lived near Paula Brito's bookshop, residing at no. 73, Praça da Constituição, it took some time for the two men to form a closer relationship. The reason for that was chiefly political, and the author in question was José de Alencar.

Alencar wrote his first novels, as well as *Cartas sobre a Confederação dos Tamoios* (Letters on the Tamoio Confederation), when he was editor-in-chief of the *Diário do Rio de Janeiro*. Indeed, after being published in that newspaper's serialized novels section, they were published in book form by the newspaper's press, Empresa Tipográfica do Diário. Alencar's procedure of engaging in literary polemics, as in the case of *Cartas,* as well as producing prose fiction, such as *A viuvinha* (The little widow) and *O guarani*, to boost the newspaper's circulation was not unfamiliar to Paula Brito, and possibly any other newspaper editor of that time. However, in his literary autobiography, Alencar wrote that he had sold the publishing rights for one thousand copies of *O guarani* to "the Brandão bookshop" for 1,400,000 réis.[41] He could have sold them to his neighbor Paula Brito, following the example of Joaquim Manuel de Macedo, a recognized author whom Alencar himself had praised. Why he chose not to may be an interesting question to pose.

José de Alencar and Paula Brito were never openly at war, unlike, for example, the dispute between the publisher and Próspero Diniz over ownership of *A marmota*. However, as Paula Brito wrote to Alencar in November

TABLE 12. Selected works by José de Alencar published between 1856 and 1861

Title	Genre	Imprint
Cartas sobre a Confederação dos Tamoios [1]	Polemic	Empresa Tipográfica Nacional do Diário, 1856
A viuvinha: Cinco minutos [1]	Novel	Tipografia do Correio Mercantil, 1860
O guarani [2]	Novel	Empresa Tipográfica Nacional do Diário, 1857
O demônio familiar [1]	Play	Tipografia Soares & Irmão, 1858 Tipografia de Soares & Irmão, Imp. de Raçon e Comp., 1858
Noite de S. João [1, 2]	Play	Empresa Tipográfic Nacional do Diário, 1857 Tipografia de Paula Brito, 1860
Mãe [1]	Play	Tipografia de Paula Brito, 1862

Sources:
1. Catálogo da Biblioteca Brasiliana (USP), www.brasiliana.usp.br.
2. Catálogo de Obras Raras da Biblioteca Nacional do Rio de Janeiro, catcrd.bn.br.

1857, "we lack the titles and close relations required to honor ourselves with the name of FRIEND,"[42] attesting to a quarrel with aesthetic and political ramifications. The roots of discord may have been set down in 1856, when Paula Brito was not at all pleased by José de Alencar's contemptuous treatment of Domingo José Gonçalves de Magalhães's *Confederação dos Tamoios* (Tamoio Confederation).

Gonçalves de Magalhães's tragedies—*Antônio José, ou, O poeta e a inquisição* (Antônio José, or, The poet and the inquisition), *Olgiato*, and *Otelo, ou, O mouro de Veneza* (his translation of Shakespeare's *Othello*)[43]—were among the first plays Paula Brito published back in the days of the Impartial Press. The same occurred with the epic poem in ten cantos *Confederação dos Tamoios*, penned by Gonçalves de Magalhães when he was serving as a diplomat in Europe. However, in this case, Pedro II made it his personal mission to transform the poem into the magnum opus of Brazilian literature, entrusting Paula Brito—then the "Printer of the Imperial House"—with the task of publishing it. Therefore, all indications are that in May 1855 the monarch hired the publisher to produce two editions. According to a report in *Correio mercantil*, "the first, luxury [edition] has a limited number of copies and belongs exclusively to His Majesty the Emperor, as it was paid for from his own purse." The second edition, which was supposed to be released one month after the Imperial edition, and for which lists of subscribers were formed, would be "produced at the publisher's expense, according to the powers invested in him for that purpose."[44]

Paula Brito's "purse" must have been delighted with the profits that would certainly fill it through the publication of that poem. The publisher worked hard and, a year later, the newspapers announced the publication of *Confederação dos Tamoios*, stressing the peerless quality of that edition. As agreed, one month before distributing copies to his subscribers, Paula Brito delivered the emperor's volumes, richly bound by the Lombaerts, who, according to the newspapers, would be sending copies to Germany. In this regard, the quality of that volume of poetry even garnered praise from France, and it was described by a reviewer from Rio de Janeiro as "clearly printed, elegant, even luxurious. It does honor to the presses and arts of Brazil, which it so ably represents and for which such efforts have been expended."[45]

Everything was going well until a certain "Ig," a pseudonym used by José de Alencar, began systematically pointing out the defects of that work. As a result, *Cartas sobre a Confederação dos Tamoios*, came on the scene—a series of eight articles published in the *Diário do Rio de Janeiro* which were so popular that they were published in a small volume in the course of the heated debate.[46] With *Cartas*, Alencar sparked a literary controversy of which the imperial publishing industry had never seen the like. The battle lines were drawn, with the editor-in-chief of the *Diário* on one side and Manuel de Araújo-Porto, Friar Francisco do Mont'Alverne, and Pedro II himself on the other. Well-known to historians,[47] there is no solid evidence that the squabble about *Confederação dos Tamoios* affected sales of the book. The publisher may even have benefited from the curiosity aroused by the dispute. But if that did in fact occur, it would have been no consolation for that loyal subject of Pedro II.

The following year, the novelist and the publisher fell out because of *O demônio familiar* (The family demon), a four-act comedy by José de Alencar staged in the Ginásio Dramático Theater. Paula Brito was in the audience on opening night, November 5, 1857, which was well attended. The curtain rises on the adventures of Pedro, a slave and the title character, who is doing everything he can to become a coachman, creating a number of embarrassing situations for his master, a doctor named Eduardo. The publisher left the theater feeling unsettled by what he had seen, so much so that, five days after the premiere, he wrote a lengthy critique in *A marmota*. In the first part of the review, Paula Brito introduced the characters and gave a summary of the plot, identifying Figaro in *The Barber of Seville* as José de Alencar's main inspiration. However, focusing on the problem of the slave's manumission at the end of the comedy, he concluded that *O demônio familiar* did not have "an entirely moral ending."

Paula Brito analyzed the play from a very specific angle. He found Eduardo to be a weak master, incapable of being "the lawmaker in his house, the competent judge to punish the lapses" of his subordinates. He also considered Pedro, the slave who "despite being a student's boy, the mistress's Creole [and] the village idiot," to be capable of developing complex reasoning, quoting aphorisms, and saying and doing anything that came to mind. Therefore, the publisher supported using manumission as a reward for good captives, but slaves like Pedro did not merit that seigneurial gift: "the best and greatest of prizes that can and should be given to a good slave, to one who dwells in our heart, well raised, that is—*freedom*." The man holding the pen and espousing these ideas was the slaveowner Paula Brito who, although he knew something about dramatic literature, was much more familiar with the institution of slavery. In sum, the publisher concluded, "The author of the comedy should note that, speaking in this manner, we accept things as our laws and our society require."[48]

The publisher also disapproved of the fact that the slave was named Pedro—after all, why not call him "Constantine" instead of naming him after the Brazilian emperor? Furthermore, he thought it inappropriate and even disrespectful for the play to have been dedicated to the empress. The response to Paula Brito's review came swiftly, published the following day in José de Alencar's newspaper. The article in the *Diário*'s arts and entertainment segment stated that the publisher suffered from "*criticomania*," and was incapable of "critiquing" but merely of "*critiquizing*," randomly spewing out baseless opinions:

> According to review, however, Mr. Alencar's comedy is no good.
>
> It is immoral; perhaps because it does not contain the *innocent graces* of cracking verses; it made Mr. Paula Brito blush: it should not have been dedicated to Her Majesty the empress, who accepted it, and for which she sought the opinion of the emperor, who, due to the protection he gives to Brazilian verses, even protected an immoral production. Finally, a [young slave] is called *Pedro*.
>
> But seriously, Mr. Paula Brito, this last observation is disgusting; and the author of the comedy does not fear it, because Mr. Paula Brito with his *Marmota*, his opinions, and his sui generis respect, will not make him accept it. Your opinions, Mr. Paula Brito, do not even have the power to influence weak minds like mine.[49]

Finally, the author of the article, which a biographer of José de Alencar has attributed to Leonel de Alencar, the novelist's brother,[50] addressed one last word to the critic: "*Let us not be angry*; frankness is repaid with frankness; we may despise a man's opinions, but we value the individual for his good qualities."

At this point, the Alencar brothers and Paula Brito disagreed not only about theatrical matters but also about politics. José and Leonel were the sons of the priest, senator, and historic liberal José Martiniano de Alencar. Protected by his father's prestige, José de Alencar ran for office as a deputy for the Liberal party in his home province, Ceará. He only won two votes in that election. Nevertheless, the novelist was far from orthodox, like his father, who had played an active role in the Liberal revolts of 1842 and 1848.[51] Upon the death of a Conservative leader, the Marquess of Paraná, José de Alencar wrote an obituary in which he praised the policy of party conciliation that the deceased politician had devised. Furthermore, when he became editor-in-chief of *Diário do Rio de Janeiro*, Alencar saw no problem with asking another prominent Conservative, Eusébio de Queirós, to grant him the concession to publish of the official acts of the province, which would bring in good money for the newspaper.[52]

Paula Brito and José de Alencar clashed openly in the political press, especially when the publisher launched *O moderador*, a newspaper which, as we have seen, fervently defended the Conservative cabinet headed by the Marquess of Caxias. The *Diário do Rio de Janeiro*, "with whom we deeply feel we do not always agree," according to one of the *Moderador*'s editorials, was then headed by José de Alencar, and had been eagerly awaiting the fall of that same cabinet since 1857. "It seems that the modern intellectual," wrote Paula Brito in one of his articles addressed to the *Diário*, "is full of curiosity to see who the new ministers will be; is impatient to wield his weapons against them, and so is angry at those who do not want to see the seats for the new opponents he awaits immediately vacated."[53]

In 1860, however, Senator Alencar's son went over to the other side.[54] After his father's death and his own departure from the *Diário*, José de Alencar's occasional flirtation with the Conservatives quickly developed into a courtship, engagement, and marriage. That year, the novelist once again ran for a seat in parliament for the province of Ceará, this time as a Conservative. In addition to getting himself elected, by forming strong links with Rio's Conservatives Alencar also established closer ties with Paula Brito who, while not being an openly declared enemy, had not considered him a friend. Indeed, it was only after José de Alencar became a Conservative that Francisco de Paula Brito published two of his books. As we can see in Table 12, they were the second edition of the libretto for the opera *Noite de São João* (St. John's Night), which came out in 1860, and the play *Mãe* (Mother), released by Paula Brito's widow in 1862. Like all books published in Rio de Janeiro, they faced obstacles to their printing and distribution.

CHAPTER 19

Rio de Janeiro's Publishing Market (1840–1850)

T HE BOOKSHOP OF Francisco Luís Pinto e Companhia, a supplier to "His Majesty the Emperor's library," specialized in scientific and legal works. Located on Rua do Ouvidor, that shop frequently received shipments of French books imported via Lisbon and, according to its newspaper ads, Francisco Luís Pinto guaranteed that he would "sell all the books adopted in the law schools of São Paulo and Recife for much less than any other establishments."[1]

In late February 1863, a resident of Rua de São Bento bought over 300,000 réis' worth of books from Luís Pinto's shop, and his purchases were duly packed up and placed in a box bearing his initials, B.J.F.V. We do not know for sure, but those initials might have belonged to an academic, or to the parent or relative of a student or lecturer. What we do know is that, on February 25, the "casket of books" was sent to the customer's address. A slave was carrying it on his head, walking behind one of the bookshop's clerks. When they had nearly reached their destination, the enslaved black man—possibly hired specifically as a porter for that shipment—fled while the clerk's head was turned, taking the books with him.[2] We cannot dismiss the possibility that the slave may have known how to read and was interested in the contents of those works, but it is also possible that he intended to sell them. After all, he could have made some 300,000 réis that way, and if they were legal or scientific works, he might have found buyers very quickly. Then again, he may have soon discovered that selling books in Rio de Janeiro was no easy task. Depending on the genre of the publication, it could be even harder.

One reviewer of *Confederação dos Tamoios* was categorical in this regard when referring to literature: "Our books, or those dealing with our matters, are not sold, or sell so slowly that not everyone can risk their capital on publishing." For the journalist, such books were doomed "to being forgotten in a dusty corner of some library shelf," for "they only occasionally receive the sincere homage of some youthful spirit, which may be enough for the poet, but not enough for the bookseller."[3] Essentially, there were two problems for the Brazilian publishing market in Paula Brito's time: first, the difficulty of producing printed matter, and second, the barriers to the distribution of these cultural goods.

Without a doubt, the producers of intellectual products and the products themselves—in other words, printed matter in different formats—were gaining more and more ground in the daily lives of residents of Rio de Janeiro and other parts of the Empire. However, in the 1840s and '50s, there could be considerable obstacles to the production of and access to those products. Except for the contents of their pages and the manpower used to produce printed matter, including slave labor, it must be considered that, to publish a book or newspaper in Paula Brito's day, everything else had to be imported. "All of the materials," complained an anonymous writer in the *Diário do Rio de Janeiro*, indignant at the increase in customs duties in March 1857, "from mechanical presses to type, from paper and ink to the common string that makes the page turn, comes from foreign parts; in this city, it is not possible to manufacture any of these objects, even to make up for a momentary lack of supply."[4] "Printers are already burdened by the size of newspapers," the *Correio da tarde*'s writer added, "paying tariffs for printing ink, because it is not manufactured here; paying tariffs for the presses, because they are not made here—[because] manufacturing here is still so far behind."[5]

As Lucien Febvre and Henri-Jean Martin observed when studying the emergence of the book in the fifteenth century, "The printing press is a major consumer of paper."[6] Therefore, the chronic problem of ensuring an adequate supply of printing paper in Rio de Janeiro is a case in point. Paula Brito felt it first-hand when printing the *Relatório da Repartição dos Negócios da Justiça* (Report of the Legal Affairs Bureau) in 1855.[7] On that occasion, having run out of paper, the publisher appealed to the *Jornal do commercio*, which promptly provided him with the necessary reams. However, disturbed by what had happened, Paula Brito published an article on the problem in *Marmota fluminense*. "There is a desperate need for a paper mill among us that meets the most urgent printing requirements," wrote the publisher, adding, "The lack of paper in Rio de Janeiro is the reason for the high price which has always been the case in the market, and it should also be noted that we have no storehouse, at the very least, for what foreign parts can send us."[8]

In 1847, there was a mill in Salvador, Bahia, that produced printing paper, but its daily output of fifty reams was only enough to meet the needs of that city's presses. That same year, in Rio de Janeiro, the Frenchman André Gaillard came up with a plan to build a large paper mill, for which he had managed to obtain government funding in the form of lottery money. Meanwhile, Zeferino Ferrez was in France, looking to purchase the machinery necessary to start up another establishment of that kind in the capital. For the lack of one, Rio de Janeiro would soon have two paper mills, both located in Andaraí.[9]

However, nothing went as expected. By 1848, all the equipment Zeferino Ferrez imported, including a "thirty-eight-foot-diameter hydraulic wheel" was still in its shipping crates, awaiting the completion of the mill. Then, the paper samples manufactured by André Gaillard that were sent to the government—"an inferior kind that can be used for wrapping, and another of better quality on which newspapers can be printed"—were considered unsatisfactory because, "in addition to creases, there are inconsistencies which the owner believes will disappear, although this is not very likely."[10] Both entrepreneurs of the Rio de Janeiro paper industry met a tragic end. Possibly because he had failed to make good-quality paper, André Gaillard shot himself in 1849. Zeferino Ferrez and his wife, as well as two of their slaves and heads of cattle, died mysteriously in 1851. Their deaths led to the deputy chief constable of Engenho Velho to exhume the bodies and order chemical tests of the water used in the mill.[11] Even so, in 1857, the two paper mills in Andaraí were still running. Despite using "water-powered machinery," according to the Report of the Minister and Secretary of State for Imperial Affairs, the mill owned by "the late Zefe-rino Ferrez . . . is limited to the production of common paper, producing thirty-two reams per day." Meanwhile, the establishment "of the widow Gaillard makes a similar kind paper but in a larger quantity."[12] Common paper was of no use to printers.

In addition to being of dubious quality, throughout most of the nineteenth century, the paper manufactured in Brazil was predominantly made from cotton or linen rags. This process made Brazilian paper even more expensive than its Belgian counterpart, for example, which was made from wood pulp.[13] In 1851, Guilherme Schüch, the Baron of Capa-nema, established the Orianda Mill in the outskirts of Petrópolis to produce good-quality paper.[14] However, four years later, as Paula Brito pointed out, "Mr. Capanema's paper mill, which we know is being built on a large scale, is reported to have struggled to achieve its aim completely, which is to manu-facture paper equal to the foreign [imports]."[15] As a result, Rio de Janeiro's presses were still being supplied by ships arriving mainly from the port of Le Havre. The cost of these imports, however, directly impacted the price of printed matter, in Paulo Brito's assessment:

> The printed matter [in our market] is not more economical because the paper and type come to us from France; and if it were not for the books they send us from Paris (which even our young people study), if we are doing badly in literature, science, and the arts, we could be much worse, seeing that not everything that we Brazilians need is printed in Brazil.[16]

Curiously enough, none of the shipments found in this study were addressed to the publisher by name. In early December 1856, for example, the French galley *Nouvelle Pauline* unloaded fifty-seven crates of paper in Rio de Janeiro, of which "thirty-two crates [belonged] to Villeneuve [of the *Jornal do commercio*], thirteen to Muniz Barreto [the owner of *Correio mercan-til*], eight to Glette, four to Laemmert." In addition to paper, the *Nouvelle Pauline* also delivered four barrels of printing ink ordered by a certain Féron, and a box of type for J. Antônio dos Santos.[17]

However, in addition to the costs of printing with imported paper, ink, and presses, there were times when the printer was also a distributor, espe-cially in the case of periodicals. When Dous de Dezembro was still active, Paula Brito printed and distributed *Guanabara*, a monthly magazine devoted to the arts, science, and literature. "Written by an association of literati," the publication was directed by Manuel de Araújo Porto Alegre, Antônio Gonçalves Dias, and Joaquim Manuel de Macedo.[18] Initially, the magazine went through some very hard times, such as the illness of two of its writers laid low by the yellow fever epidemic of 1850, as well as other problems linked to "the thousand things on which the life of a newspaper essentially depends." Paula Brito, who was very familiar with the "material life" of publications, began printing and distributing the magazine in 1851, as one of its relieved writers reported:

> Mr. Francisco de Paula Brito, to whom our subscribers should now address any complaints they may have, is responsible for everything concerning the material part of *Guanabara*: readers, who cannot fail to be aware of the solicitude and skill with which Mr. Paula Brito usually carries out such responsibilities, will undoubtedly see, in the task he has undertaken, another assurance of the future regularity of this periodical.[19]

In 1855, the *Guanabara* had a print run of 680 copies, according to Paula Brito in his reply to a letter from Francisco Freire Alemão, a doctor and writer for the magazine.[20] The following year, however, it ceased publication, and in his farewell editorial, Canon Fernandes Pinheiro, the editor-in-chief, acknowledged Paula Brito: "We express here our gratitude to the worthy publisher, Mr. Paula Brito, for the gentlemanly manner with which he has always treated us."[21]

However, in other cases, mainly due to production costs, the printing of newspapers was not devoid of conflict. This was the case with the *Auxiliador da Indústria Nacional* (Auxiliary of National Industry), the publication of the prestigious Auxiliary Society for National Industry, which had been in circulation since 1833, and which Paula Brito began printing in September 1852.[22] Relations between the publisher and the Auxiliary Society, chaired by the Viscount of Abrantes, certainly became closer as of 1851, when Paula Brito's name appeared in the list of its 365 members, while the association became a shareholder of Dous de Dezembro.[23]

The annual costs involved in the production of a periodical like *Auxiliador da Indústria Nacional*—twelve issues, with illustrations and a monthly print run of one thousand copies—were high. According to the Society's treasurer, 60 percent of its total expenses, reported to be 3,712,000 réis in 1853, went to the publication of the magazine. Printing costs came to 1,200,000 réis, followed by binding (120,000 réis), the editor's fee (600,000 réis), the delivery boy's wages (120,000 réis), and finally engravings (200,000 réis). The Society's total revenue, reported at the same time, was over 8,000,000 réis, and its main sources of income were a "provision from the National Treasury" (4,000,000 réis) and the monthly membership fees (2,400,000 réis). Only 60,000 réis of its total income came from the subscriptions and individual sales of the *Auxiliador da Indústria Nacional*. That amount covered 2.6 percent of the magazine's production costs.[24] To make things worse, a letter from Paula Brito written in July 1854 reflects the strained relations between the Sociedade Auxiliadora da Indústria Nacional and the publisher. Paula Brito complained about the "high price of everything" and asked the Society for more money. Otherwise, he would stop printing the magazine:

Dear Sir,

As a result of the high price of everything, it is not convenient for me to print the *Auxiliador*, as it has been done so far, one thousand copies with cover, binding, [etc.], for less than 150,000 réis, that is, 40,000 réis more than what it has cost so far; you will decide on this as you see fit, [and I am] certain that the engravings, drawings, etc., can be explained when convenient.

I have the honor to be

Your
[illegible] dear [illegible abbrev.]
July 25, 1854
Francisco de Paula Brito[25]

According to the figures he gave, the Sociedade Auxiliadora da Indústria Nacional was paying 110,000 réis for each monthly issue with a print run of one thousand copies, including the cover and binding. However, pressured by production costs, Paula Brito wanted to increase that amount to 150,000 réis. In this case, they failed to reach an agreement, as that same month the magazine began to be printed by the Widow Vianna Júnior, in Rua d'Ajuda.[26]

If the importation of raw materials made printing more expensive, another difficulty faced by publishers and printers who, like Paula Brito, were also responsible for distribution, was posting books and newspapers from Rio de Janeiro. Invariably, every newspaper and periodical printed in the capital had two prices, one for the capital and another for the provinces. Due to the price of postage, the printed matter cost about 1,000 to 2,000 réis more than the amount charged in Rio de Janeiro. However, all indications are that the postal system was unreliable, which made it very hard to distribute the printed matter. "*A marmota*'s editors cannot, under any circumstances, answer for the Post Office's constant failures, once the shipments are sent, which occur with customary regularity," wrote Paula Brito in April 1858, justifying himself to his subscribers in the provinces.[27] In 1860, he attempted to solve the problem by sending *A marmota* to "outside subscribers" on a monthly basis. Thus, instead of receiving separate issues twice a week, provincial readers would get all that month's issues at the end of the month. This prevented individual issues from getting lost in the post, which was a constant problem, and the "serialized novels and articles [would] arrive in full."[28]

Where books were concerned, the problem persisted. Although the records show that Paula Brito was a representative of Santos e Companhia, "printer-booksellers in Pernambuco," providing Rio's readers with "beautiful publications of excellent works, not only instructive but entertaining, in soft cover and hard cover,"[29] the inter-provincial postal service of that time was unreliable. Recalling his student days at the São Paulo Law School in the 1840s, José de Alencar observed that "In that time, the sale of books was, as it is today, [one of] luxury goods; however, although cheaper, literary works had a smaller circulation." Alencar explained that this was due to the "lack of communication with Europe and the greater scarcity of bookshops and libraries."[30] Recent studies have shown that it was not until the 1870s that, packed in the wagons of cargo trains or on steamships, books and newspapers began to circulate more freely throughout the Empire. The leading role of Baptiste Louis Garnier, the French publisher and bookseller based in Rio, in the distribution of printed matter in the last three decades of the nineteenth century is also seen as a decisive factor.[31]

In the 1879s, even exports of Brazilian books to Portugal began gaining momentum due to the efforts of Ernesto Chardron, a French bookseller based in Oporto (Porto).[32] However, until stronger links were established between Rio, Oporto, and Lisbon, the case of the *Confederação dos Tamoios* is a good example of the slack dynamics of that business. In a bibliographic essay dedicated to its author, Gonçalves de Magalhães, Inocêncio Silva wrote that he was resigned to the fact that "few Portuguese readers will have seen [*Confederação dos Tamoios*], because perhaps not even ten or twelve copies have reached Portugal."[33] Therefore, Paula Brito did not live long enough to benefit from Chardron's efforts in Portugal, or from the railways and steam ships in Brazil. Symptomatically, the list of 17,500 books in the inventory of the Rio de Janeiro publisher's estate included sixty copies of Gonçalves de Magalhães's poem, probably stranded by logistical obstacles.

CHAPTER 20

The Widow Paula Brito

BY 1861, PAULA Brito's daughters were both married women. The eldest, Rufina, who turned twenty-seven that year, had wed Leopoldo de Azeredo Coutinho in about 1853. At the time, Leopoldo was the owner of Ao Livro d' Ouro (To the Golden Book), a shop located in Praça da Constituição, no. 72, that sold office supplies, sewing supplies, tea, cigars, and other goods. The fact that his shop was located nearby must have brought the publisher's daughter and the merchant together. All indications are that Paula Brito was delighted with his first-born daughter's choice of husband. In fact, in the advertisements for the shop published in *Marmota fluminense*, he describes his son-in-law as "a young man with excellent business prospects, and worthy of all the widespread consideration he already enjoys."[1] We do not know if Leopoldo was pardo, like his wife, just as we do not know the skin-color of Eduardo Vaz de Carvalho, the husband of Alexandrina, Paula Brito's younger daughter, who was twenty-four in 1861. In any event, it is likely that, by that time, Paula Brito and Rufina lived in an empty nest at no. 32 Rua da Carioca. All the couple's belongings listed in the inventory for the publisher's estate were located at that address. The list did not include any slaves. Due to the financial difficulties he had experienced after the bankruptcy of Dous de Dezembro, Paula Brito may have sold the "good black woman who can wash and starch clothes [and] cook," a slave whom he must have owned in late March 1857, when he offered to hire out her services.[2] Without a house slave, domestic chores had probably fallen to Rufina.

The inventory describes most of the furnishings and utensils in Paula Brito's home as "ordinary." The living room contained twelve Brazilian rosewood chairs, including two with armrests, a sofa, a round table, and a plinth trimmed with stones, all described as "used." The most interesting piece in the dining room, in addition to the china closet, table, and chairs, was an American clock, valued at 8,000 réis—the same price as the wardrobe, which together with "camp beds" and "ordinary couches," made up the bedroom furniture. Finally, the household items Paula Brito had owned included four bronze candlesticks, a chandelier, and two fine jugs and spoons made of English silver for tea and table, in addition to "ordinary cutlery" for everyday use.[3] However, the publisher spent most of the day away from home. According to *Marmota*, he "was always to be found in the printing press office . . . from 8 a.m. to 3 p.m. and from 4 p.m. to 9 p.m."[4] One account quoted earlier said that anyone who passed through Praça da Constituição could see him "at the door of his workshop, wearing plain work clothes, with a smile on his face [and] a quip on his lips,"[5] which, if true, would have been the case until late November 1861, when Teixeira e Sousa fell ill.

As we know, Paula Brito and Teixeira e Sousa were friends for over twenty years. In 1840, when the novelist settled down permanently in Rio de Janeiro, it was Paula Brito who offered him a job, published his work, and made him a partner in the Teixeira e Companhia Press. Then, Teixeira e Sousa became a teacher in Engenho Velho. In the mid-1850s, he was appointed clerk of the Business Tribunal of Rio de Janeiro by the minister of justice, José Thomaz Nabuco de Araújo. On that occasion, Paula Brito, who was already publishing a series of flattering articles about the minister in *Marmota fluminense*, celebrated his friend's appointment.[6] When Teixeira e Sousa came down with the hepato-enteritis that eventually killed him on December 1, 1861, he was still working as a clerk. In an article published days after his friend's death, Paula Brito wrote that few people had attended his funeral, lamenting that "time has flown, years and months have gone by like days and hours."[7]

The novelist had left his wife and six children completely destitute—the youngest was three and the eldest, twelve. Something had to be done. Thus, in the days following Teixeira e Sousa's burial, Paula Brito worked hard to raise funds for the bereaved family. However, the publisher, who had felt a "slight discomfort" on the day of the funeral, also became seriously ill. Two weeks later, in the evening of December 15, 1861, despite the doctor's best efforts, Francisco de Paula Brito died at home, as reported by the newspapers, felled by an inflammation of the lymphatic system.[8]

The following day, his death made the news. "There is hardly a single man of letters in our country who is not today mourning the death of Paula Brito," declared the *Correio mercantil*. The Liberal newspaper *Diário do Rio de Janeiro* stressed the political distance it had always maintained from the Conservative publisher, a "devoted friend and respectful adversary." The *Jornal do commercio* opined that, "through his constancy at work, his love of his country's literature, and his beautiful personal qualities," the departed had "managed to garner many friends and great affection." The afternoon paper, *Correio da tarde*, on the other hand, reported on the crowded funeral, including "some ministers, several statesmen, and other notables."[9] According-ing to the *Correio mercantil*, "the funeral was one of the best attended ever, without distinction of class or party," including "artists, workers, ministers of state, senators, deputies, journalists, merchants, doctors, [and] lawyers." The *Courrier du Brésil*, however, pointed out the presence of Conservative party leaders, who helped carry the body of their fellow party member to its final resting place.[10]

In the days that followed, several masses were sung for the "eternal rest" of Paula Brito. They were held at the Church of Santíssimo Sacramento, the Church of Nossa Senhora da Lampadosa—the publisher had belonged to the confraternity that was based there—and even in Portugal, at Matosinhos Parish Church. None, however, was as controversial as the seventh-day mass, due to the funeral speech given on that occasion by Dr. Caetano Alves de Sousa Filgueiras, a close friend of the late publisher.[11] In addition to the long list of compliments characteristic of any eulogy, Caetano Filgueiras said that Paula Brito, "as a public man was very Brazilian," because "all his ideas, all his efforts, all his aspirations, were on behalf of his homeland, which is why he was always as an activist among the men who are guided by the great-ness and unity of all the members of this great empire"—a poorly disguised defense of the party conciliation policy implemented by the Conservatives in the 1850s. Paula Brito and Filgueiras had themselves been active members of that party, which the eulogist described as the guide of the nation. He concluded his argument by referring to the "dark hand" of Paula Brito, "which all great men shook with effusion of the soul."[12]

The seventh-day mass, Filgueiras's eulogy and even his allusion to Paula Brito's "dark hand" reverberated in the opposition press as far as Pernambuco. This is because, a few days after the mass, Filgueiras was appointed president of the province of Goiás, as reported by *O liberal*, a newspaper based in Recife, the provincial capital of Pernambuco:

> The government removed the president of Goiás, Alencastre, from his post because he advised the treasury that he had spent money on the September 7 festivities, and intended to spend more on the December 2 festivities: the government disapproved of these expenditures, because only Rio de Janeiro has the right to pour public money into the pockets of rogues: the provinces have nothing to do with the independence of Brazil, their obligation is only to produce large revenue for the rascals of Rio to waste as they will. . . . For this *plausible* reason, the president was dismissed, being appointed to replace him, Dr. Caetano Filgueiras, a young man with a very limited sphere, but who produces his little verses and is very helpful to the Vatican, adding that he was charged by Paranhos with giving the seventh-day mass speech for Paula Brito, and he did so in such a way that the entire consistory was pleased, particularly when he highlighted the circumstances of Pope Eusebius shaking Paula Brito's dark hands. . . . Tremendous pedantry is seen in this land! Paranhos was a very good friend of Paula Brito because [the publisher] supported his candidacy for senator, even in that paper for young girls, *Marmota*, and so gave this order to Filgueiras, having sent a son-in-law of Paula Brito, Leopoldo Coitinho [*sic*], manager of Rio's customs supervisors, on the same seventh day: this is what posts are created for, to make infamous payments.[13]

The Pernambuco newspaper had got the wrong son-in-law. The one that was appointed to manage the supervisors of Rio's customs department was Eduardo Vaz de Carvalho, the husband of Paula Brito's younger daughter, not Leopoldo de Azeredo Coutinho, the merchant who had married his older daughter.[14] In any event, from the outset, the article gives rise to the age-old question of the autonomy of disgruntled provinces in the face of the empire's political and economic centralization in the capital, Rio de Janeiro. According to *O liberal*, matters of the utmost importance to the provinces, such as the appointment of their presidents, were unscrupulously decided. Although he was considered "a young man with a very limited sphere," as the newspaper underscores, Filgueiras was a fine orator and well connected, which garnered him the post of provincial president. What interests us, however, is that the late Paula Brito was described in this article, borrowing an expression used in one of his obituaries, as "the most important link in a long chain of friends."[15] If, in life, he had backed Conservative party candidates, in death he still exerted some influence, from the choice of the new president of the province of Goiás to the appointment of his son-in-law to public office.

However, as O liberal alluded, in the 1861 elections the Diário do Rio Janeiro, a Liberal newspaper, referred to the Conservative José Maria da Silva Paranhos as the "marmoteiro-mor (chief groundhog) of the empire." According to a series of humorous articles published in the Diário, "Poor Mr. Paranhos! So young, so wretched, and already bald!" in his turn, had "started a new marmota (groundhog) and begun boring the readers of our Paula Brito's Marmota with little articles on the elections."[16] At the time, Paula Brito had acknowledged that "in the electoral arena," Marmota had gone a bit too far in supporting the Conservative party and its candidates, which would have caused resentment among some subscribers. However, barely apologetic, the publisher reaffirmed that "in the Conservative party, men (the leaders) represent ideas, and in politics it must always be so, and we understand it so well that that is how we do it, and we will always do it."[17]

Seeing that she had other problems, primarily how to keep the printing business going, all indications are that the publisher's widow stayed out of the political debates in the newspapers. In the months that followed Paula Brito's death, his widow, Rufina, covered the costs of the family's mourning with a loan from her son-in-law Leopoldo and appeared before the municipal judge of the first court of Rio de Janeiro in early May 1862 to begin the process of inventorying the late publisher's estate. Perhaps because he had not expected to die so soon, Paula Brito had not left a will. Thus, in June, Rufina asked the judge to appraise the couple's assets—both the press and bookshop, and the furnishings and fittings in their home.

At the same time, Leopoldo and Eduardo renounced their wives' inheritance to conduct the inventory of their father-in-law's estate—not that his daughters Rufina and Alexandrina would have received any property, real estate or otherwise. Much the opposite. Along with their mother, they had inherited nothing but debts. The buildings that housed the press and bookshop, numbers 64 and 68, Praça da Constituição, were rented, and back rents owed alone totaled more than 1,700,000 réis. Added to this were the clerks' and delivery people's pay, the workers' wages, the gas bill, the contract for the sale of stamped paper, medicine, and funeral and family mourning expenses, increasing the debt to more than 4,800,000 réis. Furthermore, the widow also stated that she owed the Viscount of Ipanema 6,000,000 réis for the mortgage. The amount owed for "bills and letters of credit" signed by the deceased reached 11,000,000, while those from the bankruptcy of Dous December exceeded 13,000,000 réis.[18]

Compared with the amount owed, the assets Paula Brito had left were insignificant. The household furniture and fixtures, as well as the store furnishings, were worth just over 400,000 réis. The entire printing establishment, assessed by the publisher Baptiste Louis Garnier and João Paulo Ferreira Dias, the administrator of the National Press, was valued at 6,500,000 réis. The shop's stock of over seventeen thousand books was worth just over 100 réis per volume, about 1,700,000 réis in total. If Rufina had managed to auction off all the assets, she could have raised approximately 8,500,000 réis, about 24 percent of a debt that added up to 35,000,000 réis.[19] However, the inventory took four years to complete, dragging on until 1866. In the meantime, Rufina did not sit still and, like other widows of printers and booksellers, such as Moré and Bertrand in Portugal, and Ogier in Rio de Janeiro, she took the helm of the business. She must have been familiar with the workings of the press and bookstore, playing a role alongside her husband that the sources hid until his death. Be that as it may, Rufina now had a considerable stock of books in addition to machinery in good condition. Therefore, all she had to do was renegotiate the back rents and wages in arrears and get the presses running again.

One of the first steps she took was renewing the contract with the city council. A few months before his death, in early March 1861, Paula Brito had attempted to extend the agreement for another four years. Until 1865, his press would supply all the printed matter used by city departments. He would also continue to print the *Arquivo Municipal*, the gazette Paula Brito had founded in 1859. Possibly foreseeing that it would cease publication, the publisher had submitted two contract options. The first, for 3,600,000 réis per year, would only change with regard to the supply of printed matter used by the bureaucracy—books and pads, receipts, notices, and so forth. The second was for 4,800,000 réis per year, for the continued publication of *Arquivo Municipal*, as well as printed matter. However, the publisher faced a serious problem at the time, because the councilmen were divided about renewing the contract. Paula Brito managed to get the second proposal approved thanks to a casting vote. Nevertheless, it was only for one year, not the four he had originally proposed.[20]

After taking charge of the printing business, Rufina kept to the agreement with the city council for the remainder of 1862.[21] However, the following year, she had to compete with H. E. Tavares e Companhia for the renewal of the contract. Rufina wanted to continue providing the Council with "all office supplies and the necessary printing" for 6,000,000 réis per year. Mr. Dias da Cruz, the councilman who analyzed her proposal based on data from the Council's accounting office, wrote a report that favored the widow.[22] Nevertheless, events took an unexpected turn when the council president decided that it was time to cut printing costs. The *Arquivo Municipal* would be canceled, as "its small circulation," the president determined, "has obliged the council, both the current and previous one, to pay more for publications in newspapers that are [actually] read." The *Arquivo Municipal* was so unpopular with readers that the Council also had to publish notices in the *Correio mercantil*, which charged 1,800,000 réis for that service. As a result, the president decided to review the entire agreement with the widow Paula Brito, proposing a new contract with the *Correio mercantil* press. Councilman José Mariano da Silva tried to save the agreement with Rufina, asking that "for equity's sake, [he give] preference to the Paula Brito [press], as long as it is subject to the same conditions imposed by the *Mercantil*, and [because they] have always satisfactorily fulfilled their contracts." However, his proposal was defeated by one vote.[23]

Despite this setback, Rufina did not give up. So much so that, from time to time, the newspapers reported a work published or about to be released by the press of the widow Paula Brito. Books such as the *Postilas de aritmética*, an arithmetic textbook by the mathematician Manuel José Ferreira Frazão adopted in several schools of Rio de Janeiro, and the *Sinopse genealógica, cronológica e histórica dos reis de Portugal e dos imperadores do Brasil* (Genealogical, chronological and historical synopsis of the kings of Portugal and the emperors of Brazil) by Henrique de Beaupaire Rohan.[24] In March 1864, Rufina also printed the *Almanaque militar*, composed entirely with type cast by inmates of the Rio de Janeiro Penitentiary. As reported in the *Diário*, "The Paula Brito [press] is giving preference to this sort of type to print the *Almanaque*, carrying on with the traditions of its late and patriotic leader," adding that "the publishing is done with great care and reveals the efforts that Paula Brito's successors do not cease to make, not only to advance their

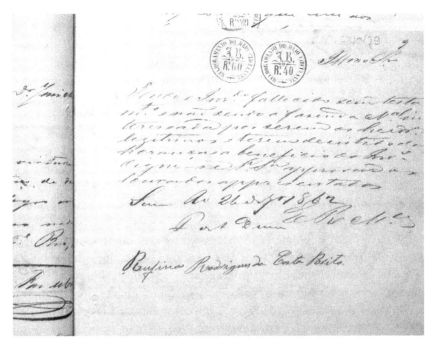

FIGURE 24. Signature of the Widow Paula Brito

art but to preserve the reputation of their establishment."[25] In January 1864, there was an attempt to bring the *Marmota* back into circulation, but the new edition of the newspaper did not survive beyond its fifteenth issue.[26]

Finally, in April 1866, Rufina asked the municipal judge of the First Court of Rio de Janeiro to auction off the assets left by her husband. At the time, the furniture was bought by its appraiser, the carpenter and master builder Antônio de Pádua da Silva. However, the printing presses and accoutrements, as well as the books, did not find a bidder. Over time, the depreciation of the presses has been increasing. In June 1866, because they had failed to sell in the previous auction, they were reappraised, and their value fell to 4,600,000 réis. A new auction was held and, once again, no one showed any interest in the press or bookstore. A third appraisal was requested, and this time the value of the estate fell to 2,200,000 réis.[27]

Along with the steady devaluation of her assets, Rufina had to deal with one of the late publisher's creditors, Manuel Rufino de Oliveira. In a petition submitted to the judge, he immediately called for the attachment and auction of the printing press, leveling serious accusations against the widow and her sons-in-law who, in his words, had disagreed "with the so-called sale purely as a whim; because the press and books, the only property of the deceased, are not included in their portion of the estate, the heirs have also opposed the sale while claiming to have given up their inheritance."[28] Rufina defended herself in a letter written in her own hand that was also sent to the judge. It stated: "As the widow and executor of the estate of the late Francisco de Paula Brito, I do not recognize the right that the claimant alleges through the seizure that was obtained as a result of false claims with which he deceived the Judge."[29] In fact, the judge had upheld the seizure proposed by Manuel Rufino and soon the print shop and bookstore would be auctioned off to repay him and the other creditors. To stop the attachment of her assets, Rufina appointed her son-in-law Leopoldo as her representative.

None of them, however, could have predicted the events that transpired on the night of September 25, 1866. At around one o'clock in the morning, a fire spread through the buildings at no. 70 and 72 Praça da Constituição. No. 70, the address of João Fortuna's photography shop, was also occupied by shoe shiners. No 72, which had once housed Leopoldo's shop, Ao Livro d'Ouro, was occupied by José Inácio do Valle's cigar store. Both buildings were gutted, and the blaze eventually reached the front and rear of the widow Paula Brito's establishment.[30] Although the interior of the bookstore and press was spared from the flames, the conflagration was followed by a flood. The water the firefighters poured on the building did serious damage to papers, books, presses, and other items used in printing. In December, the judge ordered a fresh assessment of what was left, but the inventory ends without shedding light on what happened next.

What we do know, however, is that Rufina stayed on at Praça da Constituição until 1868 when, according to the *Almanak Laemmert*, she moved to Rua do Sacramento, no. 10. Certainly with a smaller print shop, nothing compared to that of the late Paula Brito, the widow lived at that address until 1875, when the Laemmert brothers listed it for the last time among the owners of printing presses in Rio de Janeiro.

Although it is difficult to specify it exactly, if we calculate her age by determining how old Paula Brito would have been at the time, his widow must have been between sixty-five and seventy when she passed away in the early hours of March 8, 1879, eighteen years after her husband's death. In addition to her two daughters, who were also widows, she left four grandchildren.[31]

Finally, I like to think that the publisher might have been pleased with his firstborn child's career. Two years before Leopoldo's death in 1875, Rufina, then nearly forty, was appointed as a public school teacher in Macaé by the president of the province of Rio de Janeiro. Paula Brito had devoted most of his life to educating Brazil through the numerous newspapers and books he published and printed, and in a way, his daughter was carrying on his legacy. However, although she did not aim to reach the entire Brazilian Empire, as her father had aspired to doing, that parda teacher certainly made a difference to the fifty-two children she taught to read and write in 1874, and many more pupils in the years to come.[32]

A sensitive soul like the one described in chapter 34 of *The Posthumous Memoirs of Brás Cubas* may have been moved by that last paragraph. However, there is still room in this book for a reflection on the historical connections of Francisco de Paula Brito's publishing activities as an integral part of the policy of public education in the Empire of Brazil. So, let us move on to the epilogue and, if you are that sensitive soul, "clean your glasses—because that is sometimes caused by glasses."[33]

Epilogue

THE LIFE AND career of Francisco de Paula Brito allow us to grasp the historical specificity of the publisher's emergence in Rio de Janeiro at a time when similar entrepreneurs of printed cultural goods were also emerging in different Western cities, each in response to specific and varied stimuli. In the case of Brazil, two factors came together to galvanize that process. The first, given the increasing internationalization of the publishing market in the 1840s, was the need to compete with the French translations that were avidly consumed in Rio de Janeiro in different formats. The second was the political alliances that gave access to the forms of financing introduced by the Imperial government, ranging from privileges to lottery money. In this regard, it is important to stress that, in Brazil, the emergence of the publisher coincided with the formation of the nation state, which, in effect, makes this a more complex matter.

Robert Darnton's studies have pointed to the need to think about (and write) a history of books that goes beyond books. This is done through what he calls a "social and cultural history of communication by print" whose "purpose is to understand how ideas were transmitted through print and how exposure to the printed word affected the thought and behavior of mankind during the last five hundred years." Publishers played a key role in this process, and for that reason, an inquiry into the activities of those agents would "carry the history of books deep into the territory of social, economic, and political history, to their mutual benefit."[1]

One of the most influential studies on the origins of the Brazilian nation state is Ilmar Rohloff de Mattos's *Tempo Saquarema*. In it, the historian describes how the imperial state was built alongside the formation of the seigneurial class, which in turn, in a pendular motion, forged itself and the nation it led. Consisting of a small group of politicians and landowners and slaves in the province of Rio de Janeiro, the Saquarema leadership, as the historian called them, made "order" and "civilization" the watchwords of its ambitious project. However, what was meant by "order" was, above all, controlling the population, maintaining the monarchy and the vast national territory, political and economic centralization in the city of Rio de Janeiro, the perpetuation of the latifundia and slave labor, as well as the monopoly on violence against the free and poor masses. "Civilization," in turn, was viewed as the instrument for building a "good society," which was ultimately characterized by the means of transforming a coffee grower and buyer of smuggled Africans into a member of the imperial polis—that is, a worthy participant in the State and the class that was being formed. To achieve this aim, it was necessary for the Saquarema leadership to go beyond planters, ministers, and senators, encompassing other social strata that also accepted and spread the principles of order and civilization.[2]

Francisco de Paula Brito's unconditional adherence to the core of Saquaremas, who became indistinguishable from the leadership of the Conservative party, exemplifies the effectiveness of that group. Considering that the moral and intellectual formation of the "good society" was largely influenced by what it read, the recruitment of a book publisher by the seigneurial class that was forging itself and the imperial state was vital for the maintenance and reproduction of that class. Francisco de Paula Brito had himself become a Saquarema leader, intent on recruiting novelists and journalists who would ultimately serve the same purpose. Therefore, if both expressions did not essentially share similar means and almost identical ends, we can replace Ilmar Mattos's "policy of public education" in the following extract with a "policy of publishing activity":

> The close relationship between the policy of public education and the building of the imperial state was a facet of the constitution of the seigneurial class, of the mechanisms it sought to forge and set in motion in order to carry out a necessary expansion. Thus, . . . the *education of the people* consisted, first and foremost, of distinguishing each of the future citizens from the mass of slaves and rescuing them from barbarism.[3]

Considered "vehicles of civilization," novels, plays, and literary and scientific journals and magazines were believed to help maintain order through "the beliefs and ideas" they transmitted. However, that "order" was primarily based on the barbarous system of slavery. Therefore, a male or female reader who was entertained or enlightened by perusing the cultural section of a newspaper like *Marmota fluminense* may not have cared that a page replete with entertainment as well as moral and material progress could have been printed by a slave, or that an enslaved beater might have spread ink on the form used in printing.

According to Machado de Assis, the publisher who came to dominate the market in Rio de Janeiro after Paula Brito's death was a Frenchman, Baptiste-Louis Garnier. Writing as a columnist of the *Diário do Rio de Janeiro* in 1865, the novelist stressed the "vast relations" Garnier had established outside the country, implicitly referring to his brothers Auguste and Hippolyte, who were booksellers and publishers based in Paris.[4] However, the modes of reproduction of this policy on publishing activity in the Empire, which served both to consolidate the Brazilian nation state and disseminate a specific project of "civilization and order," are described in a document found in the papers of the Marquess of Olinda, currently housed in the Brazilian Historical and Geographic Institute:

> Batista Luís Garnier, bookseller-publisher, requested a decoration two years ago; the application has been found in the Office of the Ministry of Empire ever since.
>
> The petitioner has been established in the Imperial Capital for more than twenty years, having been the publisher of most of the scientific, literary, and elementary school books extant in this country.
>
> There are many Brazilian authors whose works would not have seen the light of day if it were not for the help that that publisher gave them by purchasing the publishing rights and providing them with the capital for their publication.
>
> In addition to many authors of several works and compendia for public education, those who have found in the petitioner effective help in producing their publications include, among others, senior officials of the state.
>
> The petitioner has rendered a real service by reprinting the Classics of Portuguese Literature, some of which were very difficult to find in the market.
>
> The *History of the Founding of the Brazilian Empire*, by Councilor João Manuel Pereira da Silva, the works of the Viscount of Uruguai, and many others,

which would take too long to mention, were published by the petitioner.

Other bookseller-publishers have already received honors equal to that to which he aspires; and therefore, we ask Your Excellency the Marquess of Olinda to deign to answer his plea.[5]

Although it is embedded in the grammar peculiar to such requests, this plea, which may have been read by the Marquess of Olinda when he was the head of the Cabinet of May 12, 1865, first sought to convince him that Garnier was worthy of the decoration because of the services he had rendered to public education in Brazil. From the outset, however, it touched on a point considered to be of vital importance by the administration of the imperial state. In addition to academic compendia and schoolbooks, Garnier was also reminding the minister that he had published a work by one of the most renowned Conservative historians, Pereira da Silva, as well as works by the Viscount of Uruguai, Paulino José Soares de Souza. Given that "other bookseller-publishers [had] already received honors equal to that to which he aspires," it was only fair for Baptiste-Louis Garnier's services to receive the same recognition.

In 1867, at a time when Brazilian citizens were receiving similar imperial decorations for freeing their slaves and handing them over to the army to fight in the war against Paraguay, "the French subject Baptiste Louis Garnier" finally became a Knight of the Order of the Rose "in recognition of the services he has provided to the advancement of literature and the press."[6]

Appendixes

APPENDIX 1: Slaves of Sergeant-Major Francisco Pereira de Brito found in the parish
records of the ecclesiastical archives of the Archdiocese of Diamantina (1725–1737)

Name	Year	Description in the records	Reference
Rosa*	1725	Mother of Eusébio, baptized on 11 March 1725	A, fls. 129v
Eusébio	1725	Boy baptized on 11 March 1725	A, fls. 129v
Francisco	1725	Godfather of the enslaved boy André, baptized on 8 Sept. 1725	A, fls. 112
Maria	1725	Godmother of the enslaved boy André, baptized on 8 Sept. 1725	A, fls. 112
Francisco	1728	Godfather of the girl Custódia	C, fls. 126
Luiza	1728	Godmother the girl Custódia	C, fls. 126
Rosa*	1728	Mother of the girl Maria	C, fls. 126v
Maria	1728	Daughter of the enslaved woman Rosa	C, fls. 126v
Francisco Mina	1731	Marriage of his son Domingos Pereira, a Creole freedman	C, fls. 76
Maria Pereira	1731	Marriage of her son Domingos Pereira, a Creole freedman	C, fls. 76
Josefa	1732	Baptized on 05 Apr. 1732, daughter of the enslaved woman Maria	D, fls. 13
Maria*	1732	Mother of the girl Josefa	D, fls. 13
Lourenço	1732	Son of Maria, baptized in August 1732	D, fls. 27
Maria*	1732	Mother of Lourenço	D, fls. 27

Name	Year	Description in the records	Reference
Rosa	1733	Baptized the adult Joaquim Mina on 26 May 1733	D, fls. 28
José	1734	Son of Maria, baptized on 05 Sept. 1734	B, fls. 61v
Maria	1734	Had her son José baptized on 05 Sept. 1734	B, fls. 61v
Domingos	1734	Godfather of José, baptized on 05 Sept. 1734	B, fls. 61v
Micaela	1735	Baptized on 23 Jan. 1735	B, fls. 62
Maria*	1735	Mother of the girl Micaela, baptized on 23 Jan. 1735	B, fls. 62
Maria Pereira	1737	Godmother of the girl Maria, baptized on 18 Nov. 1837	B, fls. 79v
Vitória	1737	Girl baptized on 26 Dec. 1737	B, fls. 95v
Rosa Pereira	1737	Mother of the girl Vitória	B, fls. 95v
Bernardo Pereira	1737	Father of the girl Vitória	B, fls. 95v

* Possibly the same enslaved individual shown in different records.
A. *Livro de Batismos, 1725*. AEAD, caixa 296, bloco A.
B. *Registro de Batismo de Várias Localidades, 1720-1740*. AEAD, caixa 296, bloco B.
C. *Registro de Batismos do Serro, 1727-1734; Casamentos do Serro, 1729-1734*. AEAD, cx. 296, bl. B.
D. *Registros de Batismo de Várias Localidades, 1728-1733*. AEAD, caixa 296, bloco B.

APPENDIX 2: Slaves of Captain José Pereira de Brito found in the parish records of the ecclesiastical archives of the Archdiocese of Diamantina (1724–1748)

Name	Year	Description in the records	Reference
Perpétua	1724	Mother of Vitor, baptized on 30 July 1724	B, fls. 109v
Vitor	1724	Boy baptized on 30 July 1724	B, fls. 109v
Florência	1728	Baptism of her daughter Marcela	E, fls. 129v
Marcela	1728	Daughter of Florência, recently baptized	E, fls. 129v
Damião	1732	Died on 6 Aug. 1732	F, fls. 7v
Rita	1734	Girl baptized on 11 Sept. 1734	C, fls. 45
Teresa*	1734	Mother of the girl Rita, baptized on 11 Sept. 1734	C, fls. 45
José	1735	Son of Maria Parda baptized on 5 Apr. 1735	D, fls. 61v
Maria Parda	1735	Mother of José baptized on 5 Apr. 1735	D, fls. 61v
João	1735	Died on 2 July 1735	F, fls. 5v
Mateus	1735	Died on 27 June 1735	F, fls. 5v
Basílio	1736	Baptized on 18 Sept. 1736	D, fls. 74v
Teresa*	1736	Mother of the boy Basílio, baptized on 18 Sept. 1736	D, fls. 74v

Name	Year	Description in the records	Reference
Escravo Angola	1736	Married the enslaved woman Maria on 8 May 1736	G, fls. 2v
Maria	1736	Married an enslaved man in Angola on 8 May 1736	G, fls. 2v
Antonio	1737	Godfather of the girl Maria, baptized on 6 Feb. 1737	D, fls. 96
Constantina	1737	Mother of the girl Maria, baptized on 6 Feb. 1737	D, fls. 96
Maria	1737	Girl baptized on 6 Feb. 1737	D, fls. 96
Anna do Ó	1738	Girl baptized on 8 May 1738	D, fls. 97v
Páscoa	1738	Mother of Anna do Ó	D, fls. 97v
Rosa	1739	Girl baptized on 21 Jan. 1739	D, fls. 108
Teresa*	1739	Mother of Rosa, baptized on 21 Jan. 1739	D, fls. 108
Garcia	1739	Died on 16 Aug. 1739	F, fls. 7v
Maria Gonçala	1739	Wife of the enslaved man Garcia	F, fls. 7v
Bartolomeu	1741	Father of Rita and husband of Rosa	A, fls. 29v
Rita	1741	Baptized on 1 Nov. 1741, daughter of Bartolomeu and Rosa	A, fls. 29v
Rosa	1741	Mother of Rita, and wife of Bartolomeu	A, fls. 29v
Manuel	1742	The Captain's "house" slave, died on 22 Nov. 1742	F, fls. 9v
Ignácio Pereira	1743	Baptized the boy Bernardo in Gouveia	A, fls. 42v
Antonio Sabaru	1744	Died on 19 May 1744	F, fls. 10v
Antonio Mina	1748	Died on 3 Jan. 1748	F, fls. 17v

* Possibly the same enslaved individual shown in different records.

A. *Batizados de várias localidades, 1740-1754*, AEAD, caixa 296, bloco D.

B. *Livro de Batismos, 1725*, AEAD, caixa 296, bloco A.

C. *Livro de Batizados, 1733-1734*, AEAD, caixa 296, bloco A.

D. *Registro de Batismo de Várias Localidades, 1720–1740*, AEAD, caixa 296, bloco B.

E. *Registro de Batismos do Serro, 1727-1734; Casamentos do Serro, 1729–1734*, AEAD, cx. 296, bl. B.

F. *Registro de Óbitos de Escravos do Serro, 1725-1797*, AEAD, caixa 352, bloco A.

G. *Registros de Casamentos do Serro, 1736-1772*, AEAD, caixa 338, bloco A.

APPENDIX 3: Catalog of Francisco de Paula Brito's bookshop published in *Gazeta dos tribunais* in 1845

Title	Volumes	Language
Direito Canônico por Bohemer	7	Latin
Horatius	2	Latin
Institutionum rhetoricarum ex M. Fab. Quintiliano	2	Latin

APPENDIX 3 : Catalog of Francisco de Paula Brito's bookshop published in
Gazeta dos tribunais in 1845

Title	Volumes	Language
Magnum lexicon	1	Latin
Noel dicionário latino francês	2	Latin
Salgado de protetione regia	1	Latin
Sabelli	8	Latin
Virgilius	4	Latin
Wolfh jus naturae	8	Latin
Geographia universale de Buffier	1	Italian
Lesioni de eloquenza	1	Italian
O amigo, das letras	1	Portuguese
Anatomia de Soares Franco	2	Portuguese
Anatomia de Marques	2	Portuguese
Antonio José, ou, O poeta e a inquisição	1	Portuguese
Arte de ser amado	1	Portuguese
Cânticos líricos	2	Portuguese
Cartas americanas	1	Portuguese
Cartas de Echo e Narciso	1	Portuguese
A casa mal assombrada, só o 1o volume	1	Portuguese
Coleção de leis, decretos e alvarás desde 1750 a 1808	7	Portuguese
Curso de inglês	1	Portuguese
Direito financeiro pelo desembargador José Antonio da Silva Maia	1	Portuguese
Os, dous matrimônios malogrados	1	Portuguese
As duas infelizes	1	Portuguese
Elementos de música	1	Portuguese
Elogio acadêmico da Sra. D. Maria I por J. Bonifácio de A. e Silva	1	Portuguese
Epitome das belas artes e poética por João José Maria	1	Portuguese
Escavações poéticas do Sr. Castilho, só o 1o volume	1	Portuguese
A fidalga e o Aldeão	2	Portuguese
O filho do pescador romance	1	Portuguese
História do Brasil por Constâncio	2	Portuguese

APPENDIX 3 : Catalog of Francisco de Paula Brito's bookshop published in
Gazeta dos tribunais in 1845

Title	Volumes	Language
Instituições oratórias de Quintiliano, tradução de J. S. Barbosa	2	Portuguese
Judeu errante, só o 1o, 2o, 3o e 4o volume.	1	Portuguese
Juiz de paz na Roça	1	Portuguese
Lições de química e mineralogia pelo Sr. Fr. Custódio Alves Serrão	1	Portuguese
Máquina, ou, Extravagâncias	1	Portuguese
Máximas e pensamentos praticados por Antonio Muniz de Sousa, homem da natureza	1	Portuguese
Metamorfoses de Ovídio, tradução do Sr. Castilho, só o 1o volume	1	Portuguese
Noivo em magas de camisa	1	Portuguese
Noute de S. João	3	Portuguese
Novo manual do juiz de paz	1	Portuguese
Novo método do Padre Antonio Pereira	1	Portuguese
Olgiato do Sr. Magalhães	1	Portuguese
Opinião de Becária sobre a pena de morte	1	Portuguese
Otografia de Madureira	1	Portuguese
Otelo, ou, I mouro de Veneza	1	Portuguese
Palavras de um crente	1	Portuguese
Passeio, poema	1	Portuguese
Poesias de D. Angélica Rosa César	1	Portuguese
O peregrino de Harfleur	1	Portuguese
Quadros históricos de Portugal pelo Sr. Castilho com ricas estampas	10	Portuguese
Repertório ou índice alfabético de todas as disposições dos códigos criminal e do processo, etc.	1	Portuguese
Resumo da história do Brasil pelo Sr. Bellegarde	1	Portuguese
Rudimentos de tática naval	1	Portuguese
Simão de Nântua	1	Portuguese
Sinopse cronológica	2	Portuguese
Sonhos da vida	1	Portuguese
Taquigrafia	1	Portuguese
Tancredo	1	Portuguese

APPENDIX 3 : Catalog of Francisco de Paula Brito's bookshop published in
Gazeta dos tribunais in 1845

Title	Volumes	Language
Tratado de tropos e figuras pelo Sr. Titara	1	Portuguese
Tratado do consuldado	2	Portuguese
Tratado elementar de aritmética por La Croix	1	Portuguese
Três dias de um noivado	1	Portuguese
Amelie Booth	4	French
L'amie des jeunes personnes	1	French
Anatomie des regions par Brandect avec atlas	1	French
Anecdotes de Russie	2	French
L'art de connaitre les hommes par la physionomie, par Lavater	10	French
L□autorité judiciaire em France par Henrion de Penséy	2	French
Batailles navalles	1	French
Beauté de jeune age	1	French
Beautés de l'histoire de Perse	2	French
Beautés de l'histoire de Chine	2	French
Beautés de l'histoire du Danemarck et de la Norvège	1	French
Beautés de l'histoire de Savoie	1	French
Beautés de l'histoire de Pologne	1	French
Beautés de l'histoire de Suède	1	French
Beautés de l'histoire de Turquie	1	French
Beautés de l'histoire d'Allemagne	1	French
Beautés de l'histoire de Suisse	2	French
Beautés de l'histoire de Rome	1	French
Beautés de l'histoire du Portugal	1	French
Bristed les Etats Unis de l'Amerique	2	French
Caracteres de Theofraste	2	French
Catecisme d'economie politique par Say	1	French
Causes celèbres	13	French
Le citateurs	2	French
Le conservateur	2	French
Contes à mês soeurs	2	French

APPENDIX 3 : Catalog of Francisco de Paula Brito's bookshop published in
Gazeta dos tribunais in 1845

Title	Volumes	Language
Decouverte de l'Amerique	2	French
Dialogues des morts	1	French
Diccionaire des arts er metiers	1	French
Diccionaire de la langue france par Gattel	2	French
Diccionaire des arts de police moderne	4	French
Diccionaire des arts de l'ancienne regime	1	French
Diccionaire Francês de Peigné	1	French
Diccionaire geographique de Vougien	1	French
Diccionaire Espanhol e Francês	1	French
Diccionaire Português e Francês de Fonseca	2	French
Dupin, administration des secours publique	1	French
École des jeunes demoiselles	2	French
Elements de legislation par Perraut	1	French
Elements de therapeutique par Alibert	2	French
Elements d'histoire generale par Millot	11	French
Elise	1	French
L'ermite russe	3	French
Essai sur le regime constitucionel	1	French
Ethocratie our le gouvernement fondé sur la morale	1	French
Fables de Lafontaine	2	French
Fenet, motif du code civil	15	French
La fin de temps	1	French
Les fleurs du ciel	1	French
Galerie des enfants celèbres	2	French
Gaste	1	French
Gazette des tribunaux, collection de 1830 à 1836	1	French
Grande Bretanghe en 1833	2	French
Guide de la conversation esp. e franc.	1	French
Higiene de Londe	2	French
Histoire à mês neuveux	1	French

APPENDIX 3 : Catalog of Francisco de Paula Brito's bookshop published in
Gazeta dos tribunais in 1845

Title	Volumes	Language
Histoire anciene	1	French
Histoire de Charles V	6	French
Histoire de l'Europe Moderne	2	French
Histoire de l'Impire Romain	1	French
Histoire des Naufrages	2	French
Histoire des reines de France	1	French
Histoire des voyages	3	French
Histoire naturelde Buffon	65	French
Les heures des dames, contenant les offices et priers	2	French
Imitation de Jesus Christ	1	French
Les jeunes instituteurs	1	French
Les jeunes voyageurs em Europe	2	French
Leçons de Felice	4	French
Le livre rouge	1	French
Les loix civiles	1	French
Magasin du jeunes dames	6	French
Magasin des adolescentes	4	French
Magasin pitoresque	1	French
Magendi physiologie	2	French
Manuel des juex de societés	1	French
Marins celèbres	1	French
Les martyres de Chateaubriand	2	French
Matière medical de Vavasseur	1	French
La medicine curative par le roy	1	French
Medicine portative	1	French
Memoires sur La Fayete	2	French
Memoires de Linguet	1	French
Memoires du regné de Louis XVI	1	French
Les mille et um nuit	10	French
Moliére	6	French

APPENDIX 3 : Catalog of Francisco de Paula Brito's bookshop published in
Gazeta dos tribunais in 1845

Title	Volumes	Language
Mongelas	2	French
Le nouveau Robinson	2	French
Nouvelles petits etudes	1	French
Nouvelles de Alfred de Musset	1	French
Odyssée	2	French
Oeuvres de Homère	4	French
Oeuvres de Boileau	1	French
Oeuvres de choisies de Rousseau	1	French
Le onanisme par Tissot	1	French
Les orphelins	1	French
De origine et des functions des consules	1	French
Orphela medicine legal avec altlas	4	French
Oeuvres de D'Anguesseau	12	French
Oeuvres de Montesquieu	7	French
Paul et Virgine	1	French
Petits voyageurs en Espagne et Portugal	1	French
Les petits solitaires	1	French
Pierre	1	French
Precis historique de Franc-Maçonnerie	2	French
Reglemens de l'ordre Maçonique en France	1	French
Revolutions d'angleterre par le Père d'Orléans	4	French
Revolution de suède	1	French
Richerand physiologie	1	French
Roche et sanson pathologie	1	French
Sabatier (edic. De 1832) redigé pr Begin	4	French
Les sept codes	1	French
Soirée d'Eufrosine	1	French
Systemes de philosophie comparée par Degerando	3	French
Telemaque	1	French
Traitées de legislation, extrait de Bentham	3	French

APPENDIX 3 : Catalog of Francisco de Paula Brito's bookshop published in
Gazeta dos tribunais in 1845

Title	Volumes	Language
Traites de changes	1	French
Traites de l'abus	1	French
Traites de greement	2	French
Traites elementaire ou principes de physique par Brisson	4	French
Velpeau (edic. de Brux.) avec atlas	1	French
Velpeau art des accouchemens	1	French
Le vierge	2	French
Vies des marins celèbres	2	French
Vie escandaleuse anecdotique de Charles X	1	French
Volney oeuvres choisies	2	French
Voyage moderne	2	French
Voyage dans l'Afrique	1	French
Voyage de Cortés	2	French
Voyage de Robinson	3	French
Warden, description des Etats Unis	5	French
A grammar of natural	1	English
Balistique d'Obenheim	1	English
Blairs preceptor	1	English
Didactics	2	English
District school	1	English
Emma	2	English
New elements of conversation French and English	1	English

Source: *Gazeta dos Tribunais*, n. 227, ano III, 6 May 1845, p. 3–4.

APPENDIX 4 : Conservative Party voters (1849)

1	Antonio Joaquim de Azevedo	Goldsmith
2	Antonio José Gonçalvez Fontes	Doctor
3	Antonio Rodrigues Cunha	Doctor
4	Antonio Pereira Barreto Pedroso	Councilman
5	André Antonio de Araújo Lima	Civil servant
6	Alexandre José do Rosário	Doctor

7	D. Antonio de Saldanha Gama	Civil servant
8	Euzébio de Queirós Coutinho Mattoso da Câmara	Justice minister
9	Eleutério José de Souza	Capitalist
10	Francisco de Queiróz Coutinho Mattoso da Câmara	War arsenal
11	Francisco Gomes de Campos	Senior judge
12	Francisco de Paula Brito	Printer
13	Francisco José Gonçalves Silva	Landowner
14	Francisco Manuel da Silva	Landowner
15	Francisco Manuel Ferreira	Printer
16	Geraldo Caetano dos Santos	Landowner
17	Henrique José de Araújo	Landowner
18	João de Siqueira Queirós	Lawyer
19	José Cardoso Fontes	Landowner
20	José Pereira Rego	Doctor
21	Joaquim Pereira Viana de Lima	Landowner
22	Justiniano José da Rocha	Teacher
23	José Antonio de Siqueira e Silva	Senior judge
24	Josino do Nascimento Silva	Civil servant
25	José Leite Pereira Campos	Clerk
26	João Silvério Monteiro Dias	Landowner
27	Joaquim José Barbosa	Goldsmith
28	José Siqueira Barbosa Madureira Queirós	Municipal judge
29	Manuel Pacheco da Silva	Doctor
30	João Marins Lourenço Vianna	Councilman
31	José Martins da Cruz Jobim	Councilman
32	Luiz de Siqueira Queirós	Doctor
33	D. Manuel de Assis Mascarenhas	Court judge
34	Father Manuel da Silva Lopes	Landowner
35	Mariano José de Oliveira	Doctor
36	Manuel José do Rosário	Goldsmith
37	Porfírio José Gonçaves	Civil servant
38	Sebastião José Vieira	Merchant

Source: *O Brasil*, n. 1.463, 03 Aug. 1849, p. 3.

APPENDIX 5: Shareholders of Empresa Dous de Dezembro listed in *Guanabara* magazine in 1856.

H. M. the Emperor

H. M. the Empress

João Antonio da Trindade

João Maria Pereira de Lacerda

Vicente Maria de Paula Lacerda

Pedro Maria de Lacerda

Patrício Ricardo Freire, Commander

José Maria Palhares

João Manuel da Silva

José Alves da Silva e Sá

Luiz Manuel Bastos

Brigadier Henrique M. d'O. Lisboa

Macieira & Cunha

Militão Correira de Sá

Dr. João Caldas Vianna

Councilor Angelo Muniz da Silva Ferraz

Joaquim Salomé Ramos

Antonio Carlos d'Azeredo Coutinho

João Dantas da Gama

José Francisco Pereira da Costa

Joaquim Maria de Lacerda

João Pedro da Veiga

Councilor Manuel José de Bessa

Widow Barker

Wardrobe Master José Joaquim dos Santos

Dr. José Florindo de Figueiredo Rocha

City Councilman Manuel Higino
de Figueiredo

Marquess of Abrantes

Countess of Piedade

Marquess of Mont'Alegre

Dr. Domingos d'Azeredo Coutinho
Duque-Estrada

Senador João Antonio de Miranda

João José Fernandes d'Azevedo

Dr. Carlos Antonio de Carvaho

João José de Mello Azevedo Pitada

Bernardino de Souza Ribeiro Guimarães

Canon Joaquim de Oliveira Durão

Manuel Francisco da Costa Pereira

Dr. Ludgero da Rocha Pereira Lapa

José Antonio Pinheiro

Antonio Fernandes da Costa Júnior

João Henrique Ulrich

Viscount of Rio Bonito

Dr. Vicente Joaquim Torres

Manuel José Ferreira

D. Virgínia Busti

José Fernandes de Oliveira Penna

Joaquim Rodrigues da Costa

Manuel Gomes Ferreira

Joaquim Gomes dos Santos

D. J. C. V.

D. Camilla Leonor de Lacerda

Luiz Maria Gonzaga de Lacerda

Antonio Ribeiro de Queiroga

Antonio Pereira Ribeiro Guimarães

Dr. Frederico João Ormerod

Manuel Venâncio Campos da Paz

Widow of Commander L. J. d'Almeida

Dr. Antonio Angelo Pedroso

Widow Serra

Widow Sá & Sons

Jacques Abrahão Lecesne

Dr. Antonio Pereira Leitão

Dr. José Caetano de Oliveira

João Lopes Bastos

Justino Candido Pereira de Vasconcellos

Libório José de Almeida

Antonio Ferreira de Moraes

Manuel Joaquim da Costa

Sociedade Auxiliadora da Indústria

Antonio Joaquim Xavier de Mello

Feliciano Zeofrido Rangel Maia

Baron of Parahyba

Antonio José Marques de Sá

José Carlos de Carvalho

Dr. Joaquim Candido Soares Meirelles

Peregrino Augusto dos Santos

Narciso d'Almeida Carvalho

D. Thereza Candida d'Almeida Carvalho

José Antonio de Sousa Ferreira

Marcos José Pereira do Bonfim

City Councilman José Joaquim
de Lima e Silva
Gabriel de Medeiros Gomes
Padre José Lira da Silva
Luiz Sebastião Fabregas Surigué
Camillo Lelis da Silva
Manuel Monteiro de Barros
Father Joaquim Ferreira da Cruz Belmonte
Antonio José de Freitas Júnior
Baron of Mauá
Manuel Croza
Antonio Alves Ferreira
D. Maria Thereza de Jesus Lacerda
Augusto Henrique Gonzaga
Francisco José de Sá Júnior
D. Adelaide Rosa da Silva Araújo
R. P. Bandeira
Sebastião Lira da Silva
Antonio Joaquim da Silva Freire
Henrique Beauepaire Rohan

Joaquim Soares da Costa Guimarães
Ricardo Soares da Costa Guimarães
Francisco de Paula Guedes Alcoforado
Senator Antonio Martiniano de Alencar
Dr. José Rufino Soares d'Almeida
Dr. Mateus da Silva Chaves
Francisco José de Mello e Sousa
Godinho & C.
Councilor José Maria Velho da Silva
Brigadier Gregório José de Castro Moraes
João Teixeira Bastos
Manuel José da Costa Ludovico
Hermenegildo Duarte Monteiro
José Joaquim da Silva Brum
Jeronymo Elias dos Reis
Herculado Luiz de Lima
Commander Joaquim José de Sousa Breves
Dr. J. J. de Oliveira Mafra

APPENDIX 6: Occupations of the fifty-seven shareholders of Empresa Dous de Dezembro

Shareholder	Occupation	Description	Reference in *Almanak Laemmert* (1858)
Antônio Alves Ferreira	Pharmacist	Expert or practitioner in the commercial district of the 9th session; pharmacy, pharmaceutical and apothecary laboratory	133, 416
Antônio Joaquim Xavier de Mello	Civil servant	Police clerk; clerk for police and police chiefs; justice of the peace of the 2nd district of the parish of Santa Anna	82, 83, 210
Antônio José de Freitas Júnior	Merchant	Grocery warehouses	258, 473
Antônio José Marques de Sá	Employee	Second lieutenant of the 7th Co. of the 1st Reserve Battalion; consultant at the Imperial Confraternity of Nossa Senhora da Glória do Outeiro; assistant to the treasurer of Banco de Brasil	100, 260A, 361

APPENDIX 6: Occupations of the fifty-seven shareholders of Empresa Dous de Dezembro

Shareholder	Occupation	Description	Reference in *Almanak Laemmert* (1858)
Antônio Pereira Ribeiro Guimarães	Merchant	Brazilian merchant; consignee and commissioner of import and export goods; warehouses and depots of raw tobacco in Bahia and North America [wholesaler of tobacco and cigars]	435, 439, 461
Antônio Ribeiro de Queiroga	Capitalist	Expert or practitioner in the commercial district of the 13th session; board member of the Santa Casa da Misericórdia; managing partner and manager Banco Mauá MacGregor e Cia; foreign merchant	133, 247, 363, 436
Augusto Henrique Gonzaga	Civil servant	first clerk of the 2nd Accounting Dept. of the Ministry of Finance	12, 121
Baron of Mauá	Capitalist	Session of Commerce and Means of Transport of the Auxiliary Society for National Industry; board member of the Confraternity of Nosso Senhor dos Passos	19, 57, 133, 261
Bernardino de Souza Ribeiro Guimarães	Capitalist	Sworn appraiser of slaves and livestock at the Business Court of Rio de Janeiro; capitalist, owners of buildings, etc.; hearing solicitor; judicial and hearing prosecutor; money at interest [loans] for mortgages, gold, and diamonds	66F, 392, 397, 400, 519
Countess of Piedade		Perpetual Handmaid of the Confraternity of Nossa Senhora da Glória do Outeiro; Perpetual Servant of the Imperial Confraternity of Passos de Nosso Senhor Jesus Cristo; member of the board of the St. Vincent de Paul Association	18, 261A, 261, 268

APPENDIX 6: Occupations of the fifty-seven shareholders of Empresa Dous de Dezembro

Shareholder	Occupation	Description	Reference in *Almanak Laemmert* (1858)
Canon Joaquim de Oliveira Durão	Priest	Curate of the Imperial Chapel; Synodal Examiner of the Episcopal Curia; teacher of dogmatic theology at the São José Seminary	105, 106, 107
Councilor Ângelo Muniz da Silva Ferraz	Capitalist	Member of the commercial section of the Statistical Society; director of Companhia Seguradora Contra a Mortalidade dos Escravos; secretary of the board of Companhia de Seguros Marítimos e Terrestres	33, 240, 326, 327
Councilor José Maria Velho da Silva		board member of the Imperial Confraternity of Passos de Nosso Senhor Jesus Cristo	11, 12, 261
Councilor Manuel José de Bessa	Capitalist	board member of Companhia de Navegação Macaé e Campos; capitalist, owner of buildings, etc.	345, 392
Dr. Antônio Pereira Leitão	Doctor	Adjunct of the general benefit society for civil servants; vice president of the Brazilian Pharmaceutical Society; member of the antitraffic commission of the Society against the Trafficking of Africans and Promoter of the Colonization and Civilization of the Indigenous Peoples; member of the Administration of Orphans at Santa Casa da Misericórdia; Doctor-surgeon	141, 234, 244, 247, 409
Dr. Domingos d'Azeredo Coutinho Duque-Estrada	Doctor	lieutenant surgeon of the 1st Reserve Battalion; alternate member of the City Council; Dramatic Institute treasurer	82, 94, 100, 206, 305
Dr. Frederico João Ormerod	Doctor	Doctor-surgeon	409

APPENDIX 6: Occupations of the fifty-seven shareholders of Empresa Dous de Dezembro

Shareholder	Occupation	Description	Reference in *Almanak Laemmert* (1858)
Dr. João Caldas Vianna	Lawyer	Secretary of the Imperial Confraternity of Passos de Nosso Senhor Jesus Cristo; legally qualified lawyer	261, 393
Dr. Joaquim Candido Soares Meirelles	Doctor	Head navy surgeon; navy captain; doctor-surgeon	12, 55, 160, 409
Dr. José Florindo de Figueiredo Rocha	Retired military officer	Retired captain; treasurer of the Brazilian Theater Conservatory	196, 230
Dr. Ludgero da Rocha Pereira Lapa	Doctor	Manuscript review committee of the Brazilian Historical and Geographic Institute (IHGB); Liberal and Mechanical Arts Section of the Department of International Affairs; doctor-surgeon	55, 57, 409
Dr. Mateus da Silva Chaves	Capitalist	Director of the Naval College; alternate of the board of primary and secondary public school board; alternate on the board of the Pedro II College	45, 49, 380
Dr. José Rufino Soares d'Almeida	Capitalist	Director of the Naval College	380
Feliciano Zeofrido Rangel Maia	Civil servant	Official of the Secretariat of the Supreme Official and Justice Council	168
Francisco José de Mello e Sousa	Merchant	Chairman of the board of the St. Vincent de Paul Association; member of the board of the Central Association on Colonization; director of the Banco Comercial e Agrícola; foreign merchant; cattle merchant and supplier	269, 316, 364, 436, 488
Francisco José de Sá Júnior	Doctor	Doctor-surgeon	12, 409
Gabriel de Medeiros Gomes	Teacher	First-year teacher of Latin and Portuguese grammar at Pedro II College	49

APPENDIX 6: Occupations of the fifty-seven shareholders of Empresa Dous de Dezembro

Shareholder	Occupation	Description	Reference in *Almanak Laemmert* (1858)
Guarda-Roupa José Joaquim dos Santos	Civil servant	Assistant customs agent	131, 473
Henrique Beauepaire Rohan	Merchant	Foreign merchant [*Almanak Laemmert,* Henrique B. R.]	436
Hermenegildo Duarte Monteiro	Retired military officer	Retired colonel; owner of the Companhia de Navegação a Vapor Sampaense	103, 351
Jacques Abrahão Lecesne	Merchant	[Omitted from the list of fireworks manufacturers in the almanack, but present in the name index]	641
João Henrique Ulrich	Capitalist	Director of the Banco do Brasil; board member of the general benefit society; foreign merchant; commissions on Imports and Exports	361, 365, 436, 439
João José Fernandes d'Azevedo	Merchant	Foreign merchant; lumber warehouses for civil construction and shipbuilding	436, 464
João Lopes Bastos		Board member of the Imperial Society of Friends of Education (Sociedade Imperial Amante da Instrução)	300
João Manuel da Silva	Capitalist	Capitalist, building owner, etc.; Brazilian merchant	492, 435
João Maria Pereira de Lacerda	Teacher	Lieutenant commander; teacher of geometry applied to the arts at the Navy School; officer of the Santa Tereza Convent; director of the St. Vincent de Paul Association	140, 157, 252, 268
João Pedro da Veiga	Merchant	Treasurer of the general benefit society for civil servants; treasurer of the Rio de Janeiro lotteries; justice of the peace of Candelária Parish; director of the Santa Casa da Misericórdia; Brazilian merchant	141, 142, 210, 247, 435

APPENDIX 6: Occupations of the fifty-seven shareholders of Empresa Dous de Dezembro

Shareholder	Occupation	Description	Reference in *Almanak Laemmert* (1858)
Joaquim Salomé Ramos	Military officer	Lieutenant-captain supervising construction of warehouses and workshops of the Companhia Brasileira de Paquetes à Vapor	42, 157
José Alves da Silva e Sá	Merchant	Foreign merchant	436
José Carlos de Carvalho	Military officer	Captain of the 2nd Company; captain of the corps of engineers of the War Ministry	172, 190
José Francisco Pereira da Costa	Military officer	2nd Company of the 4th Battalion of the National Guard	96
José Joaquim da Silva Brum	Merchant	Brazilian merchant [*Almanak Laemmert*, Brown]	435
José Maria Palhares	Merchant	Brazilian merchant; rubber planter	435, 683
Libório José de Almeida	Retired military officer	Retired lieutenant; captain of the police corps	196
Manuel José da Costa Ludovico	Employee	Head clerk of the Banco Rural e Hipotecário	362
Manuel Francisco da Costa Pereira	Military officer	Warship captain, commander of the navy battalion	157, 158
Manuel Gomes Ferreira	Merchant	Expert or practitioner in the commercial district of the 1st session; board member of the Imperial Confraternity of Passos de Nosso Senhor Jesus Cristo; Brazilian merchant; warehouse for imported wholesale dry goods	133, 261, 435, 139, 455
Manuel José Ferreira	Merchant	Grocery warehouses	473
Manuel Monteiro de Barros	Military officer	Paymaster at the 1st payroll office of the Finance Ministry; first lieutenant of the corps of engineers of the War Ministry	12, 128, 190
Marcos José Pereira do Bonfim	Doctor	Doctor-surgeon	409

APPENDIX 6: Occupations of the fifty-seven shareholders of Empresa Dous de Dezembro

Shareholder	Occupation	Description	Reference in *Almanak Laemmert* (1858)
Militão Correira de Sá	Capitalist	Member of the board of Companhia de Seguros Marítimos e Terrestres; director of the Banco do Brasil	327, 361
Father Joaquim Ferreira da Cruz Belmonte	Priest	Teacher of Latin grammar and language at the São José Seminary; finance committee of the Associação Ginásio Dramático	107, 236
Patrício Ricardo Freire, Comendador	Merchant	Expert or practitioner in the commercial district of the 1the session; director of the Venerable Confraternity of Apóstolo São Pedro; member of the Board of the Confraternity of Nosso Senhor Jesus Cristo; director of devotion at the Confraternity of Divino Espírito Santo of Santa Rita Parish; Brazilian merchant; merchants of gold, silver, and diamonds	133, 258, 261, 453, 662
Peregrino Augusto dos Santos	Merchant	Brazilian merchant; warehouses for raw tobacco in Bahia and North America	435, 461
Ricardo Soares da Costa Guimarães	Employee	Treasurer of the Caixa Econômica do Rio de Janeiro savings bank	366
Senator João Antônio de Miranda	Lawyer	Judge responsible for the codification of official laws; vice president of the Brazilian Theater Conservatory; member of the Public Workforce department of the Statistical Society; legally qualified lawyer	23, 165, 230, 240, 393
City Councilman Manuel Higino de Figueiredo	Retired military officer	Retired colonel	11, 103

APPENDIX 7: Businesses that went bankrupt in Rio de Janeiro (1857)

Name	Date of Bankruptcy	Assets (réis)	Liabilities (réis)
Henrique José Maria de Lima	9 Jan.	47,878,980	45,617,049
Bernardo Antonio de Meira	22 Jan.	2,288,963	10,147,923
Manuel Fernandes Barbosa	24 Jan.	—	—
José Luiz da Silva Pinto	13 Feb.	—	—
João Bento Martins	18 Feb.	—	—
Antonio Francisco da Costa Ferreira & Cia	19 Feb.	24,070,174	19,914,462
Medeiros Lobão & Cia	19 Feb.	24,070,174	25,840,419
José Ferreira Penetra	26 Feb.	3,853,680	9,145,483
João Demby Leite & Cia	27 Mar.	318,316,838	239,348,331
João Francisco Urzella Guimarães	07 Apr.	—	—
Francisco de Paula Brito	26 Apr.	43,737,282	187,131,682
José Manuel Telles	21 May	4,683,960	3,963,820
Manuel José da Silva	04 June	951,330	8,393,022
João José Pereira Guimarães	25 June	7,993,133	4,862,952
Bonniard & Cia	01st July	27,462,058	25,592,621
Antonio Cabral de Figueiredo	19 July	58,066,479	62,061,433
José Ribeiro de Meirelles	19 Aug.	2,169,733	3,338,904
Jeronimo Francisco de Freitas Caldas	24 Aug.	382,229,787	301,238,029
Manuel Marques Pereira Lima	24 Aug.	180,892,996	140,485,220
Lino Maria Urecha	23 Oct.	20,421,245	59,930,076
Charles Jugand	28 Oct.	19,889,218	31,823,960
Damião Antonio Moreira	12 Nov.	53,100,703	30,842,803
José Alexandre Soeiro de Faria	20 Nov.	579,344,546	524,616,649
José Maria Campos	11 Dec.	—	20,061,757
Arcangelo Fiorito	Unknown	Unknown	Unknown
Rosier Filho & Cia	Unknown	Unknown	Unknown
Paulo Joaquim da Silva	Unknown	Unknown	Unknown
José Mendes Guimarães de Oliveira	Unknown	Unknown	Unknown
Carlos F. Avelino	Unknown	Unknown	Unknown
Fonseca Motta & Cia	Unknown	Unknown	Unknown
José Antonio de Oliveira	Unknown	Unknown	Unknown
Albino José de Almeida	Unknown	Unknown	Unknown
Joaquim José Luiz	Unknown	Unknown	Unknown

APPENDIX 7: Businesses that went bankrupt in Rio de Janeiro (1857)

Name	Date of Bankruptcy	Assets (réis)	Liabilities (réis)
Domingo de Souza Ribeiro Leal	Unknown	Unknown	Unknown
Marques Lima	Unknown	Unknown	Unknown
Jorge Costa	Unknown	Unknown	Unknown
Moisés Gomes Travassos & Cia	Unknown	Unknown	Unknown
Marquês & Mendonça	Unknown	Unknown	Unknown
Bernardo Augusto Vieira Mendonça	Unknown	Unknown	Unknown
Fortunato Januário de Abreu	Unknown	Unknown	Unknown
Ramos & Cia	Unknown	Unknown	Unknown
Rosa Long	Unknown	Unknown	Unknown
Gouvêa & Braga	Unknown	Unknown	Unknown
José Bento de Araújo Bastos	Unknown	Unknown	Unknown
Fortunato Antonio da Silva Pinto	Unknown	Unknown	Unknown
Adriano Gabriel Corte Real	Unknown	Unknown	Unknown
Joaquim Pinto Rosas	Unknown	Unknown	Unknown
José Antonio da Silva Chaves	Unknown	Unknown	Unknown
Francisco Mauker	Unknown	Unknown	Unknown

Source: N. 22–A. Quadro demonstrativo das casas comerciais da praça do Rio de Janeiro que fizeram ponto e faliram de 1855 a 1865. In *Relatório da comissão encarregada pelo Governo Imperial por avisos de 1° de outubro e 28 de dezembro de 1864 de proceder a um inquérito sobre as causas principais e acidentais da Crise do Mês de Setembro de 1864*, Rio de Janeiro: Tipografia Nacional, 1865.

APPENDIX 8: Catalog of Paula Brito's bookshop published in late April 1858

Title	Price (réis)	Genre
Estampas do Gabinete Paraná	6,000	Prints
Retrato do Preto Simão	1,000	Prints
Figurinos, riscos de bordados, ditos de ponto de marca, paisagens, etc.	2,000	Prints
Teatro moderno de Lisboa	2,000	Play
Poesias de F. Palha	2,000	Poetry
O primo da Califórnia	1,000	Play
Retrato do Dr. Nunes Machado	2,000	Prints
Retrato do Exmo. Sr. Visconde de Uruguai	2,000	Prints
Retrato do Exmo. Sr. Marques de Olinda	2,000	Prints
Comédias do falecido Pena	600	Play

APPENDIX 8: Catalog of Paula Brito's bookshop published in late April 1858

Title	Price (réis)	Genre
Poesias do Sr. Pedro de Calasans	3,000	Poetry
Questão de dinheiro	1,000	Play
Fantasma branco	1,000	Play
Fatalidades de dous jovens	3,000	Novel
O forasteiro, novel by Joaquim Manuel de Macedo	2,000	Novel
A independência do Brasil	12,000	Poetry
Três dias de um noivado	2,000	Poetry
Carteira do meu tio	2,000	Novel
Estampa da morte de Nelson, na batalha de Trafalgar a bordo de seu navio	20,000	Prints
A confederação dos Tamoios	6,000	Poetry
História da Febre Amarela	2,000	Printed matter
Os hinos da minha alma	2,000	Poetry
Fábulas de esopo, em quadrinhas, por Paula Brito, para uso dos colégios	2,000	Poetry
Anais do Rio de Janeiro, pelo Sr. Balthasar da Silva Lisboa, 7 vols.	14,000	Printed matter
A caridade, poema pelo Sr. Pessoa da Silva	2,000	Poetry
O noviço	1,000	Play
Bilhetes de vinho do Porto	200	Paper goods
Bilhetes de vinho do Porto Feitoria (cada cento)	200	Paper goods
Listas de família, grandes	40	Paper goods
Listas de família, pequenas	40	Paper goods
Regulamentos para carros da praça	200	Regulations
Regulamentos para pedestres	200	Regulations
Regulamentos para depósitos de cadáveres	200	Regulations
Posturas da Ilma. Câmara	200	Regulations
Letras e papel selada por conta do governo desde 60 réis até	10,000	Paper goods
Olgiato	1,000	Play
Othelo, ou, O mouro de Veneza	1,000	Play
O cavaleiro teutônico	1,500	Play
Elogio histórico a Sra. D. Maria I	1,000	Printed matter
Revista literária e recreativa	500	Periodical

APPENDIX 8: Catalog of Paula Brito's bookshop published in late April 1858

Title	Price (réis)	Genre
Cartas de enterro para adultos e anjos, cento	3,000	Paper goods
As consolações	500	Printed matter
Vocabulário brasileiro	1,000	Printed matter
O jogo do burro ou a febre das ações	500	Play
O Uruguai	1,000	Poetry
Discurso de Marco Túlio contra Catilina	1,000	Printed matter
Juiz da paz da Roça	600	Play
Cantos da mocidade	2,000	Poetry
Ensaio corográfico do Império do Brasil	2,000	Printed matter
Inspirações de Claustro	2,000	Printed matter
O sete de setembro de 1857, feitos dos heróis da pátria	300	Printed matter
Tentativas poéticas por F. G. Braga	2,000	Poetry
Trovas do Dr. Larindo José da Silva Rebello	1,000	Poetry
Uma sessão de magnetismo ou as mesas falantes	300	Play
O cantico de Deus (com estampa) fato horroroso da igreja da Cruz	1,000	Religion
Guia para abertura e encerramento das lojas do Rito Escocês	200	Freemasonry
Novena de Santa Rita	300	Religion
Noções de moral para colégios	300	Printed matter
Opinião de Becária sobre a pena de morte	200	Printed matter
Oh que apuros ou o noivo em mangas de camisa	300	Play
Manuel Mendes	300	Play
O holandês ou pagar o mal que não fez	300	Printed matter
Vida de Santa Presciliana	300	Religion
A candianeida	300	Play
Quem porfia mata caça	600	Play
Judas em sábado de aleluia	600	Play
Diletanti	600	Play
Caixeiro da taverna	600	Play
Quem casa quer casa	600	Play
A poesia do amor	500	Poetry
Vicentina (3 vol.)	5,000	Novel

APPENDIX 8: Catalog of Paula Brito's bookshop published in late April 1858

Title	Price (réis)	Genre
O canário por Schimdt, trad. C. C. Bellegarde	300	Novel
Amador bueno	1,000	Play
Cartas em branco para missa de 7° e 30° dia, cento	8,000	Printed matter
Vida de Santo Antonio	200	Religion
Lembranças de José Antonio	5,000	Poetry
Decreto 736 da reforma do Tesouro	2,000	Printed matter
Libretos em italiano e português, cada um	1,000	Play
Columella, opera lírica	300	Play
Anais de medicina, jornal da academia, assinatura por 12 folhetos	6,000	Periodical
Guanabara, coleções dos 3 anos truncadas	15,000	Periodical
A fábia, pelo Sr. Palha, paródia para fazer rir	300	Play
Marmota, assinatura por ano	10,000	Periodical
Último momentos de D. Maria II	1,000	Sheet Music
Miscelânea do Sr. Moura para piano	1,000	Sheet Music
Miscelânea do Sr. Moura para flauta	300	Sheet Music
Bouquet das brasileiras, álbum musical com 14 peças de piano e canto	6,000	Sheet Music
Mauricianas, composições interessantes do Sr. Dr. José Maurício, com o retrato de seu falecido pai, por ele fielmente desenhado, um belo volume	6,000	Sheet Music
Folders of different sizes, priced up to 600 réis apiece	10,000	Paper goods
Blank books from 1 to . . .	100,000	Paper goods

Source: "Catálogo do que se vende na Rua do Cano, no. 44, nova tipografia e loja de Paula Brito e na Praça da Constituição, no. 64," A marmota, no. 946, 27 Apr. 1858.

Notes

FOREWORD TO THE BRAZILIAN EDITION

1. *Diário do Rio de Janeiro*, 24 Dec. 1861.
2. In Carlos Sussekind de Mendonça, *Salvador de Mendonça: Democrata no Império e na República*, Rio de Janeiro: Instituto Nacional do Livro, 1960, p. 21.
3. Georg Lukács, "Introdução aos Escritos Estéticos de Marx e Engels," in *Ensaios sobre Literatura*, Rio de Janeiro, Civilização Brasileira, 1965, p. 30.

INTRODUCTION

1. Although daguerreotypes and carte-de-visite photographs were very popular in Rio de Janeiro in the last years of Paula Brito's life, Moreira de Azevedo argues that, because of his excessive modesty, "they were never able to take his picture." Indeed, the dates of publication of the poetry and the unveiling of the portrait suggest that the former was inspired by the latter. *Correio mercantil*, Sept. 24, 1862, p. 4; Sept. 22, 1863, p. 4. In the days that followed, the Rio de Janeiro press gave some prominence to the unveiling of Paula Brito's portrait. Without mentioning the artist who produced the painting, Machado de Assis, for example, noted that the ceremony was "simple and modest," with "the friends of the deceased" being present, among whom "several spoke a few words about how much they missed him." *O futuro*, no. 8, Jan 1, 1863, p. 268. Regarding the daguerreotype, invented in

1839, and carte-de-visite photographs (1854), as well as their arrival and widespread use in Brazil from 1860, see Sandra Sofia Machado Koutsoukos, *Negros no estúdio do fotógrafo*, 2010, chap. 1, "A fotografia no Brasil do século XIX."

2. "Publicações a pedido: Biografia do Sr. Francisco de Paula Brito," *Correio mercantil*, 3 Mar. 1862, p. 2.

3. Pierre Nora, "Entre memória e história," *Projeto história*, 1993, p. 22.

4. Regarding portraits of free black people like Paula Brito, see Sandra Sofia Machado Koutsoukos, *op. cit.*, pp. 89—90. Regarding portraits and men's clothing, marked by bourgeois sobriety, see Ana Maria Mauad, "Imagem e autoimagem do segundo reinado," in *História da vida privada no Brasil*, edited by Luís Felipe de Alencastro, 1997, p. 228.

5. Regarding the concept of "memorialist construction," see Marcelo Balaban, "Poeta do lápis: A trajetória de Ângelo Agostini no Brasil Imperial—São Paulo e Rio de Janeiro—1864—1888," 2005. p. 7.

6. Manuel Duarte Moreira de Azevedo, "Publicações a pedido: Biografia do Sr. Francisco de Paula Brito," *Correio mercantil*, 28 Feb. 1862, p. 2; 2 Mar. 1862, pp. 2—3; 3 Mar. 1862, p. 2. Manuel Duarte Moreira de Azevedo, "Biografia," in Francisco de Paula Brito, *Poesias*, 1863. Joaquim Manuel de Macedo, *Anno biographico brazileiro*, 1876, v. 3, pp. 545—48. Eunice Ribeiro Gondim, *Vida e obra de Paula Brito: Iniciador do movimento editorial no Rio de Janeiro (1809—1861)*, 1965. José Veríssimo, *História da literatura brasileira: De Bento Teixeira (1601) a Machado de Assis (1908)*, 1969. Brito Broca, "Paula Brito: Mecenas Pobre," in *Românticos, pré-românticos, ultra-românticos: Vida literária e romantismo brasileiro*, 1979. Raimundo Magalhães Jr., *Vida e obra de Machado de Assis*, 2008. Jean-Michel Massa, *A juventude de Machado de Assis (1839—1870)*, 1971. Laurence Hallewell, *O livro no Brasil: Sua história*, 1985. Alessandra El Far, *O livro e a leitura no Brasil*, 2006, pp. 22—23. Célia Maria Marinho de Azevedo, "Francisco de Paula Brito: Cidadania e antirracismo nos inícios da nação brasileira," *Irohin—Jornal On Line*, 2007. Célia Maria Marinho de Azevedo. "Maçonaria: História e historiografia," *Revista da USP*, 1996—1997. Célia Maria Marinho de Azevedo. "Maçonaria, cidadania e a questão racial no Brasil escravagista," *Estudos Afro-Asiáticos*, 1998. Célia Maria Marinho de Azevedo, "A recusa da 'raça': Antirracismo e cidadania no Brasil dos anos 1830," *Horizontes antropológicos*, 2005. Ivana Stolze Lima, *Cores, marcas e falas*, 2003. José de Paulo Ramos Jr., Marisa Midori Deaecto, Plínio Martins Filho, eds., *Paula Brito: Editor, poeta e artífice das letras*, 2010. Cláudia Adriana Alves Caldeira, "Francisco de Paula Brito: Tipografia, imprensa, política e sociabilidade," 2010. Bruno Guimarães Martins. "Corpo sem cabeça: Paula Brito e a Petalógica," 2013.

7. *Diário do Rio de Janeiro*, 3 Jan. 1865, p. 1.

8. David Finkelstein, *The House of Blackwood: Author-Publisher Relations in the Victorian Era*, 2002. Michael Winship, *American Literary Publishing in the Mid-Nineteenth Century: The Business of Ticknor and Fields*, 2002. Jean-Yves Mollier, *Michel & Calmann Lévy ou la naissance de l'édition moderne, 1836—1891*, 1984. Ezra Greenspan, *George Palmer Putnam: Representative American Publisher*, 2000. Regarding Panckoucke's

pioneering efforts, see Christine Haynes, *Lost Illusions: The Politics of Publishing in Nineteenth-Century France*, 2010, pp. 16, 17.

9. Christine Haynes. *op. cit.*, pp. 16–17. Michael Winship, in his turn, places the publisher at the "central intersection" of the production and sale of printed goods, namely books, coordinating all activities in the trade, such as production and distribution. According to Winship, "the publisher is the entrepreneur of the book trade, the one who makes the decisions and takes the risks necessary to keep the whole enterprise in motion" (Michael Winship, *op. cit.*, p. 13).

10. Roger Chartier and Henri-Jean Martin, "Introduction," in *Histoire de l'édition française*, edited by Roger Chartier and Henri-Jean Martin, 1990, pp. 5–6. Odile Martin and Henri-Jean Martin. "Le monde des éditeurs," in Chartier and Martin, *op. cit.*, p. 196.

11. Christine Haynes, *op. cit.*, pp. 18, 25–30.

12. *Diário da Câmara dos Deputados à Assembleia Geral Legislativa do Império do Brasil*, no. 26, session of 10 Jun. 1826, p. 345.

13. Antônio de Moraes Silva's *Diccionario da língua portuguesa* (1789) defines *editor* as "One who publishes a book, that is, has published the work of an author, either through printed or handwritten copies" (p. 647). More succinctly, Silva Pinto's *Diccionario da língua brasileira* (1832) defines it as one who "takes charge of the publication of a work"

14. Laurence Hallewell, *op. cit.*, pp. 85–92.

15. Alistair McCleery, "The Return of the Publisher to Book History: The Case of Allen Lane," *Book History*, 2002, pp. 161–85.

16. Jean-Yves Mollier, *op. cit.*, 1984; Jean-Yves Mollier, *Louis Hachette (1800–1864)*, 1999. Ezra Greenspan, *op. cit.*, 2000.

17. François Dosse, *O desafio biográfico*, 2009; Sabina Loriga, *O pequeno x: Da biografia à história*, 2011. Regarding Brazilian historiography, see Maria da Glória de Oliveira, *Escrever vidas, narrar a história: A biografia como problema historiográfico no Brasil oitocentista*, 2011. Benito Bisso Schmidt, "História e Biografia," in Ciro Flamarion Cardoso and Ronaldo Vainfas, *Novos domínios da história*, 2012.

18. David Finkelstein, *op. cit.*, p. 2.

CHAPTER I

The Portuguese expression *pomba sem fel*, translated literally as "dove without gall," means both "paragon of virtue" and "gullible" (T.N.).

1. Caramuru was the indigenous name of Diogo Álvares Correia, one of Brazil's first Portuguese settlers (T.N.). Father Feijó made the following reference to the Caramurus in his report as justice minister on May 20, 1832: "On the seventeenth of the same month, the restorationist faction appeared with equal audacity, announced by the insolent [name of] *Caramuru*, and prepared at the *conservative conventicle*." Diogo Antonio Feijó, *Relatório do Exmo. Ministro da Justiça*, 1832, p. 2.

2. The chimango caracara (*Milvago chimango*) is a bird of prey of the Falconidei family (T.N.).

3. The option to use the terms "political faction" and "political identity" instead of "political party" follows the formulations of Marco Morel, *O período das Regências, (1831–1840)*, 2003, pp. 32–33.

4. Marco Morel, *op. cit.*, 2003, pp. 33–38. Marcello Basile, "Projetos políticos e nações imaginadas na imprensa da Corte (1831–1837)," in *Política, nação e edição*, edited by Eliana de Freitas Dutra and Jean-Yves Mollier, 2006.

5. *O meia-cara*, no. 1, 11 Nov. 1833, p. 6.

6. *O evaristo*, no. 5, 15 Nov. 1833, p. 4.

7. "Comunicado," *A verdade*, 17 Dec. 1833, p. 2.

8. Both versions of the fate of the Military Society's mural can be found in *A verdade*, 12 Dec. 1833, p. 4; 17 Dec. 1833, p. 3.

9. *A verdade*, 12 Dec. 1833, p. 4.

10. 1*A verdade*, 12 Dec. 1833, p. 4.

11. 1*A verdade*, 12 Dec. 1833; 17 Dec. 1833. *Sete d'Abril*, 10 Dec. 1833; 14 Dec. 1833; *Diário do Rio de Janeiro*, 12 Dec. 1833, p. 1.

12. "Ao público," *Diário do Rio de Janeiro*, 12 Dec. 1833, p. 1.

13. Francisco de Paula Brito, *Proclamação aos compatriotas*, n.d.; "Correspondência," *O carioca*, no. 12, 21 Jan. 1834, pp. 1–7.

14. Francisco de Paula Brito, *op. cit.*, n.d.

15. "Novo trama Liborianno," *Sete d'Abril*, 10 Dec. 1833, p. 4; see also: *A verdade*, 12 Dec. 1833, p. 5.

16. "Anúncios," *Sete d'Abril*, 14 Dec. 1833, p. 4. Emphasis in original. The printer-bookseller Plancher was not spared from *Sete d'Abril*'s mockery: "It is said that *Mister*. Plancher, as soon as he learned of the destruction of the presses of the daily *jurista* and Paraguaçu *Cacheu*, rushed to collect about 125,000,000 réis from Mr. José Miranda, the value of his establishment!" "Sopapo," *Sete d'Abril*, 14 Dec. 1833, p. 4.

17. "Anúncios," *Sete d'Abril*, 21 Dec. 1833, p. 4.

18. "Anúncios," *Sete d'Abril*, 1 Jan. 1834, p. 4. Emphasis in original.

19. *A Mulher do Simplício ou a Fluminense Exaltada*, no. 45, 12 Dec. 1835, p. 4.

20. As defined by Philippe Lejeune, an autobiography is "the retrospective definition in prose that a person makes of their own existence, when focused on their individual story, particularly the story of their personality." Philippe Lejeune, *O pacto autobiográfico*, 2008, p. 14.

21. Marco Morel, *As transformações dos espaços públicos*, 2010, chapter 6: "Em nome da opinião pública: a gênese de uma noção."

CHAPTER 2

1. "Correspondência," *O carioca*, 21 Jan. 1824, pp. 1, 4.

2. Hebe Mattos, *Escravidão e cidadania no Brasil monárquico*, 2000, pp. 22–23.

3. Despite their different approaches, there are important studies on the activities of these citizens of African descent in the first decades of the Empire: Keila Grinberg, *O fiador dos brasileiros*, 2002. Thomas Flory, "Race and Social Control in Independent Brazil," *Journal of Latin American Studies*, 1977. Célia Maria Marinho de Azevedo, *op. cit.*, 1998. Célia Maria Marinho de Azevedo, *op. cit.*, 1996–97.

4. Sergeant major was a rank between lieutenant colonel and captain in colonial and imperial Brazil (T.N.) The information that Sergeant Major Francisco Pereira de Brito was born in the Archbishopric of Lisbon is mentioned in the baptismal records of his grandchildren Francisco and Rosa, the children of his mixed-race daughter Marcelina Pereira da Encarnação. *Batizados de Várias Localidades, 1740–1754.* AEAD, caixa 296, bloco D, fls. 109, 128.

5. Raimundo José da Cunha Matos, *Corografia histórica da província de Minas Gerais (1837)*, 1981, p. 182. Junia Ferreira Furtado, *Chica da Silva e o contratador dos diamantes*, 2003, p. 30. Junia Ferreira Furtado, "O distrito dos diamantes: Uma terra de estrelas," in Maria Eugênia Lage de Resende and Luiz Carlos Vilalta, eds., *As Minas setecentistas*, 2007, pp. 305, 308.

6. See Appendix 1 and Appendix 2.

    Batizados de Várias Localidades, 1740–1754. Livro de Batismos, 1725. Livro de Batizados, 1733–1734. Registro de Batismo de Várias Localidades, 1720–1740. Registro de Batismos do Serro, 1727–1734; Casamentos do Serro, 1729–1734. Registro de Óbitos de Escravos do Serro, 1725–1797. Registros de Batismo de Várias Localidades, 1728–1733. Registros de Casamentos do Serro, 1736–1772.

    The *Ordenações Filipinas* ordered the owners of slaves from Guinea "to have them baptized and made Christians up to six months from the day they come into your power, on pain of losing them to anyone who demands them." Silvia Hunold Lara, ed., *Ordenações Filipinas: Livro V*, 1999, p. 308. Regarding the importance of parish records for the study of slavery, see Junia Furtado, *op. cit.*, 2003, pp. 144–45.

7. *Processo de habilitação matrimonial de Martinho Pereira de Brito e Anna Maria da Conceição, 1765,* fl. 17.

8. The information about Marcelina was obtained from the certificate of her marriage with Manuel Álvares de Passos, from Alagoas, in August 1756. Prior to their marriage, in September 1751, the couple had baptized their son Francisco, whose first name sounds like a tribute to the sergeant major who was the boy's grandfather. The records also show that it took some time for the union between Marcelina and Manuel to be blessed "in the form of the Holy Tridentine Council." *Registros de Casamentos do Serro, 1736–1772. Batizados de Várias Localidades, 1740–1754.*

9. *Registros de Batismo. Várias Localidades, 1720–1740,* AEAD, caixa 296, bloco B, fls. 97v.

10. *Processo de habilitação matrimonial de Martinho Pereira de Brito e Anna Maria da Conceição, 1765,* fl. 18v.

11. *Registro de Óbitos de Escravos do Serro, 1725–1797,* fl. 39v.

12. Maria Fernanda Bicalho, "Defesa e segurança: A cidade-capital," in *A cidade e o império,* 2003.

13. *Processo de habilitação matrimonial de Martinho Pereira de Brito e Anna Maria da Conceição, 1765*, fl. 23.

14. The documents pertaining to the manufacture of the lamps for the Benedictine Monastery were published by Clemente Maria da Silva-Nigra in 1941. D. Clemente Maria da Silva-Nigra, "Os dois grandes lampadários do Mosteiro de São Bento do Rio de Janeiro," *Revista do serviço do patrimônio histórico e artístico nacional*, 1941.

15. D. Clemente Maria da Silva-Nigra, *op. cit.*, 1941.

16. Anna Maria Monteiro de Carvalho, "A espacialidade do Passeio Público de Mestre Valentim," *Gavea*, n.d. Manuel de Araújo Porto-Alegre, "Iconografia Brasileira," *Revista do Instituto Histórico e Geográfico do Brazil*, 1856. Nireu Cavalcanti, *O Rio de Janeiro setecentista*, 2004, pp. 310–15.

17. *Processo de habilitação matrimonial de Martinho Pereira de Brito e Anna Maria da Conceição, 1765*. In the eighteenth century, these proceedings were also known as *banhos* (banns) and they often required a great deal of time and patience on the part of the engaged couple. In cases like that of Martinho, who was born in Vila do Príncipe in the Bishopric of Mariana, Minas Gerais Captaincy, the process could take months or even years. Basically, the purpose of these proceedings was to prove to the church authorities—through banns, certificates, and witnesses—that the engaged couple, or "contractors," were free to wed. For historians, the result of these processes is an invaluable trove of documents that makes it possible to conduct both serial analyses and detailed studies of individual lives.

18. *Processo de habilitação matrimonial de Martinho Pereira de Brito e Anna Maria da Conceição, 1765*, fls. 7, 9.

19. *Processo de habilitação matrimonial de Martinho Pereira de Brito e Anna Maria da Conceição, 1765*, fl. 23.

20. *Processo da habilitação matrimonial de Jacinto Antunes Duarte e Maria Joaquina da Conceição, 1795*.

21. *Índice de Batismo. N. Sra. da Candelária (1635–1781)*.

22. *Índice de Batismos de Livres. N. Sra. da Candelária (1758–1781)*.

23. "Almanaque da cidade do Rio de Janeiro para o ano de 1792," in *Anais da Biblioteca Nacional do Rio de Janeiro*, 1940, p. 245.

24. "Almanaque da cidade do Rio de Janeiro para o ano de 1794," in *Anais da Biblioteca Nacional do Rio de Janeiro*, 1940, p. 309. In 1799, the information about the "4° Regimento, dos homens pardos libertos" found in the "Almanac histórico da cidade de S. Sebastião do Rio de Janeiro" indicates that Martinho Pereira de Brito still held the post of Captain of the Company of Grenadiers: Antonio Duarte Nunes, "Almanac histórico da cidade de S. Sebastião do Rio de Janeiro. Ano de 1799," in *Revista do Instituto Histórico e Geográfico Brasileiro*, 1858, p. 83.

25. *Processo da habilitação matrimonial de Jacinto Antunes Duarte e Maria Joaquina da Conceição*, ACMRJ, fl. 8.

26. Eduardo França Paiva, "Coartações e alforrias nas Minas Gerais do século XVIII," *Revista de História*, 1995.

27. *Processo da habilitação matrimonial de Jacinto Antunes Duarte e Maria Joaquina da Conceição*, ACMRJ, fls. 9–10.

28. The records of the banns say little in this regard. According to one of the attached documents: "The supplicant, son of Anna Maria da Conceição, a slave at the time, as was the supplicant, of José Duarte, who upon his death left the supplicant free." *Processo da habilitação matrimonial de Jacinto Antunes Duarte e Maria Joaquina da Conceição*, fl. 8. Coincidentally, Jacinto's mother had the same name as his mother-in-law.

29. I found José's baptismal records in the *Livro de Batismo da Freguesia do Santíssimo Sacramento do Rio de Janeiro, Batismo entre 1794, Fev-1798*. The baptismal records for Paula Brito were transcribed by Eunice Gondim, *Vida e obra de Paula Brito: Iniciador do movimento editorial no Rio de Janeiro (1809–1861)*, p. 13. Regarding Ana Angélica, see Manuel Duarte Moreira de Azevedo, "Biografia do Snr. Francisco de Paula Brito," *Correio mercantil*, no. 59, 28 Feb. 1862, p. 2.

30. At the end of January 1819, the apparently peaceful existence that Paul Brito's family had enjoyed began to be disturbed when the overseer and some slaves of Lieutenant José Antonio Teixeira Guimarães, who owned land next to the farm, encroached on part of the leased area and, without Jacinto's consent, began to cut down trees for firewood and to form a clearing. Jacinto hired a lawyer and requested the embargo of the area, which was granted. However, Lieutenant Jose Antonio also hired a lawyer to defend his interests in Magé. A lawsuit began that dragged on until April of the following year in the Royal Court of Appeals in Rio de Janeiro. The information about the farm was obtained from the records of this lawsuit: *Apelação cível. Jacinto Antunes Duarte, apelante. José Antonio Teixeira Guimarães, apelado*. 1819–1820, ANRJ, Relação do Rio de Janeiro, no. 1236, caixa 592, gal. C.

31. Nielson Rosa Bezerra, "Mosaicos da escravidão," 2010, pp. 146–47.

32. *Apelação cível. Jacinto Antunes Duarte, apelante. José Antonio Teixeira Guimarães, Apelado*. 1819–1820, fls. 27–28v.

33. Manuel Duarte Moreira de Azevedo, *op. cit.*, 1862, p. 2.

34. Martin Lyons, "Os novos leitores no século XIX," in Roger Chartier and Guiglielmo Cavallo, *História da leitura no mundo ocidental*, 1999, p. 167. See also Robert Darnton's comment on Daniel Roche's studies of the reading of French workers in the eighteenth century: Robert Darnton, "Primeiros passos para uma história da leitura," in *O beijo de Lamourette: Mídia, Cultura e Revolucão*, 2010, p. 177.

35. *Mamelucos* were the mixed-race offspring of whites and Ameridians or *caboclos* (T.N.). João de Figueroa-Rêgo and Fernanda Olival, "Cor da pele, distinção e cargos: Portugal e espaços atlânticos portugueses (séculos XVI e XVIII)," *Tempo*, 2010. Geraldo Luiz Silva, "Esperança de liberdade: Interpretações populares da Abolição ilustrada (1773–1774)," *Revista de História*, 2001.

36. Sílvia Hunold Lara, *Fragmentos setecentistas: Escravidão, cultura e poder na América portuguesa*, 2007. p. 285.

CHAPTER 3

1. "Correspondência," *O carioca*, 21 Jan. 1834, p. 1.
2. Laurence Hallewell states that the apothecary shop was owned by Domingos Gonçalves Valle. However, I have not been able to find any references to him in the official sources for the 1820s, particularly in editions of the *Almanach do Rio de Janeiro* published in 1824, 1825, 1826, and 1827. Laurence Hallewell, *op. cit.*, p. 82. *Almanach do Rio de Janeiro para o ano de 1824*, 1824, p. 250. Francisco de Paula Brito, *op. cit.*, n.d., p. x.
3. "O ex-administrador da Tipografia Nacional," *A marmota*, no. 807, 6 Nov. 1857, p. 1. In the previous issue of *A marmota*, Paula Brito hailed the appointment of Manuel Antonio de Almeida to the post that Castrioto had previously occupied. "Assim, sim: Ça commence!" *A marmota*, no. 806, 3 Nov. 1857, p. 1. *Brás Antônio Castrioto, administrador da Tipografia Nacional e Imperial do Rio de Janeiro, pede mercê do Hábito da Ordem de Cristo, 1824–1828.*
4. *Resposta de José Bonifácio a respeito do aumento aos aprendizes da Imperial Cozinha*, 11 Mar. 1833.
5. *Gaspar José Monteiro, oficial compositor, oferece seus serviços à nova tipografia a ser instalada na Biblioteca Nacional e Pública do Rio de Janeiro*, 1822.
6. Isabel Lustosa, *O nascimento da imprensa brasileira*, 2004, pp. 52–59.
7. *José Francisco Lopes, mestre impressor na tipografia nacional da Bahia, 1823–1824.*
8. René Ogier, *Manual de typographia braziliense por René Ogier*, 1832. pp. 56–57, 63. For a study of the *Manual*, see Nelson Schapochnik, "Malditos tipógrafos," *I Seminário Brasileiro sobre Livro e História Editorial*, 2004.
9. "Correspondência," *O carioca*, 21 Jan. 1834, p. 2.
10. Octávio Tarquínio de Sousa, *História dos fundadores do Império do Brasil: Evaristo da Veiga*, vol. vi, 1957, chaps. 1, 2, and 3.
11. Francisco de Paula Brito, *Poesias*, p. x.
12. *Requerimento de Renato Ogier à Câmara Municipal do Rio de Janeiro*, 9 Mar. 1838. *Tipografias e artes gráficas. Vários papéis separados em ordem cronológica e referentes a tipografias, jornais e oficinas de artes gráficas, 1833–1887*, René Ogier. *op. cit.*, 1832.
13. Marco Morel claims that Paula Brito and Júlio Cezar Muzzi were among the newspaper's co-founders. However, I believe that Paula Brito's hiring as a lowly typesetter may have coincided with the founding of the *Jornal do commercio*. Marco Morel, *op. cit.*, 2010, p. 33.
14. "Correspondência," *O carioca*, 21 Jan.1834, p. 1.
15. Marco Morel, *op. cit.*, 2010, chap. 1, "As revoluções nas prateleiras da Rua do Ouvidor."
16. *Nova luz brazileira*, 8 Jan. 1830. In Marco Morel, *op. cit.*, 2010, p. 35.
17. Francisco de Paula Brito, *op. cit.*, 1863, pp. x-xi.
18. This is a favorite subject in Célia Azevedo's studies of the Brazilian publisher. See

Célia Maria Marinho de Azevedo, op. cit., 1998. Célia Maria Marinho de Azevedo, *op. cit.*, 1996–97

19. The exact amount was the considerable sum of 52,664,000 réis. Joaquim Manuel de Macedo, *Ano Biográfico Brasileiro*, pp. 407–10.
20. Hendrik Kraay, "The Politics of Race in Independence-Era Bahia: The Black Militia Officers of Salvador, 1790–1840," in *Afro-Brazilian Culture and Politics*, 1998, pp. 30–56.
21. "Vendas," *Diário do Rio de Janeiro*, 30 Mar. 1827, p. 1.
22. Francisco de Paula Brito, *Hino ao memorável dia 7 de abril de 1831*, 1831.

CHAPTER 4

1. *Livro de óbitos da Freguesia do Santíssimo Sacramento*, fl 127v.
2. *Almanach do Rio de Janeiro para o ano de 1824*, 1824, p. 267. *Almanach do Rio de Janeiro para o ano de 1825*, 1825, p. 248.
3. *Relação das obras que o livreiro Silvino tem encadernado na Biblioteca Imperial e Pública (Sept. 1823, Mar. 1832)*, 1832.
4. "Obras publicadas," *Diário do Rio de Janeiro*, 22 Mar. 1830, p. 2.
5. Marcelo Otávio Basile, *Ezequiel Correia dos Santos*, 2001.
6. Ibid., p. 22.
7. "Notícias particulares," *Diário do Rio de Janeiro*, 30 Aug. 1830, p. 3.
8. "Notícias particulares," *Diário do Rio de Janeiro*, 30 Aug. 1830, p. 3.
9. Gladys Sabina Ribeiro, *A liberdade em construção: Identidade nacional e conflitos anti-lusitanos no Primeiro Reinado*, 2002.
10. The events of March 13 to 15 are discussed on the basis of perspective in the statements by the bookseller Silvino José de Almeida and the apothecary Juvêncio Pereira Ferreira, both of which are transcribed in *Processo a respeito dos tumultos e desordens das garrafadas nas noites dos dias 12, 14 e 15 de março de 1831*. For a more complete analysis of this document, see Gladys Sabina Ribeiro, *op. cit.*, 2002, pp. 13–18.
11. *Processo a respeito dos tumultos e desordens das garrafadas nas noites dos dias 12, 14 e 15 de março de 1831*, fls. 19–20.
12. Ibid., fl. 17.
13. Bayonet-like weapons attached to pieces of wood. According to Silva Pinto's 1832 *Diccionário*, "*Chuço*, masculine noun. Stick with a *choupa* on the tip." "*Choupa*: feminine noun. . . . Iron implement tipped with garrocha poles, darts, and other cavalry weapons."
14. *Processo a respeito dos tumultos e desordens das garrafadas nas noites dos dias 12, 14 e 15 de março de 1831*, fls. 17–18.
15. Ibid.
16. Ibid., fls. 18–20.

17. "Correspondência," *O carioca*, 21 Jan.1834, p. 2. Emphasis in original.
18. Renasça em nós a vingança,
    Triunfe o sacro Heroísmo,
    Homens livres não se curvam
    Ao tirano despotismo

    Francisco de Paula Brito, *Hino oferecido à mocidade brasileira, no dia 25 de março de 1831*, 1831.
19. "Correspondência," *O carioca*, 21 Jan. 1834, p. 2.
20. Regarding the Portuguese quarter, see Gladys Sabina Ribeiro, *op. cit.*, 2002. References to straw hats as Exaltado symbols can be found in Marcelo Basile, "Revolta e cidadania na Corte regencial," *Tempo*, 2007. Paula Brito said that he had been *achincalhado* (mocked or derided) on Rua da Quitanda in his article in *O carioca*. See "Correspondência," *O carioca*, 21 Jan. 1834, p. 2.
21. Marco Morel, *O Período das Regências, (1831–1840)*, 2003, pp. 10–19.
22. José Murilo de Carvalho, *D. Pedro II*, 2007, p. 20.
23. "Correspondência," *O carioca*, 21 Jan. 1834, p. 2.
24. Parabéns Brasília gente,
    Floresce a LIBERDADE!
    Caiu do Trono o perverso
    Sucumbiu a iniquidade.

    Longe de nós os traidores,
    Longe o partido servil,
    Triunfou a INDEPENDÊNCIA
    No dia sete de Abril

    Francisco de Paula Brito, *Hino ao memorável dia 7 de abril de 1831*, 1831.
25. Eis que a Nação Libertada
    Aclama PEDRO SEGUNDO,
    Nascido nas férteis Plagas
    Do Brasil auri-fecundo

    Ibid.
26. José Murilo de Carvalho, *op. cit.*, 2007, p. 21.
27. Marco Morel, *op. cit.*, 2003, p. 24.
28. "Correspondência," *O carioca*, 21 Jan. 1834, p. 2.
29. Manuel Duarte Moreira de Azevedo, "Origem e desenvolvimento da imprensa no Rio de Janeiro," *Revista do Instituto Histórico e Geográfico Brasileiro*, 1865, pp. 169–224.
30. Octávio Tarquínio de Sousa, *História dos fundadores do Império do Brasil: Evaristo da Veiga*, 1957, p. 100.
31. "Correspondência," *O carioca*, 21 Jan. 1834, pp. 2–3.
32. Daniel P. Kidder and James C. Fletcher, *Brazil and the Brazilians: Portrayed in Historical and Descriptive Sketches*, 1857, p. 133.

33. The collection of the National and Public Library of Rio de Janeiro could be consulted in person for four hours in the mornings and for a few hours after 4:30 p.m. Loans had to be authorized by the minister who directed that institution. Débora Cristina Bondance Rocha, "Biblioteca Nacional e Pública do Rio de Janeiro: Um ambiente para leitores e leituras de romances," 2011, pp. 61–62.

34. Regarding São Paulo, its first printing press, and the founding of the Law School, see Marisa Midore Deaecto, *O império dos livros: Instituições e práticas de leitura na São Paulo oitocentista*, 2011, pp. 43–44, 55, 76. As regards the printers and newspapers of Rio de Janeiro in 1827, see Manuel Duarte Moreira de Azevedo, *op. cit.*, 1865, pp. 169–224.

35. *Diário mercantil, ou, Novo jornal do commercio*, 19 Apr. 1831, p. 1.

36. "Correspondência," *O carioca*, 21 Jan. 1834, p. 4.

37. José Murilo de Carvalho, *A construção da ordem: A elite política imperial / Teatro das sombras: A política imperial*, 2007, pp. 74–75.

38. "Correspondência," *O carioca*, 21 Jan. 1834, p. 3.

39. "Notícias particulares," *Jornal do commercio*, 10 Nov. 1831, p. 3.

40. "Notícias particulares," *Diário do Rio de Janeiro*, 15 Nov. 1831, p. 3.

41. Marcello Basile, "O império em construção: Projetos de Brasil e ação política na corte regencial," 2004, p. 141. Regarding opposition to the Moderates, see, for example, *Clarim da liberdade*, 14 Dec. 1831, p. 1.

42. Silvino is described in this manner in the case records for a criminal appeal in which he was the defendant in 1834. The case was filed on behalf of the parda woman Maria do Carmo, who having been charged with and acquitted of stealing slaves, accused the jailer of illegal imprisonment. *Apelação criminal. A Justiça, apelante. Silvino José de Almeida, réu*, 1834–1835, fl. 8.

43. "Relação dos presos que foram recolhidos à Cadeia desde o dia 12 do corrente até o dia 17 do mesmo," *Diário do Rio de Janeiro*, 20 Feb. 1832, p. 1; "Relação dos escravos que pelos diversos juízos têm entrado na Cadeia desde o dia 18 até o dia 25 do corrente," *Diário do Rio de Janeiro*, 28 Feb. 1832, p. 1.

44. In August and September 1842, Silvino was reportedly the jailer of the Aljube prison, for which he received 60,000 réis from the City Council of Rio de Janeiro. *Diário do Rio de Janeiro*, 11 Nov. 1842, pp. 1–2.

45. *Chimangada* was a derogatory term for the Moderates (T.N.).

CHAPTER 5

1. "Livros à Venda," *Diário do Rio de Janeiro*, 2 Dec. 1831, p. 1; 14 Dec. 1831, p. 1; 23 Dec. 1831, p. 1.

2. "Livros à Venda," "Obras a Publicarem-se," "Obras Publicadas," *Diário do Rio de Janeiro*, 21 Dec. 1831, p. 1; "Obras Publicadas," *Diário do Rio de Janeiro*, 29 Dec. 1831, p. 2.

3. "Livros à Venda," *Diário do Rio de Janeiro*, 20 Dec. 1831, p. 1.

4. "Livros à Venda," *Diário do Rio de Janeiro*, 30 Dec. 1831, p. 2; "Livros à Venda," *Diário do Rio de Janeiro*, 12 Dec. 1831, p. 1.

5. "Obras Publicadas," *Diário do Rio de Janeiro*, 13 Dec. 1831, p. 1; 15 Dec. 1831, p. 1; 21 Dec. 1831, p. 1.

6. Manuel Duarte Moreira de Azevedo, *op. cit.*, pp. 197−98.

7. "Obras Publicadas," *Diário do Rio de Janeiro*, 2 Dec. 1831, p. 1; 6 Dec. 1831, p. 1. *O ypiranga*, no. 2, 10 Dec. 1831, p. 1. *O Simplício da roça: Jornal dos domingos*, no. 5, 4 Dec. 1831, p. 44.

8. "Obras Publicadas," *Diário do Rio de Janeiro*, 1 Dec. 1831, p. 1; 6 Dec. 1831, p. 1; 17 Dec. 1831, p. 1; "Obras a Publicarem-se," *Diário do Rio de Janeiro*, 2 Dec. 1831, p. 1; 7 Dec. 1831, p. 1; 21 Dec. 1831, p. 1.

9. "Obras Publicadas," *Diário do Rio de Janeiro*, 6 Dec. 1831, p. 1; 16 Dec. 1831, p. 1; 17 Dec. 1831, p. 1; "Obras a Publicarem-se," *Diário do Rio de Janeiro*, 2 Dec. 1831, p. 1; 7 Dec. 1831, p. 1; 9 Dec. 1831, p. 1; 21 Dec. 1831, p. 1.

10. *Empresa Tipográfica Dous de Dezembro de Paula Brito*, n.d.

11. Marcello Basile, *op. cit.*, 2004, p. 130.

12. *O regente: Jornal político, literário*, no. 1, 12 Nov. 1831, p. 2; no. 2, 15 Dec. 1831, p. 3.

13. *O ypiranga*, no. 4, 17 Dec. 1831, p. 1; no. 5, 21 Dec. 1831, p. 1.

14. Regarding Cipriano Barata and the issues of *Sentinellas* published in Rio de Janeiro, see Marcello Basile, *op. cit.*, 2004. pp. 138−39.

15. *O Simplício da Roça: Jornal dos domingos*, no. 7, 18 Dec. 1831, pp. 55−56.

16. Rener Ogier, *op. cit.*, 1832. p. 12.

17. Ibid., p. 34.

18. *Documentos sobre a primeira tipografia em São Paulo*, 1823−1824.

19. "Notícias Particulares," *Jornal do commercio*, 6 Feb. 1832, p. 3.

20. The fourth issue of *Mulher do Simplício* and its *Suplemento*, both dated March 24, were printed at the press of Thomaz B. Hunt, on Rua do Sabão. (*A mulher do Simplício, ou, A fluminense exaltada*, no. 4, 24 Mar. 1832, p. 32; no. 8, 4 Sept. 1832, p. 68).

21. Moreira de Azevedo, for example, does not mention Paula Brito's business partner in his biography of the publisher, merely saying that by adding "a small printing workshop to the bookbinding shop, he began his life as a printer-publisher." "Biografia do Sr. Francisco de Paula Brito," *Correio mercantil*, no. 59, 28 Feb. 1862, p. 2.

22. *Cálculo para uma tipografia feito por Renée Ogier, para o jornal* Aurora Fluminense, *encontrado entre os papéis de João Pedro da Veiga*. Rio de Janeiro, 13 Nov. 1834.

23. *Conciliador fluminense*, 22 Nov. 1832, p. 5.

24. *Conciliador fluminense*, no. 2, 15 Nov. 1832, p. 4.

25. *O saturnino*, 2 Jul. 1833, pp. 1, 4. Regarding the Moderate ideology, see Marcello Basile, "Projetos Políticos e Nações Imaginadas na Imprensa da Corte (1831−1837)," in Eliana de Freitas Dutra and Jean-Yves Mollier (eds.), *Política, nação e edição: O lugar dos impressos na construção da vida política. Brasil, Europa e Américas nos séculos XVIII-XIX*, 2006, pp. 596−602.

26. Célia Azevedo asserts that Paula Brito was the editor of *O mulato, ou, O homem de cor*, stating, "It is interesting that the editor of *O homem de cor*, Francisco de Paula Brito (1809–1861), chose to print two opposing columns on the front page of its first issue." (Célia Maria Marinho de Azevedo, *op. cit.*, 2005, p. 303). However, Thomas Flory, a pioneer in dealing with such newspapers, takes a more cautious approach to this matter. Wondering who the editors of this mulatto press could have been, the author observes, "If racial solidarity was a possibility and if these journals were sincerely dedicated to the interests of society's mixed-bloods, then we could reasonably expect their editors to be colored themselves and leaders of their ethnic compatriots. As is the case with most of the newspapers of the day, however, the identity of the editors of the mulatto press remains a mystery" (Thomas Flory, *op. cit.*, 1977, pp. 212). Flory analyzes the case of well-known Afro-descendant journalists who worked during the Regency, Justiniano José da Rocha and Francisco de Sales Torres Homem. Ivana Stolze Lima, in turn, questions the importance of investigating the historical experience of these writers. In dealing with *O homem de cor*, she says, "I believe there would be no greater interest in unveiling in the author of the periodical *O homem de cor* the natural signs of a particular ancestry" (Ivana Stolze Lima, *op. cit.*, 2003, p. 51).

27. *O mulato, ou, O homem de cor*, 23 Oct. 1833, p. 4.

28. Ibid.

29. *O mulato, ou, O homem de cor*, 4 Nov. 1833, p. 4.

30. The model of an "anti-racist citizens' press" has been proposed by por Célia Maria Marinho de Azevedo, *op. cit.*, 2005. However, following Thomas Flory, I believe that Regency publications like *O homem de cor*, among others, articulated the concept of race in a specific political context that must also be taken into consideration (Thomas Flory, *op. cit.*, 1977).

31. Gladys Sabina Ribeiro has called attention to the limitations of Exaltado radicalism. See Gladys Sabina Ribeiro, "A radicalidade dos Exaltados em questão: Jornais e panfletos no período de 1831 e 1834," in Gladys Sabina Ribeiro and Tânia Maria Bessone Tavares da Cruz Ferreira, eds., *Linguagens e Práticas da Cidadania no Século XIX*, 2010.

32. "Pelo Brasil dar a vida; / Manter a Constituição / Sustentar a Independência / É a nossa obrigação." *O triumvir restaurador, ou, A Lima surda*, 21 Oct. 1833, pp. 3–4.

33. *A mineira no Rio de Janeiro*, 26 Jul. 1833, p. 1.

34. *A mineira no Rio de Janeiro*, 6 Aug. 1833, p. 1.

35. *A mineira no Rio de Janeiro*, 26 Aug. 1833, p. 1.

36. The witnesses stating that Paula Brito was the "Female Editor" of that publication include Moreira e Azevedo and Joaquim Manuel de Macedo, see Joaquim Manuel Macedo, *op. cit.*, 1876, p. 546. Manuel Duarte Moreira de Azevedo, *op. cit.*, 1865, p. 202.

37. Joaquim Manuel de Macedo, *op. cit.*, p. 548.

38. Sobre Política a tratar
    Onde alguns de seus versinhos
    Julgo dever refutar
    [. . .]
    Como quer salvar agora
    Amigos do Imperador,
    Que devera ser chamado
    D. Pedro Abdicador
    [. . .]
    Chama de vis assassinos
    Os que são hoje Exaltados,
    Quem tem derramado sangue
    São os cruéis moderados;
    São eles que se preparam
    Com tensões premeditadas
    Para a Jovens Brasileiros
    Irem cutilar d'espadas.
    [. . .]
    Eu não me alcunho de certo
    De Brasileira Exaltada; -
    Tenho já de Natureza
    Ódio à súcia moderada.

    "Resposta dada ao meu desconhecido marido, o Senhor Simplício poeta da roça,"
    A mulher do Simplício, ou, A fluminense exaltada, 10 Mar. 1832, pp. 23–24.
39. Ouvi os tristes lamentos
    D'uma Patrícia fiel,
    Inda imitar não podendo
    A Publicista *Stael*.
    [. . .]
    Lembrai-vos do sangue nosso,
    Que em Abril foi derramado,
    Pelo manejo da intriga
    Do partido moderado.
    Foi ele quem fez a guerra,
    Quem fez a desunião,
    E segundo a voz suprema,
    Foi que traiu a Nação.
    Por suas atrocidades
    Veio outro partido à luz;
    Dali nasceram rusguentos
    E também Caramurus.
    [. . .]

Reparai, que o bem geral
Só minha pena conduz,
Vós sabeis, quando eu detesto
Ingratos Caramurus.

"Carta que à Assembleia Geral Legislativa dirige a Redatora," *A mulher do Simplício, ou, A fluminense exaltada,* 4 Nov. 1832, p. 61.

40. "Francisco de Paula Brito. Casado com Rufina Rodrigues da Costa," in *Livro de casamentos de livres da Freguesia do Santíssimo Sacramento,* 1 May 1833. I would like to thank Eduardo Cavalcanti for providing this source. The baptismal records for the couple's second child, Alexandrina, which will be analyzed later, state that Alexandrina Rosa da Assunção was Rufina's mother.

41. Francisco de Paula Brito, *op. cit.,* n.d. "Correspondência," *O carioca,* 21 Jan. 1834, pp. 4, 6.

42. Manuel Alves Branco, *Relatório da repartição dos negócios da justiça apresentado à Assembleia Geral Legislativa na sessão ordinária de 1835,* 1835, pp. 11–12.

CHAPTER 6

1. Periodicals published in 1834: *Mutuca picante, Indígena do Brasil, Diário de Anúncios, Jornal da câmara dos deputados, Seis de Abril, Sorvete de bom gosto, Tupinambá pregoeiro.* In 1835, the following titles were available: *Rusga da carioca, Pão de açúcar, Mala de cartas, Ladrão, Anarquista fluminense, Estafeta Monárquico, Cuiabano, Fluminense, Sapateiro político, Eleitor, Dois pimpões, Justo meio, Justiceiro constitucional, Compadre de Itú, Capadócio, Revista médica, Simplício velho, A mulher do Simplício.* See Manuel Duarte Moreira de Azevedo, *op. cit.,* 1865, pp. 201–2.

2. "Novidade," *Sete d'Abril,* 25 Apr. 1835, p. 4.

3. Octávio Tarquínio de Sousa, *História dos fundadores do Império do Brasil: Diogo Antonio Feijó,* vol. vii, 1957, chap. 7.

4. Ibid., p. 240.

5. On the same page, *A novidade* observed: "we do not regard Mr. Holanda Cavalcanti as infallible or exempt from all conceivable defects—we do not know of any man in these circumstances; however, we do regard him as an honest, upstanding and intelligent citizen, a friend of his country, respectful of the laws and the Constitution. That is enough for us to prefer him to Mr. Feijó. (*A novidade,* 17 Mar. 1835, p. 12)

6. *Café da tarde,* no. 1, p. 6. The first four issues of *Café da tarde* are undated. The fifth is dated 15 May 1835.

7. *A novidade,* 3 May 1834, p. 1.

8. After a six-month wait, the results of the April 7, 1835, elections were announced on October 9. Feijó won with 2,826 votes. In his turn, Holanda Cavalcanti received 2,251 votes (Octávio Tarquínio de Sousa, *História dos Fundadores do Império do Brasil: Diogo Antônio Feijó,* vol. vii, 1957, p. 245).

9. *Carta de Diogo Antonio Feijó a Paulino José Soares*, 26 May 1836.

10. Published in Niterói, *Raio de Júpiter* argued that Feijó "was not elected by the Nation not only because he had received an absolute majority of the votes of the voters of the Empire but because it was done through secret intrigue." Consequently, also according to *Sete d'Abril*, "that was enough for the State to declare *war* and *war* to the death, persecution and extermination" (oi quanto bastou para o Poder lhe declarar *guerra* e *guerra* de morte, de perseguição e de extermínio). "Processo do *Raio de Júpiter*," *Sete d'Abril*, no. 338, 16 Apr. 1836, p. 4.

11. *Sete d'Abril*, 23 Apr. 1836, p. 1.

12. *Pão de açúcar*, 26 Apr. 1836, p. 1.

13. *Anais da Câmara dos Deputados*, 13 de maio de 1836, p. 48.
    In this regard, Bernardo Pereira de Vasconcelos warned: "The government does not oppress a press that has invincible power, which has been victorious in far more formidable battles. No, I do not want the government to grant permission, I want it to repress everywhere because that can only serve to compromise, dishonor this, the first of guarantees for free men. In this regard, I am reminded of what a celebrated writer of major importance said of Napoleon: 'Napoleon, son of liberty, you have murdered your own mother.' I will say this to our government: son of the press, and only of the press, new Nero, you conspire against the life of your own mother" (*Anais da Câmara dos Deputados*, 13 May 1836, p. 50).
    In the following session, Limpo de Abreu, Regent Feijó's justice minister, sought to justify the government's actions, implicitly referring to the case of *Raio de Júpiter*: "has been charged with crimes under the law on freedom of the press and defends itself against that charge with the articles of the code, which demonstrate that defendants can be prosecuted in their home forum or the forum where the crime was committed. It also accuses the government of unjust censorship aimed at influencing the elections and demonstrates that despite the government's strenuous efforts, it did not have many ways to influence those elections; and it greatly doubts whether the illustrious deputy can produce evidence justifying his claim; that it is a principle that recognizes that the bigwigs may be their own spawn and not creatures of the government; and how, then, can the government go against this principle, which it recognizes?" (*Anais da câmara dos deputados*, 14 May 1836, pp. 52–53).

14. *Jornal do commercio*, 9 Apr. 1842, pp. 2–3.

15. *Processo contra Nicolau Lobo Vianna e José Joaquim de Abreu Gama, impressor e responsável pelo periódico* Caramuru*, por abuso da liberdade de imprensa e sedição contra o governo*, 1832–1833, fl. 19.

16. The records listed included the following: "Francisco de Paula Brito, printer of the periodical *Seis de Abril Extraordinário* no. 1, charged on 76 June 1834" ("Relação dos Processos Apresentados na Sessão do Júri de 14 de Agosto de 1840, pelo Juiz de Paz da Cabeça do Termo José Rodrigues de Amorim," *Diário do Rio de Janeiro*, 28 Jan. 1840, p. 2).

17. "Notícias particulares," *Diário do Rio de Janeiro*, 29 Jan. 1840, p. 4. Emphasis in original.

18. In the field of History, I have not found any extensive studies of press law in Brazil similar to José Tengarrinha's enlightening work on Portugal, *Da liberdade mitificada à liberdade subvertida*, 1993. However, the summaries and compilations of the laws published by Marcello de Ipanema have been useful for the Brazilian case: *Estudos de história de legislação de imprensa*, 1949a; *Livro das leis de imprensa de D. João*, 1949; *Síntese da história da legislação luso-brasileira de imprensa*, 1949. Antonio F. Costella focuses specifically on this matter but adds little to the summaries Ipanema presented: *O controle da informação no Brasil*, 1970. The press law also receives some attention in Nelson Werneck Sodré, *História da imprensa no Brasil*, 1999; Isabel Lustosa, *Insultos impressos: A guerra dos jornalistas na Independência*, 2000.

19. Diogo Antonio Feijó, *op. cit.*, 1832.

20. Ibid., pp. 9–10.

21. "Lei de 26 de Outubro de 1831." Emphasis mine.

22. According to Article 4 of the Law of 6 June 1831, "bail shall not be granted to those caught in flagrante delicto when committing police crimes" ("Lei de 6 de Junho de 1831").

23. Paulo Domingues Vianna, *Direito criminal: Segundo as preleções professadas pelo Dr. Lima Drummond*, 1930, pp. 244–46.

24. "Decreto de 2 de Março de 1821."

25. These were the decrees of 8 May and 28 August 1821. Both can be found in Marcello de Ipanema, *Síntese da história da legislação luso-brasileira de imprensa*, 1949, p. 57.

26. "Aviso de 24 de Setembro de 1821." Ipanema, *Síntese da história*, pp. 57–58.

27. Silva Pinto, *Diccionário da língua brasileira*, 1832.

28. Marcello de Ipanema, *Síntese da história da legislação luso-brasileira de imprensa*, 1949, p. 58

29. Ibid.

30. Ibid., pp. 87–88.

31. José Murilo de Carvalho, *A construção da ordem / Teatro das sombras*, 2007, p. 54.

32. Backed by deputies José Antonio da Silva Maia, Bernardo José da Gama, Estevão Ribeiro de Resende, José Teixeira da Fonseca Vasconcelos, and João Antonio Rodrigues de Carvalho, this bill, consisting of forty-six articles, was submitted to the Constituent Assembly during the session held on October 6. *Anais da Assembleia Nacional Constituinte*, 6 Oct. 1823, p. 32.

33. Ibid., pp. 32–34.

34. The cases listed in the bill included writing against the "Roman Catholic faith," "directly inciting the people to rebellion," "attacking the representative constitutional monarchy form of government," "defaming the National Assembly," "inciting the people to disobey the laws or the authorities," acting "against Christian morals and ethics," and accusing "civil servants and private individuals of criminal acts." Ibid.

35. The deputy in question was Manuel Joaquim Carneiro da Cunha. Ibid., p. 34.

36. Ibid., p. 33.

37. Ibid., p. 32.

38. It is very interesting to follow this debate, particularly the discussion of article 3 of the bill, when deputies Francisco Jê Acaiaba de Montezuma and Antônio Ferreira França argued that not only the printer but the purchasers of publications without an imprint statement should be punished. *Anais da Assembleia Nacional Constituinte*, 8 Nov. 1823, pp. 218–19.

39. "I hereby see fit to order that the bill on this matter [freedom of the press], dated October 2 inst. . . . be fully and entirely executed on a provisional basis as of the publication of this decree until the establishment of the new Assembly which I have summoned." ("Decreto de 22 de Novembro de 1823").

40. According to Title VIII, "On the general provisions, and guarantees of civil and political rights," article 179, paragraph four, "Everyone may communicate his thoughts, in written words, and publish them in the Press, without depending on censorship; as long as they are held responsible for the abuses that they commit in the exercise of this right, in the cases, and in the form that the law determines." The law in force at the time was the Decree of 22 November 1823, which would be ratified again three years later in the Decree of 11 September 1826.

41. *Anais da Câmara dos Deputados*, 10 Jun. 1826, pp. 91–92.

42. *Anais da Câmara dos Deputados*, 3 Mar. 1830, p. 30.

43. In Marcello de Ipanema, *Síntese da história da legislação luso-brasileira de imprensa*, 1949, p. 66.

44. Provisions of articles 303 and 307. *Código Criminal do Império do Brasil*, "Lei de 16 de dezembro de 1830."

45. *Jornal do commercio*, 9 Apr. 1842, pp. 2–3.

46. "Decreto de 18 de Março de 1837."

47. In Marcello de Ipanema, *Síntese da história da legislação luso-brasileira de imprensa*, 1949, pp. 73–74.

CHAPTER 7

1. "Aproveitável aula de meninas," *O Brasil*, 22 Jun. 1844, p. 4.

2. "Notícias Particulares," *Diário do Rio de Janeiro*, 19 Oct. 1835, p. 3.

3. The following periodicals printed by Silva Sobral's Impartial Press in São Paulo can be found in the Edgard Leuenroth Archives (Unicamp): *Catolico, O periódico acadêmico* (1838), *O escandaloso* (1840), *O observador das galerias* (1838–1842), *O publícola* (1840), and *O tebyreçá* (1841).

4. *O cidadão*, 15 Mar. 1838, p. 2.

5. Cremière, Rua da Alfândega no. 135; Désiré Dujardin, Livraria Belgo-Francesa, Rua do Ouvidor no. 105; Livraria Universal de Laemmert, Rua da Quitanda no. 77; Firmin Didot Irmãos, Rua da Quitanda no. 97; Garnier Irmãos, Rua do Ouvidor no. 69; Girard e de Christen, Rua da Quitanda no. 33; Júnio Villenueve e Companhia,

Rua do Ouvidor no. 65; Luís Ernesto Martin, Livraria Portuguesa, Rua dos Ourives no. 73B; Mongie, Rua do Ouvidor no. 87 (*Almanak Laemmert*, 1850, pp. 322–23).

6. Regarding the circulation of books and the major retail networks established in the nineteenth century linking Brazil and Europe, particularly France, see Marisa Midori Deaecto, *op. cit.*, 2011, pp. 289–71.

A considerable number of French merchants were registered with the Rio de Janeiro city council in 1843. All told, there were 328 French-owned businesses. The largest urban concentration of French merchants in Rio was in Santíssimo Sacramento parish with a total of 139. (*Estatística de casas de comércio, número de rezes, embarcações, veículos terrestres e notas sobre licenças para obras, alvarás de negócio e receita e despesa*, 1843).

7. *Comércio estrangeiro. Papéis separados por ordem cronológica*, 1839–1872, fls. 36–37.

8. *Almanak Laemmert*, 1850, pp. 322–23, 419.

9. *Gazeta dos tribunais*, no. 227, 6 May 1845, pp. 3–4. See Appendix 3 in this book.

10. "Francisco de Paula Brito, Praça da Constituição, 64. This shop sells all the works of which it is the publisher—Dous de Dezembro Press—and those which are commissioned, in the form of style, both in paperback and hardcover." "Mercadores de Livros," *Almanak Laemmert*, 1852, p. 404.

11. Quem tiver *gosto* em gozar
O *gosto bom*, que o chá tem,
Pode *dar gosto* mostrando,
Que tem *bom gosto* também.

"Chá Brasileiro," *O farol*, no. 157, 28 Aug. 1844, p. 4.

12. "Notícias Particulares," *Diário do Rio de Janeiro*, 11 Sept. 1834, p. 4.

13. *Carta de Frei Camilo de Monserrate ao Ministro Luiz Pedreira do Couto Ferraz, solicitando o pagamento de uma dívida contraída com o livreiro Paula Brito pela antiga administração da Biblioteca Nacional. Rio de Janeiro*, 14 Nov. 1853.

14. "Ao publico," *O Brasil*, 31 Oct. 1844, p. 6. Emphasis in original.

15. A. Frey, *Manuel nouveau de typographie*, 1835, pp. 362–66.

16. Paul Dupont, *Histoire de l'imprimerie*, 1854. pp. 401–2.

17. "Circular do Redator do *Correio do Brasil*," *O grito nacional*, 20 Feb. 1853, p. 2.

18. "A nossa empresa," *O Brasil*, 4 Feb. 1848, p. 2.

19. Tipografia Nacional," *Anuário político, histórico e estatístico do Brasil*, 1847, pp. 206–8. Article 35 of Law 369 of 18 September 1845, which set the Empire's expenditure and income for the two-year period of 1845–1846, stipulated that "The government may apply the surpluses of the National Press, and the amounts left over from other items of expenditure to purchase a mechanical press and new type" (Lei 369 de 18 de Setembro de 1845. Fixando a Despesa, e Orçando a Receita para o Exercício de 1845–1846, *Coleção de Leis do Império do Brasil*, 1845, p. 47).

20. "The brig *Augantyre*, scheduled to depart from London on the ninth of last month, is carrying a mechanical press for the *Correio mercantil* that will enable us to complete the improvements we promised to our readers at the beginning of this year." (*Correio mercantil*, 9 Apr. 1853, p. 2).

CHAPTER 8

1. Numbers obtained from survey done at the Arquivo Edgard Leuenroth (AEL). The collection of newspapers in these archives is made up of microfilm from the collection of the National Library of Rio de Janeiro.
2. *A ortiga*, 10 Aug. 1839, p. 2. Emphasis in original.
3. "Aos Srs. Subscritores," *Arquivo médico brasileiro*, Dec. 1844, p. 120; "Academia Imperial de Medicina," *Almanak Laemmert*, 1843, p. 171.
4. "Aos Srs. Subscritores," *Arquivo médico brasileiro*, Dec. 1844, p. 120; "Aos Srs. Subscritores," *Arquivo médico brasileiro*, Feb. 1845, p. 172.
5. "Aos Srs. Assinantes," *Anais de medicina brasiliense*, 1 Jun. 1846, p. 1. Similarly, in 1851, Dr. Roberto Jorge Haddock Lobo thanked Paula Brito for his work during the physician's tenure as the journal's editor. See *Anais de medicina brasiliense*, 1 Sept. 1851, p. 288.
6. "Relatório dos trabalhos da Academia Imperial de Medicina lido na sessão anual em 30 de junho de 1846." *Anais de medicina brasiliense*, 1 Jul. 1846, p. 42.
7. Antônio Francisco de Paula Holanda Cavalcante d'Albuquerque, *Proposta e Relatório apresentado à Assembleia Geral Legislativa na 3ª Sessão da 6ª Legislatura pelo Ministro e Secretário de Estado dos Negócios da Fazenda*, 1846, p. 4.
8. Lei de 3 de Outubro de 1832.
9. "Faculdade de Medicina do Rio de Janeiro"; "Academia Imperial de Medicina," *Almanak Laemmert*, 1846, pp. 70–17, 193–94.
10. "Obras médicas," *Arquivo médico brasileiro*, Dec. 1845, p. 96; Jan. 1845, p. 144.
11. "Escola de Medicina: Colação de graus," *Arquivo médico brasileiro*, Dec. 1844, p. 120.
12. "Tipografias," *Almanak Laemmert*, 1844, p. 257.
13. "Obras publicadas: *A Moreninha*," *Diário do Rio de Janeiro*, 23 Apr. 1845, p. 2. The second edition of *A moreninha* was published in 1845 by I. P. da Costa's Americana Press.
14. The historiography of the Brazilian novel is vast. Particularly worthy of note are recent studies marked by competent empirical research such as those in Marcia Abreu (ed.). *Trajetórias do romance*, 2008. Among these studies, Ilana Heineberg described the early phase of the Brazilian serialized novel as "mimetic," because there is no clear distinction between the national and foreign narratives that occupied the same space in *Jornal do commercio*. Ilana Heineberg, "Miméticos aclimatados e transformados: Trajetórias do romance-folhetim em diários fluminenses," in Marcia Abreu (ed.), *op. cit.*, p. 502. Jefferson Cano, in turn, observes the distinction between the first Brazilian novels and their European forebears. For that historian, the national character in these narratives was built as much in opposition to the European model as in the tension between the "local and the provincial," important in times of revolts like the Farroupilha uprising. Jefferson Cano, "Nação e ficção no Brasil do século XIX," *História Social*, 2012.
15. "UM ROUBO NA PAVUNA, Brazilian novel. Distributed to subscribers at Paula Brito's shop for 500 réis and for sale for 800 réis." ("Obras publicadas," *Diário do Rio de Janeiro*, 13 May 1843, p. 3.)

16. Born in Rio de Janeiro in 1791, Azambuja Susano originally wanted to be a priest, attending the São Joaquim Seminary. After abandoning his religious studies and moving to Espírito Santo, he embarked on a successful career as a treasury agent in that province. In addition to *Um roubo na Pavuna* and compendiums and legal works, Azambuja Susano published two more fictional narratives: *O Capitão Silvestre e Frei Veloso, ou, A plantação de café no Rio de Janeiro* (1847) and *A Baixa do Matias, ordenança do Conde dos Arcos, vice-rei do Rio de Janeiro, romance-histórico-jurídico* (1858). See "Notícia sobre Azambuja Suzano," *Autores e livros*, Feb. 1950, pp. 13, 15.

17. "Folhetim: O filho do pescador, romance brasileiro original," *O Brasil*, 6 Jun. 1843, p. 1; 22 Aug. 1843, p. 1. Hebe Cristina da Silva has produced a meticulous study of the works of Teixeira e Sousa in "Prelúdio do romance brasileiro: Teixeira e Sousa e as primeiras narrativas ficcionais," 2009.

18. The first advertisement found that announces the sale of the novel was in "Obras publicadas," *Diário do Rio de Janeiro*, 25 Sept. 1843, p. 2.

19. "Obras publicadas: *Arquivo Romântico Brasileiro*," *Diário do Rio de Janeiro*, 20 Feb. 1847, p. 3.

20. Ibid.

21. Joaquim Norberto de Sousa e Silva, "Biografia dos brasileiros ilustres por amar, letras, virtudes etc.: Notícia sobre Antônio Gonçalves Teixeira e Souza e suas obras," *Revista do Instituto Histórico, Geográfico e Etnográfico Brasileiro*, 1876, pp. 202–3.

22. Ibid., p. 206

23. Teixeira e Sousa announced the founding of the Teixeira & Co. Press in the *Gazeta dos tribunais*: "Notice: New Press on Rua dos Ourives, no. 21," *Gazeta dos tribunais*, 4 Nov. 1845, p. 4. The "amicable dissolution" of the partnership was announced in 1849. On that occasion, Paula Brito observed that he was still running the establishment: "Anúncio," *O Brasil*, 3 Sept. 1849, p. 4. Regarding Teixeira e Sousa's move to Engenho Velho, see Joaquim Norberto de Souza e Silva, *op. cit.*, p. 210.

24. "Obras publicadas," *Diário do Rio de Janeiro*, 22 Dec. 1842, p. 3. *Gazeta dos tribunais*, 15 Jun. 1849, p. 4. "Anúncio," *O Brasil*, 16 Mar. 1844, p. 4. "Crítica bibliográfica: *A independência do Brasil. Poema épico em XII cantos*," *Diário do Rio de Janeiro*, 5 Nov. 1847, pp. 2–3.

25. José de Paula Ramos Jr., Marisa Midori Deaecto, and Plínio Martins Filho, eds., *Paula Brito: Editor, poeta e artífice das letras*, 2010, pp. 183–257.

CHAPTER 9

1. See Introduction, note 6.

2. *Inventário. Francisco de Paula Brito, falecido. Rufina Rodrigues da Costa Brito, Inventariante*, 1862.

3. *Marmota fluminense*, 22 Mar. 1853, p. 1.

4. "Movimento do porto," *Diário do Rio de Janeiro*, 26 Feb. 1853, p. 4.

5. "Lettres brésiliennes," *Courrier du Brésil*, 5 Oct. 1856, p. 2.

6. "Crônica diária," *Diário do Rio de Janeiro*, 21 May 1856, p. 1. "Foundation d'un etablissement de lithographie," *Courrier du Brésil*, 1 Jun. 1856, p. 4.

7. In two advertisements posted in *Marmota fluminense*, Paula Brito recommended and guaranteed the quality of his former employee's services: "For, as an artist, he is more than capable of doing all his work well, and quickly, adding to his uncommon aptitude, capability that will pass any test." ("O Tipógrafo Teixeira," *Marmota fluminense*, 18 Feb. 1853, p. 6; 22 Feb. 1853, p. 6.)

8. "Decreto no. 384 de 16 de Outubro de 1844." I would like to thank Ana Paula Cardozo de Souza for this source.

9. Ibid.

10. In August 1844, Minister Manuel Alves Branco reviewed the 15 percent tariff on products imported from Britain that had been charged since 1810. Increasing that levy, the "Alves Branco Tariff," as it became known, brought in more revenue for the government and benefited nascent domestic manufacturers because it exempted them from tariffs on imports of machinery and raw materials. See Leslie Bethell, José Murilo de Carvalho, "O Brasil da Independência a meados do século XIX," in Leslie Bethell, *História da América Latina: Da Independência a 1870*, 2001, p. 747.

11. Justiniano José da Rocha, "As patentes das imprensas," *O Brasil*, 10 Dec. 1844, p. 1.

12. Ibid.

13. Translated here as Creole, the term *crioulo* historically referred to the children and descendants of African slaves, who having been born in Brazil, were acculturated and native speakers of Portuguese (T.N.).

14. Regarding Francisco's escape from slavery, see "Atenção," *Correio mercantil*, 25 Aug. 1858, p. 4. On the role of beaters, see Robert Darnton, *O iluminismo como negócio*, 1996, p. 189.

15. "Escravos fugidos," *Jornal do commercio*, 11 Nov. 1831, p. 2.

16. "Escravos fugidos," *Correio mercantil*, 30 Aug. 1830, p. 4.

17. José Murilo de Carvalho, *op. cit.*, 2007. p. 65. According to census data for 1872, just one-fifth of the free population of Imperial Brazil was literate. Leslie Bethell and José Murilo de Carvalho, *op. cit.*, 2001, p. 695.

18. Artur José Renda Vitorino, *Máquinas e operários: Mudança técnica e sindicalismo gráfico (São Paulo e Rio de Janeiro, 1858–1912)*, 2000, p. 39.

19. *Apelação criminal. A Justiça, autor. Theodoro, crioulo escravo de Junius Villeneuve e Cia, réu*, 1863, fl. 52. I have analyzed the case of Theodoro in Rodrigo Camargo de Godoi, "Trabalho escravo e produção de impressões no Rio de Janeiro oitocentista," *Textos da Escola São Paulo de Estudos Avançados*, 2012.

20. Artur José Renda Vitorino, *op. cit.*, 2000, p. 100.

21. Ibid., pp. 71–72, 99.

22. Thomas Ewbank, *A vida no Brasil*, 1976 [1856], p. 151.

23. Regarding the many types of labor performed by slaves in Rio de Janeiro, see Mary C. Karasch, *A vida dos escravos no Rio de Janeiro (1808–1850)*, 2000, chap. 7. Luiz Carlos Soares, *O povo de "Cam" na capital do Brasil*, 2007, chap. 6.

24. Frederico Leopoldo César Burlamaqui, *Memória analítica acerca do comércio d'escravos e acerca dos males da escravidão doméstica*, 1837, p. 22.

25. "Biografia do Senhor Francisco de Paula Brito," *Correio mercantil*, 2 Mar. 1862, pp. 2–3. Joaquim Manuel de Macedo, *op. cit.*, 1876, pp. 545–48.

26. Sidney Chalhoub, *A força da escravidão*, 2012.

27. "Escravos Fugidos," *Diário do Rio de Janeiro*, 9 set. 1837, p. 4.

28. Regarding Africans from the Congo nation, see Mary C. Karasch, *op. cit.*, 2000, p. 482.

29. Foreign travelers who visited Rio de Janeiro in the first half of the nineteenth century noted the importance of hired-out slaves to the finances of families who owned one or two captives. See Roberto Guedes Ferreira, "Autonomia escrava e (des)governo senhorial na cidade do Rio de Janeiro da primeira metade do século XIX," in Manolo Florentino, *Trabalho, cativeiro e liberdade (Rio de Janeiro, séculos XVII-XIX)*, 2005, p. 234.

30. Frederico Leopoldo César Burlamaqui, *op. cit.*, p. 84.

31. "Aluguéis," *Diário do Rio de Janeiro*, 23 May 1837, p. 2.

32. *Batismo de Rofina, inocente*. Brazil, Catholic Church Records, Rio de Janeiro, Santíssimo Sacramento, Batismos 1833–1837, Image 163. *Batismo de Alexandrina, inocente*. Brazil, Catholic Church Records, Rio de Janeiro, Santíssimo Sacramento, Batismos 1833–1837, Image 249.

33. Throughout most of the nineteenth century, supplying water for Rio de Janeiro households and doing laundry were tasks performed by slave women and maids at the city's public fountains, which became important places for those women to socialize. Sandra Lauderdale Graham, *Proteção e obediência*, chap. 2, 1992.

34. "Os estrangeiros," *O grito nacional*, no. 119, 11 Jan. 1850, pp. 2–5. Paula Brito's groomsmen were Francisco Antônio de Mendonça and Mariano José de Oliveira. "Francisco de Paula Brito. Casado com Rufina Rodrigues da Costa." *Livro de casamentos de livres da Freguesia do Santíssimo Sacramento*, fl. 145v, 1 May 1833.

35. "Escravos Fugidos," *Diário do Rio de Janeiro*, 9 Sept. 1837, p. 4.

36. "Aluguéis," *Diário do Rio de Janeiro*, 18 Aug. 1838, p. 4

37. *Carregamento do Patacho Cesar*, ANRJ, IJ6 471.

38. Ibid.

39. "Declarações," *Diário do Rio de Janeiro*, 4 Aug. 1838, p. 2.

40. For obligatory reading on free Africans in Imperial Brazil, see the research of Beatriz Gallotti Mamigonian: "To Be a Liberated African in Brazil: Labour and Citizenship in the Nineteenth Century," 2002; "Revisitando a 'transição para o trabalho livre': A experiência dos africanos livres," in Manolo Florentino, *op. cit.*; "O direito de ser africano livre: Os escravos e as interpretações da Lei de 1831," in Silvia Hunold Lara and Joseli Maria Nunes Mendonça, eds., *Direitos e justiças no Brasil: Ensaios de história social*, 2006.

41. Regarding the Cassange, see Mary C. Karasch, *op. cit.*, 2000, p. 485.

42. Perdigão Malheiro, *A escravidão no Brasil: Ensaio histórico, jurídico, social*, 1976 [1867], p. 61.

43. "Sinopse dos trabalhos do júri do município do Rio de Janeiro, durante a sessão ordinária do mês de março próximo passado," *Despertador*, 22 Apr. 1840, p. 2.

44. Regarding the Sunde, see Mary C. Karasch, *op. cit.*, p. 488.

45. *Malungo* means "fellow traveler," the name given to people who survived the Middle Passage aboard the same slave ship (T.N.). Brought to Brazil on the same slave ship as Fausto, Isaac was described as "thin, toothy, with a shaved head from leaving the House of Correction," aged "11 to 12" when he escaped from his dealer in 1842. Similarly, Jovita fled from her arrematante in 1840, "aged 11 to 13." ("Escravos fugidos," *Diário do Rio de Janeiro*, 27 May 1842, p. 4. *Despertador*, 24 Feb. 1840, p. 4.) On the back of Fausto's letter of manumission, signed on June 28, 1839, we find this laconic note: "Died February 14, 1841, his services had been entrusted to Francisco de Paula Brito." (*Carta de emancipação do africano Fausto de nação Sunde.*)

46. *Relação nominal das pessoas a quem têm sido confiados Africanos livres, quantos e seu estado de dívida em 31 de dezembro de 1844, desde o segundo semestre do ano financeiro de 1840–41 em que passou a arrecadação de seus salários a ser feito pela Recebedoria do Município da Corte, até o fim do ano financeiro próximo findo de 1843–1844 na forma exigida em aviso da Secretaria de Justiça de 10 de setembro de 1844.*

47. *Relação de todos os Africanos Livres que até a presente data ainda se acham sob a responsabilidade dos particulares que foram confiados, Março de 1861*, fs. 290–344. I would like to thank Professor Daryle Williams for this reference. The destination of slave caravans from the interior, Quelimane is a seaport north of the River Zambeze in Mozambique. According to Mary Karasch, lower prices and an adequate supply of young people aged ten to fourteen also attracted Brazilian slavers to that part of East Africa. (Mary C. Karasch, *op. cit.*, pp. 61, 494.)

48. *Secretaria de Polícia da Corte, dossiê relativo a Agostinho Moçambique, September 1862.* ANRJ, IJ6 516. I am grateful to Professor Sidney Chalhoub for this document. I would also like to thank Professor Robert Slenes for his essential help in deciphering the word "Quelimane," which was abbreviated in the source.

49. *Petição de transferência dos serviços da africana livre Maria Benguela, autor Francisco de Paula Brito.* 11 Jun. 1857. I would like to thank Professor Daryle Williams for informing me about this document. Regarding Fernando Rodrigues Silva's work in "the office of notary and clerk of the court and orphans in the town of Valença," see "Expediente da secretaria do governo," *Diário do Rio de Janeiro*, 25 Mar. 1850, p. 1.

50. Beatriz Gallotti Mamigonian, *op. cit.*, 2002, pp. 103–4.

51. Carlos Eduardo Moreira de Araújo, *Cárceres imperiais: A Casa de Correção do Rio de Janeiro, seus detentos e o sistema prisional no Império, 1830–1861*, pp. 182, 186, 265–66.

52. In this regard, Paula Brito was different from the other *arrematantes* identified by Mamigonian, most of whom were engaged in nonproductive activities such as military and civil service. Beatriz Gallotti Mamigonian, *op. cit.*, 2002, pp. 88, 104.

53. *Aviso da Secretaria de Justiça ao Juiz de Órfãos.* Beatriz Gallotti Mamigonian, *op. cit.*, p. 302. Full document reproduced.

54. Ibid., 2002, pp. 88, 105.

55. *Despertador*, 14 May 1839, p. 1.
56. Ibid.
57. Ibid.
58. According to Chalhoub, granting Africans to private individuals "oiled the machine of a patronage and bribery in the Imperial government." Sidney Chalhoub, *op. cit.*, 2012, p. 55.
59. "Os Africanos," *O Brasil*, 24 Oct. 1840, p. 2.
60. Attributed to Justiniano José da Rocha by Raimundo Magalhães Jr., *Três panfletários do segundo reinado*, 2009, pp. 133–34.

CHAPTER 10

1. "Os Estrangeiros," *O grito nacional*, 11 Jan. 1850, p. 3. Joaquim Manuel de Macedo, *op. cit.*, 1876, p. 546. Between May 1839 and March 1840, Paula Brito translated some French narratives published in the satirical pages of *Jornal do commercio* and poems by Parny published in *A mulher do Simplício, ou, A fluminense exaltada* (25 Dec. 1840, pp. 12, 14–15) and (22 Dec. 1842, p. 12).
2. "Notícias particulares," *Diário do Rio de Janeiro*, 28 Nov. 1836, p. 3.
3. Henri-Benjamin Constant de Rebecque (1767–1830), the Swiss-French political activist and writer who inspired Brazilian liberalism.
4. Jefferson Cano, "Justiniano José da Rocha, cronista do desengano," in Sidney Chalhoub, Margarida de Souza Neves, Leonardo Affonso de Miranda Pereira, *História em cousas miúdas: Capítulos de História Social da crônica no Brasil*, 2005.
5. While translating this book, Sabrina Gledhill, whom I would like to thank, found an edition of *Os abrasadores* in volume 5 of *Arquivo Teatral, ou, Coleção seleta dos mais modernos dramas do teatro francês*, published in Lisbon in 1842. However, we do not know if this is the translation by Paula Brito that was staged in 1836. The Portuguese edition is available on Google Books.
6. Vivas se entoem aos Leais ANDRADAS
   Que parte houveram nessa Grande Empresa,
   E a quem o Brasil já deve tanto!
   Que alegres festejamos, saiba o Mundo:
   PÁTRIA, CONSTITUIÇÃO, PEDRO SEGUNDO
   "A constituição brasileira," *A mulher do Simplício, ou, A fluminense exaltada*, 25 Mar. 1837, p. 8.
7. "O senador," *A mulher do Simplício, ou, A fluminense exaltada*, 22 Dec. 1838, pp. 7–8.
8. José Bonifácio de Andrada e Silva, *Elogio Acadêmico da Senhora D. Maria Primeira, recitado por José Bonifácio de Andrada e Silva, em sessão pública da Academia Real das Ciências de Lisboa aos 20 de março de 1817*, 1839.
9. "O ano de 1839 e o de 1840," *A mulher do Simplício, ou, A fluminense exaltada*, 21 jun. 1840, p. 1. Emphasis in original. The poem was also published separately for

292 NOTES TO PAGES 117–118

sale or distribution. Francisco de Paula Brito, *Hino à maioridade de Sua Majestade o Imperador proclamado pela Assembleia, tropa e povo, no dia 22 de julho de 1840*, 1840.

10. Salve, por Ti, Senhor, este áureo Dia
    Da Tua Aclamação! Ó tenro Pedro
    Brasileiro Monarca—salve a glória
    Que teve em Te Aclamar Teu grato Povo!
    Pátria! Pátria feliz despe esse luto,
    Que há longo tempo teu pesar nos mostra;
    Brasílio Povo, generoso e dócil,
    Já não tens que temer o braço hediondo
    Da falaz anarquia

    "Ao dia 23 de julho de 1840, recitado em presença de Sua Majestade Imperial o Senhor Dom Pedro II, e de suas irmãs no teatro de São Pedro d'Alcântara, na noite em que se esperava a organização do novo ministério," *A mulher do Simplício, ou, A fluminense exaltada*, 1 Dec. 1840, p. 3.

11. Produz a Maioridade
    Os desejados efeitos?
    A prometida igualdade,
    Na ordem de seus preceitos
    Os povos já tendo vão?
    Ora o homem tem razão!

    "Ora o homem tem razão," *A mulher do Simplício, ou, A fluminense exaltada*, 23 Dec. 1840, p. 4.

12. Alguém O terá disposto [o Imperador]
    Entre um povo tão mesclado,
    A desprezar pelo rosto
    O cidadão devotado
    Ao Trono, às Leis e à Nação?
    Ora o homem tem razão.
    [. . .]
    Quem tiver merecimento,
    Inda tendo a cor trigueira,
    Encontrará valimento,
    Ou continua a manqueira
    De amanhã sim, hoje não?
    Ora o homem tem razão

    Ibid.
13. José Murilo de Carvalho, *D. Pedro II*, 2007, pp. 40–41
14. Teremos de ver os povos,
    E algumas autoridades,
    Traficando em negros novos,

Que nas vilas e cidades
As classes mesclando vão?
Ora, o homem tem razão.

Ou a Lei será banida,
Que proíbe a traficância,
Para então ser permitida
Essa, filha da ignorância,
Desumana escravidão!
Ora, o homem tem razão

"Ora o homem tem razão," *A mulher do Simplício, ou, A fluminense exaltada*, 23 Dec. 1840, p. 4.
15. Sidney Chalhoub, *op. cit.*, 2012, p. 72. See, in particular, the chapter entitled "Modos de silenciar e de não ver."
16. "Mudam-se as cenas, muda-se a política, / Desce o partido teu, sobe o contrário / (Partido que era meu)." "Tributo de gratidão ao Ilustríssimo e Excelentíssimo Senhor Doutor Paulino José Soares de Souza, oficial da Imperial Ordem do Cruzeiro, Ministro e Secretário de Estado dos Negócios da Justiça," *A mulher do Simplício, ou, A fluminense exaltada*, 23 Dec. 1841, p. 6.
17. Mais de uma vez, Senhor, que te ei buscado,
Sempre para valer aos infelizes,
(pois ainda para mim não pedi graças)
Acho-te franco, justo e desvelado
Quanto mais te procuro, mais te encontro.

Ibid., p. 7.
18. Roberto Schwarz, *Ao vencedor as batatas: Forma literária e processo social nos inícios do romance brasileiro*, 2000, p. 16.
19. "Soneto ao Ilustríssimo Senhor Doutor Eusébio de Queirós Coutinho Matoso da Câmara, Comendador da Ordem da Rosa, Juiz de Direito e Chefe de Polícia do Corte," *A mulher do Simplício, ou, A fluminense exaltada*, 23 Dec. 1841, p. 13.
20. "A Revista Comercial," *O grito nacional*, 8 Oct. 1856, p. 3.
21. "O regresso do herói dos chouriços," *O grito nacional*, 17 Oct. 1856, p. 3.
22. Eis, leitores, até agora
Nossas causas tais quais são:
Consiste só no *regresso*
O *progresso* da nação!

"São progressos da nação," *A mulher do Simplício, ou, A fluminense exaltada*, 1 Oct. 1842, p. 7.
23. Se outrora gritava afouta
Ferro, fogo, exaltação;

Hoje exp'riente, só peço
Ordem, paz, doce união

"Ocorrências da praça," *A mulher do Simplício, ou, A fluminense exaltada,* 23 Dec. 1843, p. 4.

24. *Constituição Política do Império do Brasil,* chap. VI, art. 94, 1824.
25. See Appendix 4.
26. "Eleições," *O Brasil,* 18 Dec. 1848, pp. 3–4.
27. *O Brasil,* 11 Nov. 1847, p. 2.
28. "Variedades," *O Brasil,* 28 Mar. 1848, p. 4. "Notícias diversas," *Diário do Rio de Janeiro,* 2 Mar. 1848, p. 2.
29. "As eleições: Notáveis acontecimentos dos dias 5, 6, 7 e 8," *O grito nacional,* 18 Aug. 1849, pp. 1–2.
30. Eduardo Silva, *Dom Obá II D'África, o príncipe do povo: Vida, tempo e pensamento de um homem livre de cor,* 1997, p. 121; Carlos Eugênio Líbano Soares, "A negregada instituição: Os capoeiras no Rio de Janeiro," 1993, pp. 281, 289; Marcelo Mac Cord, *Artífices da cidadania: Mutualismo, educação e trabalho no Recife oitocentista,* 2012, p. 185.
31. "Os Estrangeiros," *O grito nacional,* 11 Jan. 1850, pp. 2–5. Emphasis in original.
32. Ibid. Emphasis in original.
33. "Variedades," *O Brasil,* 6 Jun. 1848, p. 4.
34. Ilmar Rohloff de Mattos, *O tempo saquarema,* 2004, p. 265.
35. Ibid., p. 287.
36. "O pedido do Senhor Paula Brito," *O Brasil,* 8 Jun. 1848, p. 4.
37. Ibid.
38. "Assembleia provincial," *O americano,* 5 Jul. 1848, p. 4.
39. Ibid.
40. *Almanak Laemmert,* 1848, pp. 474–75.

CHAPTER II

1. "Os Estrangeiros," *O grito nacional,* 11 Jan. 1850, p. 3, emphasis in original.
2. Hebe Mattos, *Das cores do silêncio: Os significados da liberdade no sudeste escravista (Brasil, século XIX),* 2013, pp. 105–6. Lilia Moritz Schwarcz, *O espetáculo das raças: Cientistas, instituições e questão racial no Brasil, 1870–1930,* 1993.
3. Hebe Mattos, *Escravidão e cidadania no Brasil monárquico,* 2000, p. 20.
4. Daryle Williams, "The Intrepid Mariner Simão: Visual Histories of Blackness in the Luso-Atlantic at the End of the Slave Trade," in Agnes Lugo-Ortiz and Angela Rosenthal, eds., *Slave Portraiture in the Atlantic World,* 2013.
5. "O Preto Simão: A cor não faz o Herói, não, são seus feitos!," *Marmota fluminense,* 8 Nov. 1853, p. 3, emphasis in original.
6. Daryle Williams has analyzed the developments in Simão's life after the end of the transatlantic slave trade to Brazil. Daryle Williams, *op. cit.,* 2013, p. 408.

7. "Simão, o Herói da Pernambucana," *Marmota fluminense*, 18 Nov. 1853, p. 1.

8. "Crônica da quinzena," *Novo correio das modas*, 1853, p. 176.

9. "Club Fluminense," *Correio mercantil*, 14 Oct. 1853, p. 2.

10. Those who joined before the Club opened would be founding members, who would pay a membership fee of 30,000 réis and 6,000 réis for six months. Ordinary members would be those accepted after the official opening. In effect, they would lose the discount on the membership fee, paying 50,000 réis in addition to the monthly fee. "Occasional members" would be those who, because they did not live in Rio, would be exempt from paying the membership fee, but would make renewable monthly payments of 10,000 réis. "Club Fluminense," *Correio mercantil*, 14 Oct. 1853, p. 2.

11. See "Regulamento para o Club Fluminense," "Club Fluminense," *Correio mercantil*, 14 Oct. 1853, p. 2.

12. "Folhetim do Diário, Crônica," *Diário do Rio de Janeiro*, 20 Nov. 1853, p. 1.

13. "Club Sangue Azul," *Jornal do commercio*, 29 Dec. 1853, p. 2.

14. "Club Fluminense," *Correio mercantil*, 19 Dec. 1853, p. 2.

15. "Club Fluminense," *Correio mercantil*, 27 Dec. 1853, pp. 1–2.

16. "Aos Srs. Presidente e Diretores do Club Fluminense," *Diário do Rio de Janeiro*, 28 Dec. 1853, p. 3.

17. An article published in the *Diário do Rio de Janeiro* suggests that José Silveira do Pillar was fired from his post in the Finance Ministry in February 1852. "Ministério da Fazenda," *Diário do Rio de Janeiro*, 5 Feb. 1852, p. 1.

18. *Jornal do commercio*, 31 Dec. 1853, p. 1.

19. Ibid.

20. Unlike similar poems, this sonnet was not dated. It is signed "By the most loyal subject - Francisco de Paula Brito. / Composed and printed at the Imperial Quinta da Boa Vista in the presence of His Imperial Majesty" (Francisco de Paula Brito, *Soneto à imprensa, dedicado a Sua Majestade Imperial o senhor Dom Pedro II*, n.d.).

21. Paula Brito was a censor for the Conservatório Dramático Brasileiro. In August 1851, the publisher issued a favorable opinion on the play *A pobre louca* (The poor madwoman), by Augusto de Sá, succinctly stating: "*A pobre louca* by Mr. Augusto de Sá is in no way morally or ethically offensive and therefore / Can be performed. / Rio de Janeiro, 21 August 1851. / Francisco de Paula Brito." (*Designação de José Rufino Rodrigues de Vasconcelos para Francisco de Paula Brito examinar a peça* A pobre louca. Rio de Janeiro, 3 Aug. 1851). Regarding the Conservatório Dramático Brasileiro, see Silvia Cristina Martins de Souza, *As noites do Ginásio*, 2002, chap. 2.

22. *Relatório da comissão encarregada pelo governo imperial por Avisos de 1° de outubro e 28 de dezembro de 1864 de proceder a um inquérito sobre as causas principais e acidentais da Crise do mês de setembro de 1864*, 1865, p. 24.

23. *Requerimento de André Gailhard encaminhado ao Ministério do Império solicitando expedição de ordem para que possa receber o produto de quatro loterias a benefício de sua fábrica de papel*, 1845–1846.

24. Alongside domestic mule trading, the transfer of funds to Portugal, the reuse of part of the slaving fleet for the transport of slaves to Cuba, and Portuguese immigrants to Brazil, Alencastro states, following the indication of the Baron de Mauá, that corporations created in Rio de Janeiro from 1850 also benefited from the recycling of capital previously employed in the slave trade. See Luiz Felipe de Alencastro, "Bahia, Rio de Janeiro et le nouvel ordre colonial 1808–1860," in Jeanne Chase, ed., *Géographie du capital marchand aux Amériques*, 1987, pp. 133–34. See also Artur José Renda Vitorino, "Cercamento à brasileira: Conformação do mercado de trabalho livre na Corte das décadas de 1850 a 1880," 2002, p. 37; Maria Bárbara Levy, *História da Bolsa de Valores do Rio de Janeiro*, 1977, pp. 77–83; Maria Bárbara Levy, *A indústria do Rio de Janeiro através de suas sociedades anônimas: Esboço de história empresarial*, 1994, pp. 50–51; Eulália Maria Lahmeyer Lobo, *História do Rio de Janeiro: Do capital comercial ao capital industrial e financeiro*, 1978, p. 211. For reports of the conversion of capital produced by the slave trade in the nineteenth century, see Sebastião Ferreira Soares, *Histórico da Companhia Industrial da Estrada de Mangaratiba e análise crítica e econômica dos negócios desta companhia*, 1861, pp. 39–40.

25. "Mapa das companhias e sociedades anônimas registradas no Tribunal do Comércio da Corte do Império, desde a execução do Código Comercial até dezembro do corrente ano," "Mapa das sociedades em comandita registradas no Tribunal do Comércio da Capital do Império, desde a execução do Código Comercial até o mês de dezembro de 1865," in José Thomaz Nabuco de Araújo, *Relatório do Ministério da Justiça apresentado à Assembleia Geral da Quarta Sessão da Décima Segunda Legislatura*, 1866. Levy has produced a thorough analysis of the data from these documents and considers them "the most complete source on this matter." (Maria Bárbara Levy, *op. cit.*, 1994, pp. 55–57.) However, her study does not cover all the companies established in Rio, as many operated without government approval (Sebastião Ferreira Soares, *Esboço ou Primeiros Traços da Crise Comercial da Cidade do Rio de Janeiro em 10 de Setembro de 1864*, 1865, p. 33).

Corporations were called *sociedades anônimas* (anonymous associations) because they did not have a business name. Their origins date back to the large commercial and industrial firms that required massive sums of money to establish themselves. The capital was therefore divided into shares whose value made them affordable for a larger number of potential buyers. Limited partnerships, or *sociedades em comandita*, basically had two kinds of partners—managing partners and silent partners. Managing partners were also called *sócios solidários*, and were "entirely and jointly responsible for all debts, commitments, and tax obligations" incurred by the company, while the obligations of the silent partners were limited to the "share of capital in the stock they owned." (Antônio Bento de Faria (ed.), *Código Comercial Brasileiro anotado de acordo com a doutrina, a legislação e a jurisprudência nacional e estrangeira, e os princípios e regras do direito civil, seguido de um apêndice contendo o Regulamento n. 737 de 1850, e todas as leis comerciais em vigor, igualmente anotadas*, 1912, pp. 252, 268).

26. The copy of the "Plano da Empresa Tipográfica Dous de Dezembro" studied here was found in the Business Tribunal of Rio de Janeiro's records for a lawsuit

brought against the publisher by Father Joaquim Ferreira da Cruz Belmonte in 1857. *Ação Ordinária. Pe. Joaquim Ferreira da Cruz Belmonte, autor. Francisco de Paula Brito, réu.* 1857.

27. "Negócios Eclesiásticos." *Almanak Laemmert*, 1857, p. 157.

28. Hendrik Kraay, *Days of National Festivity in Rio de Janeiro, Brazil, 1823–1889*, 2013, p. 112.

29. Marisa Midori Deacto, *op. cit.*, 2011 p. 134.

30. "Biografia do Sr. Francisco de Paula Brito," *Correio mercantil*, 28 Feb. 1862, p. 2.

31. *Tipografia de Francisco de Paula Brito. Requerimento e informações para melhoramentos na Empresa Tipográfica*, 1851. AGCRJ, 50.3.46.

32. *Inventário. Francisco de Paula Brito, falecido. Rufina Rodrigues da Costa Brito, Inventariante*, 1862. fl. 16.

33. *Ação Ordinária. Pe. Joaquim Ferreira da Cruz Belmonte, autor. Francisco de Paula Brito, réu.* 1857, fl. 4.

34. Law no. 555 of 15 June 1850; Lei no. 668 of 11 September 1852.

35. *Almanak Laemmert*, 1850, p. 199.

36. *A marmota na corte*, 22 Jul. 1851. p. 2.

37. *Ação Ordinária. Pe. Joaquim Ferreira da Cruz Belmonte, autor. Francisco de Paula Brito, réu*, 1857, fl. 4.

38. *A marmota na corte*, 27 Jun. 1851, p. 4, emphasis in original.

39. As Maria Bárbara Levy explains, government bonds did not depreciate, even during the economic crises of the late 1850s and early 1860s. Moreover, as of the late 1860s, those bonds financed roughly 28 percent of Paraguay War expenditures. Maria Bárbara Levy, *op. cit.*, 1994, pp. 89, 91.

40. "A Empresa Tipográfica," *A marmota na corte*, 22 Jul. 1851, p. 2. Regarding the career of João Caetano, see Décio de Almeida Prado, *João Caetano: O ator, o empresário, o repertório*, 1972.

41. *A marmota na corte*, 22 Jul. 1851, p. 2.

42. Suplemento, no. 1, *Marmota fluminense*, 25 Oct. 1853, p. 1.

43. *A marmota na corte*, 2 Dec. 1851, p. 4.

44. By cross-referencing data, I was able to identify 54 of the 118 shareholders listed in *Guanabara* magazine. In 1858, the *Almanak Laemmert* introduced the "Guia do Rio de Janeiro ou indicador alfabético da morada dos seus principais habitantes," an alphabetical guide to the addresses of Rio's most prominent residents. This vast publication listed names followed by the respective addresses and a cross-reference to their appearance in different sections of the almanac. Although this method was somewhat effective, it only provides a sample of the backgrounds of Dous de Dezembro's shareholders. First, this is because the list is limited to the shareholders who received *Guanabara* magazine. Before that year, substantial changes had been made to Dous de Dezembro's shareholding plans, which excluded shareholders who did not receive that publication. Second, the *Almanak Laemmert* for 1858 only includes residents of Rio de Janeiro, which excludes

shareholders who lived outside of what was then called the Neutral Municipality. Furthermore, many of the shareholders listed in *Guanabara* in 1856 may have left Rio or even died by 1858.

See Appendix 5 and Appendix 6 of this book. "Acionistas da Empresa Dous de Dezembro que, como tais, receberam o Guanabara," *Guanabara*, vol. III, 1856. "Guia do Rio de Janeiro ou indicador alfabético da morada dos seus principais habitantes; altos funcionários, empregados, negociantes, capitalistas, proprietários, fabricantes, artistas, industriais, etc., mencionados em seus lugares competentes no Almanak Laemmert de 1858," *Almanak Laemmert*, 1858.

CHAPTER 12

1. "Aos nossos leitores e assinantes," *Marmota fluminense*, 4 May 1852, p. 1; "Empresa Dous de Dezembro," *Marmota fluminense*, 20 Jul. 1852, p. 1.

2. *Embargo de obra nova. Manuel Francisco da Silveira Freitas, autor; Francisco de Paula Brito, réu*, 1852.

3. "Júlia," *Marmota fluminense*, 21 Sept. 1852, p. 1.

4. *Marmota fluminense*, 2 Dec. 1852, p. 1.

5. "Lettres brésiliennes," *Courrier du Brésil*, 5 Oct. 1856, p. 2.

6. Gérard Martin, *L'Imprimerie*, 1966, pp. 11–13.

7. *Empreza Typográphica Dous de Dezembro de Paula Brito*. Rio de Janeiro, n.d. The wide and varied range of items sold in Francisco de Paula Brito's shop was listed on the back of the leaflet.

8. "Empresa Tipográfica," in "Suplemento," no. 1, *Marmota fluminense*, 25 Oct. 1853, p. 1. The ad was published once again in "Suplemento," no. 2, *Marmota fluminense*, 28 Oct. 1853, p. 1. References to shares valued at 100,000 réis were repeated in further issues of the biweekly publication: "Aviso," *Marmota fluminense*, 6 Dec. 1853, p. 1; *Marmota fluminense*, 9 Dec. 1853, p. 1; *Marmota fluminense*, 13 Dec. 1853, p. 1; *Marmota fluminense*, 16 Dec. 1853, p. 1; *Marmota fluminense*, 20 Dec. 1853, p. 1.

9. *Requerimento de Francisco de Paula Brito encaminhado ao Ministério do Império, solicitando que seja aprovado o estatuto de sua Empresa Literária Dous de Dezembro*, 1855.

10. *Marmota fluminense*, 26 Jun. 1855, pp. 1–2; Decreto n° 1.610, de 23 de Maio de 1855.

11. *Anais da Câmara dos Deputados*, 6 Aug. 1855, p. 58.

12. *Anais da Câmara dos Deputados*, 10 Aug. 1855, p. 97.

13. *Anais da Câmara dos Deputados*, 4 Sept. 1855, p. 333.

14. "Empresa Tipográfica Dous de Dezembro," *Marmota fluminense*, 26 Aug. 1855, p. 1.

15. Artur José Renda Vitorino, "Patrimonialismo e finanças: Política monetária de liberais e conservadores no Segundo Reinado," *Revista de História Regional*, 2010.

16. Luís Pedreira do Couto Ferraz, *Relatório do ano de 1856, Apresentado à Assembleia Geral Legislativa na 1ª Sessão da 10ª Legislatura*, 1857, p. 117.

17. "1855," *Marmota fluminense*, 30 Jan. 1855, p. 1; *Anais da Câmara dos Deputados*, 14 de maio de 1856, p. 21; Decreto n° 1.717 de 23 de Janeiro de 1856.

18. "Notícia Tipográfica," *Marmota fluminense*, 9 Oct. 1855, p. 1.

19. "Empresa Dois de Dezembro," *Marmota fluminense*, 1 Jan. 1856, p. 1.

CHAPTER 13

1. João Ferreira da Cruz Forte, *O jogo do burro, ou A febre das ações*, 1854, pp. 13–14.

2. "A febre da praça," *Marmota fluminense*, 6 Jun. 1854, p. 1.

3. Sebastião Ferreira Soares, *Esboço ou Primeiros Traços da Crise Comercial da Cidade do Rio de Janeiro em 10 de Setembro 1864*, 1865, p. 33.

4. Ibid., pp. 41–42.

5. Ibid., p. 55.

6. Artur José Renda Vitorino, *op. cit.*, 2002, p. 40.

7. Two regulations supplementing the Business Code were passed on 25 November 1850. The first, Decree no. 737, covered business processes and the second, Decree no. 738, dealt with the Business Tribunals, which had been created that year, as well as bankruptcy proceedings. See Fran Martins, *Curso de Direito Comercial*, 1986, p. 46.

8. The total amount of the purchase was 1,132,625 réis. *Ação de dez dias. Saportas e Cia, autor. Francisco de Paula Brito, réu*, 1854. *Execução. Saportas e Cia, executante. Francisco de Paula Brito, executado*, 1854. Regarding Luiz Thorey, see *Almanak Laemmert*, 1853, pp. 531–32.

9. *Almanak Laemmert*, 1856, p. 616.

10. Paula Brito bought exactly 538,300 réis worth of type from Bouchard's foundry. During the attachment proceedings, the amount was set at 582,506 réis. *Ação de dez dias. Eugenio Bouchaud, autor. Francisco de Paula Brito, réu*, 1856, fl. 2, 4. *Execução. Eugênio Bouchaud, executante. Francisco de Paula Brito, executado*, 1856, fl. 11.

11. *Ação de dez dias. Francisco José Gonçalves Agra, autor. Francisco de Paula Brito, réu*, 1854. *Execução de sentença. Francisco José Gonçalves Agra, executante. Francisco de Paula Brito, executado*, 1854. Regarding the business activities of Francisco José Gonçalves Agra, see *Almanak Laemmert*, 1854, p. 396.

12. *A marmota*, 16 Apr. 1858, p. 4.

13. *Ação de dez dias. Adriano Gabriel Corte Real, autor. Francisco de Paula Brito, réu*, 1856, fl. 8.

14. *Execução. João de Souza Monteiro, executante. Francisco de Paula Brito, executado*, 1855, fl. 13.

15. *Execução de sentença. Bernardino de Souza Ribeiro Guimarães, executante. Francisco de Paula Brito, executado*, 1854.

16. *Ação Ordinária. Mariana Augusta d'Oliveira, autora. Francisco de Paula Brito, réu*, 1855, fl. 2.

17. *Ação Ordinária. Mariana Augusta d'Oliveira, autora. Francisco de Paula Brito, réu*, 1855, fl. 9.

18. *Ação de dez dias. Bernardino Ribeiro de Souza Guimarães, autor. Francisco de Paula Brito, réu*, 1854. *Execução de sentença. Bernardino de Souza Ribeiro Guimarães, executante. Francisco de Paula Brito, executado*, 1854.

19. *Execução de sentença. Bernardino de Souza Ribeiro Guimarães, executante. Francisco de Paula Brito, executado,* 1854, fl. 20.
20. *Diário do Rio de Janeiro,* 25 Oct. 1854, p. 3.
21. The execution process ends with a certificate issued by Joaquim Antonio de Oliveira Motta, concierge of the Court's auditoriums, stating that he has posted the notice as requested by the judge. *Execução de sentença. Bernardino de Souza Ribeiro Guimarães, executante. Francisco de Paula Brito, executado,* 1854, fl. 34.
22. *Ação de dez dias. José Antonio de Oliveira Bastos, autor. Eugênio Aprígio da Veiga e Francisco de Paula Brito, réus,* 1855.
23. *Ação de dez dias. Duarte José de Puga Garcia, autor. Francisco de Paula Brito, réu.* 1855, fl. 2. *Execução. Duarte José de Puga Garcia, exequente. Francisco de Paula Brito, executado,* 1856, fl. 3.

CHAPTER 14

1. *Ação de dez dias. Francisco de Paula Brito, réu.* 1857. *Execução. Dr. Joaquim Pereira de Araújo, executante. Francisco de Paula Brito, executado,* 1857.
2. "Empresa Dous de Dezembro: Resolução definitiva tomada pela reunião de credores e acionistas da empresa," *Marmota fluminense,* 28 Oct. 1856, p. 1. *Justificação para Embargo. Dr. Joaquim Pereira de Araújo, justificante. Francisco de Paula Brito, justificado,* 1857, fl. 7.
3. Paula Brito habitually reported the payment, as well as calling shareholders' meetings for Dous de Dezembro to distribute interest in their shares in *Marmota fluminense.* See, for example: "Empresa Dous de Dezembro," *Marmota fluminense,* 20 Jul. 1852, p. 1. "Empresa Dous de Dezembro," *Marmota fluminense,* 28 Aug. 1855, p. 1.
4. *Justificação para Embargo. Dr. Joaquim Pereira de Araújo, justificante. Francisco de Paula Brito, justificado,* 1857, fl. 7.
5. Ibid.
6. *Inventário. Francisco de Paula Brito, falecido. Rufina Rodrigues da Costa Brito, Inventariante,* 1862, fls. 11–11v.
7. In the inventory for Paula Brito's estate, Antonio José Gonçalves de Souza appears in the listing regarding Dous de Dezembro's bankruptcy. José Antonio de Araújo Filgueiras, in turn, appears in the inventory in another listing, referring to creditors for "bills and promissory notes." *Inventário. Francisco de Paula Brito, Falecido. Rufina Rodrigues da Costa Brito, Inventariante,* 1862, fls. 14, 20.
8. *Justificação para Embargo. Dr. Joaquim Pereira de Araújo, justificante. Francisco de Paula Brito, justificado,* 1857, fl. 9.
9. See also articles 809, 811, and 812 of the Business Code. Antonio Bento de Faria, ed., *Código Comercial Brasileiro,* 1850.
10. *Ação Ordinária. Pe. Joaquim Ferreira da Cruz Belmonte, autor. Francisco de Paula Brito, réu,* 1857, fl. 3.

11. Ibid., fl. 17.

12. *Jornal do commercio*, 29 Apr. 1857, p. 2.

13. *Ação Ordinária. Pe. Joaquim Ferreira da Cruz Belmonte, autor. Francisco de Paula Brito, réu*, 1857, fls. 13v–14.

14. Ibid., fls. 14–14v.

15. Ibid., fls. 15–15v.

16. According to the ruling of the Business Tribunal judge: "In view of the petition, I hereby attest to the bankruptcy of the merchant Francisco de Paula Brito, on April 26 of the current year [1857], publishing this by means of edicts in the appropriate locations. . . . Rio de Janeiro, 6 Jul. 1857. João Caetano dos Santos." *Execução. Dr. Joaquim Pereira de Araújo, executante. Francisco de Paula Brito, executado*, 1857, fls. 26–26v.

17. See article 830 of Faria, *Código Commercial Brasileiro*. Regarding the appointment of the trustee, see *Execução. Dr. Joaquim Pereira de Araújo, executante. Francisco de Paula Brito, executado*, 1857, fls. 26–26v.

18. *Justificação para Embargo. Dr. Joaquim Pereira de Araújo, justificante. Francisco de Paula Brito, justificado*, 1857, fls. 2–2v. Dr. Joaquim Pereira de Araújo's petition was based primarily on Article 321 of Regulation 737 of 25 November 1850.

19. Ibid., fl. 19.

20. Ibid. fl. 21.

21. *A Pátria*, 11 and 12 May 1857, p. 3.

22. *Marmota fluminense*, 19 May 1857, p. 1.

23. *Justificação para Embargo. Dr. Joaquim Pereira de Araújo, justificante. Francisco de Paula Brito, justificado*, 1857, fl. 23.

24. Ibid., fls. 24–24v.

25. *Execução. Dr. Joaquim Pereira de Araújo, executante. Francisco de Paula Brito, executado*, 1857, fl. 17.

26. *Justificação para Embargo. Dr. Joaquim Pereira de Araújo, justificante. Francisco de Paula Brito, justificado*, 1857, fls. 29–29v.

27. Ibid., fl. 32.

28. *Execução. Dr. Joaquim Pereira de Araújo, executante. Francisco de Paula Brito, executado*, 1857, fls. 21.

29. Ibid., fl. 21.

30. Ibid., fls. 22, 27.

31. "If the defendant, being summoned for any reason whatsoever, is absent, and never appears in court, in person, or through his legal representative for the term assigned to him, and three more days, which will be expected, if summoned by Letter to the Court, or to Porto's Court of Appeals, or appearing and absent without leaving a legal representative, the plaintiff will proceed in his absence, without [the defendant] being able to appeal against him, to put him in possession of any property for the benefit of the former, nor the latter which shall follow, as we shall say in Title 20: On the Order of Judgment." *Ordenação Filipinas*, Livro III, Título XV.

32. "However, if the absent party should appear before the court before the sentence is handed down by the chancery or delivered to the party where there are no chancery proceedings, the proceedings will be taken up at the point which they have then reached." Ibid.

33. *Ação Ordinária. Pe. Joaquim Ferreira da Cruz Belmonte, autor. Francisco de Paula Brito, réu*, 1857, fls. 31–32.

34. *Inventário. Francisco de Paula Brito, falecido. Rufina Rodrigues da Costa Brito, Inventariante*, 1862, fl. 18v.

35. Ibid., fl. 19.

36. The inventory of Francisco de Paula Brito's estate contains the following lists of creditors: "List of the late Francisco de Paula Brito's creditors"; "List of creditors of the late Francisco de Paula Brito by accounts and promissory notes presented"; "List of creditors of the late Francisco de Paula Brito that are dealt with in the bankruptcy filed."

37. *Relatório da comissão encarregada pelo governo imperial pelos avisos de 1º de outubro e 28 de dezembro de 1864 de proceder a um inquérito sobre as causas principais e acidentais da crise do mês de setembro de 1864*, 1865, pp. 29–30. See Appendix 7 in this book.

38. Regarding the crisis of 1857 and its impact on Brazil, in addition to the report cited in the previous note, see Maria Barbara Levy, *op. cit.*, 1977, p. 84; Artur José Renda Vitorino, *op. cit.*, 2002, p. 55. Regarding its effect on the book publishing market in the United States, see Ezra Greenspan, *George Palmer Putnam: Representative American Publisher*, 2000, p. 374. Regarding Paula Brito, see Laurence Hallewell, *O Livro no Brasil: Sua História*, 2005, p. 165.

CHAPTER 15

1. "Discurso proferido pelo Dr. Caetano Alves de Sousa Filgueiras por ocasião da missa de sétimo dia de Francisco de Paula Brito," *Diário do Rio de Janeiro*, 24 Dec. 1861, p. 2.

2. "Ao público," *Marmota fluminense*, 1 May 1857, p. 4.

3. Regarding the conciliation of political parties, see Sério Buarque de Holanda, *Capítulos de história do Império*, 2010.

4. "Introdução," *O moderador*, 5 Feb. 1857, p. 1.

5. Among other articles, see, for example, "A insistência do *Diário*," *O moderador*, 3 Mar. 1857, p. 3. "Porque se hostiliza o ministério?," *O moderador*, 3 Mar. 1857, pp. 3–4. "O *Correio da tarde* e a colonização," *O moderador*, 6 Mar. 1857, p. 3. "As queixas do *Diário*," *O moderador*, 10 Mar. 1857, p. 4.

6. "Breves considerações sobre a política," *O moderador*, 6 Feb. 1857, p. 4.

7. "Aos Srs. Assinantes," *Marmota fluminense*, 5 May 1857, p. 1.

8. "Último figurino," *Marmota fluminense*, 22 May 1857, p. 1.

9. "Aos leitores," *Marmota fluminense*, 5 Jun. 1857, p. 1. Possibly due to the visibility of these writings, Paula Brito took up the matter of political articles in another issue

of the newspaper: "*Marmota* not being the exclusive property of its editor-in-chief, as announced in issue no. 853 of June 5 of this year; it has since been well understood that some articles, called background, would belong to the editor-in-chief and some to the newsroom; Paula Brito, however, not wanting to answer for anything he has not done, will from now sign the little he writes with his initials, being solely responsible for that. P. B." ("Retificação," *A marmota*, 20 Nov. 1857, p. 1.)

10. "Aviso tipográfico," *Marmota fluminense*, 2 Jun. 1857, p. 4.

11. Such as the "small printing shops with iron presses, very affordable, for beginners." ("Tipografias," *Correio mercantil*, 19 Mar. 1858, p. 3.)

12. "Anúncio," *A marmota*, 23 Feb. 1858, p. 4.

13. "Declaração," *Correio mercantil*, 17 Nov. 1858, p. 2. The Americans' report had appeared in the same newspaper two days earlier. See "O Brasil e os Brasileiros por Kidder e Fletcher," *Correio mercantil*, 15 Nov. 1858, p. 1.

14. *Inventário. Francisco de Paula Brito, falecido. Rufina Rodrigues da Costa Brito, Inventariante*, fl. 30. The description of Dous de Dezembro's presses can be read in "Lettres brésiliennes," *Courrier du Brésil*, 5 Oct. 1856, p. 2.

15. "Anúncio," *A marmota*, 9 Mar. 1858, p. 1.

16. Assets valued at 411,500 réis, as we will see further on. *Inventário. Francisco de Paula Brito, falecido. Rufina Rodrigues da Costa Brito, Inventariante*, 1862, fl. 29.

17. See Appendix 8 in this book.

18. "Catálogo do que se vende na Rua do Cano, no. 44, nova tipografia e loja de Paula Brito e na Praça da Constituição, no. 64," *A marmota*, 27 Apr. 1858.

19. Ibid.

20. *Anais da Câmara dos Deputados*, 31 May 1858, p. 152. *Anais da Câmara dos Deputados*, 5 June 1858, p. 47; *Anais da Câmara dos Deputados*, 8 June 1858, p. 71.

21. Paula Brito's application for lottery funding was published in *Correio mercantil*. See "Publicações a pedido: Câmara dos deputados," *Correio mercantil*, 19 May 1858, p. 2. Regarding the arrival of that document in the Chamber of Deputies, see *Anais da Câmara dos Deputados*, 17 May 1858, p. 31.

22. "Publicações a pedido: Câmara dos deputados," *Correio mercantil*, 19 May 1858, p. 2.

23. *Anais da Câmara dos Deputados*, 30 June 1858, p. 304; *Anais da Câmara dos Deputados*, 14 July 1858, p. 135.

24. "Notícias diversas," *Correio mercantil*, 27 Jan. 1858, p. 1.

25. *Anais da Câmara dos Deputados*, 26 August 1858, p. 229. It was also published in *A marmota*, see "Empréstimo a Francisco de Paula Brito," *A marmota*, 3 Sept. 1858, p. 1.

26. *Publicações de Atos Oficiais. Propostas de Justiniano José da Rocha, Editor-Proprietário do Correio do Brasil, e da Tipografia americana, do Correio mercantil e de Antônio e Luís Navarro de Andrade, Proprietários-Editores do Diário, 1853. Conta de Rodrigues e Cia, relativa a publicação das Atas da Câmara Municipal do Rio de Janeiro, 1853. Pedido de pagamento de Sebastião Gomes da Silva Belfort, empresário da tipografia do Diário do Rio de Janeiro, relativo à impressão de publicações da Câmara Municipal da corte, 5 Mar. 1868.*

27. *Proposta de Francisco de Paula Brito para imprimir um jornal que insira atos da administração municipal e os talões de expediente, sob as condições que estabelece, 1859.*

28. I have not been able to find copies of *Arquivo municipal*. The prospectus was originally published in *Correio mercantil*. See "Notícias diversas: Apareceu ontem o primeiro número do Arquivo Municipal, publicação empreendida pelo nosso patrício o Sr. Paula Brito," *Correio mercantil*, 19 May 1859, p. 1; "Arquivo Municipal," *Correio mercantil*, 21 May 1859, p. 2.

CHAPTER 16

1. "A Sociedade Petalógica," *Marmota fluminense*, 5 Jul. 1853, p. 1.
2. One of the first references to the Petalogical society found in *Marmota fluminense* is a report on its sessions in the bi-weekly. "A Sociedade Petalógica," *Marmota fluminense*, 21 Jan. 1853, p. 1.
3. Luís Maria da Silva Pinto, "Peta," *Diccionario da língua brasileira*, 1832.
4. "A Sociedade Petalógica," *Marmota fluminense*, 15 Jul. 1853, p. 1. "Sociedade Petalógica: Resumo da sessão do dia 30 de mês próximo findo." *Marmota fluminense*, 12 Aug. 1853, p. 1.
5. "Sociedade Petalógica: Resumo de uma das sessões de janeiro de 1853." *Marmota fluminense*, 28 Jan. 1853, p. 1.
6. Ibid.
7. "Sociedade Petalógica." *Marmota fluminense*, 22 Jul. 1853, p. 1.
8. Machado de Assis, "Folhetim: Ao Acaso," *Diário do Rio de Janeiro*, 3 Jan. 1865, p. 1. Emphasis in original.
9. "Sociedade Petalógica." *Marmota fluminense*, 21 Jan. 1853, p. 1. "Réplica à sarrabulhada que o amigo Cubatão intitula resposta ao meu artigo." *Marmota fluminense*, 11 Mar. 1853, pp. 1–2. "Última resposta à questão do Inverno e do Verão, na qual se empenharam dous contendores." *Marmota fluminense*, 15 Mar. 1853, p. 1.
10. "Sociedade Petalógica." *Marmota fluminense*, 10 Mar. 1857, p. 3.
11. "Sociedade Petalógica: Memória sobre as manias do Mundo da Lua, oferecida à apreciação da Sociedade Petalógica, a fim de obter-se o *honroso* título de Membro da mesma sociedade." *Marmota fluminense*, 9 Sept. 1853, p. 1; 15 Sept. 1853, pp. 1–2; 23 Sept. 1853, pp. 1–2; 30 Sept. 1853, pp. 1–2; 4 Nov. 1853, pp. 1–2; 8 Nov. 1853, pp. 1–2 (first installment of the serialization of the comedy *A. B. C. do amor, ou, A escola da roça*); 11 Nov. 1853, p. 1; 15 Nov. 1853, p. 1; 18 Nov. 1853, pp. 1–2; 22 Nov. 1853, p. 1; 6 Jan. 1854, p. 2; 4 Feb. 1855, p. 3.
12. "Sociedade Carnavalense," *Correio mercantil*, 25 Mar. 1854, p. 1.
13. "Notícias diversas," *Correio mercantil*, 20 Apr. 1855, p. 2.
14. "Uma noite artística," *A marmota*, 11 Jan. 1859, p. 2.
15. Maria Clementina Pereira Cunha, *Ecos da folia: Uma história social do carnaval carioca entre 1880 e 1920*, 2001, p. 54.
16. "Sociedades Carnavalenses," *Marmota fluminense*, 24 Mar. 1854, p. 1. Regarding Pedro II as an Entrudo reveler, see Maria Clementina Pereira Cunha, *op. cit.*, 2001, p. 54.

17. Os olhos namoradores
     Da engraçada iaiásinha
     Logo me fazem lembrar
     Sua bela marrequinha
     Iaiá, não teime,
     Solte a marreca,
     Senão eu morro,
     Leva-me a breca.
     Se dançado à Brasileira
     Quebra o corpo a iaiásinha
     Como ela brinca pulando
     Sua bela marrequinha.
     Iaiá, não teime, etc [. . .]

     "Lundu da Marrequinha," *Marmota fluminense*, 9 Aug. 1853, p. 4. Notices about lundu can also be seen in *Correio mercantil*, 4 Aug. 1853, p. 3; *Diário do Rio de Janeiro*, 7 Aug. 1853, p. 3.

18. Regarding the appointment of Alexandre Joaquim de Siqueira, see *Correio mercantil*, 16 Apr. 1853, p. 1. On the persecution of lottery ticket sellers, see "Polícia da corte," *Correio mercantil*, 2 Jun. 1853, p. 2. Regarding the registration and skills testing of free and enslaved coachmen who worked in Rio de Janeiro, see "Repartição de polícia," *Diário do Rio de Janeiro*, 2 Jul. 1853, p. 2.

19. The police chief's edict banning the Entrudo was published on different dates in Rio de Janeiro's leading newspapers: "Editais: Polícia da corte," *Correio mercantil*, 11 Jan. 1854, p. 3; 19 Jan. 1854, p. 3; 21 Jan. 1854, p. 3; 21 Jan. 1854, p. 2. "Polícia da Corte," *Diário do Rio de Janeiro*, 25 Jan. 1854, p. 2; 26 Jan. 1854, p. 2.

20. "162ª Pacotilha," *Correio mercantil*, 6 Mar. 1854, p. 1.

21. "Sabatina," *Diário do Rio de Janeiro*, 5 Mar. 1854, p. 2.

22. "Folhetim do *Correio da tarde*," *Correio da tarde*, 11 Sept. 1855, p. 2.

23. "Sociedades Carnavalenses," *Marmota fluminense*, 24 Mar. 1854, p. 1. The same article was published on the first page of *Correio mercantil* on March 25.

24. Maria Clementina Pereira Cunha, *op. cit.*, 2001, p. 66.

25. Melo Morais Filho, "O Carnaval," *Gazeta de notícias*, 21 Feb. 1887, pp. 1–2.

26. "Congresso das Summidades Carnavalescas," *Correio mercantil*, 3 Apr. 1855, p. 2.

27. "Notícias diversas," *Correio mercantil*, 18 Feb. 1857, p. 1.

28. Regarding the "triumphal float" and the petalogicians' involvement in the 1855 Carnival, see "Sociedades Carnavalenses," *Marmota fluminense*, 24 Mar. 1854, p. 1.

29. "Notícias diversas," *Correio mercantil*, 23 Feb. 1857, p. 1. See also "O Carnaval," *Marmota fluminense*, no. 825, 27 Feb. 1857, pp. 1–2.

30. "O Carnaval," *Marmota fluminense*, 27 Feb. 1857, p. 2.

31. Ibid.

32. Souza Ferreira commented on this in one of his columns: "Folhetim: Livro do Domingo," *Diário do Rio de Janeiro*, 26 Apr. 1858, p. 1. Going beyond the 1858 Carni-

val, the Petalogical Society did not take part in the revels held in 1862, as it was in mourning for its founder. "Noticiário," *Diário do Rio de Janeiro*, 2 Mar. 1862, p. 1.

33. The days excluded from the official calendar of national festivities in 1848 were January 9 ("Fico" Day, commemorating Pedro I's decision to remain in Brazil in 1822), April 7 (Pedro I's Abdication), May 3 (The Convening of the Chamber of Deputies), and July 23 (Pedro II's Majority and Acclamation). Hendrik Kraay, *Days of National Festivity in Rio de Janeiro, Brazil, 1823–1889*, 2013, pp. 112–32, 126.

34. Ibid., pp. 180–91.

35. "Notícias diversas," *Correio mercantil*, 9 Sept. 1858, p. 1.

36. "Correspondência particular do *Diário do Rio Grande*," *Correio mercantil*, 13 Oct. 1859, p. 2.

37. "Sociedade Petalógica," *Correio mercantil*, 19 Aug. 1859, p. 2.

38. "Crônica da Quinzena," *Revista popular*, T. III, 1859, pp. 333–34. The part of the column dealing with the Petalogical Society's participation in this matter was quoted in the article "O Sete de Setembro," *A marmota*, 16 Sept. 1859, p. 1. The identification of the pseudonym Carlos as being Carlos José do Rosário was suggested by Marcella dos Santos Abreu, "Moda, teatro e nacionalismo nas crônicas da *Revista popular* (1859–1862)," 2008, p. 32.

39. Hendrik Kraay, *op. cit.*, 2013, chap. 5 "The Equestrian Statue of Pedro I, 1862." Marco Cícero Cavallini. "Monumento e política: Os 'Comentários da Semana' de Machado de Assis," in Sidney Chalhoub, Margarida de S. Pereira Neves, and A. de M. Leonardo, eds., *História em cousas miúdas: Capítulos de história social da crônica no Brasil*, 2005.

40. "Estátua equestre," *Diário do Rio de Janeiro*, 21 Mar. 1862, p. 1; "Tributo de gratidão," *Diário do Rio de Janeiro*, 2 Apr. 1862, p. 1. "Ovação ao Sr. Rochet: Discurso dirigido pela Sociedade Petalógica," *Diário do Rio de Janeiro*, 4 Apr. 1862, p. 2. *Novo e completo índice cronológico da história do Brasil*, Apr. 1862, pp. 187–88.

41. Regarding Palestra Fluminense, a society that was an "affiliate or similar to the Petalogical Society," see "Notícias diversas," *Correio mercantil*, 15 Oct. 1858, p. 1. Regarding the Niterói Petalogical Society, see, for example, "O Carnaval de Niterói," *A revolução pacífica*, Niterói, 9 Mar. 1862, p. 4. Regarding the Pernambuco Petalogical Society, see "Sociedade Petalógica," *Marmota fluminense*, 9 Aug. 1853, p. 1.

42. "Folhetim: Ao Acaso," *Diário do Rio de Janeiro*, 3 Jan. 1865, p. 1; "Missas fúnebres," *Diário do Rio de Janeiro*, 15 Feb. 1864, p. 1.

43. "Herculano Lima," *Gazeta de notícias*, 1 Feb. 1888, p. 1.

44. "A Sociedade Petalógica," *Marmota fluminense*, 5 Jul. 1853, p. 1.

CHAPTER 17

1. Jean-Yves Mollier, *Michel e Calmann Lévy ou la naissance de l'édition moderne, 1836–1891*, 1984, p. 64.

2. *Anais da Câmara dos Deputados*, Session of 21 Aug. 1857, p. 45. Deputy Gavião Peixoto's bill was tabled on that occasion.
3. See Appendix 8 in this book.
4. Jean-Yves Mollier, *op. cit.*, 1984, p. 36.
5. I have presented a more detailed analysis of *Luxo e vaidade* in Rodrigo Camargo de Godoi, "Publicação e comercialização de comédias no Brasil oitocentista: O caso de *Luxo e Vaidade* de Joaquim Manuel de Macedo (1860)," *Anais do II Seminário Brasileiro Livro e História Editorial*, 2009.
6. "Lista dos senhores assinantes"; "Suplemento à lista de assinantes," in Joaquim Manuel de Macedo, *Luxo e Vaidade*, 1860. Regarding Antonio José Gonçalves Guimarães e Companhia, see *Folhinha dos sonhos para o ano de 1862*, 1862. Regarding the Universal Bookshop, see "Mercadores e lojas de livros," *Almanak Laemmert*, 1861, p. 507. Regarding José Martins Alves, see "Periódicos que se publicam na corte," *Almanak Laemmert*, 1862, p. 672. In addition to those subscribers, Garnier & Irmão subscribed for twenty-five copies.
7. "Teatro moderno," *A marmota*, 4 Dec. 1857, p. 4.
8. Macedo's column was quoted in *A marmota*. See "A Caixa Auxiliadora das Composições Dramáticas e Musicais," *A marmota*, 5 Oct. 1860, pp. 1–2.
9. Ibid., p. 2.
10. Ibid.
11. "Caixa Auxiliadora das Composições Dramáticas e Musicais," *A marmota*, 23 Oct. 1860, p. 1.
12. Ibid.
13. *Aprovação dos Estatutos do Gabinete Português de Leitura e autorização para continuar os seus trabalhos, Maranhão*, 1861.
14. *Aprovação dos Estatutos da Associação Grêmio Literário Português*, 1861.
15. Claudio H. M Batalha, "Sociedades de trabalhadores no Rio de Janeiro do século XIX: Algumas reflexões em torno da formação da classe operária," *Cadernos AEL: Sociedades Operárias e Mutualismo*, 1999.
16. Wilton José Marques, "O poeta e poder: Favores e afrontas," *Estudos Históricos*, Rio de Janeiro, 2003, pp. 33–49.
17. *Estatutos da Caixa Auxiliadora das Composições Dramáticas e Musicais*, Oct. 1860–Feb. 1861.
18. "Noticiário," *Diário do Rio de Janeiro*, 8 Mar. 1861, p. 1.

CHAPTER 18

1. *Apelação criminal. Luíza Joaquina das Neves, autora; Antônio Alexandre Lopes do Couto, réu.* 1864, fls. 58–60. Emphasis in original.
2. The Portuguese publisher followed the contract to the letter, and two years after the first edition of *Primaveras* came out, he published another in Lisbon. When the newspapers of Rio de Janeiro began to announce the sale of the Portuguese edition

and finally the steam ship *Kepler* docked in the city, carrying no fewer than 933 copies of the book, the late poet's mother and legatee, Luiza Joaquina das Neves took legal action. The lawsuit brought by her lawyer declared the Portuguese edition to be "false." *Apelação criminal. Luíza Joaquina das Neves, autora; Antônio Alexandre Lopes do Couto, réu*, 1864, fls. 3–3v.

3. *Almanak Laemmert*, 1857, p. 547.

4. Casimiro de Abreu, *Correspondência completa*, 2007, pp. 64–65.

5. "Carta de Casimiro de Abreu a Francisco do Couto Sousa Júnior, 21 abr. 1858," in Casimiro de Abreu, *op. cit.*, 2007, p. 70.

6. "Carta de Casimiro de Abreu a Francisco do Couto Sousa Júnior, 7 jul. 1858," in Casimiro de Abreu, *op. cit.*, 2007, pp. 88–89.

7. "Notícias diversas," *Correio mercantil*, 12 Jul. 1858, p. 1.

8. English words in the original letter are shown in italics [T.N.]. "Carta de Casimiro de Abreu a Francisco do Couto Sousa Júnior, 13 jul. 1858," in Casimiro de Abreu, *op. cit.*, 2007, pp. 92–93.

9. "Carta de Casimiro de Abreu a Francisco do Couto Sousa Júnior, 20 jul. 1858," in Casimiro de Abreu, *op. cit.*, 2007. pp. 96–97.

10. According to a note by Mário Alves de Oliveira, who organized Casimiro de Abreu's correspondence, "the expression used (*cum quibus* ["wherewithal"] that is, "money"), shows that Casimiro is once again relying on his father's funds to publish *Primaveras*." "Carta de Casimiro de Abreu a Francisco do Couto Sousa Júnior, 4 out. 1858," in Casimiro de Abreu, *op. cit.*, 2007, pp. 106–7.

11. Post-script in "Carta de Casimiro de Abreu a Francisco do Couto Sousa Júnior, 27 out. 1858," in Casimiro de Abreu, *op. cit.*, 2007, pp. 108–10.

12. Raimundo Magalhães Jr., *Poesia e vida de Casimiro de Abreu*, 1965, p. 235.

13. "Carta de Casimiro de Abreu a Francisco do Couto Sousa Júnior, 17 mai. 1859," in Casimiro de Abreu, *op. cit.*, 2007, pp. 146–47.

14. *O grátis da marmota*, 1 Nov. 1859, p. 1. Of excellent quality, Holland paper was made entirely of linen fiber. See Honoré de Balzac, *Ilusões perdidas*, 2011, p. 635.

15. "Cartas de Casimiro de Abreu a Francisco do Couto Sousa Júnior, 7 set. 1859 e 18 out. 1859," in Casimiro de Abreu, *op. cit.*, 2007, pp. 159–62.

16. Regarding the critical reception of *Primaveras*, see "*Primaveras* (Poesia do Sr. Casimiro de Abreu)," *O espelho*, 2 Oct. 1858, p. 5. An article by Justiniano José da Rocha also reprinted in Paula Brito's *Marmota*: "As *Primaveras* do Sr. Casimiro de Abreu," *A marmota*, 14 Oct. 1859, pp. 2–3. "Casimiro de Abreu—*Primaveras* (1 vol. 1859)," *Correio mercantil*, 19 Mar. 1860, p. 2.

17. In Raimundo Magalhães Jr., *op. cit.*, 1965, p. 250.

18. "Decreto N. 1610 de 23 de maio de 1855: Autoriza a incorporação e aprova os Estatutos da Companhia organizada nesta Corte com o título de Empresa Literária Dous de Dezembro," *Marmota fluminense*, 26 Jun. 1855, pp. 1–2.

19. Already well known in the literature, Garnier's contracts provide interesting parameters for the amounts and terms and conditions involved in Rio's publishing business

in the nineteenth century. For example, in August 1870, José de Alencar received one million réis for the rights to the novels *Guarani, Lucíola, Cinco minutos,* and *Viuvinha* "in perpetuity." Four years later, Alencar sold "the right to perpetual ownership" of the novels *Diva, Minas de Prata,* and *Iracema* for 1,100,000 réis. Macedo granted the rights to *Lições de corografia brasileira* to Garnier on condition that he receive 500 réis for each copy sold. The print run stipulated in the contract was one thousand copies. Machado de Assis, in turn, sold Garnier the rights to his novel *Helena* for 600,000 réis. The print run for that novel was 1,500 copies. The contract stipulated that Garnier would publish the novel at the Globo Press, which demonstrated the specialization—previously unheard of—of the work of a publisher.

   See *Recibo de José Martiniano de Alencar passado ao editor B. L. Garnier pela importância paga sobre os direitos autorais das obras:* Guarani, Lucíola, Cinco Minutos e Viuvinha, 23 Aug. 1870. *Contrato celebrado entre José Martiniano de Alencar e o editor B. L. Garnier para a edição das obras:* Diva, perfil de mulher, Minas de Prata e Iracema, Rio de Janeiro, 11 Dec. 1874. *Contrato celebrado entre Joaquim Manuel de Macedo e o editor B. L. Garnier para a 1ª edição da obra* Lições de Corografia Brasileira, Rio de Janeiro, 22 Dec. 1875. *Contrato celebrado entre Joaquim Maria Machado de Assis e o editor B. L. Garnier para a 1ª edição da obra* Helena do Vale, *Consta o recibo da importância paga por esse contrato,* Rio de Janeiro, 29 Apr. 1876.

   See also Marisa Lajolo, Regina Zilberman, *O preço da leitura: Leis e números por detrás das letras,* 2001. Alexandra Pinheiro. "Entre contratos e recibos: O trabalho de um editor francês no comércio livreiro do Rio de Janeiro oitocentista," in Márcia Abreu, ed., *Trajetórias do romance: Circulação, leitura e escrita nos séculos XVIII e XIX,* 2008.

20. *Marmota fluminense,* 10 Aug. 1852, p. 1. Emphasis mine.
21. *Marmota fluminense,* 10 Sept. 1852, p. 1.
22. "A Caixa Auxiliadora das Composições Dramáticas e Musicais," *A marmota,* 5 Oct. 1860, p. 1.
23. The last issue of *Marmota fluminense* published in 1854 contained an advertisement for the publication in the new year of "a major political-joco-serious work by one of our most popular writers, entitled, *A carteira de meu tio.*" *Marmota fluminense,* 29 Dec. 1854, p. 1. Regarding opposition to the conciliation policy in Macedo's work, see *Marmota fluminense,* 13 Feb. 1855, p. 2. Advertisements for the sale of the two pamphlets that made up the work published in the press described *A carteira de meu tio* as "oppositionist satire." See *Correio da tarde,* 22 Nov. 1855, p. 4.
24. "O nosso Folhetim," *Marmota fluminense,* 7 Mar. 1854, p. 1.
25. "To give *Vicentina* the number of passionate admirers it will certainly merit, we are accepting subscriptions for four months—March, April, May, and June—for the price of 3,000 réis, being including all fashion plates, sheet music, drawings, etc. Those who, instead of subscribing [to the newspaper], subscribe 100,000 réis worth of shares, will be presented with *Vicentina* organized in one volume, as interesting as possible." ("O nosso Folhetim," *Marmota fluminense,* 7 Mar. 1854, p. 1.)

26. "A nossa folha," *Marmota fluminense*, 19 Jan. 1855, p. 1.

27. "Fotografias literárias," *A regeneração*, 10 Sept. 1867, p. 3.

28. *Paulo* was first published in *Marmota* in early February 1861, appearing in book form in late April. See "Folhetim: Paulo, por Bruno Seabra," *A marmota*, 1 Feb. 1861, pp. 1–3. "Notícias diversas," *Correio mercantil*, 28 Apr. 1861, p. 1.

29. Ezra Greenspan, *op. cit.*, 2000, pp. 253, 287; Jean-Yves Mollier, *op. cit.*, 1999, p. 348; David Finkelstein, *op. cit.*, 2002, pp. 8–9.

30. "His edition [of *Marmota* has a print run of] one thousand copies, and sometimes much more, (which gives him thrice or four times the number of readers because many read it for free)." "*A marmota* e os seus," *A marmota*, no. 894, 27 Oct. 1857, p. 1.

31. "O Sr. Próspero e a Marmota," *Marmota fluminense*, 11 May, 1852, p. 1.

32. Ibid. Emphasis in original.

33. Ibid.

34. Ibid.

35. Ibid.

36. Ibid.

37. Sebastião Ferreira Soares, *Notas estatísticas sobre a produção agrícola e carestia dos gêneros alimentícios no Império do Brasil*, 1860, p. 288.

38. "O Sr. Próspero e a Marmota," *Marmota fluminense*, 11 May 1852, pp. 1–2.

39. *Recibos passados a Miguel Archanjo Galvão referentes à assinatura dos periódicos* A marmota *e* Marmota fluminense, 1859–1861. Regarding Miguel Archanjo Galvão, see *Almanak Laemmert*, 1859, p. 199; 1860, p. 204; 1862, p. 176.

40. "A marmota," *Correio mercantil*, 9 and 10 Apr. 1860, p. 2.

41. José de Alencar, *Como e porque sou romancista*, 2005, pp. 37, 59, 62.

42. "O demônio familiar," *A marmota*, 10 Nov. 1857, p. 2.

43. In a note published in the 1865 edition, Gonçalves de Magalhães wrote, "I translated this tragedy in a few days to please the renowned actor, João Caetano dos Santos, who passionately and urgently desired to perform it for a benefit." Domingos José Gonçalves de Magalhães, *Tragédias: Antonio José, Olgiato e Otelo*, 1865, p. 255.

44. "Anúncios," *Correio mercantil*, 4 May, 1855, p. 3.

45. M., "Páginas menores," *Correio mercantil*, 26 May, 1856, p. 1. "Indústrias e Artes," *Marmota fluminense*, 14 Jun. 1857, pp. 1–2. "*A Confederação dos Tamoios*," *Correio da tarde*, 29 Jun. 1856, p. 3. N. P. Chansselle, "Avis du traducteur," in Domingos J. G. de Magalhaes, *Faits de l'esprit humain*, 1860. pp. V–VI. P. de A Lisboa, "*A Confederação dos Tamoyos*: Poème épique," *Revue espagnole, portugaise, brésilienne et hispano-américaine*, 1857, pp. 193–201.

46. "Rio de Janeiro: Crônica Diária," *Diário do Rio de Janeiro*, 26 Oct. 1856, p. 1.

47. Alencar's biographies are interesting sources on the controversy surrounding *Confederações dos Tamoios*. See Raimundo de Meneses, "Primeira rusga com o Imperador," in *José de Alencar: Literato e político*, 1977. Raimundo Magalhaes Jr, "Em polêmica com o Imperador," in *José de Alencar e sua época*, 1977. Lira Neto, "Da dificuldade de esmagar percevejos," in *O inimigo do rei*, 2006. For a rhetorical analysis

of *Cartas*, see João Adalberto Campato Jr., *Retórica e literatura: O Alencar polemista nas* Cartas sobre a Confederação dos Tamoios, 2003.

48. "O Demônio familiar," *A marmota*, 10 Nov. 1857, p. 2.

49. "Folhetim," *Diário do Rio de Janeiro*, 11 Nov. 1857, p. 1.

50. Raimundo Magalhães Jr., *op. cit.*, 1977, p. 116.

51. Involvement in politics and violation of the vow of celibacy imposed by the Catholic Church had been a common practice among priests in Brazil since colonial times.

52. Raimundo de Meneses, *op. cit.*, 1977. Raimundo Magalhães Jr., *op. cit.*, 1977. Lira Neto, *op. cit.*, 2006, pp. 154–58.

53. "A imprensa política," *O moderador*, 13 Mar. 1857, p. 1; "A insistência do Diário," *O moderador*, 3 Mar. 1857, p. 3.

54. Raimundo de Meneses, *op. cit.*, 1977, pp. 156–67. Raimundo Magalhães Jr., *op. cit.*, 1977, pp. 50, 143–45; Lira Neto, *op. cit.*, 2006, pp. 195–96.

CHAPTER 19

1. Francisco Luís Pinto e Companhia was listed as a "supplier to H.M. the Emperor's Library" in the *Almanak Laemmert*, 1863, p. 523. Regarding the importation of French books via Lisbon, a subject discussed more thoroughly further on, see "Importação. Manifestos," *Correio mercantil*, 5 Feb. 1861, p. 4. Advertisements for books sold at the bookshop of Luís Pinto e Companhia can be found in "Livraria Imperial de Francisco Luiz Pinto & Comp.," *Correio mercantil*, 8 Dec. 1861, p. 4; "Na Livraria de Francisco Luiz Pinto & Comp.," *Correio mercantil*, 25 Feb. 1861, p. 4; "Livros de Direito para os Srs. Estudantes de S. Paulo," *Correio mercantil*, 28 Feb. 1862, p. 4.

2. "Roubo de livros," *Diário do Rio Janeiro*, 26 Feb. 1863, p. 1.

3. M., "Páginas menores," *Correio mercantil*, 26 May 1856, p. 1.

4. "22 de maio: Boletim do dia," *Diário do Rio de Janeiro*, 22 May 1857, p. 1.

5. *Correio da tarde*, 22 May 1857, pp. 2–3.

6. Henri-Jean Martin and Lucien Febvre, *O aparecimento do livro*, 1992, p. 59.

7. José Thomaz Nabuco de Araújo, *Relatório da repartição dos negócios da justiça apresentado à Assembleia Geral Legislativa na Terceira Sessão da Nona Legislatura*, 1855.

8. "A Indústria no Brasil," *Marmota fluminense*, 1 Jun. 1855, p. 1.

9. Joaquim Marcellino de Brito, *Relatório da repartição dos negócios do Império apresentado à Assembleia Geral Legislativa*, 1847, pp. 27–29.

10. Visconde de Macaé, *Relatório da repartição dos negócios do Império apresentado à Assembleia Geral Legislativa*, 1848, pp. 27–28.

11. "Repartição de Polícia," *Correio mercantil*, 3 Jan. 1849, p. 4. "Notícias e fatos diversos," *Correio mercantil*, 25 Jul. 1851, p. 1.

12. Luiz Pedreira do Couto Ferraz, *Relatório apresentado à Assembleia Geral Legislativa na primeira sessão da décima legislatura pelo ministro e secretário de estados dos negócios do Império*, 1857, p. 116.

13. Laurence Hallewell, *op. cit.*, p. 132.
14. Ibid. Regarding the Baron of Capanema, see Silvia Fernanda de Mendonça Figuerôa, "Ciência e tecnologia no Brasil Imperial," *Varia história*, 2005.
15. "A Indústria no Brasil," *Marmota fluminense*, 1 Jun. 1855, p. 1.
16. Ibid.
17. "Importação. Manifestos: Galera francesa *Nouvelle Pauline* do Havre," *Diário do Rio de Janeiro*, 4 Dec. 1856, p. 4. I also investigated the shipments of the following vessels: "Manifestos: Galera francesa *Empereur du Brésil*, do Havre," *Diário do Rio de Janeiro*, 11 Dec. 1851, p. 3. "Importação. Manifestos: Galera francesa *France et Brésil* do Havre," *Diário do Rio de Janeiro*, 25 Jan. 1855, p. 2. "Importação. Manifestos: Galera francesa *Ville de Rio* do Havre," *Diário do Rio de Janeiro*, 29 Mar. 1855, p. 2. "Importação. Manifestos: Galera francesa *Nouvelle Pauline* do Havre," *Diário do Rio de Janeiro*, 7 Nov. 1855, p. 4. "Importação. Manifestos: Brigue português *Joaquina*, de Lisboa," *Diário do Rio de Janeiro*, 16 Oct. 1856, p. 4. "Importação. Manifestos: Galera francesa *Imperatriz do Brasil*, do Havre," *Diário do Rio de Janeiro*, 14 Aug. 1857, p. 4.
   Imports of paper to Rio de Janeiro increased considerably between 1850 and 1852, from 117,462,389 réis between 1850 and 1851 to 689,525,725 réis between 1851 and 1852. This increase was linked to the reconversion of capital from the slave trade after the transatlantic trade was definitively banned in 1850. Artur José Renda Vitorino, *op. cit.*, 2002, pp. 44–45.
18. *Guanabara*, vol. I, 1850.
19. "Aos nossos assinantes," *Guanabara*, vol. I, 1851, p. 231.
20. On that occasion, in October 1855, Francisco Freire wrote to Paula Brito regarding the print run of *Guanabara* due to the printing of a "map that [should] accompany a Memoir." Noted on the same sheet of paper in the publisher's handwriting, we can read, "the edition is 680." *Carta a [Francisco de] Paula Brito, indagando sobre a tiragem do periódico* Guanabara. Rio de Janeiro, Oct. 1855.
21. "Epílogo," *Guanabara*, vol. III, 1856, pp. 359–60.
22. In 1848, the *Auxiliador* was printed by the Francisco Manuel Ferreira Press, located on Rua do Sabão, no. 117. In 1852, before it came to be printed by Dous de Dezembro, it was published by the press of Vianna Júnior e Paula, Rua d'Ajuda, no. 57. Paula Brito's imprint appears on the September issue of that year. *Auxiliador da Indústria Nacional*, Sept. 1852, p. 114.
23. Paula Brito was member no. 145. "Sociedade Auxiliadora da Indústria Nacional. Ano Social de 1851–1852," *Auxiliador da Indústria Nacional*, Jul. 1851, pp. 1–9. "Acionistas da Empresa Dous de Dezembro que, como tais, receberam o *Guanabara*," *Guanabara*, vol. III, 1856. There are references to Dous de Dezembro in the *Auxiliador*, when receipt of the company's publications was reported: "Os impressos da empresa—Dous de Dezembro, de que a Sociedade é Acionista." *Auxiliador da Indústria Nacional*, Jul. 1852, p. 76.
24. "Proposta fixando a despesa e orçando a receita da Sociedade Auxiliador da Indústria Nacional, para o ano de 1853–1854." *Auxiliador da Indústria Nacional*, Jul. 1853, pp. 481–82.

25. *Carta de Francisco de Paula Brito a destinatário ignorado explicando a razão de não imprimir o Auxiliador*, Rio de Janeiro, 25 Jun. 1854.
26. *Auxiliador da Indústria Nacional*, Jul. 1854.
27. "Aos senhores assinantes de fora," *A marmota*, 9 Apr. 1958, p. 1.
28. "Aos nossos assinantes de fora," *A marmota*, 20 Dec. 1859, p. 1.
29. "Livros baratos," *O Brasil*, 18 Sept. 1849, p. 4.
30. José de Alencar, *Como e por que sou romancista*, 2005, p. 38.
31. Regarding São Paulo, see Marisa Midore Deaecto, *op. cit.*, 2011. Regarding Mato Grosso, see Eni Neves da Silva Rodrigues, "Impressões em preto e branco: História da leitura em Mato Grosso na segunda metade do século XIX," 2008. Regarding Ceará, see Ozângela de Arruda Silva, *Pelas rotas dos livros: Circulação de romances e conexões comerciais em Fortaleza (1870–1891)*, 2011.
32. Patrícia de Jesus Palma, "O mercado do livro brasileiro em Portugal." Unpublished text. I would like to thank the author for sharing this article.
33. Ibid., p. 3.

CHAPTER 20

1. "Ao Livro d'Ouro," *Marmota fluminense*, 25 Oct. 1853, p. 6; 28 Oct. 1853, p. 6.
2. "Boa preta," *Correio mercantil*, 26 and 27 Mar. 1857, p. 4.
3. *Inventário. Francisco de Paula Brito, falecido. Rufina Rodrigues da Costa Brito, Inventariante*, 1862, fls. 29–29v.
4. "Tipografia de Paula Brito," *A marmota*, 13 May 1859, p. 4.
5. "Discurso Proferido pelo Doutor Caetano Alves de Sousa Filgueiras por Ocasião da Missa de Sétimo Dia de Francisco de Paula Brito," *Diário do Rio de Janeiro*, 24 Dec. 1861, p. 2.
6. "O Sr. Ministro da Justiça," *Marmota fluminense*, 3 Apr. 1857, p. 1.
7. "Morte de Antônio Gonçalves Teixeira e Sousa," *A marmota*, 6 Dec. 1857, p. 1.
8. "Biografia do Sr. Francisco de Paula Brito," *Correio mercantil*, 3 Mar. 1862, p. 2. "Crônica da quinzena," *Revista popular*, vol. XIII, 1861, p. 52. "Crônica A*** XXIII," *Correio mercantil*, 22 Dec. 1861, p. 1.
9. "Notícias Diversas," *Correio mercantil*, 16 Dec. 1861, p. 1. *Diário do Rio de Janeiro*, 16 Dec. 1861, p. 1. "Gazetilha," *Jornal do commercio*, 16 Dec. 1861, p. 1. "Notícias e Avisos Diversos," *Correio da tarde*, 16 Dec. 1861, p. 2.
10. "Notícias Diversas," *Correio mercantil*, 17 Dec. 1861, p. 1. "Chronique du moment," *Courrier du Brésil*, 22 Dec. 1861, p. 1.
11. One of the masses celebrated at the Church of Santíssimo Sacramento was ordered by the Associação Tipográfica Fluminense (Rio de Janeiro Printing Association). See "Noticiário," *Diário do Rio de Janeiro*, 30 Dec. 1861, p. 1. Regarding the mass celebrated by the Confraternity of Nossa Senhora da Lampadosa, see "Publicações religiosas," *Correio mercantil*, 24 Dec. 1861, p. 2. The mass held in Portugal

was ordered by Francisco Joaquim Correa de Brito. See "Portugal," *O português*, 16 Mar. 1862, p. 3.

12. "Discurso proferido pelo Dr. Caetano Alves de Sousa Filgueiras por ocasião da missa de sétimo dia de Francisco de Paula Brito," *Diário do Rio de Janeiro*, 24 Dec. 1861, p. 2.

13. The leaders of the Conservative Party were called "cardinals," so this reference to the Vatican is a witty political jibe, as the "pope" in this case was Eusébio de Queirós, one of the party's main leaders. "Interior," *O liberal*, Recife, 18 Mar. 1862, pp. 2–3.

14. "Notícias diversas," *Correio mercantil*, 24 Dec. 1861, p. 1.

15. "Crônica da quinzena," *Revista popular*, vol. XIII, 1861, p. 64.

16. "Comunicado: Colaboração humorística," *Diário do Rio de Janeiro*, 2 Jan. 1861, p. 2.

17. "*A marmota* e a política," *A marmota*, 26 Apr. 1861, p. 1.

18. The figures have been rounded to be more easily understood. However, the exact figures were 4,828,630 réis, for "rents for the houses in which the establishments are based, the clerks' wages, the wages of day-laborers and bill collectors, the salaries of workers, consumption of gas, liquidation of the account for the sale of stamped paper, for medication, and the cost of the funeral and mourning for the family"; 6,000,000 réis "for the mortgage"; 11,195,637 réis "for bills and letters of credit presented"; 13,675,000 "for the bankruptcy protection agreement reached by her late husband in 1857." See "Declarações que faz Rufina Rodrigues da Costa Brito, viúva e inventariante dos bens de seu casal por falecimento de seu marido Francisco de Paula Brito," in *Inventário. Francisco de Paula Brito, falecido. Rufina Rodrigues da Costa Brito, Inventariante*. 1862. fls 11, 11v.

19. The debt totaled 35,967,267 réis. The exact figures of the assessments are 411,500 réis for "household goods . . . in addition to the shelving and other office furnishings"; 6,500,000 réis for the press "and all its appurtenances"; 1,751,500, for books. *Inventário. Francisco de Paula Brito, falecido. Rufina Rodrigues da Costa Brito, Inventariante*, 1862. fls. 29–32. I have analyzed the assessments of the estate in more detail in Rodrigo Camargo de Godoi, "O espólio do editor: A 'Avaliação de Bens' do Inventário de Francisco de Paula Brito," *Anais do XXVI Simpósio Nacional de História (ANPUH)*, 2011.

20. *Vários papéis sobre o patriota Francisco de Paula Brito, dono da loja de papel da Praça da Constituição e editor; com referência a publicações mandadas fazer pela Câmara Municipal, inclusive o "Arquivo Municipal,"* 1852, 1860, 1862.

21. Ibid.

22. "Câmara Municipal: 21ª sessão em 23 de julho de 1862," *Correio mercantil*, 18 Aug. 1862, p. 2. "Câmara Municipal: 24ª sessão em 13 de agosto de 1862," *Correio mercantil*, 29 Aug. 1862, p. 2.

23. "Ilma. Câmara Municipal da Corte; 28ª sessão em 13 de setembro de 1862," *Correio mercantil*, 23 Sept. 1862, p. 2. In 1866, Rufina tendered a bid to become the printer and supplier of office materials to the Rio de Janeiro City Council. However, all indications are that, once again, she lost to the *Correio mercantil* press. *Publicações. Papéis separados em ordem cronológica*, 1838–1913.

24. *Correio mercantil*, 11 Feb. 1863, p. 2. "Publicação literária," *Diário do Rio de Janeiro*, 4 Aug. 1864, p. 3.
25. "Noticiário," *Diário do Rio de Janeiro*, 13 Mar. 1864, p. 1.
26. *A marmota*, 10 Apr. 1864.
27. Rodrigo Camargo de Godoi, *op. cit.*, 2011.
28. *Inventário. Francisco de Paula Brito, falecido. Rufina Rodrigues da Costa Brito, Inventariante*, 1862.
29. Ibid., fls. 47.
30. *Diário do Rio de Janeiro*, 27 Sept. 1866, p. 2.
31. *O repórter*, 9 Mar. 1879, p. 3; "A viúva Paula Brito," *Gazeta de notícias*, 9 Mar. 1879, p. 5.
32. "Noticiário," *A instrução pública*, 22 Jun. 1873, p. 7. "Província do Rio de Janeiro, 1874: Município de Magé; Professoras Públicas." *Almanak Laemmert*, 1874, p. 111. *A reforma*, 14 Feb. 1875, p. 4. "Província do Rio de Janeiro," *Gazeta de notícias*, 9 Dec. 1879, p. 2.
33. Machado de Assis, Joaquim Maria. *Memórias póstumas de Braz Cubas*, in *Obras completas*, v. I, 2006, p. 555.

EPILOGUE

1. Robert Darnton, "O que é a história dos livros?" in Robert Darnton, *op. cit.*, 2010, p. 122, 140; Robert Darnton, *op. cit.*, 1996, p. 13.
2. Ilmar Rohloff de Mattos, *O tempo Saquarema*, 2004, pp. 15, 170, 293–96.
3. Ibid., p. 287.
4. *Diário do Rio de Janeiro*, 3 Jan. 1865, p. 1. Regarding the Garniers in Paris, see Odile Martin and Henri-Jean Martin, *op. cit.*, 1990, pp. 180–81.
5. *Informações dirigidas ao Marquês de Olinda sobre a pessoa e trabalhos do livreiro-editor Baptista Luís Garnier que requereu uma condecoração.*
6. The decree appointing Garnier a Knight of the Order of the Rose was signed on March 16, 1867. Regarding the Imperial Order of the Rose, on the same occasion Manuel de Araújo Porto-Alegre was appointed commander; José de Alencar, Tavares Bastos, and Emílio Adet, officers; and Machado de Assis, a knight. "Noticiário: Ministério do Império," *Diário do Rio de Janeiro*, 17 Mar. 1867, p 1. Regarding citizens awarded the Imperial Order of the Rose for freeing slaves to fight in the Paraguay War, see "Atos oficiais: Ministério do Império," *Diário do Rio de Janeiro*, 3 Feb. 1867, p. 1.

References

ARCHIVES

ACMRJ. Arquivo da Cúria Metropolitana do Rio de Janeiro
AEAD. Arquivo Eclesiástico da Diocese de Diamantina-MG
AEL. Arquivo Edgard Leuenroth
AGCRJ. Arquivo Geral da Cidade do Rio de Janeiro
ANRJ. Arquivo Nacional do Rio de Janeiro
BNRJ. Biblioteca Nacional do Rio de Janeiro
IHGB. Instituto Histórico e Geográfico Brasileiro
RGPL. Real Gabinete Português de Leitura

NEWSPAPERS

O americano
Anais de medicina brasiliense
Arquivo médico brasileiro
O atlante
Autores e livros
Auxiliador da Indústria Nacional
A baboza
O brado do Amazonas
O Brasil

Café da tarde
O capadócio
O carioca
Catholico
O Católico
O cidadão
Clarim da liberdade
Conciliador fluminense: Jornal político, histórico e miscelânico
Correio da tarde
Correio mercantil
Courrier du Brésil
D. Pedro II
Despertador
Diário da Câmara dos Deputados à Assembleia Geral Legislativa do Império do Brasil
Diário do Rio de Janeiro
Diário mercantil, ou, Novo jornal do commercio
O escandaloso
O espelho
O evaristo
O farol
O filho do Brasil
Folhinha dos sonhos para o ano de 1862
O futuro
Gazeta de notícias
Gazeta dos tribunais
O gosto
O grátis da marmota
O grito da razão
O grito nacional
Guanabara
O homem de cor
O homem do povo
A instrução pública
Jornal do commercio
Justiceiro constitucional
Ladrão
O liberal
A liga americana
A marmota
A marmota na corte
Marmota fluminense
O meia-cara

Mestre José
A mineira no Rio de Janeiro
O moderador
O monarquista do século XIX
O mulato, ou, O homem de cor
A mulher do Simplício, ou, A fluminense exaltada
Nova luz brazileira
A novidade
O novo Caramuru
Novo correio das modas
Novo e completo índice cronológico da história do Brasil
O observador das galerias
A ortiga
Pão de açúcar
A pátria
O periódico acadêmico
Popular
O português
O pregoeiro
O propugnador da maioridade
O publícola
A reforma
A regeneração
O regente: Jornal político, literário
O repórter
A revolução pacífica
Revista médica brasileira
Revista médica fluminense
Revista popular
Revue espagnole, portugaise, brésilienne et hispano-américaine
O rusguentinho
O saturnino
Seleta Católica
Sete d'Abril
Simplício da roça: Jornal dos domingos
Simplício endiabrado
O Tamoio
O tebyreça
Triumvir restaurador, ou, A lima surda
A verdade
O ypiranga

MANUSCRIPTS

Ação de dez dias. Adriano Gabriel Corte Real, autor. Francisco de Paula Brito, réu. ANRJ, Coleção de processos comerciais, no. 1.406, caixa 1.355, 1856.

Ação de dez dias. Bernardino Ribeiro de Souza Guimarães, autor. Francisco de Paula Brito, réu. ANRJ, Coleção de processos comerciais, no. 664, caixa 1.199, 1854.

Ação de dez dias. Duarte José de Puga Garcia, autor. Francisco de Paula Brito, réu. ANRJ, Coleção de processos comerciais, no. 411, caixa 1.193, 1855.

Ação de dez dias. Eugenio Bouchaud, autor. Francisco de Paula Brito, réu. ANRJ, Coleção de Processos Comerciais, no. 1.303, caixa 1.345, 1856.

Ação de dez dias. Francisco de Paula Brito, réu. 1857. ANRJ, Juízo Especial do Comércio da 2ª Vara, 1857, no. 53, caixa 4.170.

Ação de dez dias. Francisco José Gonçalves Agra, autor. Francisco de Paula Brito, réu. ANRJ, Coleção de processos comerciais, no. 663, caixa 1.199, 1854.

Ação de dez dias. José Antonio de Oliveira Bastos, autor. Eugênio Aprígio da Veiga e Francisco de Paula Brito, réus. ANRJ, Coleção de Processos Comerciais, no. 427, caixa 1.193, 1855.

Ação de dez dias. Saportas e Cia, autor. Francisco de Paula Brito, réu. ANRJ, Coleção de Processos Comerciais, no. 608, caixa 1.199, 1854.

Ação Ordinária. Mariana Augusta d⊠Oliveira, autora. Francisco de Paula Brito, réu. ANRJ, Coleção de processos comerciais, no. 949, caixa 1.192, 1855.

Ação Ordinária. Pe. Joaquim Ferreira da Cruz Belmonte, autor. Francisco de Paula Brito, réu. ANRJ, Coleção de processos comerciais, no. 1.885, caixa 1.832, 1857.

Apelação cível. Jacinto Antunes Duarte, apelante. José Antonio Teixeira Guimarães, apelado. ANRJ, Relação do Rio de Janeiro, no. 1236, caixa 592, gal. C, 1819–1820.

Apelação criminal. A Justiça, apelante. Silvino José de Almeida, réu. ANRJ, no. 2729, maço 190, gal. C, 1834–1835.

Apelação criminal. A Justiça, autor. Theodoro, crioulo escravo de Junius Villeneuve e Cia, réu. ANRJ, Corte de Apelação, no. 1184, caixa 160, gal. C, 1863.

Apelação criminal. Luíza Joaquina das Neves, autora; Antônio Alexandre Lopes do Couto, réu. 1864. ANRJ, Relação do Rio de Janeiro—84, 5649/1301.

Aprovação dos Estatutos do Gabinete Português de Leitura e autorização para continuar os seus trabalhos, Maranhão, 1861. ANRJ, Conselho de Estado, Consultas do Conselho de Estado, caixa 530, pacote 2.

Aprovação dos Estatutos da Associação Grêmio Literário Português, 1861. ANRJ, Conselho de Estado, Consultas do Conselho de Estado, caixa 528, pacote 3.

Batismo de Alexandrina, inocente. Brazil, Catholic Church Records, Rio de Janeiro, Santíssimo Sacramento, Batismos 1833–1837, Imagem 249. familysearch.org.

Batismo de Rofina, inocente. Brazil, Catholic Church Records, Rio de Janeiro, Santíssimo Sacramento, Batismos 1833–1837, Imagem 163. familysearch.org.

Batizados de Várias Localidades, 1740–1754. AEAD, caixa 296, bloco D.

Brás Antonio Castrioto, administrador da Tipografia Nacional e Imperial do Rio de Janeiro, pede mercê do Hábito da Ordem de Cristo. BNRJ, Manuscritos, C-1-71-7, 1824–1828.

Cálculo para uma tipografia feito por Renée Ogier, para o jornal Aurora Fluminense, encontrado entre os papéis de João Pedro da Veiga. Rio de Janeiro. IHGB, Lata 347, Doc. 29, 13 Nov. 1834.

Carregamento do Patacho Cesar, ANRJ, IJ6 471.

Carta a [Francisco de] Paula Brito, indagando sobre a tiragem do periódico Guanabara. *Rio de Janeiro.* BNRJ, Manuscritos, I-28, 02, 028, Oct. 1855.

Carta de Diogo Antonio Feijó a Paulino José Soares. BNRJ, Manuscritos, 65, 05, 006, no. 028, 26 May 1836.

Carta de emancipação do africano Fausto de nação Sunde, ANRJ, IJ6 471.

Carta de Francisco de Paula Brito a destinatário ignorado explicando a razão de não imprimir o Auxiliador. *Rio de Janeiro.* BN, Manuscritos, I-28, 02, 028, 25 Jul. 1854

Carta de Frei Camilo de Monserrate ao Ministro Luiz Pedreira do Couto Ferraz, solicitando o pagamento de uma dívida contraída com o livreiro Paula Brito pela antiga administração da Biblioteca Nacional. Rio de Janeiro. BNRJ, Manuscritos, 30, 2, 011 no. 18, 14 Nov. 1853.

Comércio estrangeiro. Papéis separados por ordem cronológica. AGCRJ, 58.4.33, 1839–1872.

Conta de Rodrigues e Cia, relativa a publicação das Atas da Câmara Municipal do Rio de Janeiro. BNRJ, Manuscritos, II-35, 15, 10 no. 1, 1853.

Contrato celebrado entre Joaquim Manuel de Macedo e o editor B. L. Garnier para a 1ª edição da obra Lições de Corografia Brasileira. *Rio de Janeiro, 22 de dez. 1875.* BN, Manuscritos, I-7, 9, 19.

Contrato celebrado entre Joaquim Maria Machado de Assis e o editor B. L. Garnier para a 1ª edição da obra Helena do Vale. *Consta o recibo da importância paga por esse contrato.* Rio de Janeiro, 29 Apr. 1876. BN, Manuscritos, I-7, 9, 4.

Contrato celebrado entre José Martiniano de Alencar e o editor B. L. Garnier para a edição das obras: Diva, perfil de mulher, Minas de Prata *e* Iracema. *Rio de Janeiro, 11 Dec. 1874.* BN, Manuscritos, I-7, 9, 1.

Designação de José Rufino Rodrigues de Vasconcelos para Francisco de Paula Brito examinar a peça A pobre louca. *Rio de Janeiro, 3 Aug. 1851.* BNRJ, Manuscritos, Coleção Conservatório Dramático Brasileiro, I-8, 8, 50.

Documentos sobre a primeira tipografia em São Paulo. 1823–1824. Cópia. IHGB, Lata 136, pasta 22.

Embargo de obra nova. Manuel Francisco da Silveira Freitas, autor; Francisco de Paula Brito, réu. ANRJ, Juízo Municipal da 1ª Vara do Rio de Janeiro, no. 21. Maço 38, 1852.

Estatística de casas de comércio, número de rezes, embarcações, veículos terrestre e notas sobre licenças para obras, alvarás de negócio e receita e despesa, 1843. AGCRJ, 43.1.43.

Estatutos da Caixa Auxiliadora das Composições Dramáticas e Musicais, out. 1860-fev. 1861. ANRJ, Conselho de Estado, Consultas do Conselho de Estado, caixa 526, pacote 2.

Execução de sentença. Bernardino de Souza Ribeiro Guimarães, executante. Francisco de Paula Brito, executado. ANRJ, Coleção de Processos Comerciais, no. 297, caixa 1.196, 1854.

Execução de sentença. Francisco José Gonçalves Agra, executante. Francisco de Paula Brito, executado. ANRJ, Coleção de processos comerciais, no. 284, caixa 1.196, 1854.

Execução. Dr. Joaquim Pereira de Araújo, executante. Francisco de Paula Brito, executado. ANRJ, Coleção de processos comerciais, no. 68, maço 1.514, 1857.

Execução. Duarte José de Puga Garcia, exequente. Francisco de Paula Brito, executado. ANRJ, Coleção de processos comerciais, no. 1.002, caixa 1.191, 1856.

Execução. Eugênio Bouchaud, executante. Francisco de Paula Brito, executado. ANRJ, Coleção de processos comerciais, no. 1.602, caixa 1.353, 1856.

Execução. João de Souza Monteiro, executante. Francisco de Paula Brito, executado. ANRJ, Coleção de processos comerciais, no. 1.016, caixa 1.191, 1855.

Execução. Saportas e Cia, executante. Francisco de Paula Brito, executado. ANRJ, Coleção de processos comerciais, no. 371, caixa 1.195, 1854.

Gaspar José Monteiro, oficial compositor, oferece seus serviços à nova tipografia a ser instalada na Biblioteca Nacional e Pública do Rio de Janeiro, 1822. BNRJ, Manuscritos, C-1062-40, Docs 4–5.

Índice de Batismo. N. Sra. da Candelária (1635–1781). ACMRJ, I-021.

Índice de Batismos de Livres. N. Sra. da Candelária (1758–1781). ACMRJ, I-023.

Informações dirigidas ao Marquês de Olinda sobre a pessoa e trabalhos do livreiro-editor Baptista Luís Garnier que requereu uma condecoração. IHGB, Lata 214, Doc. 61.

Inventário. Francisco de Paula Brito, falecido. Rufina Rodrigues da Costa Brito, inventariante. ANRJ, Juízo Municipal da 1ª Vara do Rio de Janeiro, no. 6.210, maço 448, 1862.

José Francisco Lopes, mestre impressor na tipografia nacional da Bahia, 1823–1824. BNRJ, Manuscritos, C-937, 56.

Justificação para Embargo. Dr. Joaquim Pereira de Araújo, justificante. Francisco de P aula Brito, justificado. ANRJ, Coleção de processos comerciais, no. 557, maço 1.498, 1857.

Livro de Batismo da Freguesia do Santíssimo Sacramento do Rio de Janeiro, Batismo entre 1794, Fev-1798. familysearch.org.

Livro de Batismos, 1725. AEAD, caixa 296, bloco A.

Livro de Batizados, 1733–1734. AEAD, caixa 296, bloco A.

Livro de casamentos de livres da Freguesia do Santíssimo Sacramento. ACMRJ, AP 0134.

Livro de óbitos da Freguesia do Santíssimo Sacramento. ACMRJ, AP-162.

Pedido de pagamento de Sebastião Gomes da Silva Belfort, empresário da tipografia do Diário do Rio de Janeiro, relativo à impressão de publicações da Câmara Municipal da corte. Rio de Janeiro, 5 de março de 1868. BNRJ, manuscritos, II-35, 16, 11 no. 2.

Petição de transferência dos serviços da africana livre Maria Benguela, autor Francisco de Paula Brito. ANRJ, Diversos (GIFI) Justiça, 6D-130, 11/06/1857.

Processo contra Nicolau Lobo Vianna e José Joaquim de Abreu Gama, impressor e responsável pelo periódico Caramuru, por abuso da liberdade de imprensa e sedição contra o governo, 1832–1833. BN, manuscritos, I-31, 31, 17, no. 2.

Processo da habilitação matrimonial de Jacinto Antunes Duarte e Maria Joaquina da Conceição, 1795. ACMRJ, caixa 2514, notação 52.692.

Processo de habilitação matrimonial de Martinho Pereira de Brito e Anna Maria da Conceição, 1765. ACMRJ, caixa 1.983, notação. 33.289.

Processo a respeito dos tumultos e desordens das garrafadas nas noites dos dias 12, 14 e 15 de março de 1831. Rio de Janeiro: [s.n.], 1831. 35 p., BNRJ, manuscritos 06, 03, 012.

Proposta de Francisco de Paula Brito para imprimir um jornal que insira atos da administração municipal e os talões de expediente, sob as condições que estabelece, 1859. AGCRJ, 48.4.71.

Publicações de atos oficiais. Propostas de Justiniano José da Rocha, editor proprietário do Correio do Brasil, e da Tipografia americana, do Correio mercantil e de Antonio e Luiz Navarro de Andrade, proprietários editores do Diário, 1853. AGCRJ, 48.4.70.

Publicações. Papéis separados em ordem cronológica, 1838–1913. AGCRJ, 48.4.69.

Recibo de José Martiniano de Alencar passado ao editor B. L. Garnier pela importância paga sobre os direitos autorais das obras: Guarani, Lucíola, Cinco Minutos e Viuvinha. Rio de Janeiro, 23 de ago. 1870. BN, Manuscritos, I-7, 9, 2.

Recibos passados a Miguel Archanjo Galvão referentes à assinatura dos periódicos A marmota e Marmota fluminense. Rio de Janeiro, 1859–1861. BNRJ, Manuscritos, 37A, 04, 003, no. 008AA.

Registro de Batismo de Várias Localidades, 1720–1740. AEAD, caixa 296, bloco B.

Registro de Batismos do Serro, 1727–1734; Casamentos do Serro, 1729–1734. AEAD, cx. 296, bl. B.

Registro de Óbitos de Escravos do Serro, 1725–1797. AEAD, caixa 352, bloco A.

Registros de Batismo de Várias Localidades, 1728–1733. AEAD, caixa 296, bloco B

Registros de Batismos. Várias Localidades, 1720–1740. AEAD, caixa 296, bloco B.

Registros de Casamentos do Serro, 1736–1772. AEAD, caixa 338, bloco A.

Relação das obras que o livreiro Silvino tem encadernado na Biblioteca Imperial e Pública (Sept. 1823, Mar. 1832). Rio de Janeiro, 1832. BNRJ, Manuscritos, I-16, 04, 021.

Relação de todos os Africanos Livres que até a presente data ainda se acham sob a responsabilidade dos particulares que foram confiados, março de 1861. National Archives (Kew, United Kingdom) FO 128/48 fs. 290–344.

Relação nominal das pessoas a quem têm sido confiados Africanos livres, quantos e seu estado de dívida em 31 de dezembro de 1844, desde o segundo semestre do ano financeiro de 1840–41 em que passou a arrecadação de seus salários a ser feito pela Recebedoria do Munícipio da Corte, até o fim do ano financeiro próximo findo de 1843–1844 na forma exigida em aviso da Secretaria de Justiça de 10 de setembro de 1844. ANRJ, IJ6 471.

Requerimento de André Gailhard encaminhado ao Ministério do Império solicitando expedição de ordem para que possa receber o produto de quatro loterias a benefício de sua fábrica de papel, 1845–1846. BNRJ, Manuscritos, C-486, 5, no. 3–4. Doc. 7.

Requerimento de Francisco de Paula Brito encaminhado ao Ministério do Império, solicitando que seja aprovado o estatuto de sua Empresa Literária Dous de Dezembro. Doc. 5. BNRJ, Manuscritos, C-0803, 004. 1855.

Requerimento de Renato Ogier à Câmara Municipal do Rio de Janeiro, 9 Mar. 1838. Tipografias e artes gráficas. Vários papéis separados em ordem cronológica e referentes a tipografias, jornais e oficinas de artes gráficas, 1833–1887. AGCRJ, 44.4.16.

Resposta de José Bonifácio a respeito do aumento aos aprendizes da Imperial Cozinha. Rio de Janeiro, 11 Mar. 1833. BNRJ, Manuscritos, I-4, 35, 3.

Secretaria de Polícia da Corte, dossiê relativo a Agostinho Moçambique, setembro de 1862. ANRJ, IJ6 516.

Tipografia de Francisco de Paula Brito. Requerimento e informações para melhoramentos na Empresa Tipográfica, 1851. AGCRJ, 50.3.46.

Vários papéis sobre o patriota Francisco de Paula Brito, dono da loja de papel da Praça da Constituição e editor; com referência a publicações mandadas fazer pela Câmara Municipal, inclusive o ⊠Arquivo Municipal,⊠ 1852, 1860, 1862. AGCRJ, 47.1.60.

RARE WORKS

Albuquerque, Antônio Francisco de Paula Holanda Cavalcante de. *Proposta e Relatório apresentado à Assembleia Geral Legislativa na 3ª Sessão da 6ª Legislatura pelo Ministro e Secretário de Estado dos Negócios da Fazenda,* 1846.

Almanach do Rio de Janeiro para o ano de 1824. Rio de Janeiro: Imprensa Nacional, 1824. p. 267. memoria.bn.br.

Almanach do Rio de Janeiro para o ano de 1825. Rio de Janeiro: Imprensa Nacional, 1824. p. 248. memoria.bn.br.

Almanak Laemmert [*Almanak administrativo, mercantil e industrial do Rio de Janeiro*]. Rio de Janeiro: Eduardo e Henrique Laemmert, ed. Published annually, 1843–1889.

"Almanaque da cidade do Rio de Janeiro para o ano de 1792." In *Anais da Biblioteca Nacional do Rio de Janeiro, 1937, v. LIX.* Rio de Janeiro: Serviço Gráfico do Ministério da Educação, 1940.

"Almanaque da cidade do Rio de Janeiro para o ano de 1794." In *Anais da Biblioteca Nacional do Rio de Janeiro, 1937, v. LIX.* Rio de Janeiro: Serviço Gráfico do Ministério da Educação, 1940.

Anuário político, histórico e estatístico do Brasil. Rio de Janeiro: Casa de Firmin Didot Irmãos, 1847.

Araújo, José Thomaz Nabuco de. *Relatório do Ministério da Justiça apresentado à Assembleia Geral da Quarta Sessão da Décima Segunda Legislatura.* Rio de Janeiro: Tipografia Universal de Laemmert, 1866. brazil.crl.edu.

Branco, Manuel Alves. *Relatório da repartição dos negócios da justiça apresentado à Assembleia Geral Legislativa na sessão ordinária de 1835.* Rio de Janeiro: Tipografia Nacional, 1835. p. 11–12. brazil.crl.edu.

Brito, Francisco de Paula. *Poesias.* Rio de Janeiro: Tipografia Paula Brito, 1863.

_____. *Hino oferecido à mocidade brasileira, no dia 25 de março de 1831.* Rio de Janeiro: Tipografia Imperial de E. Seignot-Plancher, 1831. BN, Obras raras, 088, 004, 011, no. 2.

_____. *Hino ao memorável dia 7 de abril de 1831.* Rio de Janeiro: Tipografia d'E. Seignot-Plancher, 1831. BN, Obras raras, 088, 004, 010, no. 5.

_____. *Proclamação aos compatriotas*. Rio de Janeiro: Tip. Fluminense de Brito e Cia, n.d. BN, Obras raras, 102, 5, 226.

_____. *Hino à maioridade de Sua Majestade o Imperador proclamado pela Assembleia, tropa e povo, no dia 22 de julho de 1840*. Rio de Janeiro: Imprensa Imparcial de F. de Paula Brito, 1840. BN, Obras raras, 099A, 021, 096.

_____. *Soneto à imprensa, dedicado a Sua Majestade Imperial o senhor D. Pedro II*. Rio de Janeiro: Composto e impresso na Imperial Quinta da Boa Vista, n.d. BNRJ, Obras raras, 088, 004, 010, no. 6.

Brito, Joaquim Marcellino de. *Relatório da repartição dos negócios do Império apresentado à Assembleia Geral Legislativa*. Rio de Janeiro: Tipografia Nacional, 1847.

Burlamaqui, Frederico Leopoldo César. *Memória analítica acerca do comércio d▨escravos e acerca dos males da escravidão doméstica*. Rio de Janeiro: Tipografia Comercial Fluminense, 1837.

Cavalcanti d'Albuquerque, Antonio Francisco de Paula Holanda. *Proposta e Relatório apresentado à Assembleia Geral Legislativa na 3ª Sessão da 6ª Legislatura pelo Ministro e Secretário de Estado dos Negócios da Fazenda*. Rio de Janeiro: Tipografia Nacional, 1846. p 4.brazil.crl.edu.

Dupont, Paul. *Histoire de l'imprimerie*. Tome 2. Paris: Les libraires,1854. gallica.bnf.fr.

Empreza Typográphica Dous de Dezembro de Paula Brito. Rio de Janeiro: Empreza Typográfica Dous de Dezembro, n.d. BN, Obras raras, 088, 001, no. 9.

Faria, Antonio Bento de, ed. *Código Comercial Brasileiro anotado de acordo com a doutrina, a legislação e a jurisprudência nacional e estrangeira, e os princípios e regras do direito civil, seguido de um apêndice contendo o Regulamento no. 737 de 1850, e todas as leis comerciais em vigor, igualmente anotadas*. Rio de Janeiro: Jacintho Ribeiro dos Santos, editor, 1912.

Feijó, Diogo Antonio. *Relatório do Exmo. Ministro da Justiça*. Rio de Janeiro: Typ. Imp. e Const. de E. Seignot-Plancher, 1832. p. 2. brazil.crl.edu.

Ferraz, Luiz Pedreira do Couto. *Relatório apresentado à Assembleia Geral Legislativa na primeira sessão da décima legislatura pelo ministro e secretário de estados dos negócios do Império*. Rio de Janeiro: Tipografia Universal de Laemmert, 1857. brazil.crl.edu.

Forte, João Ferreira da Cruz. *O jogo do burro ou A febre das ações. Comédia em 2 atos*. Rio de Janeiro: Typ. Imparcial de M. J. Pereira da Silva Jr., 1854. BNRJ, Obras raras, 41, 17, 5. p. 13–14.

Frey, A. *Manuel nouveau de typographie*. Paris: Libraire Encyclopédique de Rorét, 1835. gallica.bnf.fr.

Kidder, Daniel P., and James C Fletcher. *Brazil and the Brazilians: Portrayed in Historical and Descriptive Sketches*. Philadelphia: Childs & Peterson, 1857.

Macedo, Joaquim Manuel de. *Ano Biográfico Brasileiro*. Rio de Janeiro: Typographia e Lithographia do Imperial Instituto Artístico, 1876.

_____. *Luxo e Vaidade*. Rio de Janeiro: Tip. de Francisco de Paula Brito, 1860.

Magalhães, Domingos José Gonçalves de. *Tragédias: Antonio José, Olgiato e Otelo*. Rio de Janeiro: B. L. Garnier, 1865, p. 255

Magalhães, Domingo José Gonçalves de. *Faits de l'esprit humain: Philosophie.* Traduit du portugais par N. P. Chansselle. Paris: Auguste Durant, Libraire. 1860. p. V-VI. gallica.bnf.fr.

Moreira de Azevedo, Manuel Duarte. "Origem e desenvolvimento da imprensa no Rio de Janeiro." *Revista do Instituto Histórico e Geográfico Brasileiro,* no. 28, v. 2, 4° trimestre de 1865.

Nunes, Antonio Duarte. Almanac histórico da cidade de S. Sebastião do Rio de Janeiro. Ano de 1799. In *Revista do Instituto Histórico e Geográfico Brasileiro.* Tomo XXI, 1° trimestre de 1858. p. 83.

Ogier, Rene. *Manual de typographia braziliense por R. Ogier.* Rio de Janeiro: Typographia de R. Ogier, 1832.

Ordenação Filipinas. Livro III. Título XV. www1.ci.uc.pt/ihti/proj/ filipinas/l3p578. htm.

Pinto, Luiz Maria da Silva. *Diccionario da língua brasileira: Por Luiz Maria da Silva Pinto natural da Província de Goyaz.* Ouro Preto: Typographia de Silva, 1832. www.brasiliana.usp.br.

Porto-Alegre, Manuel de Araújo. "Iconografia Brasileira," *Revista do Instituto Histórico e Geográfico do Brazil,* Tomo XIX, 1856, p. 349-53.

Relatório da comissão encarregada pelo governo imperial pelos avisos de 1° de outubro e 28 de dezembro de 1864 de proceder a um inquérito sobre as causas principais e acidentais da crise do mês de setembro de 1864. Rio de Janeiro: Typographia Nacional, 1865

Silva, Antônio de Morais. *Dicionário da Língua Portuguesa.* Lisboa: Simão Thaddeo Ferreira, 1789.

Silva, Joaquim Norberto de Souza e. "Biografia dos brasileiros ilustres por amar, letras, virtudes, etc.: Notícia sobre Antonio Gonçalves Teixeira e Souza e suas obras." *Revista do Instituto Histórico, Geográfico e Etnográfico Brasileiro.* Tomo XXXIX. Primeira parte. Rio de Janeiro: B. L. Garnier: Livreiro-editor, 1876.

Silva, José Bonifácio de Andrada e. *Elogio Acadêmico da Senhora D. Maria Primeira, recitado por José Bonifácio de Andrada e Silva, em sessão pública da Academia Real das Ciências de Lisboa aos 20 de março de 1817.* Rio de Janeiro: Tip. Imparcial de Francisco de Paula Brito, 1839.

Soares, Sebastião Ferreira. *Esboço ou Primeiros Traços da Crise Comercial da Cidade do Rio de Janeiro em 10 de Setembro de 1864.* Rio de Janeiro: Eduardo & Henrique Laemmert, 1865.

———. *Histórico da Companhia Industrial da Estrada de Mangaratiba e análise crítica e econômica dos negócios desta Companhia.* Rio de Janeiro: Tipografia Nacional, 1861.

———. *Notas estatísticas sobre a produção agrícola e carestia dos gêneros alimentícios no Império do Brasil.* Rio de Janeiro: Tip. Imp. e Const. de J. Villeneuve e Comp., 1860.

Visconde de Macaé. *Relatório da repartição dos negócios do Império apresentado à Assembleia Geral Legislativa.* Rio de Janeiro: Tipografia Nacional, 1848.

ANNALS, LAWS AND DECREES

Anais da Assembleia Nacional Constituinte, Sessão de 6 de outubro de 1823, pp. 32–34.

Anais da Assembleia Nacional Constituinte, Sessão de 8 de novembro de 1823, pp. 218–19.

Anais da Câmara dos Deputados, Sessão de 10 de junho de 1826, pp. 91–92.

Anais da Câmara dos Deputados, Sessão de 3 de março de 1830, pp. 30.

Anais da Câmara dos Deputados, Sessão de 13 de maio de 1836, pp. 48, 50.

Anais da Câmara dos Deputados, Sessão de 14 de maio de 1836, pp. 52–53.

Anais da Câmara dos Deputados, Sessão de 6 de agosto de 1855, p. 58.

Anais da Câmara dos Deputados, Sessão de 10 de agosto de 1855, p. 97.

Anais da Câmara dos Deputados, Sessão de 4 de setembro de 1855, p. 333.

Anais da Câmara dos Deputados, Sessão de 14 de maio de 1856, p. 21.

Anais da Câmara dos Deputados, Sessão de 21 de agosto de 1857, p. 45.

Anais da Câmara dos Deputados, Sessão de 17 de maio de 1858, p. 31.

Anais da Câmara dos Deputados, Sessão de 31 de maio de 1858, p. 152.

Anais da Câmara dos Deputados, Sessão de 5 de junho de 1858, p. 47.

Anais da Câmara dos Deputados, Sessão de 8 de junho de 1858, p. 71.

Anais da Câmara dos Deputados, Sessão de 14 de julho de 1858, p. 135.

Anais da Câmara dos Deputados, Sessão de 30 de junho de 1858, p. 304.

Anais da Câmara dos Deputados, Sessão de 26 de agosto de 1858, p. 229.

Lei de 26 de Outubro de 1831. In *Coleção das Leis do Império do Brasil*. 1831. v. I, p. 162. www2.camara.gov.br.

Lei de 6 de Junho de 1831. In *Coleção das Leis do Império do Brasil*. 1831. v. I, p. 2. www2.camara.gov.br.

Lei de 3 de Outubro de 1832. Dá nova organização às atuais Academias Medico-cirúrgicas das cidades do Rio de Janeiro, e Bahia. In *Coleção das Leis do Império do Brasil*. V. 1, 1832, p. 87. www2.camara.leg.br.

Lei n. 369, de 18 de Setembro de 1845. Fixando a Despesa, e orçando a Receita para o Exercício de 1845–1846. *Coleção de Leis do Império do Brasil—1845*, p. 47, v. I. www2.camara.leg.br.

Lei n. 555 de 15 de junho de 1850. www.senado.gov.br.

Lei n. 668 de 11 de setembro de 1852. www.senado.gov.br.

Código Criminal do Império do Brasil. Lei de 16 de dezembro de 1830. www.planalto. gov.br/ccivil_03/leis/lim/lim-16-12-1830.htm.

Constituição Política do Império do Brasil (de 25 de março de 1824). Cap. VI, art. 94. www.planalto.gov.br.

Decreto de 2 de Março de 1821. In *Coleção das Leis do Império do Brasil*. 1821. v. I, p. 25–26. www2.camara.gov.br.

Decreto de 22 de Novembro de 1823. In *Coleção das leis do Império do Brasil*, v. 1, p. 89. www2.camara.gov.br.

Decreto de 11 de Setembro de 1826. In *Coleção das leis do Império do Brasil*, v. 1, p. 12. www2.camara.gov.br.

Decreto de 18 de Março de 1837. In *Coleção das leis do Império do Brasil*, v. 1, p. 11. www2.camara.gov.br.

Decreto n. 384 de 16 de Outubro de 1844. In *Coleção das Leis do Império do Brasil*. www2.camara.gov.br.

Decreto nº 1.610, de 23 de Maio de 1855. www6.senado.gov.br.

Decreto nº 1.717 de 23 de Janeiro 1856. In Coleção das Leis do Império do Brasil, v. 1, p. 7. www2.camara.gov.br.

Bibliography

Abreu, Casimiro de. *Correspondência completa*. Coleção Afrânio Peixoto 77. Ed. Mário Alves de Oliveiro. Rio de Janeiro: ABL, 2007.

Abreu, Marcella dos Santos. "Moda, teatro e nacionalismo nas crônicas da *Revista popular* (1859–1862)." MA thesis (Literary Theory and History). IEL, Unicamp, Campinas, 2008.

Abreu, Márcia, ed. *Trajetórias do romance: Circulação, leitura e escrita nos séculos XVIII e XIX*. Campinas: Mercado de Letras, 2008.

Alencar, José de. *Como e porque sou romancista*. Campinas: Pontes, 2005.

Alencastro, Luís Felipe de, ed. *História da vida privada no Brasil: Império*. São Paulo: Companhia das Letras, 1997.

_____. "Bahia, Rio de Janeiro et le nouvel ordre colonial 1808–1860." In *Géographie du capital marchand aux Amérques: 1760–1860*, edited by Jeanne Chase. Paris: Centre d'études nord-americains; École des hautes études en sciences sociales, 1987.

Araújo, Carlos Eduardo Moreira de. *Cárceres imperiais: A casa de correção do Rio de Janeiro. Seus detentos e o sistema prisional no império, 1830–1861*. Tese de doutorado em história. Campinas, ifch, Unicamp, 2009.

Azevedo, Célia Maria Marinho. "Francisco de Paula Brito: Cidadania e antirracismo nos inícios da nação brasileira." *Irohin—Jornal On Line*, 11 Jan. 2007. www.irohin.org.br.

_____. "A recusa da 'raça': Antirracismo e cidadania no Brasil dos anos 1830." *Horizontes Antropológicos*, Porto Alegre, vol. 11, no. 34, pp. 297–320, Jul./Dec. 2005.

_____. "Maçonaria, cidadania e a questão racial no Brasil escravagista." *Estudos Afro-Asiáticos*, Rio de Janeiro, no. 34, pp. 121–36, Dec. 1998.

_____. "Maçonaria: História e historiografia." *Revista da USP*, São Paulo, no. 32, pp. 178–89, Dec./Jan./Feb. 1996–1997.

Balaban, Marcelo. "Poeta do lápis: A trajetória de Ângelo Agostini no Brasil imperial—São Paulo e Rio de Janeiro—1864–1888." PhD diss. (history). IFCH, Unicamp, Campinas, 2005.

Balzac, Honoré de. *Ilusões perdidas*. Translated by Rosa Freire d'Aguiar. São Paulo: Companhia das Letras, 2011.

Basile, Marcelo Otávio. "Revolta e cidadania na Corte regencial." *Tempo: Revista do Departamento de História da UFF*, Niterói, no. 22, Jan. 2007, pp. 31–57.

_____. "Projetos políticos e nações imaginadas na imprensa da Corte (1831–1837)." In *Política, nação e edição: O lugar dos impressos na construção da vida política. Brasil, Europa e Américas nos séculos XVIII-XIX*, edited by Eliana de Freitas Dutra and Jean-Yves Mollier. São Paulo: Annablume, 2006.

_____. "O império em construção: projetos de Brasil e ação política na corte regencial." PhD diss. (History), UFRJ, IFCS, Rio de Janeiro, 2004.

_____. *Ezequiel Correia dos Santos: Um jacobino na corte imperial*. Rio de Janeiro: Editora FGV, 2001.

Batalha, Claudio H. M. "Sociedades de trabalhadores no Rio de Janeiro do século XIX: Algumas reflexões em torno da formação da classe operária." *Cadernos AEL: Sociedades Operárias e Mutualismo*, Campinas, Unicamp, IFCH, vol. 6, no. 10, Nov. 1999.

Bethell, Leslie. *História da América Latina: Da Independência a 1870*. Vol. III. São Paulo; Brasília: Edusp; Imprensa Oficial; Fundação Alexandre de Gusmão, 2001.

Bethell, Leslie, and José Murilo de Carvalho. "O Brasil da Independência a meados do século XIX." In *História da América Latina: Da Independência a 1870*. Vol. III, edited by Leslie Bethell. São Paulo; Brasília: Edusp; Imprensa Oficial; Fundação Alexandre de Gusmão, 2001.

Bezerra, Nielson Rosa. "Mosaicos da escravidão: Identidades africanas e conexões atlânticas no Recôncavo da Guanabara." PhD diss. (History), Instituto de Ciências Humanas e Filosofia, Universidade Federal Fluminense, Niterói, 2010.

Bicalho, Maria Fernanda. *A cidade e o império: O Rio de Janeiro no século XVIII*. Rio de Janeiro: Civilização Brasileira, 2003.

Broca, Brito. *Românticos, pré-românticos, ultra-românticos: Vida literária e romantismo brasileiro*. São Paulo: Polis; Instituto Nacional do Livro, 1979.

Caldeira, Cláudia Adriana Alves. "Francisco de Paula Brito: Tipografia, imprensa, política e sociabilidade." MA thesis (History). UFRRJ, Instituto de Ciências Humanas e Sociais, Seropédica-RJ, 2010.

Campato, João Adalberto, Jr. *Retórica e literatura: O Alencar polemista nas Cartas sobre a Confederação dos Tamoios*. São Paulo: Stortecci, 2003.

Cano, Jefferson. *Nação e ficção no Brasil do século XIX. História Social*, no. 22-23, 2012.

_____. "Justiniano José da Rocha, cronista do desengano." In *História em cousas miúdas: Capítulos de história social da crônica no Brasil*, edited by Sidney Chalhoub,

Margarida de Souza Neves, and Leonardo Affonso de Miranda Pereira. Campinas: Ed. da Unicamp, 2005.

Carvalho, Anna Maria Monteiro de. "A espacialidade do Passeio Público de Mestre Valentim." *Gavea*, Rio de Janeiro, no. 1, pp. 67–76.

Carvalho, José Murilo de. *A construção da ordem: A elite política imperial / Teatro das sombras: A política imperial*. Rio de Janeiro: Civilização Brasileira, 2007.

———. *D. Pedro II*. São Paulo: Companhia das Letras, 2007.

Cavalcanti, Nireu. *O Rio de Janeiro setecentista: A vida e a construção da cidade da invasão francesa até a chegada da corte*. Rio de Janeiro: Jorge Zahar Ed., 2004.

Cavallini, Marco Cícero. "Monumento e política: Os 'Comentários da Semana' de Machado de Assis. In *História em cousas miúdas: Capítulos de história social da crônica no Brasil, edited by* Sidney Chalhoub, Margarida de S. Pereira Neves, and A. de M. Leonardo. Campinas: Unicamp, 2005.

Chalhoub, Sidney. *A força da escravidão: Ilegalidade e costume no Brasil oitocentista*. São Paulo: Companhia das Letras, 2012.

Chalhoub, Sidney, Margarida de Souza Neves, and Leonardo Affonso de Miranda Pereira, eds. *História em cousas miúdas: Capítulos de história social da crônica no Brasil*. Campinas: Ed. da Unicamp, 2005.

Chartier, Roger, and Henri-Jean Martin, eds. *Histoire de l'édition française. Le temps des éditeurs du romantisme à la Belle Époque*. Vol. III. Paris: Fayard; Cercle de la Libraire, 1990.

Chase, Jeanne, ed. *Géographie du capital marchand aux Amériques: 1760–1860*. Paris: Centre d'études nord-americains; École des hautes études en sciences sociales, 1987.

Costella, Antonio F. *O controle da informação no Brasil: Evolução histórica da Legislação Brasileira de Imprensa*. Petrópolis: Vozes, 1970.

Cunha, Maria Clementina Pereira. *Ecos da folia: Uma história social do carnaval carioca entre 1880 e 1920*. São Paulo: Companhia das Letras, 2001.

Darnton, Robert. *O beijo de Lamourette: Mídia, cultura e revolução*. São Paulo: Companhia das Letras, 2010.

———. *O Iluminismo como negócio: História da publicação da* Enciclopédia, *1775–1880*. São Paulo: Companhia das Letras, 1996.

Deaecto, Marisa Midore. *O império dos livros: Instituições e práticas de leitura na São Paulo oitocentista*. São Paulo: Edusp; Fapesp, 2011.

Dosse, François. *O desafio biográfico: Escrever uma vida*. Translated by Gilson Cézar Cardoso de Souza. São Paulo: Edusp, 2009.

Dutra, Eliana de Freitas, and Jean-Yves Mollier, eds. *Política, nação e edição: O lugar dos impressos na construção da vida política. Brasil, Europa e Américas nos séculos XVIII-XIX*. São Paulo: Annablume, 2006.

El Far, Alessandra. *O livro e a leitura no Brasil*. Rio de Janeiro: Jorge Zahar, 2006.

Ewbank, Thomas. *A vida no Brasil*. Translated by Jamil Almansur Haddad. Belo Horizonte; São Paulo: Itatiaia; Edusp, 1976.

Ferreira, Roberto Guedes. "Autonomia escrava e (des)governo senhorial na cidade do Rio de Janeiro da primeira metade do século XIX." In *Trabalho, cativeiro e liberdade (Rio de Janeiro, séculos XVII-XIX)*, edited by Manolo Florentino. Rio de Janeiro: Civilização Brasileira, 2005.

Figuerôa, Silvia Fernanda de Mendonça. "Ciência e tecnologia no Brasil Imperial: Guilherme Schüch, Barão de Capanema (1824–1908)." *Varia História*, Belo Horizonte, vol. 21, no. 34, pp. 437–55, July 2005.

Figueroa-Rêgo, João de, and Fernanda Olival. "Cor da pele, distinção e cargos: Portugal e espaços atlânticos portugueses (séculos XVI e XVIII)." *Tempo*, no. 30, 2010.

Finkelstein, David. *The House of Blackwood: Author-Publisher Relations in the Victorian Era*. University Park, PA: Penn State University Press, 2002.

Florentino, Manolo. *Trabalho, cativeiro e liberdade (Rio de Janeiro, séculos XVII-XIX)*. Rio de Janeiro: Civilização Brasileira, 2005.

Flory, Thomas. "Race and Social Control in Independent Brazil." *Journal of Latin American Studies*, vol. 9, no. 2, Nov. 1977.

Furtado, Junia Ferreira. "O Distrito dos Diamantes: Uma terra de estrelas." In *As Minas setecentistas, I*, edited by Maria Eugênia Lage de Resende and Luiz Carlos Vilalta. Belo Horizonte: Autêntica; Companhia do Tempo, 2007.

_____. *Chica da Silva e o contratador dos diamantes: O outro lado do mito*. São Paulo: Companhia das Letras, 2003.

Godoi, Rodrigo Camargo de. "Trabalho escravo e produção de impressões no Rio de Janeiro oitocentista." *Textos da Escola São Paulo de Estudos Avançados*. Campinas, 2012. www.espea.iel.unicamp.br.

_____. "O espólio do editor: A 'Avaliação de Bens' do inventário de Francisco de Paula Brito." *Anais do XXVI Simpósio Nacional de História (ANPUH)*, São Paulo, July 2011.

_____. "Publicação e comercialização de comédias no Brasil oitocentista: O caso de *Luxo e Vaidade* de Joaquim Manuel de Macedo (1860)." *Anais do II Seminário Brasileiro Livro e História Editorial*. Niterói, UFF, 2009.

Gondim, Eunice Ribeiro. *Vida e obra de Paula Brito: Iniciador do movimento editorial no Rio de Janeiro (1809–1861)*. Rio de Janeiro: Livraria Brasiliana Editora, 1965.

Graham, Sandra Lauderdale. *Proteção e obediência: Criadas e seus patrões no Rio de Janeiro, 1860–1910*. São Paulo: Companhia das Letras, 1992.

Greenspan, Ezra. *George Palmer Putnam: Representative American Publisher*. University Park, PA: Penn State University Press, 2000.

Grinberg, Keila. *O fiador dos brasileiros: Cidadania, escravidão e direito civil no tempo de Antonio Pereira Rebouças*. Rio de Janeiro: Civilização Brasileira, 2002.

Hallewell, Laurence. *O livro no Brasil: Sua história*. Translated by Maria da Penha Villalobos and Lólio Lourenço de Oliveira. São Paulo: T. A. Queiróz; Edusp, 1985.

Haynes, Christine. *Lost Illusions: The Politics of Publishing in Nineteenth-Century France*. Harvard Historical Studies 167. Cambridge, MA: Harvard University Press, 2010.

Heineberg, Ilana. Miméticos, aclimatados e transformados: Trajetórias do romance-folhetim em diários fluminenses. In *Trajetórias do romance: Circulação, leitura e escrita nos séculos XVIII e XIX*, edited by Márcia Abreu. Campinas: Mercado de Letras, 2008.

Holanda, Sério Buarque de. *Capítulos de história do Império*. Ed. Fernando A. Novais. São Paulo: Companhia das Letras, 2010.

Ipanema, Marcello de. *Estudos de história de legislação de imprensa*. Rio de Janeiro: Gráfica e Editora Aurora, 1949.

———. *Livro das leis de imprensa de D. João*. Rio de Janeiro: Gráfica e Editora Aurora, 1949.

———. *Síntese da história da legislação luso-brasileira de imprensa*. Rio de Janeiro: Gráfica e Editora Aurora, 1949.

Karasch, Mary C. *A vida dos escravos no Rio de Janeiro (1808–1850)*. Translated by Pedro Maia Soares. São Paulo: Companhia das Letras, 2000.

Koutsoukos, Sandra Sofia Machado. *Negros no estúdio do fotógrafo: Brasil, segunda metade do século XIX*. Campinas: Editora da Unicamp, 2010.

Kraay, Hendrik. *Days of National Festivity in Rio de Janeiro, Brazil, 1823–1889*. Stanford: Stanford University Press, 2013.

———, ed. *Afro-Brazilian Culture and Politics: Bahia, 1790s to 1990s*. New York: M. E. Sharpe, 1998.

———. "The Politics of Race in Independence-era Bahia: The Black Militia Officers of Salvador, 1790–1840." In *Afro-Brazilian Culture and Politics: Bahia, 1790s to 1990s, edited by* Hendrik Kraay. New York: M. E. Sharpe, 1998.

Lajolo, Marisa, and Regina Zilberman. *O preço da leitura: Leis e números por detrás das letras*. São Paulo: Ática, 2001.

Lara, Sílvia Hunold. *Fragmentos setecentistas: Escravidão, cultura e poder na América portuguesa*. São Paulo: Companhia das Letras, 2007.

———, ed. *Ordenações Filipinas: Livro V*. São Paulo: Companhia das Letras, 1999.

Lara, Sílvia Hunold, and Joseli Maria Nunes Mendonça, eds. *Direitos e justiças no Brasil: Ensaios de história social*. Campinas: Editora da Unicamp, 2006.

Lejeune, Philippe. *O pacto autobiográfico: De Rousseau à Internet*. Edited by Jovita Maria Gerheim Noronha, translated by Jovita Maria Gerheim Noronha and Maria Inês Coimbra Guedes. Belo Horizonte: Editora UFMG, 2008.

Levy, Maria Bárbara. *A indústria do Rio de Janeiro através de suas sociedades anônimas: Esboço de história empresarial*. Rio de Janeiro: Editora UFRJ, 1994.

———. *História da Bolsa de Valores do Rio de Janeiro*. Rio de Janeiro: IBMEC, 1977.

Lima, Ivana Stolze. *Cores, marcas e falas: Sentidos da mestiçagem no Império do Brasil*. Rio de Janeiro: Arquivo Nacional, 2003.

Lobo, Eulália Maria Lahmeyer. *História do Rio de Janeiro: Do capital comercial ao capital industrial e financeiro*. Rio de Janeiro: IBMEC, 1978.

Loriga, Sabina. *O pequeno x: Da biografia à história*. Translated by Fernando Scheibe. Coleção História e Historiografia 6. Belo Horizonte: Autêntica, 2011.

Lugo-Ortiz, Agnes, and Angela Rosenthal, eds. *Slave Portraiture in the Atlantic World.* New York: Cambridge University Press, 2013.

Lustosa, Isabel. *O nascimento da imprensa brasileira.* 2nd ed. Rio de Janeiro: Jorge Zahar Ed., 2004.

_____. *Insultos impressos: A guerra dos jornalistas na Independência.* São Paulo: Cia das Letras, 2000.

Lyons, Martin. "Os novos leitores no século XIX: Mulheres, crianças, operários." In *História da leitura no mundo ocidental,* vol. 2, by Roger Chartier and Guiglielmo Cavallo. São Paulo: Ática, 1999.

Mac Cord, Marcelo. *Artífices da cidadania: Mutualismo, educação e trabalho no Recife oitocentista.* Campinas: Ed. da Unicamp, 2012.

Machado de Assis, Joaquim Maria. *Obras Completas,* v. i. São Paulo, Nova Aguilar, 2006.

Magalhães, Raimundo, Jr. *José de Alencar e sua época.* Rio de Janeiro; Brasília: Civilização Brasileira; INL, 1977.

_____. *Três panfletários do segundo reinado.* Rio de Janeiro: Academia Brasileira de Letras, 2009. (Coleção Afrânio Peixoto, 86).

_____. *Vida e obra de Machado de Assis.* Rio de Janeiro: Record, 2008.

_____. *Poesia e vida de Casimiro de Abreu.* São Paulo: Editora das Américas, 1965.

Malheiro, Perdigão. *A escravidão no Brasil: Ensaio histórico, jurídico, social.* vol. II. 3rd ed. Petrópolis; Brasília: Vozes; INL, 1976.

Mamigonian, Beatriz Gallotti. "O direito de ser africano livre: Os escravos e as interpretações da Lei de 1831." In *Direitos e justiças no Brasil: Ensaios de história social,* edited by Silvia Hunold Lara and Joseli Maria Nunes Mendonça. Campinas: Editora da Unicamp, 2006.

_____. "Revisitando a 'transição para o trabalho livre': A experiência dos africanos livres." In *Trabalho, cativeiro e liberdade (Rio de Janeiro, séculos XVII-XIX),* edited by Manolo Florentino. Rio de Janeiro: Civilização Brasileira, 2005.

_____. "To be a Liberated African in Brazil: Labour and Citizenship in the Nineteenth Century." PhD thesis (History). University of Waterloo. Waterloo, Ontario, Canada, 2002.

Marques, Wilton José. "O poeta e poder: Favores e afrontas." *Estudos Históricos,* Rio de Janeiro, no. 32, 2003, pp. 33–49.

Martin, Gérard. *L'Imprimerie.* Paris: Presses Universitaires de France, 1966.

Martin, Henri-Jean, and Lucien Febvre. *O aparecimento do livro.* São Paulo: Editora Unesp, 1992.

Martin, Odile, and Henri-Jean Martin. "Le monde des éditeurs." In Chartier and Martin, *Histoire de l'édition française.*

Martins, Bruno Guimarães. "Corpo sem cabeça: Paula Brito e a Petalógica." PhD diss. (Literature). Pontifícia Universidade Católica do Rio de Janeiro, Rio de Janeiro, 2013.

Martins, Fran. *Curso de Direito Comercial.* Rio de Janeiro: Forense, 1986.

Massa, Jean-Michel. *A juventude Machado de Assis (1839–1870): Ensaio de biografia intelectual*. Rio de Janeiro: Civilização Brasileira, 1971.

Matos, Raimundo José da Cunha. *Corografia histórica da província de Minas Gerais (1837)*. Vol. 1. Belo Horizonte: Editora Itatiaia, 1981.

Mattos, Hebe. *Das cores do silêncio: Os significados da liberdade no Sudeste escravista (Brasil, século XIX)*. Campinas: Editora da Unicamp, 2013.

_____. *Escravidão e cidadania no Brasil monárquico*. Rio de Janeiro: Jorge Zahar Ed., 2000.

Mattos, Ilmar Rohloff de. *O tempo saquarema*. São Paulo: Hucitec, 2004.

Mauad, Ana Maria. "Imagem e autoimagem do segundo reinado." In *História da vida privada no Brasil: Império*, edited by Luís Felipe de Alencastro. São Paulo: Companhia das Letras, 1997.

McCleery, Alistair. "The Return of Publisher to Book History: The Case of Allen Lane." *Book History*, vol. 5, 2002, pp. 161–85.

Meneses, Raimundo de. *José de Alencar: Literato e político*. Rio de Janeiro: Livros técnicos e científicos, 1977.

Mollier, Jean-Yves. *Louis Hachette (1800–1864): Le foundateur d'un empire*. Paris: Fayard, 1999.

_____. *Michel & Calmann Lévy ou la naissance de l'édition moderne, 1836–1891*. Paris: Calmann Lévy, 1984.

Morel, Marco. *As transformações dos espaços públicos: Imprensa, atores políticos e sociabilidades na cidade imperial*. São Paulo: Hucitec, 2010.

_____. *O período das Regências, (1831–1840)*. Rio de Janeiro: Zahar Ed., 2003.

Neto, Lira. *O inimigo do rei: Uma biografia de José de Alencar, ou, A mirabolante aventura de um romancista que colecionava desafetos, azucrinava d. Pedro II e acabou inventando o Brasil*. São Paulo: Globo, 2006.

Nora, Pierre. "Entre memória e história: A problemática dos lugares." *Projeto história*, São Paulo, no. 10, Dec. 1993.

Oliveira, Maria da Glória de. *Escrever vidas, narrar a história: A biografia como problema historiográfico no Brasil oitocentista*. Rio de Janeiro: Editora FGV, 2011.

Paiva, Eduardo França. "Coartações e alforrias nas Minas Gerais do século XVIII: As possibilidades de libertação escrava no principal centro colonial." *Revista de História*, no. 133, São Paulo, Dec. 1995.

Palma, Patrícia de Jesus. "O mercado do livro brasileiro em Portugal." Unpublished manuscript.

Pinheiro, Alexandra. "Entre contratos e recibos: O trabalho de um editor francês no comércio livreiro do Rio de Janeiro oitocentista." In *Trajetórias do romance: Circulação, leitura e escrita nos séculos XVIII e XIX*, edited by Márcia Abreu. Campinas: Mercado de Letras, 2008.

Prado, Décio de Almeida. *João Caetano: O ator, o empresário, o repertório*, 1972.

Ramos, José de Paulo, Jr., Marisa Midori Deaecto, and Plínio Martins Filho, eds. *Paula Brito: Editor, poeta e artífice das letras*. São Paulo: Edusp; Com Arte, 2010.

Resende, Maria Eugênia Lage de, and Luiz Carlos Vilalta, eds. *As Minas setecentistas, I.* Belo Horizonte: Autêntica; Companhia do Tempo, 2007.

Ribeiro, Gladys Sabina. "A radicalidade dos exaltados em questão: Jornais e panfletos no período de 1831 e 1834." In *Linguagens e práticas da cidadania no século XIX*, edited by Gladys Sabina Ribeiro and Tânia Maria Bessone Tavares da Cruz Ferreira. São Paulo: Alameda, 2010.

———. *A liberdade em construção: Identidade nacional e conflitos antilusitanos no Primeiro Reinado.* Rio de Janeiro: Relume Dumará; Faperj, 2002.

Ribeiro, Gladys Sabina, and Tânia Maria Bessone Tavares da Cruz Ferreira, eds. *Linguagens e práticas da cidadania no século XIX.* São Paulo: Alameda, 2010.

Rocha, Débora Cristina Bondance. "Biblioteca Nacional e Pública do Rio de Janeiro: Um ambiente para leitores e leituras de romances." MA thesis (Literary Theory and History). IEL, Unicamp, Campinas, 2011.

Rodrigues, Eni Neves da Silva. "Impressões em preto e branco: História da leitura em Mato Grosso na segunda metade do século XIX." PhD diss. (Literary Theory and History). IEL, Unicamp, Campinas, 2008.

Schapochnik, Nelson. "Malditos Tipógrafos." *I Seminário Brasileiro sobre Livro e História Editorial.* Rio de Janeiro, 2004. www.livroehistoriaeditorial.pro.br/pdf/nelsonschapochnik.pdf.

Schmidt, Benito Bisso. "História e Biografia." In *Novos domínios da história*, edited by Ciro Flamarion Cardoso and Ronaldo Vainfas. Rio de Janeiro: Elsevier, 2012.

Schwarcz, Lilia Moritz. *O espetáculo das raças: Cientistas, instituições e questão racial no Brasil, 1870–1930.* São Paulo: Companhia das Letras, 1993.

Schwarz, Roberto. *Ao vencedor as batatas: Forma literária e processo social nos inícios do romance brasileiro.* São Paulo: Duas Cidades, Ed. 34, 2000.

Silva, Eduardo. *Dom Obá II D'África, o príncipe do povo: Vida, tempo e pensamento de um homem livre de cor.* São Paulo: Companhia das Letras, 1997.

Silva, Hebe Cristina. "Prelúdio do romance brasileiro: Teixeira e Sousa e as primeiras narrativas ficcionais." PhD diss. (Literary Theory and History). IEL—Unicamp, Campinas, 2009.

Silva, Ozângela de Arruda. *Pelas rotas dos livros: Circulação de romances e conexões comerciais em Fortaleza (1870–1891).* Fortaleza: Expressão Gráfica e Editora, 2011.

Silva-Nigra, D. Clemente Maria da. "Os dois grandes lampadários do Mosteiro de São Bento do Rio de Janeiro." *Revista do serviço do patrimônio histórico e artístico nacional*, Ministério da Educação e Saúde, Rio de Janeiro, no. 5, pp. 285–97, 1941.

Silva, Geraldo Luiz. "'Esperança de Liberdade': Interpretações Populares da Abolição Ilustrada (1773–1774)." *Revista de História*, no. 144, pp. 107–49, 2001.

Soares, Carlos Eugênio Líbano. "A negregada instituição: Os capoeiras no Rio de Janeiro (1850–1890)." MA thesis (History). IFCH, Unicamp, Campinas, 1993.

Soares, Luiz Carlos. *O povo de "Cam" na capital do Brasil: A escravidão urbana no Rio de Janeiro do século XIX.* Rio de Janeiro: Faperj; 7 Letras, 2007.

Sodré, Nelson Werneck. *História da Imprensa no Brasil.* 4th ed. Rio de Janeiro: Mauad, 1999.

Sousa, Octávio Tarquínio de. *História dos fundadores do Império do Brasil: Evaristo da Veiga*. Vol. vi. Rio de Janeiro: José Olímpio, 1957.
_____. *História dos fundadores do Império do Brasil: Diogo Antonio Feijó*. Vol. vii. Rio de Janeiro: José Olympio, 1957.
Souza, Silvia Cristina Martins de. *As noites do Ginásio: Teatro e tensões culturais na Corte (1832–1868)*. Campinas: Editora da Unicamp; Cecult, 2002.
Tengarrinha, José. *Da liberdade mitificada à liberdade subvertida: Uma exploração no interior da repressão à imprensa periódica de 1820 a 1828*. Lisbon: Edições Colibri, 1993.
Veríssimo, José. *História da literatura brasileira: De Bento Teixeira (1601) a Machado de Assis (1908)*. Rio de Janeiro: Livraria José Olympio Editora, 1969.
Vianna, Paulo Domingues. *Direito criminal: Segundo as preleções professadas pelo Dr. Lima Drummond*. Rio de Janeiro: F. Briguet e Cia. Editores, 1930.
Vitorino, Artur José Renda. "Patrimonialismo e finanças: política monetária de liberais e conservadores no Segundo Reinado." *Revista de História Regional*, 15 (1), 131–68, Summer, 2010.
_____. "Cercamento à brasileira: Conformação do mercado de trabalho livre na Corte das décadas de 1850 a 1880." PhD diss. (History). IFCH, Unicamp, Campinas, 2002.
_____. *Máquinas e operários: Mudança técnica e sindicalismo gráfico (São Paulo e Rio de Janeiro, 1858–1912)*. São Paulo: Annablume; Fapesp, 2000.
Williams, Daryle. "The Intrepid Mariner Simão: Visual Histories of Blackness in the Luso-Atlantic at the End of the Slave Trade." In *Slave Portraiture in the Atlantic World*, edited by Agnes Lugo-Ortiz and Angela Rosenthal. New York: Cambridge University Press, 2013.
Winship, Michael. *American Literary Publishing in the Mid-Nineteenth Century: The Business of Ticknor and Fields*. Cambridge Studies in Publishing and Printing History. Cambridge, UK: Cambridge University Press, 2002.

Image Credits

1. Posthumous portrait of Francisco de Paula Brito (1863). [BRITO, Francisco de Paula. *Poesias.* Rio de Janeiro: Tipografia Paula Brito, 1863].
2. The Brazilian Empire (1846)
3. Rio de Janeiro, the Imperial Capital (1858). [Acervo Brasiliana Fotográfica]
4. Praça da Constituição [Constitution Square] (1845–1846). Rio de Janeiro, RJ: [n.n.], [1845–1846]. 1 print, lithography, b&w, 17.5 × 26.8 cm on a support measuring 24.4 × 32.8 cm. objdigital.bn.br/objdigital2/acervo_digital/div_iconografia/icon1424738/icon1424738.html. Accessed on 1 Nov. 2019.
5. Caminho Novo [New Road] (ca. 1750)
6. Signature of Captain Martinho Pereira de Brito, Paula Brito's grandfather (1787). [SILVA-NIGRA, D. Clemente Maria da. "Os dois grandes lampadários do Mosteiro de São Bento do Rio de Janeiro." *Revista do serviço do patrimônio histórico e artístico nacional*, Ministério da Educação e Saúde, Rio de Janeiro, no. 5, p. 285–97, 1941].
7. Signature of the freedman Jacinto Antunes Duarte, Paula Brito's father (1819). [*Apelação cível. Jacinto Antunes Duarte, apelante. José Antonio Teixeira Guimarães, apelado.* 1819–1820. ANRJ, Relação do Rio de Janeiro, no. 1236, caixa 592, gal. C, fls. 10].
8. Genealogy of Francisco de Paula Brito
9. Signature of Silvino José de Almeida, Paula Brito's cousin (1834). [*Apelação criminal. A Justiça, apelante. Silvino José de Almeida, Réu.* ANRJ, no. 2729, maço 190, gal. C, fls. 8, 1834–1835].
10. Fluminense Press of Brito & Co. production (1832–1835)

11. Portrait of Francisco de Paula Brito by Louis Alexis Boulanger (1842). Drawing for lithograph, 12 × 15 cm, Collection of the Instituto Histórico e Geográfico Brasileiro.
12. Portrait of Rufina Rodrigues da Costa Brito, Paula Brito's wife, by Louis Alexis Boulanger (1842). Drawing for lithograph, 13 × 16 cm, Collection of the Instituto Histórico e Geográfico Brasileiro.
13. Portrait of Rufina, Paula Brito's "fille Aimée" (beloved daughter), by Louis Alexis Boulanger (1842). Drawing for lithograph, 12 × 14 cm, Collection of the Instituto Histórico e Geográfico Brasileiro.
14. Portrait of Alexandrina, Paula Brito's younger daughter, by Louis Alexis Boulanger (1842). Drawing for lithograph, 12 × 14 cm, Collection of the Instituto Histórico e Geográfico Brasileiro.
15. Newspapers printed by Francisco de Paula Brito's Impartial Press (1835–1851)
16. Title page of *Considerações sobre a nostalgia* (On nostalgia), thesis by Joaquim Manuel de Macedo (1844). archive.org/details/101498902.nlm.nih.gov/page/n5. Accessed on 1 Nov. 2019.
17. Title page of *Um roubo na Pavuna* (A robbery in Pavuna), novel published in 1843. Acervo do Real Gabinete Português de Leitura.
18. Title page of Antonio Gonçalves Teixeira e Sousa's novel *Tardes de um pintor* (Afternoons of a painter), and the author's portrait on the frontispiece, published in the "Brazilian Romantic Series" by Paula Brito. Collection of the Real Gabinete Português de Leitura.
19. Portrait of Simão the mariner, given to the *Marmota fluminense*'s subscribers
20. Dous de Dezembro press plan. [*Ação Ordinária. Pe. Joaquim Ferreira da Cruz Belmonte, autor. Francisco de Paula Brito, réu.* ANRJ, Coleção de processos comerciais, no. 1.885, caixa 1.832, 1857].
21. Profile of fifty-four shareholders of Dous de Dezembro.
22. Stock exchange fever. [*Marmota fluminense*, no. 476, 06/06/1854, p. 1].
23. Constitution Square shortly after the unveiling of an equestrian statue of Pedro I in 1862. [CASTRO Y ORDOÑEZ, Rafael. Praça de D. Pedro I. 1 foto: papel albuminado, p&b; 25 × 18.2 cm. In: *La comision cientifica destina al Pacífico*, 1862. BN Digital, Coleção Thereza Christina Maria].
24. Signature of the Widow Paula Brito. [*Inventário. Francisco de Paula Brito, falecido. Rufina Rodrigues da Costa Brito, Inventariante.* ANRJ, Juízo Municipal da 1ª Vara do Rio de Janeiro, no. 6.210, maço 448, 1862].

Index

The letter *t* following a page number denotes a table; the letter *f* following a page number denotes a figure.

Abreu, Casimiro de, 204–8
Alencar, José de, 116, 214–15, 15t, 217–19, 226, 309n19, 315n6
"Ig" (pseudonym), 216
Almanach do Rio de Janeiro, 29, 34–35, 274n2
Almanak Laemmert, 80, 82–83, 144–45, 45t, 191, 236, 297n44
Almeida, Silvino José de, 9, 29, 35–40, 46–47, 275n10
Anais de medicina brasiliense, 87–90, 140, 266t
Araújo, Joaquim Pereira de, 163, 165, 167–68
Arquivo médico brasileiro, 87–88, 88t, 90t, 145
Arquivo Municipal, 186, 233–34, 304n28
Arquivo romântico brasileiro, 94–95
Assis, Machado de, 188, 191, 198, 214, 241, 309n19, 315n6
Aurora Fluminense, 31, 43, 54

Auxiliary Fund for Dramatic and Musical Works, 200–3
Azevedo, Moreira de, 1, 25, 33, 43, 50, 214, 267n1 (introduction), 278n21

Barata, Cipriano, 51
Belmonte, Joaquim Ferreira da Cruz, 136, 146, 166, 168, 174, 255t (appendix 5), 261t (appendix 6)
book market, 4, 10, 81
Brasil, O, 75, 84, 86, 93, 102, 112, 123–25
Brito, Francisco de Paula
  career start, 30
  carnival lyrics, 192–93
  childhood, 19, 27
  and cousin. *See* Almeida, Silvino José de
  and daughter Alexandrina, 76, 79f, 106–8, 135, 228, 232, 281n40
  and daughter Rufina, 76, 78f, 106–8, 135, 228, 232
  death, 1, 230

Brito, Francisco de Paula (*continued*)
  debts, 232–33
  as "free printer", 16, 18, 80, 86
  genealogy, 20–27, 27f
  government loan, 123–25
  inventory, 100–101, 138, 167, 175, 182,
    185, 227–29, 232–33
  and Joaquim Manuel de Macedo, 57,
    113, 209
  and José de Alencar, 216–18
  and Machado de Assis, xi–xii, 3, 8, 100
  military service, 33–34
  poetry, 17, 31, 34, 39, 41, 116–20, 132
  political stance, 65, 120–22
  portrait, 1, 2f, 76f
  as publisher, 3, 9
  and racism, 129–30, 135
  and sister Ana Angélica, 25, 28
  skin color, 19–20
  and slavery, 9, 101, 104–10, 135, 229
  and Teixeira e Sousa, 98, 101
  as translator, 113, 291n1
  and wife. *See* Brito, Rufina Rodrigues
    da Costa
Brito, Rufina Rodrigues da Costa, 59,
  77f, 106–8, 135, 228–29, 232–35
  death, 236
Brito's Impartial Press, 33, 53, 72, 80–82,
  87, 98–99, 125, *209t*
  catalog, 82–83, *83t, 245–52t (appendix 3)*
  periodicals, 86, 88t, 89t, 93
  plays, 215
  theses, 90t, 90–91

Cânticos líricos, 82, 98, 246t
Caramuru, O, 66, 282n15
Caramurus, 13–15, 51, 56, 58–60, 269n1,
  280n39
*carioca: Jornal político, amigo da liberdade e
  da lei, O*, 17, 19, 31–33, 39, 42–43, 45,
  54t, 54–55, 59
Cartas sobre a Confederação dos Tamoios
  (Alencar), 214–16

carteira do meu tio, A (Macedo), 209t,
  209–10, 264t
Carvalho, Eduardo Vaz de, 228, 231
Cavalcanti, Holanda, 63–64, 281n5
Chimangos. *See* Moderates
cidadão, O, 80, 86, 88t
Confederação dos Tamoios (Magalhães),
  215–16, 221, 226, 264t
Congresso das Sumidades Carnavalescas,
  194–95
Considerações sobre a nostalgia (Macedo),
  91f, 209t
Correio da tarde, 84, 180, 221
Correio mercantil, xii, 3, 85, 104, 133–34,
  180–82, 215, 223
Coutinho, Leopoldo de Azeredo, 228,
  231–32, 236–37

demônio familiar, O (Alencar), 215t, 215–
  17
Dias, Gonçalves, xii, 206, 224
Diário do Rio de Janeiro, 16–17, 66, 163,
  180, 203, 230, 232
  advertisements, 34, 49, 91, 106, 108,
    168
  articles, 15, 36, 46, 48, 133–34, 188, 221
  and José de Alencar, 214, 216, 218
  and Machado de Assis, xi, 198, 241
Diniz, Próspero, 122, 211–14
Dous de Dezembro Company, 9, 83, 101,
  135, 138
  administration, 166
  bankruptcy, 110, 161–62, 164–65, 175,
    179, 229, 300n7
  catalog, 263–66t (appendix 8)
  company shares, 138, 140, 142, 144, 150,
    152, 156, 185
  distribution business, 223
  liquidation, 167, 179–80
  literary publishing house, 99, 150, 154,
    200–201, 208, 210
  printing business, 125, 136, 137f, 155,
    160, 182

Dous de Dezembro Company
(*continued*)
property auction, 168–71, 173, 183
shareholders, 141, 145–46, 168, 170,
224, 254–55t (appendix 5), 255–61t
(appendix 6`), 297n44
workshops, 147–48

Emperor Pedro I, 16, 32–33, 40–41, 56,
60, 70–71, 196f, 196–97, 306n33
abdication, 9, 13, 36, 42
Emperor Pedro II, 14, 42, 56, 119, 130,
135, 192, 216
majority, 9, 80, 87, 115–17, 119
and Paula Brito, 132, 138, 150, 172, 196
Entrudo, 192–94
Evaristo, 14, 54–55
Exaltados, 13, 36–37, 40, 48, 51, 55–57,
59, 280n39

Farroupilhas. *See* Exaltados
Father Feijó. *See* Feijó, Diogo Antonio
Feijó, Diogo Antonio, 51, 63–67, 71,
281n5
fall, 115–16
regency, 9, 84, 115
Filgueiras, Caetano Alves de Sousa, 230–
32
filho do pescador, O, 82, 94–95, 98, 246t
Fluminense Club, 132–35
Fluminense Press of Brito & Co., 16–17,
52, 54, 56, 59, 61, 80
closing, 78
crisis, 83
inception, 53
newspapers printed by, 54t, 54–55, 63t
production of periodicals, 62f
Forte, João Ferreira da Cruz, 157

Gaillard, André, 136, 222–23
Garnier, Baptiste Louis, 3, 208, 226, 233,
241–42, 308n19, 315n6

Gazeta dos tribunais, 82–83, 83t, 88t,
245–52t (appendix 3), 287n23
Grito da pátria, 49–50
grito nacional, O, 107, 113, 119–24, 129
Guanabara, 140, 144, 223, 224, 254, 266,
297n44, 312n20
guarani, O (Alencar), 214–15

Heaton & Rensburg, 81, 105

Imperial and National Press, 30–31
independência do Brasil, A, 98, 264t
ipiranga, O, 50–51

jogo do burro, ou, A febre das ações, O
(Forte), 157–58
Jordão, Albino, 49–50, 81
Jornal do commercio, 50, 54, 82, 93, 134,
188, 223, 286n14
advertisements, 53
articles, 33, 44, 46, 65
foundation, 32, 274n13
slaves, 105

Laemmert brothers, 80, 82–83, 90, 93,
236
Leão, Honório Hermeto Carneiro. *See*
Marquess of Paraná
Ledo, Joaquim Gonçalves, 70–71
Lessa e Pereira Press, 51–53
liberal, O, 231–32
Luxo e vaidade (Macedo), 200, 209t

Macedo, Joaquim Manuel de, xii, 91, 144,
169, 190–91t, 214, 224
selection of works, 209t
Magalhães, Gonçalves de, 169, 203, 215,
227, 310n43
*Manual de typographia braziliense by René
Ogier* (Ogier), 30, 52
Marmota fluminense, 166, 179–81, 191, 194,
209, 213, 241

Marmota fluminense (continued)
  advertisements, 149–50, 156, 162, 228
  announcements, 101, 148, 155
  articles, 130, 172, 192, 208, 210, 222, 229
  social columns, 187–89
marmota na corte, A, 122, 140–41, 144, 211–13
Marmota, A, 186, 211, 213–14, 226, 231, 235
  advertisements, 182–83, 199
  articles, 201–2, 216
Marquess of Olinda, 183, 203, 241–42
Marquess of Paraná, 63, 119, 160, 179–80, 189, 218
moderador, O, 180, 218
Moderates, 13–14, 48, 51–52, 55–57, 59, 66
moreninha, A (Macedo), 91, 93, 209t
mulato, ou, O homem de cor, O, 20, 55–56, 129, 279n26
mulher do Simplício, ou, A fluminense exaltada, A, 17, 53, 56–57, 62, 115–17, 119–20

novidade, A, 62–64, 281n5

Odes ao Barata (Macedo), 209
Ogier, René, 30–32, 52–54, 233
Olgiato (Magalhães), 82, 215, 247t, 264t
ortiga, A, 86, 88t

Pena, Martins, 98, 183, 199
Petalogical Society, 1, 9, 201, 304n1
  Carnival festivities, 194–95
  creation, 187
  members, 189–91, 190–91t, 199
  philanthropic activities, 192
  sessions, 188
Plancher, Pierre, 31–33, 35, 46, 113, 122, 270n16. *See also* Seignot-Plancher, Émile

presses
  iron, 52, 84
  mechanical, 84–85, 99, 123
  wooden, 9, 52–53, 84
Primaveras (Abreu), 204–8
printing paper, 221–23
Proclamação aos compatriotas (Brito), 16
publishing market, 221–23

Queirós, Eusébio de, 119–20, 191t, 191–92, 197
  Eusébio de Queirós Law, 136, 161

Raio de Júpiter, 64, 282n10, 282n13
Real, Adriano Gabriel Corte, 162, 165, 167
regeneração, A, 86, 88t, 211
Regent Feijó. *See* Feijó, Diogo Antonio
regente: Jornal político e literário, O, 50–51
Restorationists. *See* Caramurus
Revista médica brasileira, 87, 88t
Revista médica fluminense, 87, 88t, 91
Rocha, Justiniano José da, 75, 84–85, 93, 214, 279n26
  articles, 102–3, 112, 114, 124
roubo na Pavuna, Um (Susano), 92f, 93–94

Santos, Ezequiel Correia dos, 32, 36, 186
Santos, João Baptista dos, 50
Saquarema(s), 122, 124, 240
Seignot-Plancher, Émile, 32–34, 41, 50, 52
Sentinella da liberdade, 50–52
Sete d'Abril, 16–18, 62–64, 270n16, 282n10
Simplício da roça: Jornal dos domingos, 50–52
Simplício velho, 49, 281n1

slave(s),
  market, 108
  in Paula Brito's family, xiii, 5, 9,
    18, 20–21, 23–28, 132, 243–44t
    (appendix 1), 244–45t (appendix 2)
  in Paula Brito's household, 106–10,
    129, 228–29
  in press companies, 102, 104–5, 221,
    241
  trade, xiii, 6, 9, 110, 118–19, 135–36,
    159, 161
slavery, 1, 6, 9, 28, 105, 217, 241, 288n14
Sousa, Antônio Gonçalves Teixeira e, 9,
  82, 93, 95, 96–97f, 98, 208–9, 214
  death, 229–30
Sousa, Paulino José Soares de. *See*
  Viscount of Uruguai
Sousa, Teixeira e. *See* Sousa, Antônio
  Gonçalves Teixeira e
Staël, Madame de, 32, 58
stock market, 142, 157–58, 160

Susano, Luís da Silva Alves de Azambuja,
  93, 287n16

Tardes de um pintor (Sousa), 96–97f
Teixeira & Co. Press, 95, 98, 229,
  287n23

Veiga brothers, 31, 49–50. *See also* Veiga,
  Evaristo da; Veiga, João Pedro da
Veiga, Evaristo da, 18, 31, 39, 43, 49–50, 54
Veiga, João Pedro da, 31, 40–41, 45, 49–
  50, 81, 254, 259
Vianna, Nicolau Lobo, 15–17, 52, 65,
  71, 141
Vicentina (Macedo), 209t, 209–10, 265t,
  309n25
Villeneuve, Junius, 33, 82, 105, 223
Viscount of Uruguai, 98, 119, 123–24,
  183, 241
viuvinha, A (Alencar), 214–15

CPSIA information can be obtained
at www.ICGtesting.com
Printed in the USA
LVHW111351111220
673933LV00007B/185

9 780826 500168